The Role of Leadership Educators

Transforming Learning

A Volume in
Contemporary Perspectives on Leadership Learning

Series Editor
Kathy Guthrie
Florida State University

Contemporary Perspectives on Leadership Learning

Kathy Guthrie, Editor

The Role of Leadership Educators: Transforming Learning (2018)
by Kathy L. Guthrie and Daniel M. Jenkins

The Role of Leadership Educators

Transforming Learning

by

Kathy Guthrie
Florida State University

and

Daniel M. Jenkins
University of Southern Maine

INFORMATION AGE PUBLISHING, INC.
Charlotte, NC • www.infoagepub.com

Library of Congress Cataloging-in-Publication Data

CIP record for this book is available from the Library of Congress
http://www.loc.gov

ISBNs: 978-1-64113-098-1 (Paperback)

978-1-64113-099-8 (Hardcover)

978-1-64113-100-1 (ebook)

CONTENTS

**SECTION III: DESIGNING OPPORTUNITIES FOR LEADERSHIP
LEARNING INTRODUCTION**

FOREWORD

Jay A. Conger

When I began my career as a leadership educator in the late 1980s, it was a field dominated by a relatively small number of academic frameworks and constructs—from the task and social roles to the contingency/situational/path goal models to the transactional versus transformational models to the "big picture" frameworks related to leading change. These models were the cornerstones of how we thought about leadership and ultimately what we taught in course work. The purpose of the leadership educator was relatively straightforward—explore the thinking behind these constructs and find ways to link them to 'real world' situations that students would face.

Today, the field of leadership has become far richer and as a result more complicated to teach. We can now take deep dives into what had been a singular dimension of leadership (for example, emotional intelligence is the richer and more nuanced variant of the early "social roles" of leaders). Our notion of leadership embodied primarily in a single individual has given way to the importance of a complicated process called shared leadership. We are now equally curious about the other side of the equation—followership—and what it takes to be a "good" follower. Reflecting a growing cynicism about institutional leaders, we adamantly talk about the importance of authenticity. Yet our understanding of this attribute is incomplete like so many new constructs that have normative appeal. We also still struggle with drawing meaningful distinctions between the activities of managing versus leading. For example, when is coaching a managerial activity or a leadership activity? The implication is that we as educators work in a field that is evolving, expanding and incredibly

The Role of Leadership Educators: Transforming Learning, pp. xv–xvii
Copyright © 2018 by Information Age Publishing

dynamic. We must be continually refreshing our perspectives as well as making sense of an ever growing, complex universe of research that under-pins what we teach.

The second demand facing leadership educators is the breadth of choices in pedagogy that we have today. These choices are the result of innovations and "borrowed" pedagogies from fields such as adult education and psy-chotherapy that appeared in the 1980s and 1990s. As a doctoral student, I can recall thinking that teaching leadership was primarily a choice of which case studies and readings to use and how best to structure a compel-ling lecture that would follow a classroom discussion. In my first year as a professor, I had the good fortune to join the faculty at McGill University where experiential learning methods were being honed to teach leader-ship to MBA students. Simultaneously, the Center for Creative Leadership was pioneering powerful instruments such as 360 assessments to provide more reliable feedback on perceptions of an individual's leadership style as well as launching leadership simulations like the Looking Glass. I began to experiment with both innovations. Today I realize that I was standing at the dawn of a new age of pedagogy for leadership development. The tradi-tional classroom experiences suddenly appeared too narrow and limiting. My personal challenge became one of growing my repertoire of pedagogies beyond those that I had honed so well. I had to make significant invest-ments in new ones often without experienced mentors to guide me.

These two forces rising up in the 1980s and 1990s—expanding bodies of research and emerging nontraditional pedagogies—have created the Renaissance that we enjoy today in leadership education. They have pushed education beyond traditional classrooms resulting in an explosion of co-curricular programing. As the authors note, there are now more than 2000 programs worldwide. At same time, they are redefining in powerful ways how we must think and act as leadership educators. In this book, Guthrie and Jenkins have taken this remarkable moment in our field to help us reflect more deeply on what this era demands of us as leadership educators.

While there are many lessons to be learned from reading this book, I want to highlight several that resonate with me so personally. As leadership educators, we must hold ourselves to a higher standard than our colleagues in other fields. Our classroom explorations of leadership often focus on the demonstration of exemplary behavior, the content of an individual's character and the role of decisions guided by a moral compass. To be credible as leadership educators, we have to model these very behaviors, worldviews, and values that we teach. I can think of few academic disci-plines that require this demanding standard of behavior. In addition, we are on parallel personal journeys of learning with our students. Most of us were drawn to the field because of a deep interest in human potential. We see leadership as a primary means to achieve that end. By necessity, we are curious about human behavior and often about our own. As a result, it is incumbent upon us to explore and understand who we are and how our multiple identities influence our roles as educators. After all, the teaching of leadership requires "engaged pedagogy." While I believe most of us practice this form of pedagogy, it is a demanding practice. We appreciate the fact that the models of leadership we teach are often in a format of abstractions—generic competencies, linear frameworks. Their "translations" require a blend of pragmatism and creativity. More challenging is the fact that learning of leadership requires extensive practice. Yet our classrooms are structured for episodic learning in settings that are often removed from real world leadership challenges and offer limited opportunities for practice. While working within the constraints of a college or university setting, we have to be far more thoughtful and creative about how we bridge learning beyond the classroom.

Hand in hand with engaged pedagogy is the notion of *agitation*. Guthrie and Jenkins describe this as the practice of disrupting our students thinking and frames of reference to deepen their engagement around learning leadership. This is not easy to do. Ronald Heifetz at the Harvard Kennedy School is one of the rare masters at this skill. If anything, most of us err on the side of creating learning environments that are far removed from agitation. So how do we balance the seeming opposing forces of surprise and challenge with learning environments that are psychologically safe?

Finally, we live in a world where most individuals will have to lead masterfully across departments, functions, organizations, and cultures. Most of this leadership requires influence without authority. It is therefore an imperative for us as educators to create more integrative learning situations for our students to prepare for this demand. Ideally, we should be structuring learning experiences built around collaboration across departments/programs as well as combining curricular and co-curricular activities. To pull this off as educators, we have to be more adept at building powerful partnerships across our campuses. We have to cultivate our own networking and persuasion skills to enroll other departments and program owners to join along.

Welcome to the new world of the leadership educator. If you wish to be one, it is no longer enough to be an effective classroom teacher. We all need to be agents of change who can rally our campus colleagues to rethink how we teach leadership to young people in the context of educational institutions. We must think expansively so that learning stretches far beyond the classroom and reaches into every nook and cranny of a student's life.

Guthrie and Jenkins have provided us with a wonderful rich resource to reflect deeply on who we are and who we need to become. This book will challenge you to become the best leadership educator you can possibly be. You will be inspired to do so.

FOREWORD

Susan R. Komives

There is an old Kenyan proverb that sticks tied together in a bundle are unbreakable. Higher education has many "sticks"—courses, majors, departments, activities, residence halls, bands, athletics, recreation—that bring quality education and experience to students. The institution also has many "threads"—transcendent values and learning outcomes like critical thinking, multiculturalism, and leadership—that weave among those sticks and bind them together. Those threads belong everywhere across the college environment.

Treads like leadership development are not just the responsibility of the campus's leadership program, Center for Student Involvement, or the business school but by every major, student employment position, and area for student learning and involvement. Kathy Guthrie and Dan Jenkins have masterfully captured how leadership learning can be enhanced in these diverse experiences across the whole environment. Indeed, every single student experience is and must be an opportunity to develop leadership in every student.

Just as any student has the potential to develop leadership capacity, all educators have the potential to expand their educator identity to include being a leadership educator. Indeed, Guthrie and Jenkins define leadership educators as "… anyone who intentionally develops and delivers leadership initiatives" (p. 4, this volume). This book provides the foundation perspective and scaffolds the experiences of educators to make that

The Role of Leadership Educators: Transforming Learning, pp. xix–xxi
Copyright © 2018 by Information Age Publishing

a reality. Users of this book must be open to mindfully confront their own leadership philosophies and perspectives and enhance their own leadership practices. It starts with you!

Guthrie and Jenkins affirm that developing students' leadership capacity is a transformative experience symbolized by the butterfly on the cover of this book. Educators must remember that one does not grow a butterfly by merely sticking wings on a caterpillar. True transformation changes a person by adding perspective and complexity that fundamentally changing what Kegan (1994) called changing one's stage of consciousness. It is a developmental process. Our leadership identity development research (LID; Komives, Owen, Longerbeam, Mainella, & Osteen, 2005) indeed showed that one's leader identity changed as one developed a more complex view of leadership often through learning the language of leadership. That evolution happened in the context of reflection on meaningful engagement with supports from adults and peers.

I challenge readers to focus on four important dimensions of their own leadership educator development and in the development of capacity in their students that are dimensions of this book.

(1) Educators must address their own and their students' leadership self-efficacy. No amount of study of leadership or skill building in leadership will be enacted if one does not have the leadership efficacy to be willing to engage with others, try new skills, and think "I can do this" or "I can learn how to do this!" This involves two types of developmental readiness- one to learn and one to engage in the leadership behavior (Reichard & Walker, 2016). These important aspects of readiness are related to current scholarly work presented in this book on fixed and growth mindsets (Dweck, 2008).

(2) Admittedly, educators' mindset about teaching and developing leadership is to influence *individual* students to develop their leadership awareness and capacity. Individuals do need to understand themselves, enhance their awareness of others, and build their individual capacities. We are good at that. It is a bigger challenge to develop the personal mindset that leadership happens among people working together in groups. We must move from an entity ("the leader") approach to a leadership approach ("the group's process") (Komives, Lucas, & McMahon, 2013; Uhl-Bein & Ospina, 2012). This means teaching groups how to work more effectively together and developing student organizations to be leader-full environments not just leader-led environments.

(3) I applaud and encourage readers to develop their skills to design and facilitate meaningful discussions particularly to enhance students' capacity to engage in discussions around difficult social and cultural issues. Dan Jenkins' research, presented in this book, identified "discussion" to be the signature pedagogy for leadership education. Our Multi-institutional study of Leadership identified the high impact practice of engaging in

cultural conversations to be critical to leadership development (see Dugan, Kodama, Correia & Associates, 2013). Meaningful discussion teaches listening skills, dialogue skills, develops social perspective taking, clarifies worldview, and supports developing a growth mindset. Take this seriously!

(4) All kinds of mentoring matters and educators should ensure that mentoring is part of their own and their students' experience. This book emphasizes the role of faculty, staff, and peer mentors in developing leadership capacity. A powerful finding in our LID research was that peers who served as mentors actually developed further leadership capacity through being mentors (Komives et al., 2005). Developing peer leadership mentor programs in academic majors, among office staff, and in organizations supports the continued leadership development of all students.

This book thoughtfully abounds with scholarship, research, good practices, and resources to support the development of each leadership educator and diverse leadership programs on each campus. The comprehensive treatment of the range of teaching, learning, and developing leadership is impressive. Treat yourself to a personal journey of becoming a better leadership educator and a better leader. Your students will benefit by your commitment to the goals of engaging with this fine book.

REFERENCES

Dugan, J. P., Kodama, C., Correia, B., & Associates. (2013). *Multi-Institutional Study of Leadership insight report: Leadership program delivery*. College Park, MD: National Clearinghouse for Leadership Programs.

Dweck, C. S. (2008). *Mindset: The new psychology of success*. New York, NY: Ballentine Books.

Kegan, R. (1994). *In over our heads: The mental demands of modern life*. Cambridge, MA: Harvard University Press.

Komives, S. R., Lucas, N., & McMahon, T. R. (2013) *Exploring leadership: For college students who want to make a difference* (3nd ed.). San Francisco, CA: Jossey-Bass.

Komives, S. R., Owen, J. E., Longerbeam, S. D., Mainella, F. C., & Osteen, L. (2005). Developing a leadership identity: A grounded theory. *Journal of College Student Development, 46*, 593–611.

Reichard, R. J., & Walker, D O. (2016). In pursuit: Mastering leadership through leader developmental readiness. In R. J. Reichard & S. E. Thompson (Eds.), *New Directions for Student Leadership: No. 149. Leader developmental readiness* (pp. 15–26). San Francisco, CA: Jossey-Bass.

Uhl-Bien, S., & Ospina, S. (Eds). (2012). *Advancing relational leadership research: A dialogue among perspectives*. Greenwich, CT: Information Age.

PREFACE

Leadership as a discipline, leadership education as a field, and leadership educator as a profession are still in their infancy and rapidly evolving. For the last 30 years, the field of leadership studies has continued to expand. Guthrie and Osteen (2016) challenged higher education to reclaim their role in development leadership capacity of students. Further, Chunoo and Osteen (2016) argued that higher education's purpose, mission, and context directly align with the environment and resources necessary to provide quality leadership education in both academic/curricular and co-curricular contexts.

Because of this alignment, as professionals in higher education, we are constantly asked to provide opportunities for students to learn leadership. However, little if any professional development occurs in how to create such learning opportunities. Jenkins (2017) found that fewer than one-quarter of leadership educators have a terminal degree in leadership or a related field, and fewer than half of leadership educators have completed any graduate-level coursework in leadership, higher education, college teaching, college student development, or a closely related field.

This book is written to fill that gap. Its primary audience is leadership educators in a variety of contexts, including student affairs professionals who work with co-curricular leadership programs in higher education. Often times student affairs professionals are called on to provide student leadership education for positional leaders including student organization officers, student employees, conduct board members, orientation leaders, peer mentors, and so on. Divisions of student affairs also often provide

The Role of Leadership Educators: Transforming Learning, pp. xxiii–xxv
Copyright © 2018 by Information Age Publishing

trainings to the larger student body in various forms, for example, a lecture on being engaged through campus activities, offering self-assessments through a career center, or leadership workshops on various knowledge, skills, and values through the leadership office. This book would also benefit any college instructor who has been tasked with teaching a leadership course at either an undergraduate or a graduate level. Because leadership is multidisciplinary, this cuts across colleges, majors, departments, and programs. Finally, this book was written for anyone seeking to advance capacity to facilitate leadership learning. This could be graduate students who will be facilitating such leadership learning opportunities in future positions, those in current positions who have been tasked to develop and deliver leadership education programs, or those simply interested in learning more.

With our focused audience in mind, the overall organization of this book provides resources for leadership educators in three sections. The first section, *Leadership Can Be Taught: Education and Educator*, sets the stage for leadership education and the professional work of leadership educators. Chapter 1 provides a broad view of leadership education and the historical underpinnings of the field and profession. Exploring how our multiple identities influence our professional identity as a leadership educator is in Chapter 2. Culminating in Chapter 3 is a variety of professional development resources for leadership educators, including professional associations, journals, potential books and textbooks, and other interesting resources.

Designing Opportunities for Leadership Learning, the second section, collectively provides information, resources, and examples of leadership program design with learning at the center. Chapter 4 introduces a leadership learning framework that focuses on six aspects of leadership learning: content, development, training, observation, engagement, and metacognition. The importance of context is explored in Chapter 5, examining multiple layers of context, as well as institutional settings such as academic/curricular, co-curricular, undergraduate, graduate, discipline-specific, interdisciplinary, and integrated. After in-depth review of literature, five characteristics of distinctive programs emerged, which is discussed in Chapter 6. Next, Chapter 7 provides examples of distinctive programs in various contexts. Finally, Chapter 8 addresses assessment of both individual leadership learners and leadership education programs. Together these five chapters provide in-depth information on leadership education program design.

The third and final section, *Delivering Leadership Education*, offers specific instructional and assessment strategies for leadership learning. With the Leadership Learning Framework introduced in Chapter 4, this section aims to provide an array of instruction strategies with facilitate transformational leadership learning. Chapters 9 to 17 focus on a range of instructional strategies, including discussion, case study, reflection, team-based learning, service learning, self-assessments, role-play, simulation, games, and art, to fulfill learning outcomes. Each of these chapters provides an overview of the instructional strategy, situates it in leadership education, provides specific examples, and finally provides summary points and ways to put it into practice.

Much like the butterflies on the cover of this book, we hope the information provided can help leadership educators transform leadership learning. We have enjoyed our journey as leadership educators and are excited for you to join us in this community of practice.

ACKNOWLEDGMENTS

No book is ever written "in a vacuum" or in isolation without a lifetime of influence from multiple factors. It takes countless conversations, listening, thinking, reflection, and learning to develop ideas and concepts into something worthy of others reading. When I think about all of the individuals who have been there for me to engage in these conversations about leadership, taught me about what it means to be a leader, taken chances on me, and role model what true, authentic leadership is, I could write a book on just those lessons. However, some people directly influenced this book, and I cannot miss the opportunity to mention them. My co-author, Dan, I am thankful you agreed to go on this journey with me. Besides our shared love for FSU, I appreciate our common appreciation for all things leadership, connecting others, engaging in discourse for the sake of moving forward, and just having fun!

I am incredibly grateful for the professionals in the Leadership Learning Research Center, I am continually in awe of being able to work collectively with such an intelligent, passionate, fun group of people. Every day I learn from our conversations, and I am a better person because of you all. I am fortunate to have colleagues who "have my back," such as Maritza Torres for her multiple suggestions, insights, love, and support on this project—you kept me motivated and reminded me why we do this work every day; V. Chunoo and Trisha Teig for providing meaningful feedback on an abbreviated timeline; and Sally Watkins for her design and concept brilliance. Yes, feedback does equal love! I am also fortunate to have strong women in my life who individually and collectively support and love me

The Role of Leadership Educators: Transforming Learning, pp. xxvii–xxix
Copyright © 2018 by Information Age Publishing

unconditionally: Janet Guy (who I am lucky to call mom), Sara Thompson, Elizabeth Swiman, Laura Osteen, Mary Reynolds, Phyllis McCluskey-Titus, and Susan Komives.

Mostly, I am thankful for Team Guthrie. I am nothing without you. Every author knows the sacrifice it takes to write a book. Brian, you have always been the love of my life, my biggest fan, and the greatest partner I could ask for. The words "thank you" do not express my love and gratitude for you and all you give me each day of our lives. Kinley, you have sharpened my focus, given me purpose, and motivate me every day to be the best version of myself.

Kathy L. Guthrie
July 2017

This book is a product of passionate pursuits and is influenced and supported by compassionate family members, incredible mentors, and loyal colleagues. When I think about the myriad conversations with new and seasoned leadership educators that affirmed the need for this book; the colleagues, co-authors, and co-facilitators who helped me explore both the scholarly and applied sides of leadership education; and the students, faculty, and other professionals who I learned from along the way, I realize how lucky I have been on this academic expedition. From my own leadership learning journey as a high school band officer to an undergraduate fraternity executive board member and student senate president pro tempore to leadership roles in hospitality, finance, and higher education, this book represents those crucible moments where I become a better leader as a result of my experiences and the support and opposition of those I met along the way. Equally, many people directly influenced this book, and I am grateful for the opportunity to thank them.

My co-author, Kathy, thank you for taking a risk on me. Your work ethic and passion for leadership education are as contagious as they are inspiring. I was lucky to have volunteered to co-facilitate with you all those years ago, that you work at my blessed alma mater FSU, and that we share a sense of humor and the drive needed to connect and develop others for the betterment of our field. To my mentors and colleagues at USF, Bob Sullins, Jody Conway, Jennifer Espinola, Todd Wells, Amanda Cutchens, Susan MacManus, Don Dellow, and Jim Eison, thank you for showing me the "higher ed ropes" and seeing my potential to teach leadership. To the amazing staff of the ILA and LEMIG volunteers, fellow LEA creators, ALE board members, and ILEC team, Corey Seemiller, Tony Andenoro, Nicole Stedman, Matt Sowcik, Dave Rosch, Kerry Priest, Scott Allen, Paige Haber-Curran, Craig Slack, Susan Komives, Julie Owen, Eric Buschlen, Jackie

Bruce, Mindy McNutt, Sherry Early, Melissa Rocco, Eric Kaufman, Sara Brierton, Nicole Stedman, Jill Arensdorf, Barry Boyd, Tony Middlebrooks, Rian Satterwhite, Lisa Endersby, Shelly Wilsey, Bridget Chisholm, Debra DeRuyver, and Anita Marsha, thank you for architecting and sustaining our communities of practice. To my colleagues at USM, Tara Coste, Liz Turesky, Joyce Gibson, Pam Roy, Mary Anne Peabody, Sharon Timberlake, Betty Robinson, and Marv Druker, I am thankful for your care, support, and collegiality.

Chiefly, I am thankful for the support of my wife and two daughters. For the ludicrously early mornings, late nights, and days spent in front of my MacBook writing this book instead of with you, I thank you. Stacey, your patience, encouragement, and respect during this journey reminds me why I am the luckiest husband. Ava and Macie, you have taught me what it means to also lead as a father, you have reminded what is most important in life, and you keep a smile on my face.

Daniel M. Jenkins
July 2017

SECTION I

LEADERSHIP CAN BE TAUGHT:
EDUCATION AND EDUCATOR

In Parks (2005) book, *Leadership Can Be Taught: A Bold Approach for a Complex World*, she outlines and interprets the teaching approach of Ronald Heifetz, who is arguably currently the most influential teacher and theorist of leadership. Through Parks' observations, she challenges leadership educators to practice and teach leadership in more inspired, skilled, and effective ways.

This first section focuses on the notion that leadership can be taught in ways that cover intentionally designed learning outcomes as well as create environments where students can thrive. Building off the work of the National Clearinghouse for Leadership Programs and Komives, Dugan, and Owen's (2011) *The Handbook for Student Leadership Development*, Chapter 1 sets the stage for the field of leadership education by introducing leadership broadly, discussing the power of language in leadership, and providing a historical overview of leadership education in both the co-curricular and academic/curricular contexts.

Emerging scholarship on the professional identity development of leadership educators is discussed in Chapter 2. Exploring and honoring our multiple identities and how that influences our professional identity as a leadership educator is complex. This chapter scratches the surface in the identities of educators teaching leadership and encourages us to all think how we bring our multiple identities into our work.

Chapter 3 builds upon the notion introduced in the leadership educator professional identity research of the importance of a community of practice. Leadership educator resources are discussed in depth in this chapter. Although not an exhaustive list, it hopefully provides resources for educators to continue to learn about teaching leadership and engage in various communities of practice.

CHAPTER 1

SETTING THE STAGE

Importance of Leadership Education

As educators, we are constantly asked to provide leadership learning opportunities for students. Whether this is in the context of academic classrooms or occurring outside of the class in co-curricular contexts, in all facets of our work we are working toward developing leaders—leaders in various industries, leaders in social change, global leaders. Although this text is focused on the context of the United States, specifically in higher education, some, if not most, of the topics we discuss could potentially be transferable to contexts outside of higher education and the United States. We honor that leadership education is different internationally, but we hope that global audiences can take pieces of our discussions and apply them to their varying contexts. Much work needs to be done in the areas of teaching and learning of leadership. Therefore, we chose to focus on these contexts as a starting point.

In this text, we define leadership education, taken from the National Leadership Education Research Agenda: "Leadership Education is the pedagogical practice of facilitating leadership learning in an effort to build human capacity and is informed by leadership theory and research. It values and is inclusive of both curricular and co-curricular educational contexts" (Andenoro et al., 2013, p. 3). As Guthrie and Osteen (2016) clearly state, higher education needs to reclaim their purpose in leadership development. One way of reclaiming this purpose is to continually expand the discussion on the leadership education field and the role of leadership

The Role of Leadership Educators: Transforming Learning, pp. 3–18
Copyright © 2018 by Information Age Publishing

educators. This text intends to do just that. A myth is that the title "leadership educator" is only for those who work directly in offices of leadership or those who instruct leadership courses. We push against this notion and propose that anyone who intentionally develops and delivers leadership initiatives is a leadership educator.

Leadership educators are positioned to provide transformative learning opportunities for students, and we hope you join us in the conversation in how we can best do just that. This chapter starts by setting the stage regarding leadership education. It includes a discussion on defining leadership and the history of leadership education. By understanding how leadership education has evolved, we are able to better see where the field is currently and where we need to go.

DEFINING LEADERSHIP

In 2012, Kellerman stated that more than 1,500 definitions and 40 models of leadership exist. Over time, the definition of leadership has become more debated than agreed on and ranges from ideas rooted in "Great Men" to efforts toward social and community change. Individuals may define this complex concept differently based on personal identities, experiences, traits, behaviors, or worldviews. As Guthrie, Bertrand Jones, Osteen, and Hu (2013) assert, leadership is socially constructed and therefore holds different meanings to different people. Appropriately acknowledging the seminal book *Leadership*, Burns (1978) should be credited with creating a dramatic shift in the conversation among Western leadership scholars. Explored in detail by Rost in 1991, Burns' work moved the conceptualization of leadership from an industrial to a postindustrial model of leadership. Industrial definitions equated leadership with position, being at the top of power hierarchies and directing others. Rost (1991) simplified this by framing industrial ideas of leadership as simply good management. Burns (1978) challenged the notions of a lone individual being a leader who single handedly creates and executes a vision. This led to postindustrial conceptions of leadership—those rooted in reciprocal relationships as essential components of leadership processes. Postindustrial concepts and models introduced a new paradigm in leadership studies, one that differentiates leader and leadership, the person and the process.

Additionally, Rost (1991) explored the historical evolution of the word *leadership* and the accompanying definitions. He attempted to develop a definition of leadership that met six criteria: "clear, concise, understandable by scholars and practitioners, researchable, practically relevant, and persuasive" (p. 99). After much deliberation, Rost settled on this definition: "Leadership is an influence relationship among leaders and followers who intend real change that reflects their mutual purposes" (p. 102). Rost's definition of leadership makes it operational for all engaged in the process of leadership. This includes leaders, followers, and those who want to create real change, not just for those who are in positions of power.

This foundational belief that anyone may engage in the process of leadership, regardless of positional power, aligns with leadership development programs in higher education that seek to advance all students' leadership. Leaders are the individuals, with or without formal positions of authority, who work collectively to tackle social problems. Leadership is the collaboration of these leaders, interactions between leaders and followers, and the process occurring among and between them. The challenge for higher education scholars and practitioners is how to best develop these outcomes within students. An issue closely related to defining leadership is describing how we talk about leadership, the language we use regarding this complex process.

Language of Leadership

Language is important. The words we use, how we phrase them, and the intent behind our language are often undervalued concepts. As Guthrie et al. (2013) describe, language is not only used for communication but also provides insight into our individual and collective worldviews. When describing self, it is important to interrogate the assumptions that might ground use of language when discussing salient social identities. For example, choices between girl and woman, Cuban or Hispanic, or deaf as opposed to hearing impaired represent differences beyond the semantic. Words and underlying definitions matter in the language of leadership, just as in the descriptions we construct of ourselves.

Common parlance and writing on leadership often confuse or conflate *leader* and *leadership*, two words often mistakenly switched with little clarification or distinction (Dugan & Komives, 2011). Confusion frequently results in carelessly interchanging the language of the person (leader) and the process (leadership). When used interchangeably, leadership becomes the work of one versus all, which is not in alignment with postindustrial models of leadership. The tension of this confusion impedes clarity in the literature. More important, the lack of clarity on the language of leader and leadership has confused learners and most likely left out diverse students who never saw themselves in the language and definitions provided. Komives (2011) noted the "Perennial problems in the 'languaging of leadership' may distance the concept from some of the very groups of students who could most benefit and/or contribute to leadership development" (p. 13). Specifically, assumptions of what leadership is and how we talk about leadership determine the ability to reach diverse populations (Warner & Grint, 2006). These assumptions ground observations of who is considered a leader and how the process of leadership is defined. Leaving these beliefs unexamined is dangerous and can lead educators to ignore the diversity of leaders and leadership processes on college campuses (Ostick & Wall, 2011). The language of leader and leadership directly influences who is identified as a leader, the development of leadership capacity (potential) in students, and the ability to reach students from all backgrounds.

Leadership as Interdisciplinary and Multidisciplinary

Around the world and for the past several centuries, different societies have expressed interest in developing leaders (Ayman, Adams, Fisher, & Hartman, 2003). This topic is not new or one only discussed in the United States. Some argue that all modern philosophy and education have evolved from the teachings of Plato and Aristotle (Birkelund, 2000), including leadership. The first recorded teaching in higher education dates back more than 2,300 years ago to Plato's Academy (Hartz, 1998). Plato's most famous student, Aristotle, agreed with the importance of higher education. In fact, in *Nicomachean Ethics*, Aristotle wrote, "That is why we need to have had the appropriate upbringing—right from early youth, as Plato says—to make us find enjoyment or pain in the right things; for this is the correct education" (Irwin, 1999, p. 21). It is fascinating to think about how higher learning has been important since the days of Plato and Aristotle. Although rooted in philosophy, Plato's teaching was interdisciplinary and multidisciplinary in nature. Burkhardt and Zimmerman-Oster (1999) discuss how Aristotle placed importance on educating future leaders, which can be seen in his teaching and mentoring of Alexander the Great. This brief historical look at early philosophers provides a foundational context for the interdisciplinary and multidisciplinary nature of leadership as a discipline.

Riggio, Ciulla, and Sorenson (2003) make a case for leadership learning as benefitting from the use of various constructs from multiple perspectives and diverse contexts. Therefore, if learning is to be enhanced, then leadership education should be multidisciplinary. Studying leadership from political, linguistic, psychological, historical, cultural, and sociological perspectives enhances students' understandings of various leadership approaches (Harvey & Riggio, 2011). Exploring leadership in action from these multiple processes is foundational for effective leadership education programs (Wren, 1994). Structuring leadership education as an interdisciplinary and multidisciplinary process opens the door to integrate skills and knowledge learned in various contexts. It is also important to note how leadership has evolved in the U.S. context.

Leadership in the United States

Although the notion of leadership has been discussed since Plato and Aristotle's time, the term *leadership* did not come into use, in the English language, until the late 19th century (Brungardt, 1998). It was not until the beginning of the 20th century that leadership became a pursuit of the U.S. government, U.S. businesses, and academia (Riggio, Ciulla, & Sorenson, 2003). The first glimpse of leadership as a field of study emerged in 1940 from research projects funded by the U.S. government in an effort to gain advantages during World War II. Postwar funding allowed academic institutions the opportunity to continue the empirical study of leadership. The research conducted in the 1950s produced the Ohio State and Michigan State studies, two seminal investigations of the field (Stech, 2007) that still continue to influence leadership studies. These two academic institutions laid the foundation for the study of leadership and management as a scientific venture within academia (Riggio et al., 2003; Stech, 2007).

In an effort to increase productivity, private enterprises funded leadership research within higher education institutions. An example of corporate involvement in promoting leadership research is the Smith Richardson Foundation, which funded research that led to one of the most influential books in the field of leadership, Stodgill's *Handbook of Leadership* (Riggio et al., 2003). In addition to larger educational institutions, small liberal arts colleges became increasingly involved in leadership research. In 1978, the groundbreaking book, *Leadership*, by Burns appealed to both academics and the general public for its "interdisciplinary efforts" (Klenke, 1993; Riggio et al., 2003). Burns' (1978) writing transformed the way scholars and ordinary citizens viewed the process of leadership. Tracing the roots of leadership education is important for us, as educators, to understand where the field has been and how it continues to evolve.

LEADERSHIP EDUCATION: RESPONSIBILITY OF LEADERSHIP EDUCATORS

Leadership education is often narrowly defined as learning activities and educational environments intended to enhance and foster leadership abilities (Brungardt, 1996). Leadership education programs can be either co-curricular or curricular. Co-curricular leadership education includes programs, activities, and services that occur outside of the classroom environment, where students do not earn an academic grade or credit. In contrast, curriculum delivery methods include courses based on facilitated discussion (Jenkins, 2012), content focused on theory and practical application, retreats, and co-curricular programs (Eich, 2007;

Sowcik, 2012). Holistically, these instructional techniques are considerably different than those found in most academic disciplines. In a theoretical analysis of leadership education, Billsberry (2009) posited that leadership is socially constructed, and there are myriad ways of viewing it. Similarly, Burns (1978) described leadership as one of the most observed and least understood phenomena. Billsberry (2009) suggests that teaching the postindustrial leadership paradigm (see Rost & Barker, 2000) of leadership theory may be more art than science.

Theoretical Framework for Leadership Education

As we have discussed, we believe that leadership is socially constructed. However, a growing consensus exists around generally effective leadership practices. Members of this growing consensus believe that leadership is a combination of knowledge, skills, traits, abilities, and behaviors of individuals who engage in the leadership process (Northouse, 2009). As Harvey and Jenkins (2014) discuss, at the programmatic level, these elements are captured through the elements of knowledge (i.e., being technically sound and understanding the significant theories and models of leadership), praxis (i.e., learning by doing and understanding the theoretical by engaging in daily practice), and reflection (i.e., critical thinking and questions about the tensions between leadership constructs and experiences and observations). With this in mind, more leadership educators are developing and adapting their programs around a three-tiered structure focused on student attitudes, knowledge, and behaviors (Rosch & Anthony, 2012). Leadership development programs such as the Harvard Business School (Nohria & Khurana, 2010), the U.S. Army Official Leadership Manual (Hesselbein & Shinseki, 2004), and the widely used textbook, *Exploring Leadership* (Komives, Lucas, & McMahon, 2007), all demonstrate the importance of a leader's being, knowing, and doing.

Being (attitudes) includes inner qualities. Inner qualities such as character, credibility, optimism, and integrity were first and foremost fundamental for successful leaders across government, business, and education (Kouzes & Posner, 2010). Leadership programs focused on building student leadership capacity should emphasize developing these inner qualities in students. Knowing (knowledge) is gaining information that reflects contemporary contexts and situations. Current leaders must know how to build relationships with diverse individuals (Kezar & Moriarty, 2000) and understand the complexities of organizations (K. E. Allen & Cherry, 2000). Knowing how to do this is critical in successful leadership. Doing (skills) stems from Katz's (1955) description of needing technical, interpersonal, and conceptual skills to be an effective leader. Helping students practice these three skill areas in different contexts in order for them to apply them, regardless of environment, is fundamental in leadership education. Being, knowing, and doing are much more than leadership skills, but skills that can be carried into all aspects of life.

Most leadership education programs do not explicitly distinguish whether they focus on being, knowing, or doing. Yammarino, Dionne, Uk Chun, and Dansereau (2005) describe four interrelated "levels of analysis" for leadership education. The first is the individual level, where the focus of education is on the person, including his or her traits, skills, abilities, and behaviors. Second, the dyad level, focuses on interpersonal relationships. Next is the group/team level, which includes hierarchical groups with supervisors and nonhierarchical social groups. Finally, at the collective/system level, leadership education programs are focused on leadership within systems, communities, and society as a whole. According to Yammarino et al. (2005), leadership education should incorporate each of these four levels to provide high-quality leadership learning opportunities.

In Chapter 4, we offer our expanded framework for leadership learning, which focuses on the learner. As we know, teaching and learning are inextricably linked. Many insights provided from a leadership education framework are built on in our leadership learning framework. However, we felt that flipping the current emphasis of leadership education to offering a focus on leadership learning was critical to placing the learner at the center of our conversation.

Co-curricular and Extracurricular Leadership

Students develop leadership skills through such disparate aspects of the co-curriculum as informal interaction with faculty, participation in clubs and organizations, time spent utilizing campus resources, and peer interaction (Astin, 1984; Kuh, 2008). For the purposes of this book, we define co-curricular and extracurricular leadership involvement as activities, programs, and services that happen outside of the classroom environment, where students do not earn an academic grade or credit. The curriculum of leadership programs should be explicitly linked to the knowledge, behaviors, or attitudes intended for students to possess after attending. The outcomes of the programs must be clearly stated prior to attending and reiterated during the experience to help students make meaning of their learning. Similar to curricular experiences, learning outcomes help organize our resources and hold students responsible for their learning by helping them make sense of their experience in logical and intentional ways. Students must be given regular opportunities to succeed and struggle in various contexts if they are to ever learn to apply the intended behavior, knowledge, or attitude outcomes after the experience has ended.

As leadership educators, it is necessary to create a menu of opportunities for students to experience the multiple levels of leadership discussed previously—individual, dyad, group, and organizational approaches. Distinguishing among them and offering skill development sessions targeted at each can help educators design programs that develop students' capacities for the diversity of experiences they are likely facing both while in college and upon graduation. To illustrate, campuses that have first-year emerging leadership programs provide individual attention to students and have a focus on personal skill building. Students on these campuses may then transition into programs that focus on interpersonal or community development as a leader. A lack of intentional structure applied to programs leaves many students unable to grasp the difference in capacity necessary for personal success and organizational or societal leadership.

Co-curricular or extracurricular contexts provide three distinct advantages and are important spaces where students learn and practice leadership. Student leaders often have multiple advisors, additional role models, alumni, or community allies whom they can contact for support, advice, and guidance. In this environment, leadership educators can provide structure to a student's education, help make meaning, and connect an understanding of developmental theory to one's lived experience in more informal ways not tied to any academic coursework or only within the four walls of a classroom.

The second advantage of the co-curricular context is the opportunity for extended learning opportunities beyond one semester. Student affairs professionals have the opportunity to arrange interactions with students and groups of students across multiple semesters. In addition, these professionals can work with students across different contexts (i.e., different organizational settings and within different types of leadership experiences). This provides powerful learning opportunities for both the student and the practitioner.

The third advantage of teaching leadership through the co-curriculum is the opportunity for involvement with a large and diverse peer group. Several scholars have pointed out that peer group interaction produces student gains across many psychological, psychosocial, and cognitive outcomes (Astin, 1993; Cuyjet, 2006; Pascarella & Terenzini, 2005). Indeed, for some groups of students (e.g., students of color), the extracurricular or co-curricular context may be the first venue by which students experience leadership development and socialization within the college context (Museus, 2008; Sutton & Kimbrough, 2001).

HISTORY OF POSTSECONDARY LEADERSHIP EDUCATION

Twenty years ago, it was argued that leadership, as an academic field of study in higher education, was in its infancy (Hackman, Olive, Guzman, & Brunson, 1999). Similarly, how educators teach and individuals learn leadership is an even younger field. As the discipline of leadership studies evolves, so does the field of leadership education and the profession of leadership educator (Komives, 2011). With any developing field, there is opportunity for creativity but potential instability as well. To better understand where we are going, it is important to know the path we have traveled thus far. While developing simultaneously and informing each other, co-curricular- and curricular-based leadership education in higher education both have rich histories.

History of Co-curricular Leadership Education

Student affairs professional organizations, various institutions, and specific individuals have played significant roles in bringing attention to creating resources for and supporting further investment in leadership education as a component of student affairs and as an emerging professional field. The conversation about the importance of leadership education in higher education began in the 1970s when several student affairs professional associations urged their members to embrace the central role that student personnel administrators could and should play in the process of leadership education. Understanding how the emergence of student affairs practitioners as leadership educators transpired and informed academic student affairs preparation programs shaped the efforts of professional organizations, ultimately influencing the programming efforts at institutions.

Beginning in the 1970s

The American College Personnel Association (ACPA) was the first student affairs professional association to address leadership development as a needed area of research. As 1 of 12 commissions founded in 1961, the focus of Commission IV was students, colleges, and universities and their environments to develop a deeper understanding of students. In 1975, the Commission established the goal of creating a Task Force on Leadership Development to study approaches to leadership development on campuses, research efforts in progress, needs, developments, and share findings with ACPA membership (Watkins, in press).

The Commission IV Task Force issued a call for resources from across the country and a monograph, *Towards Modern Concept of Leadership* (1971), was produced by Overholt. This call for resources resonated with the members of the Task Force. Prior to assuming the role of Associate Dean, Overholt served as the Protestant Chaplain and taught in the Higher Education program at Boston University. As a young man, he participated in 4-H camp (youth programs based in agricultural areas) and the American Youth Foundation (Christian-based leadership training program). These foundational experiences, coupled with work in student affairs, the YMCA, and the U.S. Army Air Forces, shaped Overholt's perspectives on leadership and developing leaders. International travel across his career informed his perspective calling for the modern university "to motivate young people for world citizenship" (Overholt, 1971, p. 92).

Between 1976 and 1977, the ACPA's Commission IV set a goal "to develop a Task Force on Leadership Developments for Commission IV in order to study approaches to leadership development on campuses, research efforts in progress, needs, developments, and so forth, and share findings with ACPA membership" (History of Commission IV, February 17, 1977). As Watkins (in press) states, other professional organizations, such as the Association of College Unions-International (ACUI), National Association for Campus Activities (NACA), National Association of Women Deans, Administrators, and Counselors (NAWDAC), and Association of College & University Housing Officers-International (ACUHO-I), were also having conversations about leadership training and development. However, none had so purposefully identified this as a goal nor had they actively disseminated their work beyond their specific professional organization.

The ACPA's Task Force on Leadership Development for Commission IV was chaired by Dennis C. Roberts from 1976 to 1979. Roberts led a comprehensive survey of the leadership development activities at colleges and universities. At this beginning stage of the Task Force, its main goal was to be a resource repository. In 1978, Jan Greenwood, Chair of the ACPA Media Board, expressed interest in a monograph on student leadership development in higher education and authorized Roberts to proceed with plans for developing the publication (ACPA Commission IV Directorate Update from November 20, 1978, p. 3). Richard N. McKaig, then ACPA Commission IV chairperson, stated, "…[the] Task Force shifted from collecting and analyzing information regarding leadership development programs offered at colleges and universities toward creating a resource and referral file for Association members and developing a monograph on student leadership development in higher education" (p. 8). The 1970s was a decade filled with discussion about the need for leadership education in higher education and the beginning of collecting information of what co-curricular programs were happening on college campuses.

Resource Development in the 1980s

The 1980s were filled with efforts toward developing the first resources for co-curricular leadership educators. In 1981, after conducting research for three years on student leadership programs on campuses, the ACPA Commission IV released *Student Leadership Programs in Higher Education*, an edited volume by Dennis Roberts, who was the Task Force chair for three years. This volume was a compilation of the resource files and collective ideas of the Leadership Development Task Force, putting leadership on the national agenda of the higher education community. In *Student Leadership Programs in Higher Education*, advocated for a comprehensive and purposeful leadership development strategy that would include numerous approaches and multiple purposes and would be offered to various populations. The multiple purposes of training, education, and development were derived from Nadler's (1970) model of training, education, and development with regard to human resource development

D. C. Roberts' (1981) *Student Leadership Programs in Higher Education* was a foundational resource for leadership educators. Written for application by working professionals, the final product was divided into five parts: rationale, models, process, program types, and populations. Relevant at the time for administrators, academics, consultants, and individuals interested in leadership training, education, and development, the book established the "how-to" of developing leadership programs and formalized procedures for evaluating the effectiveness of existing programs (Watkins, in press). In 1985, Commission IV published the initial *National Leadership Programs Resource Guide* distributed at national conferences and via the mail when requested by commission members.

As the 40th president of ACPA, Phyllis Mable actively pursued efforts to support interassociation collaboration across student affairs professional organizations—specifically between ACPA and National Association of Student Personnel Administrators (NASPA). Commission IV was one of several ACPA commissions working to improve the communication and collaboration among the associations to address salient professional issues, including student leadership development. In 1984, fifteen associations were invited to participate in an interassociation meeting. Seven groups— ACPA, ACUHO-I, NASPA, NAWDAC, ACUI, National Association of College and University Business Officers (NACUBO), and National Orientation Directors Association (NODA)—met in Washington, DC. At this meeting, association representatives were asked to share potential areas where associations could partner, and leadership development emerged as an area for collaboration. Dennis Roberts, then-President-elect of ACPA, followed up with ACUI President LeNorman Strong and Pat Brown of the University of Vermont, who was the active chair of the Commission

IV Leadership Task Force, to initiate conversations about developing an interassociation group focused on student leadership development. The Inter-Associational Leadership Project was formed in 1986 (Watkins, in press). Many individuals from this group participated in the Association of American Colleges (AAC; now the American Association of College and Universities) Institute on the Study and Practice of Leadership in Washington, DC, in June 1987. The Inter-Association Leadership Project group actively pursued developing a comprehensive model for academic and student affairs staff, options to establish a clearinghouse for leadership programs, and strategies to evaluate program effectiveness. At the time, Nance Lucas served as the Chair of the Commission IV Leadership Task Force, in which the first edition of *The Leadership Exchange* was published utilizing funds and resources provided by the University of Vermont and Ohio University.

During this same timeframe, Susan R. Komives came to the University of Maryland as a graduate faculty member in the College Student Personnel Program. Charged from Vice President William "Bud" Thomas to find ways that University of Maryland could support the development of college student leadership locally and nationally. In 1989, Maryland's Vice President Bud Thomas approved Komives' recommendation for the establishment of the National Clearinghouse for Leadership Programs (NCLP) by providing support through a graduate assistant, assigning responsibility of the Assistant Director of Student Programs in the Office of Campus Programs, as well as designating Komives as the Faculty Associate for the Division of Student Affairs with the project (S. R. Komives, personal communication, January 6, 2017).

Scholarship in the 1990s

In 1990, the newly founded NCLP, the Inter-associational Task Force, and NACA were concurrently planning initiatives to advance co-curricular leadership education. Their interests converged, and the three entities co-hosted the first National Leadership Symposium (NLS), which was held at the University of Maryland in 1990. The attendees shared ideas, generated new programs, defined terms, challenged conventional theory, and began to develop a plan to advance student leadership programs. The National Leadership Symposium meetings became annual, and at the second NLS, the need to develop standards was first discussed and drafted. Susan R. Komives, Dennis Roberts, Nance Lucas, and Tracy Tyree began the process of developing a proposed standard for leadership education for consideration by the Council for the Advancement of Standards in Higher Education (CAS) in the early 1990s. During this time, the NCLP was developing and became a member of CAS. From this, NCLP and CAS redrafted the CAS standards for Student Leadership Programs, and it was published in 1996 (S. R. Komives, personal communication, January 6, 2017).

Along with the release of the Student Leadership Programs CAS standard in 1996, two seminal pieces of scholarship were also published in the same year: the social change model of leadership development (Higher Education Research Institute [HERI], 1998) and the Relational Leadership Model (Komives, Lucas, & McMahon, 1996). The social change model of leadership development was created by a group of leadership and student affairs scholars and practitioners known as the *Ensemble*. The model describes three domains of values: individual, group, and community, which include seven related capacities (HERI, 1998). The Individual Domain focuses on personal skills and identity, the Group Domain focuses on interpersonal skills leaders should effectively use, and the Community Domain emphasizes how leaders should display "citizenship" through positive engagement with the larger society.

Exploring Leadership (Komives, Lucas, & McMahon, 1996) introduces the relational leadership model, which focuses on the idea that leadership effectiveness relates to the leader's ability to create positive relationships within the organization. Inclusiveness, empowerment, and purposeful, ethical, and process orientations are all components of this model. The social change model of leadership development and the relational leadership model are two of the most widely used resources in co-curricular leadership programs (Rosch & Anthony, 2012).

Two professional leadership educator associations were developed in the 1990s. Coming from the agriculture and extension community, the Association of Leadership Educators (ALE) was created in 1990 (Walker, 2002). Today, the ALE has more than 400 members and hosts more than 180 attendees at their annual conference (ALE/Membership, 2017). In 1999, the International Leadership Association (ILA) was created to focus on leadership from a global context and to expand the conversation of leadership into many contexts. Today, the ILA has more than 3,000 members and hosts more than 1,200 attendees from more than 50 countries at their annual conference (ILA/About, 2017). For more about these professional associations, related associations, and the resources they provide, see Chapter 3.

Due to the efforts of pioneers such as Dennis Roberts, Susan R. Komives, and many others, an increase of interest in student leadership development in higher education was apparent. Riggio et al. (2003) states that the number of ACPA, NASPA, and conference participants interested in leadership development doubled from the mid-1980s to the mid-1990s. Starting in the 2000s and continuing today, student affairs practitioners as leadership educators continue to move forward as a profession. In Chapter

3, leadership educator resources are provided, many of which started in the 2000s, continuing the rich history of leadership education as a field and profession.

Scholarship in the 2000s and 2010s

The 2000s catapulted leadership studies from a collection of curricular and co-curricular programs to a discipline. Harvey and Riggio (2011) argue that, by this point, the discipline had matured, boasting widespread presentation of scholarship at professional conferences (i.e., ILA, ALE, NASPA, ACPA), and several peer-reviewed journals had emerged (see Chapter 3). These efforts paved the way for collaborative scholarly efforts, including multiple professional associations such as *National Leadership Education Research Agenda* (Andenoro et al., 2013) and the Critical Considerations for Leadership Education (*Inter-association Leadership Education Collaborative*, 2016).

History of Academic/Curricular-Based Leadership Education

In the 1980s, higher education institutions began offering credit-based leadership-focused courses, and the academic discipline of Leadership Studies began to emerge. In 1980, Gonzaga University in Spokane, Washington, was the first institution to offer liberal arts-based doctoral courses in Leadership Studies (Riggio et al., 2003). A few years later, in 1987, Marietta College in Marietta, Ohio, created the McDonough Leadership Program. This program was the first undergraduate liberal arts leadership-based program (Perruci & Schwartz, 2002). Throughout the 1980s and into the 1990s, curricular leadership education programs began to emerge in both undergraduate and graduate education.

In 1992, the Jepson School of Leadership Studies at the University of Richmond in Virginia became the first degree-granting school of Leadership Studies (Riggio, Ciulla, & Sorenson, 2003). Since 1992, numerous institutions of higher learning responded to the demand for undergraduate leadership development (R. L. Welch, 2000). The W. K. Kellogg foundation, Ford Foundation, and Carnegie Foundation helped fund and produce comprehensive examinations and research into the development of leadership-based programs in higher education (Zimmerman-Oster & Burkhardt, 1999).

Since the founding of the Jepson School, leadership development programs within higher education have grown at an incredible rate (Brungardt,

Greenleaf, Brungardt, & Arensdorf, 2006; Sorenson, 2007). Today, more than 2,000 programs exist worldwide (ILA/Directory, 2017). Perhaps the growth of leadership studies lies within its unique characteristics and the inter- and multidisciplinary nature of the undertaking (Harvey & Riggio, 2013; Rost, 1991; Yukl, 2006). Many scholars argue that leadership studies transcend the disciplines and prepare students for all professions (e.g., Doh, 2003; Wren, Riggio, & Genovese, 2009; Zimmerman-Oster & Burkhardt, 1999).

Academic/Curricular-Based Leadership Program Research

Exploring the phenomenon of academic/curricular-based leadership programs, Brungardt et al. (2006) employed a qualitative study to compare and contrast the leadership major in identified programs from public and private universities in the United States (undergraduate enrollment at these institutions ranged from 700 to more than 69,000). Specifically, the research team looked at school profiles, program profiles, mission, purpose (including theory and application), and curriculum (as well as pedagogy). Notable differences included varied school sizes, host departments, and credit hour requirements. Other inconsistencies included the focus of the program, the major scholars evident within the curricula, and the disparity between theory and skill development. Notable findings from their study include: (a) leadership programs are not limited to a particular type or size of institution; (b) most programs are located in professional and adult studies program, followed by colleges of arts and colleges of business and leadership; (c) all programs in the study were created between 1993 and 2003; (d) careers of graduating students varied greatly, showing occupations in government, social service, religion, business, and industry; (e) an overwhelming majority focused on both theory and application as well as civic and/or organizational objectives; and (f) several universities focused their learning objectives on cognitive theories, whereas others focused on the development of skills and behaviors (with only a few schools focusing on service learning as pedagogy).

Recent research suggests that leadership studies remains inter- and cross-disciplinary. Jenkins' (2017a) study of the instructional strategy use of 836 leadership educators from 41 countries reported leadership studies program delivery from an assortment of academic colleges and departments ranging from business, arts and sciences, education, the humanities, and student affairs. Brungardt et al. (2006) estimated that more than 1,000 curricular-based leadership studies programs existed in the forms of advanced professional, doctorate, and graduate degrees to major, minor, or certificate programs. Similarly, the ILA's Directory of

Leadership Programs contains information for more than 2,000 leadership studies programs from around the globe (ILA/Directory, 2017). These programs include leadership studies, higher education, global studies, outdoor education, and theology. Arguably, this programmatic and curricular growth will engender corresponding leadership scholarship and research. Seeing the growth and overall evolution of both co-curricular and curricular leadership education shows us where leadership has been as a field. It also provides glimpses on where we are headed.

CONCLUSION

Leadership is a unique discipline because it draws from multiple disciplines and is, in fact, interdisciplinary. Leadership studies is distinctive in this regard, and its uniqueness presents endless opportunities for teaching and learning. Leadership education as a field and a profession are both in their infancy and continue to evolve. This book will hopefully add to the conversation. As we mentioned before, although this text is focused on higher education in the U.S. context, we hope that some, if not most, of the topics we discuss are transferrable. However, we understand leadership education internationally is different and needs to be further explored.

This chapter provided a foundational and historical overview of leadership studies as a discipline and leadership education as a field. Hopefully this helps explain the current state of the field and how we got to this point. As we dig into our role of leadership educators, it is vital to think about where we are headed as a field. Although we will discuss this notion throughout the book, it is worth mentioning the importance of looking at leadership through a critical lens (Dugan, 2017) and how we create leadership learning environments for diverse students (Bertrand Jones, Guthrie, & Osteen, 2016; Guthrie et al., 2013). With this in mind, Chapter 2 provides a brief introduction to leadership educator as a professional identity to begin the conversation on identity.

CHAPTER 2

LEADERSHIP EDUCATOR AS A PROFESSIONAL IDENTITY

Leadership education and development occur across high school and college experiences in diverse settings from student organizations, classroom settings, athletics fields, internships, residence halls, service-learning sites, class group meeting spaces, and many others. The term *leadership educator* refers to all educators who intentionally design and foster leadership development. Providing intentional leadership education can be a small part of the main responsibilities (such as student organization advisor, residence hall director, or business course instructor) or as the main focus of full-time responsibilities (e.g., director of a leadership center or leadership course instructor). In the context of higher education, in *The Handbook for Student Leadership Development*, Komives (2011) discusses the professionalization of leadership education and how "...all leadership educators are responsible for this shared journey of advancing the college student leadership agenda" (p. 2). We want to emphasize our deeply held belief that leadership education is for everyone. We all come to being leadership educators from different pathways and contexts, and we bring our personal experiences and multiple identities into this work.

Every educator who interacts with students, in any setting, should think about leadership education—how it emerges for his or her specific role as an educator, program of study design, and instructional and assessment strategies. Developing a personal leadership philosophy and leadership educator philosophy are helpful to consider how the complexities of

The Role of Leadership Educators: Transforming Learning, pp. 19–31
Copyright © 2018 by Information Age Publishing
All rights of reproduction in any form reserved.

leadership and identity intersect and emerge personally as a leadership educator. We honor that this is easier said than done as we continue on our own personal journeys as leadership educators, and we have our own narratives of how our identities influence our professional identities. We have observed colleagues and friends engage in this journey to identifying as a leadership educator.

Social identities have become increasingly significant in conceptualizing leadership as a relational process of understanding both self and others (Guthrie et al., 2013; Ostick & Wall, 2011). Identity is a large part of how we show up as educators and administrators. Discussing how we lean into our leadership educator identities while honoring our other social identities, how they intersect, and which identities become salient when facilitating leadership learning opportunities for different student populations helps us be the best educators we can be. Leadership educators should consider how they teach and show up in the context of influencing student learning (Mahoney, in press).

Palmer (2007) discusses how educators need to teach beyond technique but to bring in their identity, which he defines as the "intersection of diverse forces that make up (my) life" (p. 14). This identity is profound in how we see the world. Palmer (2007) also discusses the "hidden wholeness" in the role of an educator. One of the paradoxes that Palmer suggests we need to reconsider is how we often separate teacher and learner. The teacher has knowledge and the student receives it. However, the wholeness is celebrating that we are all teachers and learners. This wholeness is where education can truly and deeply influence lives. Leadership is a thoughtful discipline where educators are encouraged to join students' journeys of learning. One way we can do this is by exploring our own identity. This chapter introduces leadership educator as a professional identity through discussing multiple dimensions of identity, concepts, and models that inform leadership educator identity and our emerging understanding about leadership educator identity. Much more conversation is needed about this development, as well as spaces where we can explore how our personal identities influence our roles and identities as leadership educators. This chapter gets the conversation started.

IDENTITY

Identity exploration has been a hallmark of higher education research and practice for decades. The basic question of "Who am I?" has plagued humankind since its origins and remains as compelling as it was when Erikson (1959) conceptualized identity and provided foundational work for many theorists, researchers, and practitioners to contribute to the evolution of the concept. As concepts of identity evolved, many frameworks and perspectives emerged. However, depending on the framework, historical context, and disciplinary focus, definitions of identity and the process of how identity development occurs vary. As we frame identity for leadership educators, it is important to consider how theories are socially constructed and reflect the historical, political, cultural, and societal contexts from which they develop (Jones & Abes, 2013).

Reflecting on one's own identity, especially salient identities, is necessary for better understanding experiences in different contexts. Focusing on social identities represents how individuals see themselves as well as how they are perceived by others. Additionally, the salience of certain social identities changes with time and as a result of varying contexts. Salience means "the prominence or importance attached to a particular experience, idea, feeling, or in this case social identity" (Jones & Abes, 2013, p. 40). Although the term *social identities* is relatively new in the landscape of higher education literature, it has a longer history of scholarship in the disciplines of sociology, social psychology, and cultural studies (Jones & Abes, 2013).

Model of Multiple Dimensions of Identity

The Model of Multiple Dimensions of Identity (MMDI) was first introduced by Jones and McEwen (2000) but originated from Jones' (1997) dissertation research. More recently, Jones and Abes (2013) shared scholarship and further thoughts on how the MMDI influences identity development and our work in higher education. The MMDI represents multiple social identities as intersecting rather than just a set of multiple individual, distinct identities and is ever changing as a person evolves in various contexts. As Jones (2016) states, "…the MMDI is intended as a developmental snapshot, rather than a fixed portrayal of identity, and suggests perceptions of one's identities and relative salience are constantly shifting in relation to changing contexts" (p. 26).

The MMDI contains four elements, including the core, multiple social identities, identity salience, and contextual influences (see Jones & McEwen, 2000; Jones & Abes, 2013, for in-depth descriptions). The core is at the center of the MMDI. It represents an individual's personal identity—anything the person considers important to his or her sense of self (e.g., personal attributes, characteristics, qualities, and values). Multiple social identities are represented in the MMDI as intersecting circles around the core. All individuals possess multiple social identities, and these social identities intersect regardless of whether we experience them as such. Identity salience in the MMDI is represented by dots on each of the social identity circles. The more salient a social identity is to an individual, the closer to the core it appears. It is important to note that context makes a difference in how salient certain social identities are experienced, which brings us to the fourth element of the MMDI. Core, social identities, and identity salience are all elements of the MMDI that are situated in a larger context. Placing these elements within a larger context proposes that identities may never be fully understood without taking external forces into consideration (Jones & Abes, 2013).

Intersectionality

Issues of intersectionality have become increasingly common in the fields of education, higher education, and leadership studies. Intersectionality is the study of intersections between different minority and disenfranchised groups specifically studying the interactions of multiple systems of oppression (Crenshaw, 1991). As Jones (2016) states, intersectionality, "… captures the complexities in lived experiences of a diverse array of students and makes an explicit connection between identities and larger structures of inequality" (p. 29). Conceptualizations of identity grouped in the intersections of social identities are a critical consideration, especially in interrogating these identities within larger structures of privilege and oppression. An intersectional lens helps us analyze and more fully understand the lived experiences of individuals across differences and contexts. Exploring the intersectionality of our own multiple identities has implications for how we perceive and interpret the world, as well as our place in it. These perspectives are critical for leadership educators because our facilitation and use of instructional strategies are greatly influenced by our multiple identities and intersections of those identities regardless of whether we recognize it.

INFORMING LEADERSHIP EDUCATOR IDENTITY

Building on Jones and Abes' (2013) work on multiple dimensions of identity and the concept of intersectionality, additional theoretical frameworks, models, and concepts can assist leadership educators in honoring personal identities while developing their own leadership educator identity. Different pedagogies allow educators to differentially explore and reflect on their personal identities, as well as how their identities influence their teaching. Considering engaged pedagogy (hooks, 1994), sentipensante pedagogy (Rendón, 2009), counter-storytelling (Solórzano & Yosso, 2002), public narratives (Ganz, 2011), and culturally relevant leadership learning

(Bertrand Jones et al., 2016) can each further honor and explore how multiple social identities influence our roles as leadership educators. Each of these instructional strategies can have profound influence on how personal identities intersect with leadership educator identity and emerge in a leadership program context. These pedagogies and learning frameworks put the educator at the center, implicitly recognizing the influence of educators to provide learning opportunities in authentic ways.

Engaged Pedagogy

From a holistic learning framework, engaged pedagogy is a practical theory with components of critical theory and feminist theory (hooks, 1994). Engaged pedagogy views education as a liberating force that is not measured through memorization and often challenges standard pedagogical practices. Education is often approached as separate from real life, but engaged pedagogy works to connect learning and learners' lives (hooks, 1994). Often, traditional pedagogy holds knowledge as a possession and not a way of life. It can be seen as temporary and can be difficult to see how to integrate classroom lessons with life outside of college. Ultimately, through engaged pedagogy, students and educators participate in processes that connect their lives and empower them to live deeply.

Engaged pedagogy emphasizes freedom, wisdom, and hope. Freedom is created when the students "see" how information can transform their lives. Through this strategy, educators create environments where learning is engaged in the reality of life and gives students the opportunity to ask probing questions about the status of content and how it applies to individual lives and current events. Wisdom is another component of engaged pedagogy because it employs aspects of critical thinking, which is essential to making people independent learners. Hope gives a sense of possibility, helps foster community, and lets learners look at problems in order to be innovative in the development of creative solutions.

Engaged pedagogy focuses on creating instructional strategies and learning environments where the learner is excited to learn and has interest in the subject due to immersion with the content. hooks (1994) describes engaged pedagogy as a practice in which educators are encouraged to fully immerse themselves in the classroom experience. Engaged educators are vulnerable and transparent with students, especially if there is an expectation for students to share their own lived experiences. These aspects are important in developing learning spaces where educators are able to facilitate dialogue and reflection for students to understand how content is reflected in their own lives.

Sentipensante Pedagogy

Considering sentipensante (sensing and thinking) pedagogy (Rendón, 2009) as an instructional and learning strategy can have a profound influence on how personal identities intersect with a leadership educator identity and emerge in a leadership program, in both academic and co-curricular settings. Rendón (2009) defines sentipensante pedagogy as a "...teaching and learning approach based on wholeness, harmony, social justice, and liberation" (p. 132). One goal of this instructional strategy is to embrace teaching and learning approaches that symbolize wholeness and appreciate personal truth. With this in mind, this approach cultivates well-educated and well-rounded individuals or, as Rendón (2009) describes, "personas educadas" (educated people). The ultimate goal of sentipensante is to instill a commitment to sustain life, maintain the rights of all people, and preserve nature and the harmony of our world in all learners.

Rendón (2009) believes that educators serve many roles, not just the one of imparting knowledge to a student. According to Rendón (2009), an educator is a:

- Teacher/learner (knowledgeable but recognizes he or she is still learning)
- Artist (embraces innovative thinking and creativity)
- Healer/liberator (restores students self-confidence and heals self-doubt)
- Humanitarian (views teaching for the greater good)
- Activist/social change agent (cares about equality and justice for all)

Furthermore, Rendón (2009) states that, using the sentipensante pedagogy, learning environments need to be relationship-centered, foster community, be caring and supportive, and invite emotion. Additionally, these environments should incorporate ways for students to work collaboratively and have both academic and interpersonal validation. Educators have a responsibility to create this type of learning environment, which can be done by being vulnerable and open themselves. By role modeling this type of openness, students are less likely to be afraid of being vulnerable; thus, sharing and making meaning will become more comfortable. However, we acknowledge that being open can be difficult and is different from the professional distance educators are expected to keep between educator and student. For example, we offer our own stories in leadership learning to the students we work with. We discuss how we fail, continue to learn, and daily evolve as leaders, and our journey is best engaging in the process of leadership.

Storytelling

Ganz's (2011) model of public narrative and counterstories (Solórzano & Yosso, 2002) are two frameworks where social identities of educators and learners can be explored and shared. Ganz's (2011) model of public narrative includes three forms of storytelling: story of self, story of us, and story of now. Ganz (2011) writes:

> Story of self communicates the values that move us to lead. A story of us communicates values shared by those whom you hope to motivate to join us. And a story of now communicates the urgent challenge to those values that demand action now. (p. 282)

These forms of storytelling are drawn from a series of choice points that have created the plot of your life. These points include challenges faced, choices made, and outcomes experiences.

Mahoney (in press) discusses how he uses Ganz's (2011) public narratives as a leadership educator. Mahoney (in press) frames Ganz's model as a framework to establish leadership educators as "action facilitators" who "practice what we teach in the way we teach it" (Ganz & Lin, 2011, p. 359). Educators sharing stories of self can help students with possible feelings of anxiety and give them confidence to share their own stories of self as a leadership learning skill. Essentially, Ganz's model of public narrative allows leadership educators and learners to engage each other more fully.

In addition to public narratives, sharing counterstories is another powerful storytelling strategy. A counterstory occurs when stories of those who have been silenced can finally use their voice to tell their story and be acknowledged. Examples of counterstories are personal stories, narratives, other people's stories or narratives, and composite stories or narratives (Solórzano & Yosso, 2002). Counterstories can be used to expose, analyze, and challenge deeply entrenched narratives. They humanize the lived experiences of members of often marginalized groups and teach others about the realities of those lived experiences. As educators develop curriculum, creating their own stories of self and counterstories allows for personal identities to emerge as an important part of the leadership learning process. It also allows content to come alive and often makes it more relatable. As Mahoney (in press) asserts, "...storytelling can be another effective critical pedagogical practice which draws its strength in a comprehension of embodied emotions" (p. xx).

Culturally Relevant Leadership Learning

The culturally relevant leadership learning (CRLL) model (Bertrand Jones, Guthrie, & Osteen, 2016) challenges and aims to transform previous leadership learning paradigms. CRLL considers learning environments in terms of campus contextual dimensions and broader environmental factors by focusing on leader identity, capacity, and efficacy of diverse learners. The CRLL model (Bertrand Jones et al., 2016; see Figure 2.1) recognizes the power inherent in leadership, with distinct considerations on the use of language, and leadership educators' power to influence students' identity, capacity, and efficacy through institutional culture and climate. It relies on intersectional frameworks of identity development (Guthrie et al., 2013; Jones, 2016; Ostick & Wall, 2011) to create learning environments where everyone is welcome and can engage in the leadership learning process. Grounded in the work of Hurtado, Milem, Clayton-Pederson, and Allen (1999) and Milem, Chang, and Antonio (2005), the five domains of cultur- ally relevant leadership learning include: (a) historical legacy of inclusion/ exclusion; (b) compositional diversity; (c) psychological climate; (d) behav- ioral climate; and (e) organizational/structural aspects.

Educational scholars (Meixner & Rosch, 2011; Rosch & Anthony, 2012; Thompson & Couto, 2016) have argued that effective pedagogy should reflect the leadership content being taught. Additionally, parallels between relational models of leadership and teaching, as well as critical pedago-

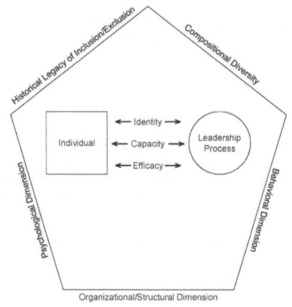

Source: Bertrand Jones et al. (2016.

Figure 2.1.   Culturally relevant leadership learning model.

gies, have been found to be effective teaching tools for leadership learning (Guthrie et al., 2013, 2016; Mahoney, 2016; Pendakur & Furr, 2016). Mahoney (in press) eloquently remarks:

> CRLL harnesses diverse and often overlooked leadership thought and prac-
> tice to enhance all students' identity, capacity and efficacy in leadership de-
> velopment for social change. These "subjugated knowledges" of leadership,
> experiences and theories put forth by women, people of color and sexual mi-
> norities, work on, against, and alongside dominant paradigms to challenge
> students' conceptualization of leadership and make space for marginalized
> students. (p. XX)

CRLL provides a learning framework that can be influential on students' learning as well as our own journeys as leadership educators and how our identities matter.

Our review of hooks' (1994) engaged pedagogy, Rendón's (2009) sen-tipensante pedagogy, Solórzano and Yosso's (2002) counter-storytelling, Ganz's (2011) public narrative, and the Bertrand Jones et al. (2016) cul-turally relevant leadership learning model is by no means an exhaustive treatment of the pedagogies that leadership educators can employ in their search for understanding their own social identities or the intersectional identities of others. However, they do represent significant starting points for those about to embark on such a journey, and they serve as helpful reminders to those who are already entrenched in this work. Recognizing where we are in our own journey better prepares us as leadership educators to provide the space and grace others may need to do their own identity work. This includes our students, who, in addition to learning leadership, are constructing their own leader identities. The manner in which we are able to make meaning from the multiples dimensions of our visible and invisible identities can only help create more impactful learning environ-ments for our students.

LEADERSHIP EDUCATOR IDENTITY

We still know little about the professional identities of leadership educators. However, research regarding leadership educator identity (Harding, 2011; Seemiller & Priest, 2015, 2017; Jenkins, 2017b) offers promising findings. These studies are foundational to further conversations and additional research about this topic. However, we do know that individuals enter the task of becoming a leadership educator from different disciplinary lenses, contexts, and experiences. For example, the authors had different personal journeys in becoming leadership educators.

Our two stories provide a small snapshot of just how different journeys can be to becoming a leadership educator. Kathy started facilitating leadership programs as a graduate assistant during her master's degree work at Illinois State University. She transitioned into working as the director of the Office of Volunteer Programs at University of Illinois at Urbana-Champaign, where she worked closely with the Illinois Leadership Center. Although she had an undergraduate minor in leadership, she learned how to develop programs and curriculum through trial and error. Dan started teaching leadership during the first year of his doctoral program at University of South Florida after teaching political science courses at a local community college for a year. The first class he taught was an undergraduate introductory leadership course. He had only taken one undergraduate course almost a decade prior, but he loved teaching and drew on his experiences as an involved undergraduate student at Florida State University. Although both were involved undergraduate students, one had minimal academic training, and the other had classroom teaching experience. Kathy and Dan started as leadership educators through different contexts: Kathy in co-curricular and Dan in academic/curricular contexts. These differences are significant even at a cursory level because they show how educators come into this work with such varying experiences, causing the way they teach to differ greatly. These differences also demonstrate the need to better understand how leadership educators enter the field, their experiences, and how their professional identity develops.

Harding's (2011) dissertation is the first known research on experiences of leadership educators. His phenomenological study was aimed at describing the experiences of 12 leadership educators who taught in an undergraduate leadership development program. All participants in Harding's (2011) study had at least three years of experience teaching leadership at the undergraduate level. From his qualitative study, four themes emerged "(a) 'I teach leadership. What does that mean?'; (b) 'not dancing alone' in the learning community; (c) helping students make a difference; and (d) the educator's journey: 'a place of becoming'" (Harding, 2011, p. ii). This study found that teaching leadership was about both the student's (leadership learning) and educator's (self-development) parallel journeys of learning. Harding's (2011) research provided a foundation for further exploring the journeys and professional identities of leadership educators.

LEADERSHIP EDUCATOR PROFESSIONAL
IDENTITY DEVELOPMENT

A deeper understanding of leadership educator professional identity has potential benefits for leadership educators, their students, and the entire field of leadership education. Harding (2011) offered, "...identities of the leadership educators would be expected to develop as they participate in a community of practice with the students and their colleagues" (p. 93). Communities of practice that support new professionals and engage experienced practitioners can create more learning opportunities for educators to share resources, provide formal and informal mentoring, and offer various professional development experiences (Seemiller & Priest, 2017). As we discussed in Chapter 1, leadership education is a relatively young field. Therefore, exploring how to best develop the capacity of leadership educators will assist in their individual professional identity development, as well as prove vital to the continued development of competent, confident, passionate, and effective leadership educators.

Seemiller and Priest (2015) began to explore identity development by synthesizing professional identity literature and developing the Leadership Educator Professional Identity Development (LEPID) model. This model includes identity spaces, influences, and critical incidents. The authors suggest that leadership educators are situated in four identity spaces, including exploration, experimentation, validation, and confirmation. Individuals can move forward and backward through these four spaces depending on influences and critical incidents that occur (Seemiller & Priest, 2015). In the exploration identity space, an individual explores whether the leadership identity is a fit for them. Experimentation occurs when an individual tries out the leadership educator identity, often emulating a more experienced person in the field to see whether it fits his or her own identity. Validation occurs through both self-validation and validation from others, and confirmation is found when an individual feels a part of a leadership educator community of practice (Seemiller & Priest, 2015).

Expanding their proposed model, Seemiller and Priest (2017) analyzed stories from participants of a professional leadership educator development experience. They uncovered additional elements of leadership educator identity, resulting in a more holistic understanding of one's professional identity development. One major finding in their study was the role of leader in leadership education (Seemiller & Priest, 2017). Of the 22 leadership educators in this study, every participant mentioned prior leadership experience as part of their professional journey. Most participants discussed the influence of serving in a formal leadership role, whereas others described failing as a leader. Both the positive and negative experiences served as foundational elements for their professional identity as a leadership educator. This confirms Harding's (2011) findings that "leadership educators shared that their interests in leadership, which eventually led to their interest in teaching leadership" (p. 94).

Experiences of Becoming and Being a Leadership Educator

Jenkins (2017b) added to the limited literature on the experiences associated with becoming and being a leadership educator. He conducted a phenomenological study utilizing a snowball sample of 13 leadership educators (eight female and five male) from 11 various institutions. Participants ranged in role and experience from adjunct faculty to department head. The study's interviews included questions about what motivated them to be a leadership educator, what professional development they engage in, how they would describe the learning environment they create, and what it is like to teach leadership among other questions.

From the data collected, four major themes emerged from participants' journey of becoming a leadership educator: (a) impact; (b) serendipity; (c) "fake it till you make it"; and (d) developing others. Participants described needing to make a positive impact on their students' lives, and this need influenced their chosen career path of a leadership educator. Serendipity emerged from participants' discussion about how finding their way to this profession was because of earlier experiences with leadership or engaging with others in the process of leadership. The theme "fake it till you make it" is what one might guess: most leadership educators had little to no formal teaching preparation or education in leadership prior to facilitating or teaching a leadership program. Finally, developing others was discussed as an important part of entering this profession.

Through further examination of the data, Jenkins (2017b) revealed six subthemes regarding participants' understanding of being a leadership educator:

- A helping field (participants described leadership educator as a selfless profession)
- Trial and error (participants learned teaching strategies from observing others and experimenting)
- Creating a "safe" space (participants felt creating environments that were safe for exploration of ideas was critical for leadership learning)
- Modeling the way (participants described that modeling leadership through facilitating and teaching was important for being a leadership educator)
- I'm loving it (participants had a deep affection for the work they do)
- Agitators (participants articulated the importance of disrupting students' thinking in order to engage and dig deeper into concepts and how they apply to students' lives)

By practicing transparent instructional strategies and embracing their own learning processes and identity development, leadership educators can fully engage in their professional identity. It is important for leadership educators to model the type of leadership skills and values they are teaching (Rosch & Anthony, 2012). Students may notice inconsistencies if leadership programs are based on teaching practices in which educators are disengaged from the experience. If the content received is not integrated into the educators' personal practices and identity, then the overall learning experience will be disconnected.

BRINGING THE WHOLE SELF TO THE LEADERSHIP LEARNING ENVIRONMENT

It is important for both majority and minority populations to bring their whole selves to leadership education and learning processes. How educators show up in leadership programs, both co-curricular and academic/curricular in nature, is critical. As educators, we all need to spend time reflecting on how we present ourselves as well as the space we take up in the learning environment. Frankly, we have a lot of responsibility for creating a learning environment where all students feel welcomed and validated in their own leadership learning journey.

As educators, we need to remember how our identity is at the core of our teaching leadership journey (Harding, 2011). It influences the way we engage students, teach leadership, and make decisions on how we build intentional learning environments. How we bring our whole selves to this work as leadership educators while continuing to learn about ourselves is complex. As our students are evolving, so are we as educators. It is important to center our work on deep reflection, connecting with mentors, and debriefing experiences as educators to develop our professional identities and bring the best versions of ourselves as possible. We must honor and acknowledge those complexities of bringing our whole selves as we focus on the leadership discipline with love and dedication to our students, ourselves, and leadership learning.

CHAPTER 3

LEADERSHIP EDUCATOR RESOURCES

In talking with colleagues, we realize only a small percentage of leadership educators are plugged into the most pragmatic resources for teaching leadership. In fact, according to a 2015 internal benchmarking survey administered by the Inter-Association Leadership Education Collaborative (ILEC), including 416 members of ILEC professional associations who identified as leadership educators, the resources on the International Leadership Association's (ILA) website (http://www.ila-net.org/) were only used regularly by more than half (57.4%) of the respondents. The next most regularly used resources were those found on the websites of the National Clearinghouse for Leadership Programs (NCLP, http://nclp. umd.edu/) (33.0%), Association of Leadership Educators (ALE, https:// www.leadershipeducators.org/) (29.2%), and the Center for Creative Leadership (CCL, https://www.ccl.org/; 28.1%). Although respondents were aware of resources such as the Greenleaf Center for Servant Leadership, (https://www.greenleaf.org/) more than half (50.9%) said they do not use it. In fact, more than half of respondents reported having never heard of eight of the 20 resources included in the survey: ACPA: College Student Educators International, ACUI I-LEAD Program, ACUI I-LEAD Connect, Association of College Unions International, ALE, Campus Compact (State or National), CCL, Center for Ethical Leadership, Colorado Leadership Alliance, Commercial Student Affairs Resource Groups (e.g., PaperClip Communications, Magna), Discipline-based association(s),

The Role of Leadership Educators: Transforming Learning, pp. 33–52
Copyright © 2018 by Information Age Publishing
All rights of reproduction in any form reserved.

Greenleaf Center for Servant-Leadership, ILA, LeaderShape Inc., NACA, NCLP, National Conference on Race and Ethnicity (NCORE), National Association of Campus Activities, NASPA Student Leadership Institute, and the NASPA: Student Affairs Administrations in Higher Education (we will provide coverage of many of these resources in this chapter and empower you to explore those we do not). There appears to be either a lack of useful leadership educator resources or a significant marketing and awareness gap. This divide was just one of the many impetuses for this text.

In our own scan, we learned of some potentially underutilized resources for teaching and learning leadership. We wanted to provide practical resources that all leadership educators can use while developing and teaching curricular and co-curricular programs. This chapter outlines resources including, but not limited to, professional associations, academic journals, printed manuals and classroom texts, useful instructor's guides, centers, and other helpful items. By no means do we claim this list as exhaustive, but it will hopefully provide additional supportive resources for leadership educators.

PROFESSIONAL ASSOCIATIONS AND THEIR RESOURCES

Professional associations provide ongoing support as well as a plethora of resources accessible to members and sometimes nonmembers. We will explore both leadership- and student affairs-focused associations and the resources they provide.

Leadership-Focused Associations

Three associations specifically focused on leadership will be discussed below: the Association of Leadership Educators, International Leadership Association, and the National Clearinghouse for Leadership Programs.

Association of Leadership Educators (ALE)

In 1990, the ALE (https://www.leadershipeducators.org/) was officially created after discussion of such a professional association developed over three annual leadership seminars of agricultural faculty and extension specialists in the late 1980s (Walker, 2002). During the third seminar, held in Milwaukee, Wisconsin, ALE was officially formed, and the following year, in 1991, the first official conference and annual meeting of ALE was held in Denver, Colorado (Walker, 2002).

ALE is a practitioner-based professional association for leadership educators. The purpose of ALE is to strengthen the leadership skills and competencies of leadership educators who work to develop the leadership capabilities of others as well as strengthen and broaden the knowledge base that supports research, teaching and outreach, student services, consulting, and other programs in leadership (ALE Purpose, 2017). Its membership includes more than 400 leadership educators, including scholars, postsecondary faculty, and college student affairs professionals (ALE Member Directory, 2017).

The conference proceedings from ALE's annual conference are a rich source of information. They include numerous application briefs, peda-gogy-in-practice pieces, educator workshops, and peer-reviewed research papers. These proceedings can be accessed at www.leadershipeducators. org/ConferenceProceedings.

In the fall of 2011, the inaugural National Leadership Education Research Agenda 2013–2018: Providing strategic direction for the field of leadership education (NLERA) was conceived, and the ALE stepped forward to develop a practical resource to supplement the scholarship informing leadership education (Andenoro et al., 2013). The two over-arching goals of the NLERA include providing research priorities that can guide applied scholarship in contributing to the development of future leaders and managers through higher education, and offering key elements to further define leadership education as a discipline. The NLERA includes the following seven research priorities as well as practical applications and future steps:

1. Teaching, Learning, & Curriculum Development
2. Programmatic Assessment & Evaluation
3. The Psychological Development of the Leader, Learner, and Follower
4. The Sociological Development of the Leader, Learner, and Follower
5. The Influences of Social Identity
6. Social Change and Community Development
7. Global and Intercultural Capacity

The following professional associations, member groups, and organizations offered public support of this collaborative effort: ACPA, ACUI, NCLP, NACA, ALE, ILA Leadership Education Member Interest Group, NASPA Student Leadership Programs Knowledge Community, *The New York Times* in Leadership, and Jossey-Bass Publishing.

International Leadership Association (ILA)

Throughout the mid-1990s, participants of the Kellogg Leadership Studies Project discussed the need for a unifying and overarching organization to support the field of leadership studies. Supported by the W. K. Kellogg Foundation, the Kellogg Leadership Studies Project convened a group of 50 leadership scholars and practitioners from around the world to create and publish cross-disciplinary leadership scholarship. At the end of this project, a conference was organized: the Leaders/Scholars Association. The purpose of this meeting was to bring together those who study leadership and those who practice it. After this first meeting, it was decided that this association should be for anyone who shared an interest in leadership and the association was to be driven by diversity in thought, discipline, culture, sector, and geography (ILA, 2017).

The ILA is the largest international and interdisciplinary association dedicated to the study and development of leadership. Its membership includes more than 3,000 top scholars and practitioners from more than 70 countries and is one of the few organizations to actively embrace academics, practitioners, consultants, private industry, public leaders, not-for-profit organizations, and students (ILA Member Benefits, 2017). Additionally, the ILA provides annual conferences where presentations are internationally quadruple blind peer reviewed. In addition to yearly conferences, specific topical conferences are held internationally depending on interests of the membership.

ILA Member Communities. ILA comprises three types of member communities: Member Interest Groups (MIGs), Learning Communities (e.g., Arts and Leadership, Doctoral Program Faculty and Leaders), and Affinity Groups (e.g., Leadership Education Program Directors, Deans, and Chairs), which provide specific support to members. The two largest member communities are the Leadership Education and Leadership Scholarship MIGs. The Leadership Education MIG facilitates the sharing of leadership ideas, methods of teaching and learning, programs, and curricula. The Leadership Scholarship MIG creates opportunities to share research and theories, encourages rigor and relevance, and fosters collaboration for both seasoned and new scholars (ILA Member Interest Groups, 2017).

ILA Publications. The ILA also provides its membership with a variety of published resources. The ILA monthly newsletter, *ILA Intersections*, provides various points of information for members—from interviews with members and scholars around the world to job postings and association events. A reoccurring column in the ILA Intersections newsletter is "PAUSE for Pedagogy." "PAUSE for Pedagogy" aims to connect leadership education theory to practice and takes lessons learned in the classroom to expand our theoretical knowledge of teaching and learning. The ILA also publishes an annual *Building Leadership Bridges* books series (2001–present), with topics ranging from grassroots leadership, arts, and social change (Erenrich & Wergin, 2017) to future trends (Sowcik, Andenoro, McNutt, & Murphy, 2015).

National Clearinghouse for Leadership Programs (NCLP)

In 1989, the NCLP was established by the support of University of Maryland's Vice President for Student Affairs, Bud Thomas, when he provided funding for a 12-month graduate assistant and designated Dr. Susan Komives' role as Faculty Associate for the Division of Student Affairs to the project (S. R. Komives, personal communication, January 6, 2017). Still based at the University of Maryland, the NCLP supports the development of cutting-edge resources, information sharing, and symposia on leadership development for college students. With more than 300 institutional members, the NCLP is a hub for leadership educator and program development and aims to connect leadership educators to one another (NCLP, 2017).

The NCLP provides an abundance of leadership educator resources, including assessment tools, bibliographies on cutting-edge research, access to foundational scholarship, leadership book reviews, syllabi, and a tri-annual newsletter. It also provides sample syllabi for leadership-focused courses and descriptions of co-curricular leadership development programs. *Concepts and Connections* is another publication of the NCLP and serves as a place for scholarly content, campus program spotlights, book reviews, and research updates to be shared. One of the critical contributions the NCLP offers to leadership educators beyond resources is providing conferences and various events for leadership educators to gather. We will discuss some of these conferences and events later in this chapter.

Student Affairs-Focused Associations

Throughout the history of U.S. higher education, student affairs professionals have both designed and supported the goals of student learning. With a focus on the holistic development of students (American Council of Education, 1937), student affairs is now defining learning and development as intertwined (ACPA & NASPA, 2004). Learning needs to be at the center of the student affairs profession.

With roots in student affairs, leadership educators continue to be supported by field-specific professional associations. In 2009, the two primary student affairs professional associations—ACPA: College Student Educators

International and the NASPA: Student Affairs Administrators in Higher Education—collaborated to establish a set of professional competencies for student affairs practitioners. A considerable amount of research has identified core competencies for the various work done by student affairs professionals (Herdlein, 2004; Lovell & Kosten, 2000; Pope & Reynolds, 1997). From this collaborated effort, 10 competency areas were initially adopted by both associations in July 2010 and then revised in 2015. One of the consistent core competencies for student affairs professionals between the two editions is Leadership. As described by the *Professional Competency Areas for Student Affairs Educators* (ACPA & NASPA, 2015), the Leadership competency:

> addresses the knowledge, skills, and dispositions required of a leader, with or without positional authority. Leadership involves both the individual role of a leader and the leadership process of individuals working together to envision, plan, and affect change in organizations and respond to broad-based constituencies and issues. This can include working with students, student affairs colleagues, faculty, and community members. (p. 13)

The proposed professional development for the Leadership competency should reflect the shift from knowledge of leadership theories and concepts to critical application, ultimately leading to the development of leadership within and among others (ACPA & NASPA, 2015). The development of leadership is the work of leadership educators—a critical responsibility of student affairs professionals.

ACPA: College Student Educators International

As you may recall from Chapter 1, ACPA was instrumental in supporting the beginning of co-curricular leadership development through leading conversations, establishing task forces, and publishing the first documents sharing leadership development resources. ACPA has a rich history dating back to 1924 (History of ACPA, 2017). At this same time, two important organizational purposes were articulated for ACPA. The first was to establish specific areas within the larger organization that support different types of personnel work. The second was to focus on the promotion and development of members.

The Commission for Student Involvement supports leadership educators by providing a supportive community of student Aaffairs professionals committed to providing meaningful co-curricular and curricular experiences for today's college students. A major emphasis of the commission's work is integrating out-of-class activities of on-campus students with formal academic curriculum. By providing access to unique resources, networking events, distinguishing recognitions, and professional development opportunities, this commission works to enhance the knowledge and practice of educators specifically focused on Fraternity and Sorority Life, Leadership Development, Student Organizations and Activities, as well as Community Service and Service Learning.

NASPA: Student Affairs Administrators in Higher Education

In the fall of 1918, NASPA's founding members discussed the need for a group to support college student personnel. A year later, the Conference of Deans and Advisers of Men was founded, eventually becoming NASPA (The History of NASPA, 2017). This association focuses on the advancement, health, and sustainability of the student affairs profession. With more than 13,000 members across all 50 states, 29 countries, and 8 U.S. territories, it serves a full range of professionals who provide programs, experiences, and services to cultivate student learning and success in concert with the missions of its member colleges and universities (About NASPA, 2017).

Within the NASPA structure, knowledge communities (KCs) provide access to information in particular subject areas, connect members, and facilitate sharing of that knowledge. With more than 5,000 members, SLPKC is the largest knowledge community in NASPA. SLPKC's mission is to serve as a resource for higher education professionals interested in leadership training, education, and development of college students (NASPA Knowledge Communities, 2017). This community of leadership educators share best practices; examine standards for leadership programs; support international, national, and regional efforts to develop student leadership programs; and contribute to leadership scholarship and literature (Student Leadership Programs, 2017).These goals are met through monthly electronic newsletters, sponsored programs at the annual convention, and podcasts that provide opportunities to learn and engage with scholars and innovative ideas.

As you can see, professional associations offer various resources from conferences, focused communities to engage with, and access to scholarship and examples of practice. Broadly, associations are essential to the community of practice for leadership educators. They offer structured support whether specifically focused in leadership or the higher education context.

PROFESSIONAL INSTITUTES, WORKSHOPS, AND SYMPOSIA

Beyond annual conferences, several professional development opportunities are available for leadership educators to gain knowledge, apply theory to practice, and build community with other leadership educators.

Although this list is not exhaustive, we will discuss a few focused gatherings specifically for leadership educators, including the National Leadership Symposium, the Leadership Educators Institute, the Leadership Educators Academy, and Lead 365. We provide a brief overview here but encourage you to visit each program's website for the most current information.

National Leadership Symposium (NLS)

Since 1993, the annual NLS has offered a professional development experience for faculty, administrators, and other educators involved with leadership education at colleges and universities. It is situated around major topics such as pluralistic leadership, leadership education, authenticity, and student development. NLS is coordinated by the National Association for Campus Activities (NACA) and the National Clearinghouse for Leadership Programs (NCLP). It is designed to be an intimate learning environment, with about 50 participants, and includes a variety of presentation formats, exercises, and conversations to engage different learning styles and preferences. Participants are expected to have read several selected readings in advance of arriving to NLS. Craig Slack, director of the NCLP, is instrumental in the continued development of NLS (NCLP History, 2017).

Leadership Educators Institute (LEI)

The LEI is a biennial, innovative forum intended to address the needs of entry- to mid-level leadership educators. In 2004, NCLP, ACPA, and NASPA held the first LEI at the University of North Caroline at Greensboro with approximately 400 people in attendance. Most recently, LEI 2016 was held in Long Beach, California, with approximately 500 in attendance (C. Slack, personal communication, February 17, 2017).

Leadership Education Academy (LEA)

Sponsored by the ILA and co-chaired by Corey Seemiller and Dan Jenkins, LEA (http://www.ila-net.org/lea/) was designed over a two-and-a-half-year period by leadership educators in higher education from a variety of educational backgrounds, programming and classroom experiences, and association involvement. The biennial academy, introduced in 2015, is intended to be a complementary experience to other established professional development programs for leadership educators. LEA is a cohort-style program, limited to 72 participants, and specifically designed to advance one's ability to teach leadership in a variety of capacities. LEA is unique because it is an immersive, cohort-based, experiential, and intentional opportunity for learning, mentoring, and feedback to maximize professional development (Leadership Educators Academy, 2017).

LEAD 365

LEAD 365 is a two-day leadership program held annually in early November in Orlando, Florida. Focusing on student experiences, LEAD 365 has two professional development tracks for graduate students, leadership educators, advisors, and professional staff members focusing on the development of college student leaders. This leadership educator program is provided simultaneously to a student-focused workshop series so educators can be learning while their students are learning.

Whether it is learning a new program design or instructional strategy or getting new ideas for program enhancement, professional development opportunities are vital for leadership educators. Opportunities to learn with other leadership educators in a community of practice provides space to engage with other educators, connect for potential collaboration, and exchange best practices.

ACADEMIC JOURNALS AND MONOGRAPHS

Access to high-quality scholarship is critical for the continuous development of leadership educators. Searching academic journals often results in a plethora of results from higher education and its related subfields. However, given the relative novelty of leadership as a discipline and the role of leadership educator as an emerging profession, few journals focus on leadership. Although they are growing in both circulation and prominence, specific academic outlets for student leadership, leadership education, and the broader field of leadership remain elusive. We choose to highlight a few examples of journals that could be of particular interest to leadership educators: *New Directions for Student Leadership*, *Journal of Leadership Education*, *Journal of Leadership Studies*, and *The Leadership Quarterly*. We encourage working with your institution's library to ensure access to these high-quality leadership scholarship outlets.

New Directions for Student Leadership (NDSL)

The *NDSL* monograph series explores leadership conceptually and pedagogically with topics of interest to high school and college leadership educators. Issues in this series are grounded in scholarship featuring practical applications and good practices in youth and adult leadership education. Prior to becoming *NDSL* in 2015, this *New Directions* series was formally *New Directions for Youth Development*. Table 3.1 shows the available issues from the first three years of publication.

Table 3.1.   New Directions for Student Leadership Published Issues

Issue Editor(s)	Year	Volume	Issue Title
Seemiller, C.	2017	156	A competency-based approach for student leadership development
Rosch, D.	2017	155	The role of student organizations in developing leadership
Tillapaugh, D., & Haber-Curran, P.	2017	154	Gender and leadership
Ahlquist, J., & Endersby, L.	2017	153	Going digital in student leadership
Guthrie, K. L., Bertrand Jones, T., & Osteen, L.	2016	152	Developing culturally relevant leadership learning
Roberts, D., & Bailey, K.	2016	151	Assessing student leadership
Wagner, W., & Pigza, J.	2016	150	Leadership development through service learning
Reichard, R., & Thompson, S.	2016	149	Leader developmental readiness: Pursuit of leadership excellence
Evans, M., & Knight Abowitz, K.	2015	148	Engaging youth in leadership for social and political change
Stenta, D., & McFadden, C.	2015	147	Developing leadership through recreation and athletics
Schwartz, A. J.	2015	146	Developing ethical leaders
Owen, J. E.	2015	145	Innovative learning for leadership development

NDSL, co-edited by Susan R. Komives and Kathy L. Guthrie, aims to be innovative in student leadership education and learning. In the short time it has been in publication, it has already started to influence how leadership educators design and develop leadership learning opportunities.

Journal of Leadership Education (JOLE)

In 2002, *JOLE* (http://www.journalofleadershiped.org/) began with support from the ALE. *JOLE* is an international, refereed journal that provides a forum for scholars and professional practitioners engaged in leadership education to develop knowledge to put into practice. *JOLE*'s editorial focus is on applied research, reinforcing the notion that feedback between theory and practice tests and strengthens both. Accordingly, *JOLE* offers scholarly and empirical feature articles as well as application briefs focused on practice, programs, and pedagogy. The journal sits at the nexus of education theory and practice, as well as leadership theory and practice.

Journal of Leadership Studies (JLS)

JLS aims to publish leadership research-based and theoretically driven contributions that bridge the gap between scholarship and practice. *JLS* promotes interdisciplinary and interorganizational approaches, fosters dialogue to transcend industry-specific contexts, and explores leadership's role in improving organizational practices and human life (*Journal of Leadership Studies*, 2017). Although not focused primarily on leadership education, the journal includes articles and symposia related to the practice of teaching, learning, and assessing leadership development.

Leadership Quarterly (LQ)

LQ is a social-science journal (https://www.journals.elsevier.com/the-leadership-quarterly) devoted to advancing the understanding of leadership as a phenomenon. This includes the study of leadership, as well as leadership's practical implications. *LQ* incorporates a variety of disciplinary perspectives and seeks to amplify multidisciplinary perspectives. This journal aims to publish empirical, scholarly, and applied manuscripts from diverse fields of inquiry about leadership. The editorial board is open to research of both formal and informal leaders from various walks of life (*The Leadership Quarterly*/Editorial Board, 2017).

BEYOND JOURNALS AND MONOGRAPHS

Resources are available for leadership educators or those interested in learning more about leadership education, but many remain underutilized. Table 3.2 provides additional reference material for leadership educators. Furthermore, potential leadership education textbooks for use with students are provided in Table 3.3. It is important to note that classroom texts do not have to have the word *leadership* in the title to directly connect with the established learning outcomes. Instructional manuals we have used in a variety of capacities and contexts are in Table 3.4. As leadership educators, we often need to look across disciplines to find the best resources.

Table 3.2.   Leadership Educator Books and Reports

Author(s)	Title	Year Published	Brief Overview
Adams, M., Bell, L. A., & Griffin, P.	*Teaching for Diversity and Social Justice* (2nd ed.)	2007	Provides theoretical and curricular frameworks for teaching diversity and social justice, which can translate to elements of the leadership classroom and curriculum.
Guthrie, K. L., Bertrand Jones, T., Osteen, L., & Hu, S.	*Cultivating Leader Identity and Capacity in Students From Diverse Backgrounds*	2013	Addresses the intersection of undergraduate leadership development and student diversity to provide insight on effective programming and intentional interventions, offering paths to optimize the development of all students' identity and capacity to lead.
Guthrie, K. L., Bertrand Jones, T., & Osteen, L.	*New Directions for Student Leadership:* No. 152. Developing Culturally Relevant Leadership Learning	2016	Provides a model and conceptual framework for assisting leadership educators in intersecting concepts of culture and leadership.
Kezar, A. J., Carducci, R., & Contreras-McGavin, M.	*Rethinking the L Word in Higher Education: The Revolution of Research on Leadership*	2006	Summarizes research and literature about conceptualizations of leadership from a postmodern and postindustrial paradigm to inform practice in higher education leadership.
Komives, S. R., Dugan, J. P., Owen, J. E., Slack, C., Wagner, W., & Associates.	*The Handbook for Student Leadership Development*	2011	Contains a history of student leadership programs in higher education and provides practical tools for building student leadership development programs on college campuses.
Kouzes, J. M., Posner, B. Z., & Biech, E.	*The Leadership Challenge Activities Book*	2010	Focused on experiential engagement to engender learning about the practices; meant to accompany teaching and learning the five practices of the Leadership Challenge.

(Table continues on next page)

Table 3.2. (Continued)

Author(s)	Title	Year Published	Brief Overview
Landreman, L. M.	*The Art of Effective Facilitation: Reflections of Social Justice Educators*	2013	Includes useful, practical guides for teaching and facilitating topics of social justice.
Lozano, A., Barcelo, N., & Beatty, C. C.	*Latina/o College Student Leadership: Emerging Theory, Promising Practice*	2015	Addresses leadership development for Latina/o college students. Grounded in research from student development theory and experiences of Latina/o students.
Rost, J. C.	*Leadership for the 21st Century*	1991	Review of the study of leadership over a 75-year range; highlights distinctions between leadership and management; establishes a recommended postindustrial definition of leadership.
Seemiller, C.	*The Student Leadership Competencies Guidebook*	2013	Based on learning outcomes of a number of programs; highlights 60 leadership competencies educators can explore for encouraging and understanding student leadership development.
Shankman, M., Allen, S., & Haber-Curran, P.	*Emotionally Intelligent Leadership for Students: Facilitation and Activity Guide*	2015	Provides activities and facilitation guides for curriculum in conjunction with Emotionally Intelligent Leadership for Students.
Skendall, K. C., Ostick, D. T., Komives, S. R., & Wagner, W. (Eds.)	*The Social Change Model: Facilitating Leadership Development*	2017	Provides leadership educators with classroom and workshop activities, discussion and reflection questions, assignment suggestions, and additional resources, including video clips, supplementary readings, and several case studies.
Tillapaugh, D., & Haber-Curran, P.	*New Directions for Student Leadership*: No. 154. Gender and Leadership	2017	Considers research and practice on how students' intersectional social identities, in particular gender identity, influence their leadership development and experiences.

(Table continues on next page)

Table 3.2. (Continued)

Author(s)	Title	Year Published	Brief Overview
Wagner, W., Ostick, D., & Associates	*Exploring Leadership: For College Students Who Want to Make a Difference-Facilitation and Activity Guide*	2013	Contains teaching strategies and active learning modules that can be used for organizing a course or workshop series focusing on student leadership development, specifically related to content from the book, *Exploring Leadership: For College Students Who Want to Make a Difference,* 3rd edition.

Table 3.3.   Potential Classroom Texts

Author(s)	Title	Year Published	Brief Overview
Astin, H. S., & Leland, C. L.	*Women of Influence, Women of Vision: A Cross -Generational Study of Leaders and Social Change*	1999	A narrative exploration of influential women leaders and their experiences.
Avolio, B.	*Leadership Development in Balance: Made/Born*	2008	Focuses on leadership competencies of developing authentic leadership; challenges made vs. born controversy; integrates case studies from a variety of contexts.
Bolman, L. G., & Deal, T. E.	*Reframing Organizations: Artistry, Choice, and Leadership* (5th ed.)	2013	Considers leadership from an organizational theory and behavior perspective.
Bordas, J.	Salsa, Soul, and Spirit: Leadership for a Multicultural Age	2012	Emphasizes the importance of incorporating Latino, African American, and American Indian approaches to leadership learning to strengthen leadership practices and leadership education.
Bordas, J.	*The Power of Latino Leadership: Culture, Inclusion, and Contribution*	2013	Shares perspectives, stories, and ideas about how Latino leadership has developed and how everyone can learn from Latino leadership practices.

(Table continues on next page)

Table 3.3. (Continued)

Author(s)	Title	Year Published	Brief Overview
Bridges, W.	*Managing Transitions* (2nd ed.)	2009	Provides practical, step-by-step strategies for minimizing the disruptions caused by workplace change. It is a managerial tool for navigating uncertainty.
Cronin, T. E., & Genovese, M. A.	*Leadership Matters*	2012	Covers concepts of leadership through history, business, politics, the military, and Hollywood from the idea of a leadership paradox.
DuBrin, A. J.	*Leadership: Research Findings, Practice, and Skills*	2015	Provides a strong practical foundation by introducing relatable leaders and knowledge with skill-building activities, vignettes, and end-of-chapter cases.
Dugan, J. C.	*Leadership Theory: Cultivating Critical Perspectives*	2017	An interdisciplinary survey text on leadership theory using critical perspectives. Intended for use in undergraduate classrooms.
Greenleaf, R.	*Servant Leadership*	1977	Introduces the concept and theory of the leader as a servant first, with narrative examples to connect to the concepts.
Heifetz, R., & Linsky, M.	*Leadership on the Line*	2004	Presents concepts of the dangers of navigating leadership in complex contexts; utilizes the theory of adaptive leadership
Komives, S. R., Lucas, N., & McMahon, T.	*Exploring Leadership: For College Students Who Want to Make a Difference* (3rd ed.)	2013	Designed for college students to help them understand that they are capable of being effective leaders and guides them in developing their leadership potential, integrating the Relational Leadership Model (RLM).

(Table continues on next page)

Table 3.3.   (Continued)

Author(s)	Title	Year Published	Brief Overview
Komives, S. R., Wagner, W., &Associates.	*Leadership for a Better World* (2nd ed.)	2016	Provides an approachable introduction to the Social Change Model of Leadership Development (SCM), giving students a real-world context through which to explore the seven Cs of leadership for social change as well as approaches to socially responsible leadership.
Kouzes, J. M., & Posner, B.	*The Leadership Challenge: How to Make Extraordinary Things Happen in Organizations*	2017	Provides new cases and examples based on the five practices of exemplary leadership.
Kouzes, J. M., & Posner, B.	*The Student Leadership Challenge* (2nd ed.)	2014	Includes an overview based on research of student leaders of five leadership practices students can apply to develop their leadership skills; contains narrative examples of student leaders' experiences.
Northouse, P.	*Introduction to Leadership: Concepts and Practice* (3rd ed.)	2014	A practical introduction guide to leadership with interactive items including quizzes and reflections for each chapter.
Northouse, P.	*Leadership: Theory and Practice* (7th ed.)	2016	A survey text of leadership theory from historical to modern perspectives and research. Includes case studies with each chapter to assist in understanding the theories.
Pittinsky, T. L. (Ed.)	*Crossing the Divide: Intergroup Leadership in a World of Difference*	2009	Scholarly essays from intergroup development and leadership researchers discussing group development, conflict, and diversity to create better interactions and collaboration within group leadership.
Sensoy, O., & Di'Angelo, R	*Is Everyone Really Equal: An Introduction to Key Concepts in Social Justice Education*	2013	Introduction and practical guide to understanding issues of social justice education geared toward students.

(Table continues on next page)

Table 3.3. (Continued)

Author(s)	Title	Year Published	Brief Overview
Shankman, M., Allen, S., & Haber-Curran, P.	*Emotionally Intelligent Leadership for College Students* (2nd ed.)	2015	Covers a conceptual model of emotional intelligence geared toward college student development; also has companion workbook and inventory available.
Wilson, M. C.	*Closing the Leadership Gap: Why Women Can and Must Help Run the World*	2004	Advocates the need for more women's leadership for the betterment of the social good.
Wren, T. (Ed.)	*The Leader's Companion*	1995	Provides an overview of leadership throughout history and across cultures.

Table 3.4. Instructor Guides

Accompanying Text	Access
The Leader's Companion: Insights on Leadership Through the Ages	http://scholarship.richmond.edu/bookshelf/35/
Exploring Leadership: For College Students Who Want to Make a Difference (2nd ed.)	https://nclp.umd.edu/include/pdfs/publications/exploringleadershipguide.pdf
Leadership for a Better World (2nd ed.)	https://nclp.umd.edu/include/pdfs/publications/leadership_for_a_better_world.pdf
Leadership Challenge	https://www.researchgate.net/publication/242601322_An_Instructor%27s_Guide_to_The_Leadership_Challenge

ADDITIONAL LEADERSHIP EDUCATOR RESOURCES

Professional development support comes in a variety of formats, which is essential to tailoring to the various needs with which and contexts in which leadership educators operate. In this chapter, we discussed professional associations, professional development opportunities, academic journals, printed resources, classroom texts, and instructor guides. The following additional resources range from research centers to large data sets to specific reports and newsletters.

Center for Creative Leadership (CCL)

This international, nonprofit, educational organization was established in 1970 and currently has 10 offices around the world. CCL traces its history back to Lundsford Richardson, a pharmacist and creator of Vicks VapoRub. Through the generosity of the Smith Richardson Foundation and based on Richardson's vision and philosophy centered on boldness and what he called "cross-country thinking," CCL was born. Its mission is to "advance the understanding, practice and development of leadership for the benefit of society worldwide" (Center for Creative Leadership, 2017). CCL is dedicated to creating knowledge that positively transforms the way leaders, organizations, and overall societies tackle difficult tasks.

Greenleaf Center for Servant Leadership

The Greenleaf Center for Servant Leadership has provided resources for leadership educators since 1964, when it was first established as the "Center for Applied Ethics." Greenleaf (1977) published the landmark *The Servant as Leader*, which coined the phrase servant leader. The Greenleaf Center has been a thought leader regarding leadership, specifically servant leadership, and provides international conferences, online learning opportunities, and speaking and workshop engagements (Greenleaf Center, 2017).

The Interassociation Leadership Education Collaborative (ILEC)

In 2012, the ILEC was established to bring professional associations together around leadership education. Currently, the ILEC includes the following professional associations: NCLP, NACA, ALE, Association for College Unions International (ACUI), ILA, ACPA, NASPA, and the American Association of University Women's (AAUW) Collegiate Women's Leadership Educators Alliance (CWLEA). Since 2013, a representative from each member association attends an ILEC Summer Summit to discuss challenges and opportunities facing leadership educators. Recently, ILEC published the *Collaborative Priorities and Critical Considerations for Leadership Education* white paper, which serves as an invitation to all who engage in the work of leadership education to consider: What is required of us to collectively build capacity of leadership learners?" (NCLP, 2017). It includes three priority areas: building inclusive leadership learning communities, expanding evidence-based practice through assessment and evaluation, and enhancing our community of practice through professional development and resources. Each priority area includes a rationale or general description of the background or needs, as well as potential action steps for engaging in each through research and practice, including learning design, capacity creation, and critical considerations (NCLP, 2017).

MESTIZA Leadership International

Established by Juana Bordas in the early 1990s, MESTIZA Leadership International's mission is to "prepare collaborative leaders for the multicultural and global age" (MESTIZA Leadership, 2017, http://www.mestizaleadership.com/). This organization provides diversity and leadership programs for thousands of people and hundreds of organizations across the country. Two of those resources include *Salsa, Soul, and Spirit: Leadership for the Multicultural Age* (Bordas, 2012) and *The Power of Latino Leadership* (Bordas, 2013).

Multi-institutional Survey of Leadership

In 2005, John C. Dugan and Susan R. Komives launched the first national study of college student leadership based on a theoretical approach to leadership. Using a revised version of the Socially Responsible Leadership Survey (Tyree, 1998), the Multiinstitutional Study of Leadership invites campuses to apply for participation. This growing database of information is a partnership with the Center for Student Studies and NCLP. Information on this study can be found on the NCLP website and on www.leadershipstudy.net.

Additional Conferences of Interest

Several additional conferences and gatherings of scholars and practitioners further develop knowledge, skills, and values regarding their roles as educators. A few conferences are not directly focused on leadership educators but have provided incredible training:

- The National Conference of Race and Ethnicity in Higher Education (https://ncore.ou.edu)
- The White Privilege Conference (www.whiteprivilegeconference.com)
- Social Justice Training Institute (http://www.sjti.org)
- U.S. Hispanic Leadership Institute (www.ushli.org)

CONCLUSION

We realize this is a lot of information. We are also certain we have missed many resources that leadership educators find vital to their professional development and use in facilitating leadership programs. We hope you discovered some new resources, whether it be a professional organization, an academic journal, a printed resource, an instructor's guide, or another helpful resource.

With leadership studies and leadership education both being in their infancy, it is evolving at a rapid pace. As a leadership educator, you have the opportunity to contribute your knowledge and expertise toward enhancing the field of leadership education. We encourage you to immerse yourself in areas of leadership that are missing and fill any gaps in knowledge, theory, and practice of leadership education. Please remember to share resources you have found useful in delivering leadership programs. By doing so, you are assisting to build our community of practice further. Our field can only improve if we work collectively, and your voice is important in the continual development of resources and the field as a whole.

SECTION II

DESIGNING OPPORTUNITIES FOR
LEADERSHIP LEARNING

One of the hardest things for leadership educators to learn and understand is how to intentionally design effective leadership education programs. The five chapters in Section II collectively assist leadership educators to design leadership learning opportunities. Chapter 4 proposes a leadership learning framework that shifts the focus from the educator and teaching to the learner and learning. To design influential leadership education programs, we should be focusing on how learning occurs and design programs from the learner perspective, not what the educator feels like teaching. The five leadership learning aspects of content are development, training, observation, engagement, and metacognition.

In designing learning opportunities, considering the multiple contexts and the various layers present is critical in situating the program appropriately, as we will discuss in Chapter 5. Institutional factors such as academic/curricular, co-curricular, undergraduate, graduate, discipline-specific, interdisciplinary, and integrated models matter when intentionally designing, delivering, and assessing leadership programs.

From an extensive literature review, five characteristics of distinctive programs emerged, which are critical for consideration in designing opportunities. Chapter 6 discusses these characteristics, including intentionally designing programs, creating authentic leadership learning environments, focusing on application of knowledge, skills, and values, making meaning through planned reflection, and including continuous program improvement in overall program design. Chapter 7 provides examples of distinctive programs in various contexts. These examples from various leadership education programs around the country demonstrate how programs can implement distinctive characteristics in different contexts.

Finally, Chapter 8 focuses on assessment, which at a program level is a characteristic of distinctive leadership programs. Various assessment types, including individual learning and program-wide assessment, are discussed. Collectively, these five chapters provide in-depth information on leadership education program design and hopefully give better understanding to crafting influential leadership learning opportunities.

CHAPTER 4

LEADERSHIP LEARNING FRAMEWORK

The true success of effective leadership programs is measured by students' ability to apply their learning to the challenges they will face after program completion, not whether they have a relationship with the instructor (Baxter Magolda & King, 2004). With this in mind, educators should attend to student learning more than teaching (Barr & Tagg, 1995), which is generally not how educational programs are developed (Fink, 2013). Unfortunately, leadership development programs are often created from a buffet of activities educators experienced themselves or observed while working with other students. Consequently, many leadership program schedules are filled with entertaining activities generated around the availability of facilitators and are void of any sense of content or curricular sequencing. Likewise, learning outcomes may not have been created, let alone integrated as a focus of the program. Further, students' context, lived histories, or intersectional student social identities are rarely taken into consideration.

However, when the focus is placed on learning, student- and learning-centered approaches emerge (Barr & Tagg, 1995). This focus places educators in the role of conduit rather than distributor and requires attention to collaborative learning practices, personal responsibility for growth and development, and construction of an inclusive learning community. Merriam and Caffarella (1999) described learning as "a process by which behavior changes as a result of experiences" (p. 250). Leadership is a

The Role of Leadership Educators: Transforming Learning, pp. 55–77
Copyright © 2018 by Information Age Publishing

process of learning in which individuals make sense of their experiences, uncover leader identities within themselves, and work in communities of leadership practice with others (Antonacopoulou & Bento, 2004). This chapter will focus on the student-centered approach by introducing a leadership learning framework in which educators can develop programs with learning at the forefront.

Leadership learning has become central to the work of student affairs and academic affairs divisions within American colleges and universities (Dugan, 2006; Thompson, 2006). Institutional mission statements are increasingly focused on creating global leaders, which Chunoo and Osteen (2016) state requires realigning the purpose, mission, and context of post-secondary education within student leadership learning. To meet this goal, Astin and Astin (2000) recommend a renewed focus on social responsibility in collegiate leadership learning programs. However, questions still remain regarding how to best develop leadership learning opportunities for an ever-evolving, diverse body of student.

In 1989, Roberts and Ullom provided one model of training, education, and development (TED model) as the way to approach leadership learning. Expanding on the TED model, Guthrie and Osteen (2012b) added engagement as critical to learning leadership. As aforementioned, it is important to distinguish leadership terminology such as training, education, development, and engagement. Despite seeming conceptually simple, the extant literature discussing leadership learning outside higher education is inconsistent in terminology (Sowcik & Allen, 2013) and often uses terms such as *leadership education, leadership studies, leadership training,* and *leadership development* interchangeably with little intentionality behind their use. Although these terms are often used interchangeably (Ayman, Adams, Fisher, & Hartmen, 2003), each has distinct applications and implications. Here, we build off previous efforts in this area to propose a leadership learning framework that leadership educators can use theoretically, conceptually, and in practice to create programs that intentionally connect pedagogy with learning outcomes. This can aid leadership educators in critically thinking about the best assessments for potential leadership learning.

Leader identity development and leadership development are also integral to leadership learning. Guthrie, Bertrand Jones, Osteen, and Hu (2013) drew clear distinctions between the two: "*Leader* development [which] focuses on individual students' capacity and identity, with or without formal authority, to engage in the leadership process ... [and] ... leader*ship* development is a collective focus on a group's relationships and process" (p. 15; italics original). Therefore, leadership learning can be understood as a dynamic, multifaceted, and integrated phenomenon where individuals are influenced in a variety of ways by numerous experiences.

Subsequently, we define leadership learning as changes in knowledge, skills, behavior, attitudes, and values resulting from educational experiences, both co-curricular and curricular in nature, associated with the activity of leadership. This definition of learning, as an outcome, opens the conversation for a more complex, thoughtful, and intentional approach to the design of educational opportunities. By retaining leadership learning as the intended outcome, we can design more intentional, thoughtful, and purposeful leadership education programs.

UNSEEN LEADERSHIP PROGRAM ARCHITECTURE

For this book, we focus on six aspects of leadership learning: knowledge, development, training, observation, engagement, and metacognition, all within the context of leadership. These six areas build on many scholars' work in various facets of learning, teaching, and education, resulting in a framework that challenges leadership educators to rethink leadership learning.

Using the metaphor of a steering wheel, the Leadership Learning Framework provides a mechanism for students to steer their own learning, but also for educators to better understand the multiple ways in which students learn. Educators can then create programs with student learning at the forefront of development. As seen in Figure 4.1, leadership knowledge encompasses the entire wheel. Knowledge of leadership theories, concepts, and skills is foundational for all leadership learning and needs to be adjoined to all of its aspects. We believe leadership knowledge acquisition occurs in all programs, even if only by using language about leadership that may not have been used previously. Working in from the leadership knowledge rim of the framework, the four aspects of development, training, observation, and engagement all contribute to metacognition. Metacognition sits at the heart of leadership learning because, without critical thought and reflection of the learning experience, we cannot make meaning or begin to apply and adapt what we learn. In the following section, each of these six aspects of leadership learning is discussed in detail, along with a review of attendant instructional strategies and possible ways to assess student learning. Suggested instructional and assessment strategies are informed by the extensive work of Conger (1992), Allen and Hartman (2009), and Jenkins (2017a), who explored in-depth sources of learning in leadership education, as well as the author's collective personal experiences in teaching leadership for several years.

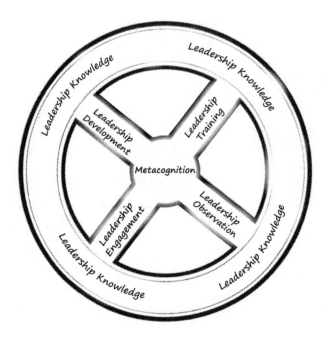

Figure 4.1. Leadership learning framework.

LEADERSHIP KNOWLEDGE

Leadership knowledge is the "interdisciplinary, academic and applied field of study that focuses on the fluid process and components of the interaction between leaders and followers in a particular context" (Sowcik, 2012, p. 193). To learn leadership knowledge is to acquire information and critical insights about the process of leadership. This process is cognitive in nature and places a heavy emphasis on knowledge acquisition and mental processing. In more detail, according to Allen and Shehane (2016):

> the cognitive orientation is often declarative ('knowing what' or Aristotle's notion of *Episteme*) and is often delivered by an "expert." This type of information is often delivered in a formal educational setting (e.g., university, high school) via lecture, reading, and case study. Tests, exams, and quizzes measure the level of learning that has taken place. Likewise, this type of intervention is associated closely with degrees such as a major or minor and may include learning leadership from the perspective of diverse disciplines. (p. 42)

Thus, developing leadership knowledge is an essential aspect of overall leadership learning.

Leadership Knowledge Development

Knowledge development via learning leadership theories and concepts represents a critical part of leadership education in curricular and co-curricular programs. As Harvey and Jenkins (2014) state, developing a leadership program begins with identifying what knowledge is to be learned by students. "The 'necessary' knowledge...falls into two broad categories: technical knowledge of the expertise and skills deemed requisite to leadership either generally or in particular areas and humanistic knowledge about people, both as individuals and as members of groups" (Harvey & Jenkins, 2014, p. 77). Therefore, effective leadership educators situate themselves and create their teaching environments to contribute meaningfully to leadership learners' inventory of technical and humanistic information.

Gaining leadership knowledge transcends classroom experiences and can occur through the lens of a leader as well as a follower. Learning also occurs when applying leadership theories and concepts to personal experiences, which completes a praxis model. A praxis model is practical in nature and is put into action. Although learning in a traditional classroom setting provides structure, established learning outcomes, and assessment, leadership learning in a co-curricular context is also essential for students to learn in a holistic manner. As Ludvik, Gardner, and Hickmott (2012) tell us, outcome-based knowledge assessment is not only done in a classroom setting, specific experience, or event. Thus, intentional mapping of a student's co-curricular knowledge development creates an opportunity for leadership educators to assess leadership learning. Mapping can be done well for all leadership educators, from both academic and student-affairs frameworks, which can lead to shared language linking leadership knowledge development through the application of a shared leadership framework (Buschlen & Dvorak, 2011).

Most Widely Utilized Leadership Frameworks

As previously discussed, gaining leadership knowledge includes learning foundational theories and concepts. Rosch and Anthony (2012) discuss three of the most frequently used leadership frameworks: (a) the social change model of leadership development (Higher Education Research Institute, 1996); (b) the relational leadership model (Komives, Lucas, & McMahon, 2013); and (c) the Five Practices of Exemplary Leadership (Kouzes & Posner, 2012). The social change model of leadership development was created to aid in the individual development of personal values, group values, and citizenship and serves as both curriculum and/or co-curriculum for diverse programs. Buschlen and Dvorak (2011) found that when undergraduate leadership education programs use the social change model of leadership development as the overarching theoretical framework, student success was noted. The relational leadership model views leadership as a complex process that should be inclusive of others and diverse points of view, ethical in practice, and empowering of group members (Komives et al., 2013). The Leadership Challenge describes five exemplary practices that successful leaders have exhibited when they were at their "personal best" (Kouzes & Posner, 2012) and was developed from data of thousands of leaders. These practices are organized into categories of Modeling the Way, Inspiring a Shared Vision, Challenging the Process, Enabling Others to Act, and Encouraging the Heart (Kouzes & Posner, 2012). These models are easily adaptable to both co-curricular and curricular programs and vital for leadership knowledge development.

Instructional and Assessment Strategies

Educators can use several instructional strategies to best provide opportunities for students to learn leadership knowledge. The third section of this book provides in-depth discussion on leadership education pedagogies, but we want to mention some teaching strategies that link with each aspect of leadership learning. Instructional strategies well suited for developing leadership knowledge may include but are not limited to:

- Lectures
- Reading
- Pair-Share-Report
- Case Studies
- Peer Facilitation
- Bringing in Current Articles
- Guest Speakers
- Art Creation of Leadership Artifacts
- Dramaturgy (acting theory)
- Flipped Classroom
- One-minute Papers

Once instructional strategies and content are provided, how do we know whether students actually *learned* the leadership knowledge we intended for them to learn? Strategies for assessment of learning are also critical in the process of teaching and learning and are covered in-depth in Chapter

8. Intentional assessment for learning leadership knowledge may include but are not limited to:

- Tests
- Quizzes
- Written Assignments
- Poster Presentations
- Blogs
- Papers
- Discussion (Face-to-Face and Online)
- Application of Theory to Practice
- Reading Critiques

LEADERSHIP DEVELOPMENT

Leadership development refers to the human and intrapersonal aspects of leadership learning. This is where learning focuses on individuals and their values and needs (Maslow, 1970), personal motivation and readiness to lead (Avolio & Hannah, 2008), identity (Day, Harrison, & Halpin, 2009; Guthrie et al., 2013; Komives, Owen, Longerbeam, Mainella, & Osteen, 2005), and multiple other dimensions of self (Allen & Shehane, 2016). As Allen and Shehane (2016) state, leadership development is "characterized by new insights and progression, can include an individual's motivations, values, identity, emotions, and potential in relation to the activity of leadership" (p. 43). This aspect of leadership learning may include knowledge of and experiential exposure of ethics, consciousness of self, authenticity, citizenship, receiving feedback, engaging in reflection, healthy self-esteem, flexibility, and emotional self-regulation (Shankman, Allen, & Haber-Curran, 2015).

It is important to note that, although we describe it as leadership development, leader development is also included. It is important to further explore the differences between leadership and leaders to fully understand what we include in the leadership development aspect of learning. Day (2001) defines leadership development as "expanding the collective capacity of organizational members to engage effectively in leadership roles and processes" (p. 582). In other words, leadership development focuses on relationships as well as opportunities to integrate and understand a group. In contrast, leader development focuses on the individua—one's intrapersonal growth and opportunity to understand the self (Day, 2001). Through enhancing one's knowledge, skills, and values, one can build human capital as a leader. Complimentary leadership development builds social capital,

the "networked relationships among individuals that enhance cooperation and resource exchange in creating organizational value" (Day, 2001,
p. 585). Within Day's conceptualization, leadership roles may be formal or
informal, whereas leadership processes are how people come together to
work in meaningful ways.

Moreover, a future- and person-centered definition of development is
offered by Nadler (1984): "learning for growth of the individual but not
related to a specific present or future job" (p. 22). Nadler (1984) offered
that the personal growth emphasis, joined with the minimization of tasks,
sets development far apart from training or education. These distinctions
are echoed by Roberts and Ullom (1989), who applied these concepts
directly to leadership education, while adding the notion of leadership
engagement—the application and practice of leadership skills (from training), knowledge (from education), and values (from development) to solve
problems or change conditions. As you can see from this discussion, the
different aspects of leadership learning are intertwined and integrated in
many ways.

Instructional and Assessment Strategies

Instructional strategies for leadership development are personal and
often reflective in nature. Focusing on the best ways to integrate personal
aspects into co-curricular and academic/curricular teaching is critical to
support different aspects of leadership learning, especially leadership
development. Below are a few instructional strategies leadership educators may want to consider for leadership development learning.

- Personal Mission Statements
- One-on-One Discussions
- Values-Based Boards/Videos
- Visioning Boards
- Mind Mapping
- Storytelling
- Participating in Service Learning

Because leader identity and leadership development are personal,
implementing specific assessment strategies can be as challenging for educators to implement as it is for students to engage. However, intentional
and strategic assessments can help maintain or correct the trajectory of
leadership development initiatives. Some assessment strategies for leadership development learning include but are not limited to:

- One-Minute Papers
- Assessment Instruments
- Role-Plays
- Social Identity Activities
- Reflective Journals
- Small-Group Discussions

From our perspective, effective leadership educators choose assessments that are reflective of their learning outcomes, responsive to the needs of their students, and authentic to their own values as well. We recommend employing assessments appropriate for the leadership learning context and combining strategies in innovative and creative ways to better determine what and how students learn leadership.

LEADERSHIP TRAINING

Leadership training is central to leadership learning and education given its focus on the skill- and competency-based behavioral aspects of learning. This type of leadership learning places heavy emphasis on scaffolding learning so students can practice and build on lessons toward mastery and observable behavioral change. Specifically, leadership training is the space where "...proficiency in demonstrating specific tasks associated with the activity of leadership" (Allen & Shehane, 2016, p. 43) are practiced and assessed. This is most often the aspect of leadership learning co-curricular leadership programs are built around, especially when programs are created for training positional student leaders. In many ways, leadership training focuses on what leadership learners are *able to do* when they leave our leadership programs. These skills and competencies may include meeting management, facilitation, decision making, negotiation, public speaking, listening, establishing vision, providing feedback, and supervision. This echoes Nadler's (1984) definition of training as "learning related to the present job" (p. 18), which places emphasis on improved performance on specific tasks.

Micari, Gould, and Lainez (2010) found that some specialized leadership programs attract students who want to gain expertise in a specific disciplinary area. Leadership training, when coupled with a disciplinary focus and intentional program design, is more likely to develop students in meaningful ways and provide learning opportunities specific to their field of study. Helpfully, Nandan and London (2013) provided a rationale for developing interprofessional competencies, mainly in graduate programs designed to prepare individuals as global leaders and change agents. They argue that, to prepare leaders to deal with complex challenges, leadership training must include opportunities to sharpen interdisciplinary competencies. Clearly, implementing interprofessional educational models to teach critical competencies is vital to comprehensive leadership training efforts. Nandan and London (2013) argue this approach to training constitutes an ethical responsibility of educators to prepare future leaders of social change.

Instructional and Assessment Strategies

Leadership training focuses on skill-building and competency-based learning. Thus, instructional strategies to foster leadership training should focus on behavioral characteristics and integrate them into the process of leadership. Integrating skill-building into curricular and co-curricular teaching is critical. Below are a few instructional strategies leadership educators may want to consider for leadership training learning.

- Simulations
- Practice/Repetition
- Role-Play
- Skill-Based Instruments
- Debate
- Games
- Peer Critical Feedback Sessions
- Icebreakers

Intentional assessment of skill-building can vary depending on the curricular and co-curricular format. Some assessment strategies for learning through the leadership training aspect can include but are not limited to:

- Rubrics
- Checklists
- Role-Plays
- Ropes Course
- Online Feedback for Group
- Mentorship
- Art/Visual Representation of Learning
- Scenario Practice
- Peer/Instructor Evaluation

From this brief review, the message seems clear: behaviorally based and competency-focused leadership training is a valuable and necessary component of leadership learning. Effective leadership educators are those who have clear intentions regarding the skills and capacities their students should develop, can articulate strategies to impart those practices, create opportunities for students to practice leadership behaviors and habits, and provide timely, accurate, and frequent feedback regarding students' training progress.

LEADERSHIP OBSERVATION

Leadership observation refers to the social, cultural, and observational aspects of leadership learning. This type of learning is constructivist in nature because the learner is making meaning about how effective and ineffective leaders and followers act in relation to others in sociocultural contexts. However, in this space, the learner is a passive recipient of the learning. Bandura (1977) states that through the social learning orientation context and culture are key to learning. In this section, we will elaborate on the impact that leadership educators can have on shaping observational leadership learning.

Learning is always culturally bound (Merriam & Caffarella, 1999). Whether it is observing specific leaders in a culture, an elder in another culture, or the process of leadership with many individuals in a collectivist society, observation of others and the consequences of their actions are central stimuli for learning. For example, when watching members of parliament in the United Kingdom debate, neighbors in an African community come together, or a community leader in Mexico City bringing a group of citizens together to discuss a building a neighborhood playground, we learn by observing these culturally contextual interactions. Looking involves learning to interpret, and like other practices, looking involves relationships of power (Sturken & Cartwright, 2003). Observing naturally leads to reflection and making meaning from what is seen.

"The ways of observing (or looking with intentionality) require us to go another step (or two) and to use our judgement and inference-making abilities to arrive at something resembling knowledge" (Mitra, 2011, p. 185). The learning that occurs from looking with intention provides leaders with knowledge as well as practice in reading their environments with accuracy. With complex situations, the onslaught of information we have access to, and hard-to-discern patterns in data and behaviors, it is critical to see clearly to learn leadership and provide effective leadership. The ability to read with clarity the complex environments we interact with and then find solutions to issues is at the core of leadership education.

Mitra (2011) introduces two ways of observing or "looking with intentionality" (p. 185): inductive and deductive looking. Inductive looking is when we look to make sense of the world. It is a way of being introduced to new concepts, interactions, and relationships. Inductive looking is focused purely on description. Deductive looking, in contrast, is observing in which inferences are made from previous experiences. In deductive looking, conclusions are from either general or universal principles we infer. Effective observational learning incorporates both inductive sense-making and deductive conclusions about ourselves, others, and the world around us.

Instructional and Assessment Strategies

Because leadership observation is a passive way to receive information, instructional strategies for this type of learning center on providing space for the learner to intentionally and methodically observe leadership processes, interactions, and relationships. It is important for educators to guide reflections related to how leadership is socially constructed. Included here are a few instructional strategies educators may want to consider for creating observational leadership learning opportunities:

- Lectures
- Shadowing
- Witnessing Group Dynamics
- Service-Learning
- Videos/Movie Watching
- Field Assignments
- Observing Simulations and Role-Plays
- Observation Instruments
- Environmental Scans

To make meaning from passively receiving information, reflective blogs, journal entries, essays, and discussions can serve as highly effective ways of assessing whether learning occurred. It is important to provide prompts or guiding questions to assist learners in the meaning-making process. Assessment strategies for leadership observation learning include but are not limited to:

- Reflective Blogs
- Reflective Journal Entries
- Reflective Essays

- Presentations on Findings
- One-on-One Discussions
- Article Critique
- Papers
- Rubrics

Example

Environmental Scan

Environmental scans can be particularly powerful in learning leadership through observation. Dr. Paige Haber-Curran provides this example in a Gender and Sexuality in Higher Education class, which can be easily altered to focus on various levels of leadership education in both curricular and co-curricular frameworks.

The instructional strategy includes guiding students to observe things around them. In addition to having conversations with her students regarding observation, Paige provides this in her syllabus:

> You will want to notice, capture, and reflect on things that you interact with in your daily life, especially those on campus or those that college students may be exposed to: news, advertisements, media, social media, discussions and conversations, clothing, jokes, your feelings or expectations for yourself or others, other peoples' expectations for you or themselves, interactions with friends, family, partners, peers, etc. (P. Haber-Curran, Personal Communication, May 3, 2017)

In this example, students are given an opportunity to observe the environment around them, especially regarding gender. Assessment of this learning is a virtual project creation, which could be a blog, video, or webpage, and includes images, reflections, links, or anything else that assesses what they observed through the environmental scan. Similar to this in-class example, a co-curricular-based example is asking leaders in a student organization to attend another organization's meeting and without talking to anyone observe the organizational dynamics. Discussing this experience at the next executive board meeting could be enlightening to learning leadership through observation.

LEADERSHIP ENGAGEMENT

Leadership engagement refers to the experiential, relational, interactional, and interpersonal aspects of leadership learning. Like leadership observation, leadership engagement is constructivist in nature. However, in leadership engagement, the learner is an active participant. Specifically, learners construct meaning in response to direct and personal encounters with the activities of leadership. That is, "the purpose is to provide the learner with new experiences, and the role of the educator is often to help individuals capture and make sense of planned or naturalistic experiences (constructivism) following an activity" (Allen & Shehane, 2016, p. 44).

Conversations about the importance of engagement emerged with Astin's (1984) research on the benefits of student involvement on college campuses. However, student involvement, broadly, is an investment of time, effort, and other resources by students and institutions to optimize the overall student experience, often with implications for student retention and persistence to a degree. Ultimately, the purpose of engagement is to enhance the development of students—specifically for our conversation, the leadership learning outcomes. Trowler (2013) discussed that leadership engagement has both behavioral and cognitive dimensions; when an institution supports engagement for leadership learning, desirable outcomes drastically improve.

Engaging with others to achieve change has never been more critical in postsecondary education (Drew, 2010). This includes both administrator and student perspectives. Drew (2010) found interpersonal engagement was vital in meeting key challenges for leaders. Learning from an engagement perspective through interpersonal means is effective for learners globally, not just the highly researched Western context (Krauss & Hamid, 2015). As Trowler (2013) suggests, higher education should intentionally design opportunities for students to engage with leadership opportunities, thereby learning critical aspects of leadership with implications for future careers and additional academic pursuits.

Instructional and Assessment Strategies

Instructional strategies for leadership engagement should focus on experiential learning and relational aspects of leadership and be interactional and interpersonal in nature. A foundational component of leadership engagement is that the learner is an active participant in receiving the information. This has been a focus of co-curricular leadership development since the beginning but can also be influential for curricular-based learning. Shared here are a few instructional strategies for the engagement aspect of leadership learning.

- Action learning
- Case-in-Point
- Problem-Based learning
- Internships

- Service Learning
- Reflective Practice
- Positional and Nonpositional Experiences
- Games
- Simulations
- Internships
- Debate
- Theatre of the Oppressed (Social Justice Theatre)
- Team-Building Activities

Assessing engagement from both curricular and co-curricular frameworks can be similar in nature. Providing opportunities for students to assess their own learning through experiential and relational means in which engagement offers is imperative. It is not just for the learner to make meaning from their experiences, but for the educator to better understand what and how the learning outcomes are or are not being met. Some assessment strategies for leadership engagement learning include but are not limited to:

- Presentations
- Discussion (Large and Small Group)
- Feedback Cards-Reading Out Loud
- Synthesis Paper
- Group Paper
- Reflective Blogs/Journal Entries
- Reflective Essays
- Video Diaries

LEADERSHIP METACOGNITION

Leadership metacognition refers to the reflective, systemic, organizational, analytical, evaluative, adaptive, processual, mindful, and complex aspects of leadership learning. In this space, the learner is critically aware and understands his or her own thought progressions about the leadership process and the learning of leadership. In other words, the learner is practicing mindfulness with respect to leadership.

Meichenbaum (1985) referred to metacognition as the mindfulness of one's own knowledge and the ability to recognize, control, and employ one's cognitive processes. This understanding includes knowing when, where, and why to use particular strategies for problem solving and learning. Using prior knowledge to design a strategy for learning, taking necessary steps to problem solve, reflecting on and evaluating results, as well as modifying one's approach as needed are all aspects of metacognition. Flavell (1976), who coined the term metacognition, offered the following example: "I am engaging in metacognition if I notice that I am having more trouble learning A than B; if it strikes me that I should double check C before accepting it as fact" (p. 232).

Cognitive strategies are the basic mental abilities we use to think, study, and learn and include recalling information from memory, analyzing images, comparing and contrasting different pieces of information, and making inferences. These cognitive strategies help an individual achieve a particular goal, such as comprehending text or solving a math problem, which can be individually identified and measured. In contrast, metacognitive strategies are used to ensure that an overarching learning goal is being or has been reached (Flavell, 1976).

Critical Thinking Is Essential to Metacognition

Critical thinking from a leadership perspective entails complex thinking (Flores, Matkin, Burbach, Quinn, & Harding, 2012; Jenkins & Cutchens, 2011), which is connected to the metacognition aspect of leadership learning. In fact, a majority of modern leadership theories support the development of cognitive abilities, critical knowledge, and intellectual stimulation (Northouse, 2016). In an effort to address this leadership need of developing cognitive ability and complex thinking, many classrooms are turning to critical thinking (Stedman, 2009) to organize their pedagogy and activities. Critical thinking is comprised of both skill and disposition. Although skill is malleable, a critical thinking disposition is one's naturally occurring attitude or preference for critical thinking and is not easily changed. In many instances, there is an assumption that students are different in disposition. However, leadership education offers a unique platform inherently designed to improve critical thinking by cultivating self-regulatory judgment through interpretation, analysis, evaluation, and inference of a leader's own decisions and actions (Facione, 1990; Jenkins & Andenoro, 2016), which goes beyond disposition. Leaders deal with complex problems that require complex solutions. Thus, leaders who can think critically will be more effective in developing and implementing creative solutions. Leaders also need critical thinking skills flexible enough to adapt to rapidly changing environments. Although higher education emphasizes critical thinking across disciplines, many undergraduates do not effectively utilize this skill (Burbach, Matkin, & Fritz, 2004). Leadership studies curricula maximize effectiveness when they emphasize building metacognitive skills, such as critical thinking, through student-centered experiential and active learning (Eich, 2008; Moore, Boyd, & Dooley, 2010). The use of critical thinking skills provides an in-depth and forward-thinking reflection process (Rudd, Baker, & Hoover, 2000). Further, the development of critical thinking capacity allows for a more purposeful and effective reflection process in leadership development (Stedman, 2009).

Using Ennis's (1993) 10 actions that a learner must take to think critically, Jenkins and Cutchens (2011) created 12 actions that a leader can take to lead critically:

1. Be aware of the context of your situation and evaluate the implications of your decisions.
2. Ask questions and listen appropriately.
3. Take the time to understand the diversity of others' decisions, values, and opinions.
4. Be flexible and open minded in your decision making.
5. Accept, internalize, and apply constructive criticism.
6. Evaluate assumptions before you try to challenge them.
7. Understand processes before you try to change them.
8. Know the strengths and weaknesses of your followers and direct or empower accordingly.
9. Be purposeful and take into account your organization's mission and values when making decisions.
10. Engage others where they are, not where you want them to be.
11. Encourage critical followership.
12. Take informed action. (p. 7)

Although we recognize that no simple list of factors can adequately address the variations in leadership learning environments, we nonetheless endorse these recommendations as starting points for leadership educators who seek to improve the metacognition of leadership learners under their charge.

Leadership Metacognition Can Be Taught

Akin to many other aspects of leadership, metacognitive strategies can be taught (Halpern, 1996) and are associated with successful learning (Borkowski, Carr, & Pressley, 1987). Effective learners have various strategies to choose from and can transfer them between settings (Pressley, Borkowski, & Schneider, 1987). If students understand metacognition strategies in general, then they may more easily transfer those approaches to various situations they experience in the leadership process.

Few college instructors explicitly teach strategies for monitoring learning (McKeachie, 1988); they assume that students have learned these strategies in high school. However, many undergraduate students are unaware of metacognitive processes and their importance to learning. Memorization is the predominant and often the only learning strategy that high school students have used when they enter college (Brown, Roediger, & McDaniel, 2014). In a review of the literature on strategic learning, Simpson and Nist (2000) emphasized the need for college instructors to provide specific study strategies and practical recommendations regarding their use in specific courses.

Appropriate support and challenge (Sanford, 1962, 1966) is also important when teaching metacognition. Educators need to select and implement activities and assignments at an appropriate level of difficulty. In other words, they need to be challenging enough so students need to apply metacognitive strategies but not so challenging that students become overwhelmed or frustrated. As Biemiller and Meichenbaum (1992) point out, educators need to prompt learners to think about what they are doing; however, educators also need to be careful not to do the thinking for their students. There is a delicate balance in making students experts at seeking help rather than experts at thinking about and directing their own learning. Effective educators continually prompt learners by asking: "What should you do next?" Students need to understand that they have various strategies to use depending on their surrounding context.

Instructional and Assessment Strategies

Educators can encourage leadership metacognition by teaching learners to become more strategic thinkers. This goal can be achieved by helping them focus on the ways they process information. Self-questioning, reflective journal writing, and discussing their thought processes with other learners are among the ways that students can be encouraged to explore and develop their leadership metacognitive processes.

To be successful thinkers, Fogarty (1994) suggests a three-phase metacognition process consisting of planning, monitoring, and evaluation. Effective leadership educators take these phases into consideration for the leadership learning of our students. The first phase is to develop a plan before approaching a learning activity. The second phase is to monitor students' understanding. Evaluating students' thinking after completing the learning activity is the third step in this process. As seen in Table 4.1, educators can model the application of questions and prompt learners to ask themselves questions during each phase. Hence, incorporating opportunities for learners to practice in curricular and co-curricular programs by using specific questions during learning activities and tasks can benefit students in their leadership metacognition.

Table 4.1.   Three-Phase Metacognition Process

Phase	Action	Guiding Questions for Learners
Planning	Developing a plan to approach learning activity prior to starting	• What am I supposed to learn? • What do I already know that will help me? • What should I do first? • How much time to do I have to complete this activity?
Monitoring	Monitoring actual understanding of learning during process	• How am I doing? • What is important to remember from this activity? • Should I adjust my pace in completing this activity? • If I do not fully understand, what can I do to assist in my learning?
Evaluation	Assessing actual learning after completing activity	• How well did I do? • What did I learn? • What could I have done differently? • Is there anything I do not understand? • How might I apply this learning to other situations and/or problems?

Beyond the three-phase process, intentional instructional strategies for metacognition focus on seeking meaning from knowledge gained and experiences. Here are a few pedagogical ideas for learning leadership metacognition:

- Simulations
- Role-Play
- Case Study Analysis
- Field Work
- Team-Based Learning
- Environmental Assessment
- Group Discussion
- Group Facilitation
- Provocative Statements
- Feedback
- What? So What? Now What?

Because metacognition is essentially thinking about thinking, reflective practices are foundational for the assessment of the metacognition aspect of leadership learning—not only guiding students through their making meaning process but also demonstrating to themselves and the instructor(s) that learning outcomes have been achieved. Some assessment approaches for learning leadership metacognition include but are not limited to:

- Reflection Essays
- Reflective Blogs
- Reflective Journal Entries
- Poster Presentations
- Start-Stop-Continue
- Values Self-Portrait
- Synthesis Paper
- Intergroup Dialogue
- Observation Instruments
- Poster Presentations

CONCLUSION

We hope this chapter ignited your thinking regarding how students learn leadership. It is vital that leadership educators put students and their learning at the center of education. When we shift to deeply understanding how students learn leadership, we are able to create better learning environments that can enrich their leadership capacity and help them think critically and strategically about engaging in the process of leadership and being leaders.

Regardless of context, whether you choose to use these instructional and assessment strategies in co-curricular programs or academic/curricular programs, it is important to understand the need for adaptability as an educator. Not only do we need to remember that each student is an individual and has unique needs but also that the learning environment is based on how students are receiving the information given. The complexity of how students are taking in information is influenced by multiple factors. As educators, we need to be prepared to adjust our instructional and assessment strategies when students need something different.

The examples we provided are not inclusive of all pedagogy and learning assessment but are meant to give leadership educators ideas as they are developing programs. Hopefully, these examples are a starting point for you to be innovative in your own leadership initiatives. Instructional strategies and assessment utilizing technology, various media outlets, and current events tap into all of these aspects of leadership learning. In closing, Table 4.2 provides the instructional and assessment strategies of the Leadership Learning Framework: Knowledge, Development, Training, Observation, Engagement, and Metacognition provided in this chapter.

Table 4.2.   Three-Phase Metacognition Process

Aspects of Leadership Learning	Definition	Pedagogies (Teaching Strategies)	Assessment (of Learning)
Knowledge	Knowledge acquisition and mental processing.	Lectures	Tests
		Reading	Quizzes
		Pair-Share-Report	Written Assignments
		Case Studies	Poster Presentations
		Peer Facilitation	Blogs
		Bringing in Current Articles	Papers
		Art Creation of Leadership Artifacts	Discussion (Face-to-Face and Online)
		Dramaturgy (acting theory)	Application of Theory to Practice
		Flipped Classroom	Reading Critiques
		One-Minute papers	
Development	Intrapersonal aspects of leadership.	Personal Mission Statements/Philosophies	One-Minute Reflections
		One-on-One Discussions	Self-Assessment Instruments
		Values-Based Boards/Videos	
		Visioning Boards	Role-Plays
		Mind Mapping	Survey
		Storytelling	Social Identity Activities
			Reflective Papers
			Small-Group Discussions

(Table continues on next page)

Table 4.2.   (Continued)

Aspects of Leadership Learning	Definition	Pedagogies (Teaching Strategies)	Assessment (of Learning)
Training	Interpersonal, Skill-, and competency-based behavioral aspects of leadership learning.	Simulations	Rubrics
		Practice/Repetition	Checklists
		Role-Plays	Role-Plays
		Skill-Based Instruments	Ropes Course
		Debate	Online Feedback for Group
		Peer Critical Feedback	Mentorship
			Art/Visual Representation of Learning
			Scenario Practice
			Peer/Instructor Evaluation
Observation	Constructivist in nature, where learner is passive recipient of information.	Lectures	Reflective Blogs
		Shadowing	Reflective Journal Entries
		Witnessing Group Dynamics	Reflective Essays
		Service-Learning	Presentations on Findings
		Videos/Movie Watching	One-on-One Discussions
		Field Assignments	Article Critique
		Environmental Scans	Papers
			Rubrics

(Table continues on next page)

Table 4.2. (Continued)

Aspects of Leadership Learning	Definition	Pedagogies (Teaching Strategies)	Assessment (of Learning)
Engagement	Learner is active participant, constructivist in nature.	Action Learning Case-in-Point Problem-Based learning Discussion Groups Service Learning Reflective Practice Positional and Nonpositional Experiences Games Debate Theatre of the Oppressed (Social Justice Theatre) Team-Building Activities	Presentations Discussion Feedback Cards- Reading Out loud Synthesis Paper Group Paper
Metacognition	Learner is critically aware and understands own thought processes about leadership. Construction of meaning occurs through facilitation of the process or activity of leadership.	Reflection Essays Case Study Analysis Simulation and Role-Plays Field Work Environmental Assessment Group/Discussion Facilitation Critical Leadership Provocative Statements Feedback What? So What? Now What?	Reflection Essays Reflective Blogs Reflective Journal Entries Intergroup Dialogue Poster Presentations Start-Stop-Continue Values Self-Portrait Synthesis Paper

CHAPTER 5

LEADERSHIP EDUCATION AND LEARNING CONTEXTS

As we have discussed in previous chapters, the context in which a leadership program is being developed and delivered is a critical consideration from the start. The International Leadership Association's (2009) Guiding Questions begin with understanding which context you are working within. More often than not, it is assumed that context matters and is important, but more than likely it is not taken into full consideration. We may intuitively know that context is always there—influential and ever-changing—but we don't always explicitly name it or explore how it impacts learning. In other words, context is something we know exists but is often glossed over because it is always in the background. However, context is one of the most important pieces of developing and delivering a leadership program. Effective educators continuously think about context, as well as bring it to the forefront of planning, delivery, and assessment of leadership programs. These various aspects of context need to be continually questioned because of its ever-changing nature. In this chapter, we will discuss the complexities of context and then explore seven more specific contexts that significantly influence development and delivery of leadership programs.

The Role of Leadership Educators: Transforming Learning, pp. 79–93
Copyright © 2018 by Information Age Publishing
All rights of reproduction in any form reserved.

LEVELS OF CONTEXT

Leadership as an engaged process is a socially constructed, cultural phenomenon and varies according to an individual's particular context (D. Roberts, 2007). Contextual differences in understanding leadership are indicative of the underlying meaning-making process. This recognition is critical to appreciating a learner's journey, such that they can simply be and lead from a true place of understanding. Bolman and Deal (2017) contend that the ability to understand multiple environments and subsequently reframe context provides a "liberating sense of choice and power" (p. 17).

Guthrie et al. (2013) described college campuses as having several levels of context embedded in the institution, much like a Russian nesting doll (Kellerman, 2013). Beyond institutional walls, there are also several contexts to consider such as the international, national, and institutional. Within the institution, there are multiple contexts to examine, as well as the specific program learning environment (see Figure 5.1). Day-to-day contexts change and influence institutional cultures, campus climates, and learning environments. As postsecondary institutions invest resources in student leadership programs, awareness of the multiple contexts that shape learning environments is vital to providing quality leadership learning opportunities for students.

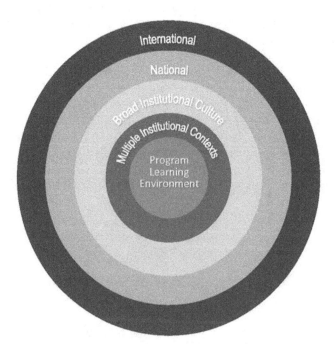

Figure 5.1.   Levels of context in higher education.

BRIEF HISTORY OF
AMERICAN HIGHER EDUCATION CONTEXT

Before digging into broad institutional contexts and specific contexts within an institutional setting, providing a brief historical overview of American higher education is helpful. American higher education has gone through continuous transformation over the past three centuries. The higher education system has emerged as a result of changes to the environment within America and the U.S. context (Hofstadter & Hardy, 1952). Prior to the Civil War, U.S. higher education consisted of small liberal arts colleges that focused on a few areas of study (Lucas, 1994). After the Civil War, criticism surfaced related to the lack of growth in college enrollment (Hofstadter & Hardy, 1952). This drop in growth from the years 1838 to 1869 prompted the president of Columbia University to point out, "American colleges have been steadily losing their appeal to young men" (Hofstadter & Hardy, 1952, p. 29). This was a direct result of various factors. First, the traditional U.S. college was rigid, providing an inadequate schedule of classes in only classic literature and mathematics, which were required of every student (Lucas, 1994). Teaching was unimaginative, and students tended to be taught by repetition, with a heavy reliance on memory. Professors were not encouraged to provide intellectual leadership in any specific academic field but were required to know a little bit about numerous fields of study. Finally, criticism emerged from the public, which believed college should provide the necessary tools to help students make a living in the new industrial society (Blackburn & Conrad, 1986; Hofstadter & Hardy, 1952).

Resulting from the dissatisfaction with higher education, late 19th-century research universities were established to mimic the German model of higher education (Lucas, 1994). The research university, different from the liberal arts college, contained a number of different units, including a professional school, a liberal arts college, and programs of graduate education (Hofstadter & Hardy, 1952). Furthermore, the newly formed U.S. institutions benefitted from a newfound emphasis on research and knowledge in specialized fields of study (Cohen, 1998). Research universities established laboratories and experiment stations to provide advancements in the acquisition of knowledge. However, while the research university concentrated on theoretical learning, it was also able to continue as a center for practical and applied learning (Lucas, 1994). The need to provide technical training for adults was primarily driven by the demand caused by the dynamic growth of the American industrial age. The meteoric rise of the U.S. research university in the mid-20th century had two major implications for U.S. higher education as it exists today: the increase in size of higher education (both in more institutions and larger-sized institutions) and the impact the research university model had on the curriculum. The rest of the chapter will discuss contextual influence on the development of leadership education programs and their modes of delivery.

BROAD INSTITUTIONAL CULTURE

Numerous aspects of context are worth mentioning at an institutional level. For example, is the institution public or private? Is it considered small, medium, or large? Is it religiously affiliated? Are the majority of enrolled students traditional age (18 to 22 years old) or nontraditionally aged, transfer, and commuter students? Are most students taking academic courses online? What Carnegie classification does it hold regarding its level of research activity? In 2016, the ILA provided full access to its leadership directory program database to the Leadership Learning Research Center (LLRC) at The Florida State University. The staff at the LLRC engaged in a descriptive analysis of the data provided from ILA and collected additional missing data (Leadership Learning Research Center, 2017) to gain a better sense of what types of leadership programs are currently being offered in the United States and internationally.

The data included in the ILA directory represents academic, for-credit, curricular-based programs in the United States that self-selected to be listed. The current directory has 1,570 academic programs from U.S. institutions of higher education (International Leadership Association, 2016). These programs represent a diverse group of credential types, including associates ($n = 13$), certificates ($n = 250$), bachelor's (majors and minors; $n = 324$), master's ($n = 654$), and doctoral ($n = 329$; see Table 5.1). Within these varying options, degree programs are housed within a wealth of different disciplines or are interdisciplinary in nature, which is challenging information to capture.

The programs represented in the directory can also be considered from public and private and religious or nonreligious affiliated perspectives. Currently, the directory overrepresents private institutions ($n = 1,003$) compared with public ($n = 472$). There are a large number of religious affiliated institutions ($n = 923$) compared with nonreligious affiliated ($n = 647$) that elected to place their program in the directory (see Table 5.2).

Reviewing the Carnegie classifications of the institutions listed in the directory yields data regarding what types of schools have leadership-related programs. The Carnegie classification system was created in 1970 to help identify institutions with similarities for educational and research purposes. Larger master's degree-granting colleges and universities have the largest share of programs ($n = 432$), followed by the moderate research doctoral universities ($n = 292$). Doctoral universities have the largest number of leadership-related programs overall ($n = 714$; see Table 5.3).

Table 5.1.   ILA Directory Degrees

Associates	Bachelor's		Master's		Doctoral		Certificates
Total	*Total*		*Total*		*Total*		*Total*
13	324		654		329		250
	Degree	*Number*	*Degree*	*Number*	*Degree*	*Number*	
	Major	207	MS	190	DMin	19	
	Minor	117	MA	219	EdD EdSEdM	167	
			MEd	63	PhD	125	
			MBA	50	Other	18	
			MDiv	7			
			Other	125			

Source: International Leadership Association (2016).

Table 5.2.   ILA Directory Affiliations

Affiliation	Number
Private	1,003
Public	472
Religious Affiliated	923
Nonreligious Affiliated	647

Table 5.3.   ILA Directory Carnegie Classifications

Carnegie Classification	Number
Associate's Colleges: High Transfer-High Nontraditional	1
Associate's Colleges: High Transfer-Mixed Traditional/ Nontraditional	7
Baccalaureate Colleges: Arts & Sciences Focus	51
Baccalaureate Colleges: Diverse Fields	51
Doctoral Universities: Highest Research Activity	266
Doctoral Universities: Higher Research Activity	156
Doctoral Universities: Moderate Research Activity	292
Master's Colleges & Universities: Larger Programs	432
Master's Colleges & Universities: Medium Programs	134
Master's Colleges & Universities: Small Programs	48

(Table continues on next page)

Table 5.3.   (Continued)

Carnegie Classification	Number
Special Focus Four-Year: Medical Schools & Centers	1
Special Focus Two-Year: Other Fields	1
Special Focus Four-Year: Business & Management Schools	8
Special Focus Four-Year: Faith-Related Institutions	29
Special Focus Four-Year: Other Health Professions Schools	33
Not Applicable	60
Total	1,270

Sources: ILA Directory Carnegie Classifications (2016; Leadership Learning Research).

MULTIPLE INSTITUTIONAL CONTEXTS

Deconstructing the institutional layers of context leads to better understanding and negotiation of these environments. Effective educators develop and deliver programs with multiple contexts in mind. Unfortunately, we are unable to discuss all of the varying higher education contexts that are present in a broad institutional context, such as whether institutions are private or public, whether they have a religious affiliation, or what their Carnegie classification is in depth. For this chapter, we chose to further discuss seven important contexts within most if not all institutional environments when it comes to developing, delivering, and assessing leadership programs. Contexts that fall within multiple institutional frameworks and are broader than a specific program learning environment will be the focus of the rest of this chapter. Thus, the institutional contexts we will discuss include co-curricular, academic/curricular, undergraduate, graduate, interdisciplinary, integrative, and discipline-specific (see Figure 5.2).

Co-curricular Programs

As academia evolved, a philosophy of educational delivery and additional environmental factors emerged in response, including an increase in women and people from racial and ethnic minority backgrounds participating in higher education—the "look" of higher education dramatically changed (Lucas, 1994). Although societies and social clubs were always a part of higher education, they also grew within this new type of institution. The number of students participating in activities outside of the classroom (i.e., co-curricular offerings) increased, and this unique form of activity and experience took shape. In 1937, the American Council of Education

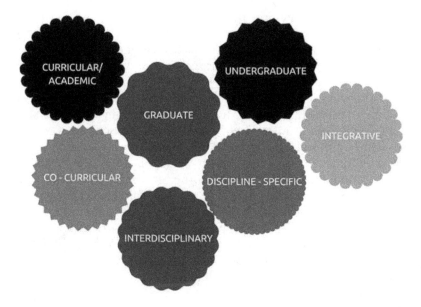

Figure 5.2. Multiple institutional contexts for consideration in leadership programming.

published a statement—the Student Personnel Point of View—underscoring the need to view higher education students in a holistic manner, The Student Personnel Point of View (American Council of Education, 1937) formally established the need for student services and learning outside of the classroom for students to develop life skills to become contributing members of society. This document is considered by many to be the birth of the student affairs profession with an emphasis on out-of-classroom learning also known as co-curricular programming.

Most often led by student affairs professionals, co-curricular leadership programs are delivered in a variety of formats and target members of different populations. College student leadership development has become a clear focus of student affairs work (Roberts, 1981). A scan of student affairs divisions reveals that often undergraduate co-curricular leadership development programs occur across the division with students in formal leadership positions and those engaged in the leadership process not attached to formal positions. According to Smist (2011), co-curricular leadership programs vary in both context and placement in an institution. These various initiatives include recreation and athletics, campus activities, student organizations, identity programming, community engagement, international education, and professional preparation. Co-curricular formats may include one-time programs and workshops or a speaker to a short-term program such as a conference or retreat. There are also longer co-curricular leadership program formats that may include a series of workshops or programs, certificate programs, or multiyear programs (Smist, 2011).

As discussed in Chapter 1, leadership programs had a strong beginning in co-curricular programming, with student affairs taking the lead on facilitating this type of learning. Often, part of the job description of student affairs administrators includes providing some type of leadership programming, usually in a co-curricular context. Although still widely absent from graduate student affairs preparation programs, some institutions, such as The Ohio State University and The Florida State University, require a course on being a leadership educator to train future administrators how to develop and deliver leadership programs in a co-curricular format. Yet in most of these cases, the courses are contingent on the availability of particular faculty with an appropriate set of experiences. These courses provide students with foundational knowledge of the theories and concepts in leadership studies. With this knowledge, emerging student affairs professionals will be well equipped to structure, format, and assess their co-curricular programs in a theoretical context.

Academic/Curricular-Based Programs

Throughout history, the priorities represented in the academic curriculum have shifted drastically. During the antebellum period, higher education curriculum was stagnant and consistent across the nation (Blackburn & Conrad, 1986; Hofstadter & Hardy, 1952). The curriculum consisted of an identical path for each student, regardless of interest or professional pursuits. After the Civil War, educational philosophies and views on a prescribed curriculum changed, and higher education was not exempt from these influences. In the late 19th century, universities started to remove liberal arts requirements in the curriculum (Hofstadter & Hardy, 1952). Over the 20-year period from the 1870s to the 1890s, schools such as Harvard and Columbia first eliminated prescribed classes for seniors and juniors and then removed most general education classes throughout the entire undergraduate curriculum.

It was only after the rigid curriculum of a liberal arts education was discredited that the elective system emerged in higher education (Blackburn & Conrad, 1986). Proponents of the elective system believed students would be the most qualified to make wise decisions about the classes that matched their interests and anticipated professional careers (Hofstadter & Hardy, 1952). Hofstadter and Hardy (1952) eloquently stated:

By the end of the first decade of the twentieth century, when the elective system reached its apogee, its benefits were widely agreed upon. It had blown through the American college like a gust of fresh air, and had swept out innumerable features of the old regime that could hardly be justified—its rigidity, its archaic content, its emphasis on discipline and memory rather than inquiry and criticism, its tendency to constrict the lives of faculty members as well as students by limiting their opportunities to deepen themselves in a special field of learning. (p. 53)

However, by 1930, the educational system had ventured too far from its liberal arts beginnings in favor of a completely elective-based curriculum (Hofstadter & Hardy, 1952). In an effort to address some of the educational issues brought about by a strict liberal arts education, the elective system became a catalyst for other problems. This new, unstructured system, which allowed students to choose classes, was criticized for being too vocational in nature and for having lowered higher education standards, thereby allowing students to graduate with classes that only required minimal conceptual material. The metaphorical pendulum swung from an extremely rigid to a completely unstructured curriculum. Currently, academic curriculum holds the middle ground. Broadly speaking, a general and liberal arts curriculum provides elective options for students to fill specific established competencies within a structured discipline of study.

In the specific context of leadership education, Brungardt, Greenleaf, Brungardt, and Arensdorf (2006) compared and contrasted undergraduate academic majors focused on leadership in self-identified programs within the United States. Their study examined school profiles, program profiles, mission and program purpose, and curriculum. Notable differences included varied school sizes, host departments, and credit hour requirements. Other variations included the focus of the program, the major scholars evident within the curricula, and the disparity between theory and skill development. Important findings from the Brungardt et al. (2006) study include: (a) programs are not limited to a particular type or size of institution; (b) careers of graduating students varied greatly, showing occupations in government, social service, religion, business, and industry; (c) an overwhelming majority focusing on both theory and application as well as civic and/or organizational objectives; and (d) several universities focused their learning objectives on cognitive theories whereas others focused on the development of skills and behaviors. The Brungardt et al. (2006) study provides an overview of undergraduate academic programs. However, an increasing number of co-curricular programs are being developed at an undergraduate level (Komives et al., 2011).

Undergraduate Programs

Undergraduates are participating increasingly in co-curricular programming. As indicated by Table 5.1, only 337 of 1,570 (21%) academic programs were offered at the undergraduate level. However, as discussed in the co-curricular context section, co-curricular undergraduate leadership development is happening across student affairs divisions in the majority of institutions. In fact, student affairs programs and services have primarily focused on undergraduate students (Haber, 2011). Therefore, leadership programming delivered by student affairs administrators is focused on undergraduate students.

The majority of student development theories and models on creating learning environments, such as leadership identity development (Komives, Owen, Longerbeam, Mainella, & Osteen, 2005), culturally relevant leadership learning (Bertrand Jones et al., 2016), and the relational readership model (Komives et al., 2013), are focused squarely on undergraduate students. Although these leadership theories and models can be transferable to graduate students, their primary focus is on undergraduate students. Additionally, student leadership research efforts are also mostly focused on undergraduate students, such as the Multi-Institutional Study of Leadership (Dugan, Kodama, Correia, &, Associates, 2013) and the Student Leadership Challenge (Kouzes & Posner, 2014).

Graduate and Professional Programs

As seen in Table 5.1, the majority of academic leadership programs offered in the United States are at the graduate level. Data collected from the ILA's Program Directory (2016) yielded 654 master's programs and 329 doctoral programs. Of 1,570 total programs included in this analysis, 983 (62.6%) were graduate programs. This figure demonstrates the large number of graduate academic programs focusing on leadership studies. However, the experiences of graduate and professional students in higher education differ greatly when compared with their undergraduate counterparts.

Socialization and involvement of graduate and professional students assists in understanding the context for leadership programs. Gardner and Barnes (2007) used Astin's (1984) conceptualization of involvement to specifically describe graduate student involvement. The emphasis of graduate student involvement is the professional experiences that ultimately tie directly to professional socialization. Socialization experiences are those that prepare graduate students for the values and cultures associated with their chosen profession, participation in an academic community, as well as the functions of their specific role (Golde, 1998; Weidman, Twale, & Stein, 2001). We can also define professional development experiences as socialization because these experiences assist in increasing graduate students' involvement in and understanding of professional behavior and expectations.

Arguably, the professional development of graduate students is a form of leadership education. Professional involvement, as a form of professional development, can be viewed in multiple ways: local, regional, state, and national. Local activities encompass those at the student's home academic institution. National activities include involvement in professional associations. Gardner and Barnes (2007) discussed a continuum of involvement for both local and national levels. Involvement can range from paying membership dues to attending and presenting at national conferences or even committee or task force work. This conceptualization of involvement differs from traditional definitions of undergraduate involvement. Understanding how graduate students define and practice leadership is one way to get a better understanding of how to assist in their leadership development.

Interdisciplinary Programs

Defining interdisciplinary studies has proven to be a difficult task because it remains an ambiguous term that applies to both the borrowing of ideas across disciplines and the creation/development of new academic categories based on the ideas and concepts of numerous fields of study (Klein, 1990). However, this problem has been addressed in the research (Keesey, 1988; Payne, 1998), and one definition that has surfaced is "the bringing together and interweaving of content, methods, and research strategies of various existing fields of study" (Payne, 1998, p. 176). The emergence of interdisciplinary studies came about from the need to more holistically understand problems that could not be solved from just one discipline. During the latter half of the 20th century, another factor arose that promoted a different perspective on this type of study. The positive reception and application of both general systems theory and complexity theory provided higher education with a new lens with which to view interdisciplinarity (Newell, 2001). These new views also brought to light many of the similarities these theories share with interdisciplinary programs and the process of integration. As Newell (2001) stated, "An interdisciplinary approach is justified only by a complex system. So if a behavior is not produced by a system or the system is not complex, interdisciplinary study is not required" (p. 1).

There are a number of positive outcomes of interdisciplinary studies including: (a) development of cognitive and affective skills; (b) precision in reading, writing, speaking, and thinking; (c) appreciation of different perspectives; (d) tolerance for ambiguity; (e) increased sensitivity to ethical issues; (f) ability to synthesize and integrate; and (g) more creative, original, and unconventional thinking skills (Payne, 1998). However, interdisciplinary programs did not come without their own set of issues and problems. The first problem is represented by the politics related to individual disciplines (Klein, 1990). It is seen as defection within higher education to leave one's discipline and cohabitate with members of a different discipline (Knights & Willmott, 1997). However, probably the greatest problem of interdisciplinary studies is the organizational structure of colleges and universities (Klein, 1990).

However, prominent scholars have argued, "The study of leadership is not limited to a single discipline" (Riggio, Ciulla, & Sorenson, 2003, p. 228). Correspondingly, this interdisciplinarity creates opportunities to bring together typically siloed disciplines and give voice to multiple perspectives on leadership (Harvey & Riggio, 2011; Jenkins & Dugan, 2013). Leadership learning is enhanced through various constructs, multiple perspectives, and diverse contexts. Therefore, it follows that leadership education should be interdisciplinary (Riggio et al., 2003). Furthermore, leadership studies is mostly composed of scholars who are primarily trained in a single, specific discipline—the majority of whose advanced degrees are outside leadership or leadership studies (Jenkins, 2017a)—whereas much of the work done in studying leadership crosses disciplinary lines (Harvey & Riggio, 2011). Within this framework, leadership education has the potential to revolutionize the academic world. As Guthrie and Callahan (2016) state, framing leadership education as multi- and interdisciplinary processes provides the opportunity to integrate skills and knowledge learned in both the liberal arts and general curriculum.

Integrative Programs

Increasing emphasis has been placed on developing undergraduate students' integrative learning through multiple forms of engaged educational experiences. Disciplinary integration is a distinctive characteristic of leadership programs, and leadership learning across academic and student affairs boundaries is a signature characteristic of 21st-century liberal education, curricular, co-curricular, and pedagogical innovations. Integrative learning involves developing capacities to reflect, connect, and make positive change (Schneider, 2003) and calls for innovative partnerships between faculty and administrators to develop integrative programs to provide learning opportunities for students. Such partnerships and innovative integrative program development requires understanding the effectiveness of curriculum in individual departments and across an institution. To aid in this effort, the Association of American Colleges and Universities is providing leadership research, faculty training, and conferences in the area of integrative undergraduate learning (Association of American Colleges and Universities /Integrative-Learning, 2017).

Peden, Reed, and Wolfe (2017) provide 13 examples of undergraduate student projects focusing on complex questions that are meaningful to individual students and society. These projects require students to integrate, apply, demonstrate, reflect on, and communicate their cumulative learning, requiring input from multiple disciplines and perspectives. Purposefully guided curriculum and co-curricular experiences where students develop and connect their knowledge and skills across broad and specialized study have the most significant influence on student learning (Peden et al., 2017). Expanding the conversation into technological spheres, Bass and Eynon (2016) explored the implications of emerging digital capacities and the influence of overall higher education culture. They argued that higher education, and specifically liberal education, needs to be reimagined by using networked and adaptive systems to connect learning experiences by technologies that may have been disconnected. Technology would open the boundaries of institutions and create new integrative contexts for transformative learning.

Integrative leadership education programs should weave together various experiences, content areas, and learning opportunities to create holistic learning experiences. This form of leadership learning opportunity should include experiences on and off campus, both in- and out-of-class experiences, across disciplines, and across campus. The strength in integrative leadership education programs derives from the connections that foster deeper learning (Haber, 2011).

Discipline-Specific Programs

The emergence of academic disciplines occurred due to higher education's move to an elective curricular structure and the increase in the population of students, faculty, and higher education institutions. The specialized nature of an academic discipline naturally differentiates itself from other disciplines through the use of particular language, symbols, artifacts, research, and ways of communicating that are specific to that discipline (Frost & Jean, 2003). The boundaries created through these differences influence individual and group attitudes, behaviors, and relationships with others in higher education (Becher, 1989). The increase in academic disciplines throughout higher education in the 20th century prompted the competition for power, resources, and prestige and created a hierarchy among the different fields of study (Davies & Guppy, 1997). The ranking of disciplines exists primarily in the differences between the disciplines that concentrate on "hard" versus "soft" subjects and between "pure" and "applied" fields of study.

In an effort to move away from the liberal arts college, higher education found itself on the opposite end of the spectrum by the mid-20th century. The formerly overstructured liberal arts education was now a chaotic and disorganized elective system, which had a number of disciplinary problems, including the lowering of educational standards and a lack of connection between disciplines in higher education (Hofstadter & Hardy, 1952). The aim of a discipline was no longer to connect and contribute to higher education or society but to impress others within the academic field. The criticism for this new specialized education began to surface in the mid-20th century. These critiques, centered on the education of "scientifically-illiterate humanists" and "culturally-illiterate scientist," spread throughout higher education and led to the abandonment of "liberal learning because it was too difficult to conceptualize or administer … without having anything coherent to replace it" (Lucas, 1994, p. 295).

In the analysis of the ILA Program Directory, more discipline-specific leadership programs and individual courses are beginning to emerge (Leadership Learning Research Center, 2017). As Riggio et al. (2003) introduced more than 15 years ago, subfields within specific disciplines, including education, political science, engineering, business, and others, are providing "academic niches" for leadership development within higher education. Discipline-specific leadership programs, whether in an undergraduate, graduate, curricular, or co-curricular framework, provide a space and place for specific leadership competencies (Seemiller, 2013) to be applied to specific career and industry values.

CONCLUSION

In simple terms, context matters. Recognizing various frameworks, naming them, and intentionally discussing the challenges and assets of various contexts will only provide a more solid foundation for developing and delivering leadership programs. As you can see, context is critical for consideration in seven frameworks mentioned in this chapter: co-curricular, academic/curricular, undergraduate, graduate, interdisciplinary, integrative, and discipline-specific. Leadership educators who are aware of the context in which they are working from can better understand the stakeholders, including student learning, and therefore can better construct learning objectives that meet learners' needs.

Because leadership and leadership education have their roots in inter- and multidisciplinary thinking, it is uniquely positioned to champion continued efforts in this vein and lead the charge in breaking down the siloes that actually hinder student learning across the academy. However, at the same time, increases in discipline-specific leadership programs provide focused opportunity for leadership learning that will translate into new fields. This adds to the overall complexity of context, especially if discipline-specific programs do not explore the possibility of initiatives in an interdisciplinary nature. No matter which way you look at this complex issue of multiple contexts and the potential tension they create, it is important to remember that higher education is always evolving. As educators, we must be prepared to tailor our programs to deal with the changes occurring in the multiple contexts in higher education.

CHAPTER 6

CHARACTERISTICS OF DISTINCTIVE LEADERSHIP PROGRAMS

When developing an academic/curricular or co-curricular leadership program, understanding context is critical; however, it is only one variable. After an extensive literature review, five major characteristics for distinctive leadership programs emerged. For the purposes of our conversation, distinctive programs are those that have a positive influence on student leadership learning. This encompasses both co-curricular and curricular programs and may include but is not limited to student satisfaction. Distinctiveness is based on high-quality, well-developed programs that demonstrate the ability to meet their stated learning outcomes. Eich (2008) suggested high-quality leadership programs focus on opportunities for students to practice leadership, whether it is through specifically practicing skills and concepts learned in the program, engaging in out-of-classroom projects, or participating in positions related to the leadership program responsible for developing and teaching. Building off Eich's (2008) work, we found five characteristics of distinctive leadership programs, including:

1. Intentionally Designed Programs
2. Authentic Leadership Learning Environments
3. Application of Knowledge, Skills, and Values
4. Meaning Making through Reflection
5. Continuous Program Improvement

The Role of Leadership Educators: Transforming Learning, pp. 95–115
Copyright © 2018 by Information Age Publishing

This chapter deeply explores these five characteristics of distinctive leadership programs to better understand how to create and sustain high-quality programs, in both curricular and co-curricular contexts, and how leadership educators as program architects can create such programs.

INTENTIONALLY DESIGNED PROGRAMS

The first characteristic of a distinctive leadership program is intentionality in design. Developing a leadership program with purpose is critical to overall program success and the achievement of student learning. We have all attended programs, workshops, and speakers where it felt more like time filler than a well-planned, intentional learning experience. Because of limited resources, such as time, qualified educators, and/or money, programs are often built strictly on what is readily available or what has worked in the past, with little consideration of developing learning outcomes, connecting appropriate instructional strategies, or the characteristics of the learners. A scaffolding approach, where you plan and execute the design of program curriculum and learning experiences to meet specified purposes (Wiggins & McTighe, 2005), is a specific strategy to produce an intentionally well-designed program. To that end, we will introduce the creation of learning outcomes, connect learning outcomes to pedagogy, and offer guiding questions to motivate effective leadership educators' thinking and acting toward constructing new programs and revising those already in existence.

Learning Outcomes Creation

Morgan, King, Rudd, and Kaufman (2013) point out, "Curriculum planning and revision is often neglected by faculty and administrators for lack of an effective method to undertake this effort" (p. 140). Strategic curriculum planning starts by developing a set of learning outcomes—essentially beginning with the end in mind. This kind of "backwards design" (Wiggins & McTighe, 2005, p. 56) is critical to the effectiveness of any learning experience. Harvey and Jenkins (2014) agree that creation of a leadership program begins with specifying what knowledge is to be learned by students. Unfortunately, at times, program planning starts by developing a schedule of activities or list of readings you want students to accomplish. By organizing resources in this fashion, learning outcomes are overlooked and often times never articulated.

As you can imagine, high-quality learning outcomes are critical in curricular planning and intentionally designing a leadership program. Specific learning outcomes also influence the quality of the learning environment and the perceptions of learners regarding whether they encourage learning in a deep way rather than just at a surface level (Trigwell & Prosser, 1991). Harvey and Jenkins (2014) further explain that learning outcomes should "...fall into two broad categories: technical knowledge of the expertise and skills deemed requisite to leadership either generally or in particular areas and humanistic knowledge about people, both as individuals and as members of groups" (p. 77). Incorporating these types of learning outcomes when developing an initiative creates a solid foundation for an intentionally well-designed program.

Designing Outcomes With Learning Taxonomies

Learning taxonomies are widely used to describe the learning stages at which a learner is operating for particular content and can include elements such as knowledge, skills, and abilities. Two of the most widely used learning taxonomies come from Bloom (1956) and Fink (2013). Bloom's taxonomy moves stepwise in a hierarchical sequence, increasing in higher levels of learning: (a) knowledge, (b) comprehension, (c) application, (d) analysis, (e); synthesis, and (e) evaluation. A design strategy aligned with particular outcomes of Bloom's Taxonomy would consider, for example, how leadership education is delivered and assessed as part of an overall leadership development program—that is, how it fits into the broader organizational plan—as opposed to an independent activity with independent outcomes (Lindsay, Foster, Jackson, & Hassan, 2009). Thus:

> ... leadership education could be used to provide the requisite knowledge that could then be coordinated with an experiential setting where the individual is required to apply that knowledge in particular scenarios. The combined influence of leadership education and leadership application would be identified through a unified assessment goal of individual development. Knowledge for knowledge sake does not necessarily benefit the individual or the organization, but knowledge and application could be enhanced when personal leader development is part of a broader developmental program that extends well beyond the classroom. (Lindsay, Foster, Jackson, & Hassan, 2009, p. 167)

Fink's (2013) taxonomy is not hierarchical but instead interactive, meaning that each of the following kinds of learning may stimulate one or more of the others: (a) foundational knowledge; (b) application; (c) integration; (d) human dimension; (e) caring; and (f) learning how to learn. For example, when a leadership educator finds a way to help students apply a particular leadership model to the case studies in an assigned textbook reading (application), this makes it easier for them to get excited about the value of leadership (caring). When students learn how to effectively relate leadership to other subjects, ideas, or areas of their lives (integration), this makes it easier for students to see the significance of course material for themselves and others (human dimension; Fink, 2013). Through using this learning outcome design process, leadership educators can develop learning objectives for their educational programs, provide ways of assessing learning outcomes, select and adapt assignments that are more challenging for engaged students, and spark their own creativity in developing activities and projects. Instructors are encouraged to select the learning activities that best support their teaching goals, class size, and other situational factors (Fink, 2013). Table 6.1 is a template for designing a leadership course or workshop within a leadership program—adapted from Fink (2013) and Northouse (2014)—as well as two lists of sample learning objectives. In Chapter 8, include an example of an assessment process for learning outcomes across an entire academic leadership program, such as a leadership major or minor.

Table 6.1.   Learning Taxonomy and Outcomes Template

Learning Outcomes for Course/Workshop	Procedures for Assessing Student Learning	Learning Activities
Foundational Knowledge: Understand and remember key assumptions and components of various leadership models		
Application: Know how to apply leadership models to real-life situations		
Integration: Be able to relate leadership theory to other academic subjects and current events		
Human Dimension: Understand the personal and social implications of knowing about leadership		
Caring: Care about leadership and learning more about it		
Learning how to Learn: Know how to keep on learning about leadership		

Examples

Learning Outcomes: Leading in Teams Workshop/Student Organization Training

Foundational Knowledge:

- …remember some of the terminology associated with teams and teamwork (e.g., groupthink, roles)
- …be able to identify the key elements of team and group processes (e.g., forming, storming, norming, and performing; Tuckman, 1965)

Application:

- …be able to do a formal analysis of team roles in order to meet specific goals
- …be able to observe a team in the real world and identify specific group dynamics

Integration:

- …identify some of the differences between effective and ineffective team leaders and how context affects each
- …relate ideas about teamwork to group processes (e.g., communication, shared decision making)

Human Dimension:

- …come to see themselves as people more educated about teams and teamwork than the average person
- …be able to inform and educate other organizational members about the roles and responsibilities of team members in group work

Caring:

- …value the importance of assigned roles in group work as a part of effective team leadership
- …be anxious to critically evaluate group dynamics that they encounter regularly in the public media

Learning How to Learn:

- …be able to identify important resources for their own subsequent team-based work
- …have a clear sense of what they would like to learn or develop next about leadership

Learning Outcomes: Leading in Teams Workshop/Student Organization Training

Foundational Knowledge:

- …remember some of the terminology associated with teams and teamwork (e.g., groupthink, roles)
- …be able to identify the key elements of team and group processes (e.g., forming, storming, norming, and performing; Tuckman, 1965)

(Examples continue on next page)

Examples (Continued)

Learning Outcomes: Leading in Teams Workshop/Student Organization Training

Application:

- …be able to do a formal analysis of team roles in order to meet specific goals

- …be able to observe a team in the real world and identify specific group dynamics

Integration:

- …identify some of the differences between effective and ineffective team leaders and how context affects each

- …relate ideas about teamwork to group processes (e.g., communication, shared decision making)

Human Dimension:

- …come to see themselves as people more educated about teams and teamwork than the average person

- …be able to inform and educate other organizational members about the roles and responsibilities of team members in group work

Caring:

- …value the importance of assigned roles in group work as a part of effective team leadership

- …be anxious to critically evaluate group dynamics that they encounter regularly in the public media

Learning How to Learn:

- …be able to identify important resources for their own subsequent team-based work

- …continue to be proactive with team-based work and shared decision making, for example, what group roles to take on and how to delegate responsibilities

---

Connecting Learning Outcomes to Appropriate Pedagogies

Once learning outcomes are established, connecting appropriate instructional strategies helps to create an intentionally designed leadership program. These pedagogies put the leadership learning framework in action by considering how participants learn and grow via the programs in which they participate. As discussed in Chapter 4, the six aspects of leadership learning—knowledge, development, training, observation, engagement, and metacognition—should be taken into consideration when developing program curricula. In order to select and implement appropriate pedagogies and their attendant activities, experiences, and ways to gain knowledge, it is imperative to first look at the articulated learning outcomes associated with the initiative, then shifting focus onto how learners will receive content, and finally consider the overall and individual characteristics of participants. To these ends, two approaches are suggested. The first involves aligning aspects of leadership learning with the selection of appropriate instructional strategies. For example, what instructional strategies will best facilitate growth in the areas of knowledge, development, training, observation, engagement, and metacognition for social justice? An effective instructional strategy to teach the engagement aspect of social justice might differ from an effective strategy to teach metacognition. The second approach to electing instructional strategies is to consider how students might demonstrate learning outcomes simply by experiencing an instructional strategy, regardless of content. That is, leadership educators do not have to find a perfect instructional strategy to fit particular content but consider how instructional strategies provide learning in and of themselves; they can be consider both the means and ends of learning. For example, service-learning experiences can develop the learners' observation skills and capacity for engagement, regardless of the site or community partner.

In order for leadership educators to maximize students' leadership learning and capacity building, they "must be intentional in matching their intended program or course outcomes with relevant student and leadership development theory, and then apply effective strategies for the delivery of material to a diverse student population" (Rosch & Anthony, 2012, p. 38). Part of bridging learning outcomes to pedagogies is applying appropriate conceptual frameworks, leadership theories, models, and concepts. Having reliable and valid leadership frameworks are key in connecting these two critical components in curriculum.

International Leadership Association Guiding Questions

An incredible resource for designing and revising leadership programs is the International Leadership Association (ILA) Guiding Questions. After a 5-year collaborative process, the ILA (2009) published *Guiding Questions: Guidelines for Leadership Education Programs*. As Ritch and Mengel (2009) discuss, the open-ended format of ILA's guiding questions document was meant to be applicable to any leadership educator (practitioner or faculty) developing a student leadership program. The ILA guiding questions were the framework for Guthrie and Osteen's (2012a) *New Directions in Student Services* monograph "Developing Students' Leadership Capacity." Using the five standards outlined in the ILA Guiding Questions—context, conceptual framework, content, teaching and learning, and assessment—the monograph was developed to assist leadership educators in their understanding, conceptualization, and implementation of leadership programs. The five overarching questions that focus on the standards and created Guthrie and Osteen's (2012a) framework include:

- Context: "How does the context of the leadership education program affect the program?"
- Conceptual Framework: "What is the conceptual framework of the Leadership education program?
- Content: "What is the content of the leadership education program and how was it derived?"
- Teaching and Learning: "What are the students' developmental levels and what teaching and learning methods are most appropriate to ensure maximum student learning?"
- Outcomes and Assessment: "What are the intended outcomes of the leadership education program and how are they assessed and used to ensure continuous quality improvement?"

Taken together, this organizing framework and its questions help form a conceptual bridge that leadership educators can use to connect their specific learning outcomes to their broader pedagogical orientations, with implications for course readings, assignments, activities, reflective exercises, and assessment strategies. We highly encourage all leadership educators to adapt this type of framework, or ones like it, to critically interrogate their own educative initiatives. The results of such an exercise, we anticipate, will at least improve cohesion in your work and at most lead to improved gains in student leadership learning.

LEADERSHIP LEARNING ENVIRONMENTS

Creating an authentic learning environment is another characteristic of distinctive leadership programs. Just as leadership is contextual, so is developing a positive learning environment. The changing dynamics of learners, their interactions, and engagement in a leadership program can all influence program architects' ability to create positive learning environments. However, thinking broadly when developing a program can yield great benefits to creating a positive learning environment. We want to further explore a few key considerations in learning environments, including the influence of instructors, supportive and challenging environments, integrative learning environments, and incorporating culturally relevant leadership learning.

Role of Instructors

As architects of learning, whether that is in the role of a classroom instructor or program facilitator, educators are essential in both the development and delivery of the curriculum. As Morgan et al. (2013) state, "faculty are experts in their discipline, possessing a deep knowledge of the subject matter, which is the basis of how they establish the knowledge, skills, and practicum required for degree attainment" (p. 143). They are seen as experts of knowledge, and they completely control how the curriculum is delivered. This includes presentation of material, which topics are emphasized and how, as well as which learning activities are used to impart knowledge and make meaning, which results in particular forms of growth and learning (Morgan et al., 2013). Harding (2011) clearly states this by "What we teach may not nearly be as important as ... how we teach" (p. 76). In fact, a leadership educator's behavior, language used, and engagement become part of the curriculum.

The influence that educators have on establishing a positive learning environment cannot be overstated. Effective leadership educators who construct distinctive leadership programs purposefully cultivate environments that are supportive yet challenging, are integrative of students' lived experiences, and appropriately respond to learners' social and personal identities. In the following sections, we consider each of these elements in turn, providing recommendations related to building and maintain these signature environmental characteristics.

Supportive Yet Challenging Environments

One of the things that educators should consider when constructing learning spaces is a supportive yet challenging environment. Sanford (1962, 1966) introduced a student development theory rooted in the tension between support and challenge, which has since become widely used in postsecondary education. Sanford theorized that effective educators strike a careful balance between the level of support and challenge they provide students to assist in development. In other words, a student who is overly supported may not be motivated toward growth, yet a student who is overly challenged may be too overwhelmed to move forward. Therefore, it is the instructor's responsibility to create and maintain environments that are optimally supportive and challenging. This feat is all the more complicated when we consider this balance must be stuck for individual students, as well as the group of students who participate in our leadership learning initiatives. Figure 6.1 depicts the tensions between challenge and support alongside individual and group needs to more accurately depict where we believe effective leadership educators should position themselves and the environments they strive to create. With these balances in mind, supportive yet challenging environments empower students to stretch beyond what they believe is possible (see also Dweck, 2007).

Source: Created by V. Chunoo, Leadership Learning Research Center.

Figure 6.1.   The balance among challenge, support, and individual and group needs.

An effective instructor can be instrumental in creating supportive and challenging environments, but this unseen architecture is co-created by program participants. The underlying culture of support and challenge is often invisible to the casual observer but can be felt throughout the program by participants and organizers. Eich (2008) discusses two elements that foster learning and engage learners in a culture of support and challenge. First, participants must be made to feel safe in an encouraging environment to challenge others, learn from mistakes, think critically, and ask difficult questions. Second, facilitators of learning are positioned to set community standards encouraging participants to be positive, open minded, approachable, and helpful.

Arao and Clemens (2013) advocate implementing a learning environment of brave space. Moving beyond the safe space conceptualization, a brave space entreats participants to engage in the struggle of understanding across difference in creative and productive ways. These include engagement in controversy with civility (Higher Education Research Institute, 1996); awareness and ownership of one's intentions and impact; implementation of an environment of respect, with the caveat for a need to discuss expectations of respect within the group, as respect looks different in various cultures; and encouraging participants to step into and wrestle with the uncomfortable (Arao & Clemens, 2013). Frequently facilitators begin a difficult conversation with the understanding of challenge by choice, allowing participants to disengage if they feel unsafe with the topic. The brave space contention dissuades this overarching tenant; instead brave space calls to challenge participants to consider why they may choose to not engage and if possible step into the discomfort to achieve individual and group growth (Arao & Clemens, 2013).

Creating a supportive yet challenging environment is critical, especially when engaging participants about and across differences in personal and social identities. Dugan et al. (2013) reported that the strongest predictor of socially responsible leadership capacity included informal and formal conversations and interactions about and across differences. Engagement about difference with a diverse group can be made tangible in leadership programs in several ways. Intentionally or organically, engagement can occur by participants articulating perspectives, worldviews, and how their past experiences influence their ways of being and perspectives about the future. Distinctive programs contribute to student learning by recruiting, selecting, and supporting diverse and engaged participants. Participatory culture, interactive teaching and learning, and adequate access to resources are critical to discussions about and across differences (Haworth & Conrad, 1997). Eich (2008) also discussed how students encourage difference through programs by exposure to different experiences, contexts, groups, and people, as well as an opportunity to practice various ways of leading and engaging with diverse individuals. Creating supportive yet challenging environments can be a difficult balance to achieve; however, it is essential in providing a learning environment that invites all to engage in deep leadership learning.

Integrative Learning Environments

Building on the role of instructors and a supportive and challenging environment, integrative learning environments provide an incredible opportunity for leadership learning. Working to create an integrative, also sometimes referred to as a seamless, learning environment, where both curricular and co-curricular work together to maximize leadership learning is ideal. Owen (2015) clearly states, "If leadership educators want to create leaders who make connections across silos, structures, and disparate activities, they need to be practicing integrative leadership development" (pp. 52–54). Because leadership is an interdisciplinary topic, students need to understand leadership theory, develop leadership skills and competencies through practical application, and reflect on learning to grow and evolve as learners (Guthrie et al., 2013). This type of learning can be enhanced by focusing on how to integrate curricular and co-curricular learning environments for students to reach their maximum leadership capacity.

Collaborative efforts to create integrative leadership learning environments across an institution, which are mutually beneficial and respectful, are critical but often difficult to achieve (D. Roberts, 2007). A shared vision for combining curricular and co-curricular education, which benefits students, academic programs, and administrative bodies, is important to the construction of such environments (Westfall, 1999). To fully create a multidimensional integrative learning environment, constant anticipation of successes and challenges, precise attention to detail, appropriate communication, and continuous clarification is needed for all groups represented (Guthrie et al., 2013). More often in higher education, coordination occurs where academic and students affairs work together to organize efforts but do not truly commit to integrate a program where learning flows between curricular and co-curricular contexts.

Ideally, integrative leadership learning environments are created with the psychosocial and educational needs of students as top priorities. Collaborations should focus on creating the best environment for students to have the enlightening moments, also known as those "aha!" moments (Guthrie et al., 2013). Kuh (1995) reminds us that context continues to be important, and an institution needs to consider its campus culture, recognize appropriate theoretical content, and determine the best instructional strategies and assessments of learning. Guthrie and Thompson (2010) regard the potential influence of integrative learning environments as "… partnerships … for leadership knowledge acquisition, practical application of leadership skills and knowledge, and reflection on the experiences in light of the education adding, "Student experiences are strengthened and learning is deepened when institutions intentionally create environments…" (p. 54). With this sentiment in mind, we challenge leadership educators to cultivate and maintain these types of partnerships to enhance their effectiveness and improve their students' leadership learning success.

Culturally Relevant Leadership Learning Environments

Bertrand Jones et al. (2016) introduced the culturally relevant leadership learning (CRLL) model, which is another critical piece of a distinctive leadership learning environment. CRLL focuses on contextual dimensions of a learning environment, most often a campus climate, while incorporating a leadership learner's identity, capacity, and efficacy. This model seeks to challenge and ultimately transform previous paradigms of leadership learning. CRLL confronts the myriad ways that racism, sexism, religious oppression, heterosexism, cisgenderism, and classism advantages and disadvantages individuals' lives (Bertrand Jones et al., 2016; Guthrie, Bertrand Jones, & Osteen, in press).

Guthrie et al. (in press) uses the metaphor of a house to describe the CRLL model. The role of campus and/or organizational climate creates the structure of the house, including the floor, walls, and roof. Essentially, the architecture of the house represents the environment of leadership learning and its degree of culturally relevance. The foundational architecture creating the floor, walls, and roof include five domains from Hurtado, Milem, Clayton-Pederson, and Allen (1999) and Milem, Chang, and Antonio (2005): (a) historical legacy of inclusion/exclusion; (b) compositional diversity; (c) psychological climate; (d) behavioral climate; and (e) organizational/structural aspects. Taken together, the CRLL model provides a comprehensive approach to diagnosing and altering the leadership learning environments we construct to enhance their effectiveness toward student learning.

In creating a strong learning environment, just as when building a house, structural components such as floors, walls, and roof need to provide a solid foundation. Without the foundation we have described here, the learning activities that occur in the environments (i.e., in our houses) are more limited in their abilities to enhance leadership learning. Just as when a solid culturally relevant learning environment is created, all feel welcome to participate. The other critical components of the CRLL model (Bertrand Jones et al., 2016) are individuals' ways of understanding through identity, capacity, and efficacy. As discussed in Chapter 2, identity is answering the question of "Who am I?" (Erikson, 1959). Capacity is an individual's reflection on their overall ability to behave effectively in the leadership process (Dugan, 2011). Efficacy, as Bandura (1997) defines, is the belief that an individual can "organize and execute the courses of action required to produce given attainments" (p. 3). Identity, capacity, and efficacy are interconnected and together motivate students to engage in the leadership process (Reichard & Walker, 2016). Identity, capacity, and efficacy act as doorways into engagement, in which students will enter into the house in order to grow.

APPLICATION OF KNOWLEDGE, SKILLS, AND VALUES

Another distinctive program characteristic involves providing opportunities for learners to apply leadership knowledge, skills, and values to real-life situations. Studying Plato's Republic, we can learn a great deal about applying knowledge, skills, and values for aspiring leaders. Harvey and Jenkins (2014) discussed aspiring leaders in Plato's Republic do not only receive instruction but engage with practice for years to follow. In fact, the Greek word "praxis" means to apply to context (Merriam-Webster, 2017). As you can see, this notion of applying knowledge is not new to leadership learning. However, this critical aspect is sometimes missing from leadership programs. Eich (2008) underscores the recommendation: "high-quality leadership programs incorporate student-centered experiential learning experiences that include leadership practice, reflection activities, application in meetings, meaningful discussions, episodes of indifference, civic service, and discovery retreats" (p. 180). To further explore these ideas, we discuss some pivotal aspects of how leadership programs can intentionally incorporate experiential learning, as well as other activities and experiences to encourage application of knowledge, skills, and values.

Experiential Learning

McCall (2004) stated that experience should be the primary mechanism for learning leadership. Therefore, leadership educators should look to experiential learning theories to ground leadership learning. Building from the works of Dewey (1933), Lewin (1951), and Piaget (1970), Kolb (1984) created the experiential learning theory. According to Kolb (1984), learning is defined as "the process whereby knowledge is created through the transformation of experience. Knowledge results from the combination of grasping and transforming experience" (p. 41). The four phases in Kolb's (1984) Cycle of Experiential Learning include: concrete experience, reflective observation, abstract conceptualization, and active experimentation. Learners can enter the cycle at any point and actually learn best when they are engaged in all four modes. Concrete experience is learning from specific experiences. Reflective observation is making meaning of experiences. Abstract conceptualization is logically analyzing ideas, planning systematically, or acting on an intellectual understanding of a situation. Active experimentation is revealed by demonstrating skills, ability to get things done, and influencing people and events through action (Kolb, 1984). We expand on the unification of leadership education and experiential learning in the introduction to Section III of this book.

Service Learning

Service learning is an increasingly popular experiential learning pedagogy in leadership programs. Incorporating service into meaningful leadership practices, students are more able to make positive contributions to their communities as well as their own development. Well-developed service-learning programs create spaces for students to exercise their leadership development for civic purposes, as well as build bridges within and between communities. A critical consideration of service-based leadership learning is the process of self-awareness in context of the communities they are working in. With thoughtful guidance from instructors, students perform leadership and better understand by engaging with those around them to work towards positive sustainable change. Chapter 14 will explore specific instructional strategies in service-learning and community engagement work.

Experiences in Leadership

Building off the importance of experiential learning in leadership education, structuring leadership experiences in program design is an important way to include application of knowledge, skills, and values. Students can experience leadership in a variety of ways including but not limited to researching with a professor, working at an internship, studying abroad, serving as a student organizational officer, or working on campus. Intentionally designing learning opportunities that provide structure for application of knowledge, skills, and values within a specific example can enhance a student's learning.

Example

Academic/Curricular-Based Leadership Experience Course

LDR 3263: Leadership Experience at Florida State University is an experiential based course that offers participants an opportunity to put into practice the knowledge, theory, and skills. Students will participate in a chosen experience that is either a service-learning project, internship, or research for 120 hours in one semester. In this course, students complete an experiential learning contract, extensively reflect on their experience, and apply learned theory to their personal experience throughout the course. Additionally, students prepare a research poster that demonstrates their leadership learning from previous leadership courses and how it connects with their leadership experience. Further, discussing what their leadership experience in this course has taught them more about leadership is required.

Framing leadership learning as theory-to-practice-to-theory for students can help them conceptualize this ongoing process of learning leadership knowledge, skills, and values, applying them to practice, then back to the theories and concepts. Often times we use theory-to-practice language in applying content knowledge we learn to our lived experiences, but we stop there. By looping students experiences back to learned content, we validate their experience and help them make meaning from what they are experiencing.

MAKING MEANING THROUGH REFLECTION

Reflection, much like metacognition, is making meaning of knowledge and experiences to learn and grow. Often reflection is interchanged with "meaning making" or "processing," but all refers to enhancing learning by thinking of past experiences. Dewey (1933) discussed reflection as a goal of education, which he envisioned as a cycle learners spiraled through, gaining depth with each rotation. Reflection has been conceptualized as the primary process through which learners extract knowledge from their experiences (Illeris, 2007). For leadership educators, the challenge is best understanding how students "mine" their experiences to learn and develop leadership knowledge and skills (Guthrie & Bertrand Jones, 2012).

Learners who go through a cycle of reflection create new meaning that leads to growth and serves both themselves and a greater good (Rodgers, 2002). A critical point about reflection is that it is a continual process not about reaching an end point. Framing reflection as a continual process elevates it as part of the learning process rather than relegating it to a single activity (Volpe White & Guthrie, 2016). Educators need to do their part by creating the tension necessary to encourage growth-producing encounters (Guthrie & Bertrand Jones, 2012). For reflection to be useful in the meaning-making process, it needs to be guided and purposeful. Harvey and Jenkins (2014) define *critical reflection* as "an iterative process of returning to what one has studied, thought, experienced, done, and felt, and an autonomous but still relatively structured and disciplined process of synthesizing lessons, conclusions, uncertainties, and questions" (p. 79). Critical reflection pushes students beyond a surface-level understanding of their leadership experience to an analytical and a thorough approach of synthesizing one's experiences with one's perspective and ways of knowing.

Over the last two decades, reflection models based in research and experience have emerged. These models provide leadership educators guidance to enhance leadership learning through reflection. Volpe White and Guthrie (2016) provided a summary of themes from effective reflection models, and an overview is provided in Table 6.2.

Depending on context, group, and nature of experience, how leadership educators should structure reflection differs. Although meaningful reflection can take place in various settings, educators need to provide space and intentional structure to facilitate reflection. It is important for those

Table 6.2. Common Themes of Effective Reflection Models

Effective Reflection Model Characteristics	References
Ongoing	Eyler & Giles, 1999; Eyler, Giles, & Schmeide (1996); Hatcher & Bringle (1997)
Contextual	Eyler & Giles (1999); Eyler et al. (1996); Hatcher & Bringle (1997)
Provides Feedback	Hatcher & Bringle (1997)
Promotes Critical Thinking	Ash & Clayton (2004); Eyler & Giles (1999); Eyler et al. (1996)
Values Clarification Included	Astin, Vogelgesang, Ikeda, & Yee, (2000); Hatcher & Bringle (1997)
Connected to Experience	Eyler & Giles (1999); Eyler et al. (1996); Hatcher & Bringle, (1997)

who administer leadership programs to make explicit connections between experiences and learning outcomes, otherwise students may not readily see the associations (Volpe White & Guthrie, 2016). Drawing on Kolb's (1984) learning styles, Eyler, Giles, and Schmeide (1996) divided reflection activities into four categories: reading, writing, doing, and telling. Guthrie and Bertrand Jones (2012) furthered these distinctions by discussing connected reflection (integrating experience with learning), challenging reflection (producing new understanding and ways of problems solving), and contextualized reflection (context specific). Different reflective methods have value for diverse learning styles, program structures, and learning outcomes (Volpe White & Guthrie, 2016).

In a qualitative study with undergraduate students enrolled in a leadership certificate program, which included structured reflection, students indicated understanding reflection and developing greater self-awareness led to creating and applying reflective pedagogy to their leadership learning (Volpe White & Guthrie, 2016). Respondents from this study stated that the intentional reflection in leadership courses provided them with an awareness of reflection, as well as opportunities to make meaning from experiences and gain skills for deeper reflection. Students also reported a direct link between reflection and a greater self-awareness. This increase in self-awareness resulted in more self-confidence and practiced self-care (Volpe White & Guthrie, 2016). The importance of a reflective environment also emerged from Volpe White and Guthrie's (2016) study. Establishing a reflective culture through instructors, class sizes, and seating arrangements and having discussion-based courses were all significant for this supportive, reflective environment.

Reflection is an essential instructional strategy for leadership educators (Guthrie & Bertrand Jones, 2012) and leadership development in general (Eich, 2008). As Volpe White and Guthrie (2016) demonstrate, instructors can support meaningful reflection by creating environments encourage and value reflection as a continuous process. By connecting reflection to leadership education, students may have an increased self-awareness, which might help them be more effective leaders. Distinctive leadership programs have reflective environments, created through intentional spaces and instructional strategies throughout the program.

CONTINUOUS PROGRAM IMPROVEMENT

Developing and delivering distinctive leadership programs requires architects to engage in continuous assessment, feedback, and improvement. Although we will explore assessment tools and strategies in depth in Chapter 8, it is important to note here how critical assessment is for continuous program improvement as a characteristic of a distinctive program. Including assessment with the goal of program improvement should not be an afterthought but should be intentionally designed when establishing the learning outcomes, instructional strategies, and overall program design.

Program-level assessment focuses on a specific program. Accordingly, this type of assessment goes well beyond a participant's satisfaction with a program (Janke et al., 2007), which often refers to whether food provided was delectable or the chairs in the classroom were comfortable. Recommendations offered by Martineau and Hannum (2004) include measuring more than just the participant's perception of the program but should instead focus on what was learned. However, this makes evaluation of leadership programs more difficult because most programs do not always produce immediately recognizable results and growth may take time to be realized. Goertzen (2012) clearly states "program level assessment is only effective to the degree of alignment between intended learning outcomes, content, and assessment strategies" (p. 59). As suggested, connecting program assessment to learning outcomes can provide more actionable feedback and result in overall program improvement.

Morgan et al. (2013) draw special attention to several aspects to consider in assessment and evaluation, such as instructors, resources, and the curriculum, which are differentially influenced by a variety of environmental factors throughout an administrative hierarchy, such as university, community, and industry effects. Soliciting feedback from experts, outstanding practitioners, and scholars in the field to keep curriculum current (Diamond, 1989) is not a new concept. However, all too often the feedback loop fails to recognize important suggestions for program improvement.

Eich (2008) found that educators often knew the most detail of how programs are developed and implemented but lacked in knowledge of how to best assess learning for program improvement. Chapter 8 will provide specific strategies in how to implement such assessments and overcome the challenges of assessment discussed next.

Assessment Challenges

Challenges abound when it comes to collecting data for assessment and evaluation purposes. In our experience, lacking money, knowledge, or time is the most frequent reason that leadership program personnel do not engage in comprehensive program reviews. Ironically, the information that could be gleaned from such reviews is often exactly what is needed to advocate for more of each of those resources. As the battle for institutional resources continually intensifies, effective leadership educators cannot ignore the need for valid and reliable data if they are to sustain this important work. As most, if not all, available resources are allocated toward program delivery, we encourage leadership educators to think and work collaboratively and creatively to support the evaluation and assessment of their programs to attain a distinctive leadership initiative.

Another challenge is represented by knowledge gaps among leadership educators regarding how to appropriately collect assessment information for program improvement. Martineau and Hannum (2004) review advanced considerations when collecting data, such as response-shift bias when using quantitative methods. These complexities largely are unknown to untrained educators. However, leveraging the knowledge that may already exist in offices of institutional research and seeking consultation from those professionals may help bridge the knowledge gap that leadership educators face when attempting to collect evaluation information.

Lack of time is another challenge when focusing on assessment. For many leadership educators, especially those in co-curricular programs, teaching is not intended to be their full-time responsibility. However, effective leadership educators will dedicate the time necessary to deeply consider most of the recommendations we put forth in this text. With various demands on educators' time, program evaluation can be a low priority. It becomes an "after thought" as the next program coming up becomes the focus. We suggest leveraging the human capital represented by undergraduate teaching and program assistants (and program participants themselves) to alleviate the constraints associated with the lack of time. Many of our students are already in academic programs where they get specialized training and experience in assessment and evaluation. Consider reviewing the academic backgrounds of your students, regardless of role, for technological and administrative support in collecting assessment information.

Most often leadership programs will gather evaluation data as participants go through the programs or right at the conclusion of the program. However, typically a collective evaluation mechanism does not often exist, something to determine outcomes after participants leave the program (Black & Earnest, 2009). It is challenging to have a satisfactory response rate after participants leave a program, and they are not required to complete one, although learning and growth could be continuing to occur well after the program's conclusion. Consider offering incentives to program participants to motivate their adherence to assessment initiatives, both immediately after programs as well as toward the ends of semesters or academic years. Although many students may be motivated by physical objects, some may be moved to share their experiences by simply understanding how their feedback could be used to shape programs for future participants. Being transparent about why we assess in the first place may stimulate intrinsically motivated individuals to offer their insights.

Broadly speaking, it is essential that distinctive leadership programs engage in continuous program improvement. Doing this by intentional program assessment followed by looping feedback to reevaluating the program learning outcomes, redesigning curriculum, and revising delivery can provide a structure for continuous program improvement. By juxtaposing best practices of assessment with redesigning programs should be a high priority for leadership educators (Goertzen, 2012).

CONCLUSION

Distinctive programs create spaces to help students learn about leadership, practice leadership, and better understand what they are doing in concert with others. Creating these spaces includes an intentional design of an overall program, developing a positive learning environment, applying knowledge, skills, and values to the learner's lived life, engaging in continuous reflection, and making ongoing program improvement a priority.

Intentionally designing all aspects of a leadership program cannot be overstated. This designing of a program includes developing learning outcomes, connecting learning outcomes to appropriate instructional strategies, creating a positive learning environment, implementing opportunities for theory-to-practice to emerge, structuring reflection opportunities, and developing assessment for program improvement. Although assessment occurs at the end of a program, it needs to be planned in the overall program design. Often assessment is last minute and does not actually respond to student needs and feedback. As mentioned, Chapter 8 will continue the discussion on assessment techniques for leadership programs.

Eich (2008) so eloquently states the importance for well-designed programs, "... leadership development can be fostered and accelerated as a result of a program educational intervention rather than leaving leadership development to chance through life experiences" (p. 186). Developing, delivering, and assessing high-quality programs for students needs to role model purpose, inclusivity, empowerment, reflection, and the process-oriented framework of leadership to advocate for students to become the best leaders they can be. As leadership educators, we need to look critically at our programs; we want to provide distinctive programs to provide the best leadership learning opportunities so our students can be the best versions of themselves.

CHAPTER 7

DISTINCTIVE CONTEXTUAL LEADERSHIP PROGRAM EXAMPLES

This chapter will provide specific examples of some distinctive contextual leadership programs. As discussed in previous chapters, leadership educators need to consider many contexts when developing and delivering a leadership program. We chose to provide some examples that reflect broad institutional contexts as well as specific institutional contexts such as academic, discipline-specific, interdisciplinary, and integrative programs. All of these examples have multiple institutional contexts (see Chapter 5) in which they reside, as well as several characteristics that make them distinctive. In Chapter 6, five characteristics of distinctive leadership programs were discussed: (a) intentionally designed programs; (b) authentic leadership learning environments; (c) application of knowledge, skills, and values; (d) meaning making through reflection; and (e) continuous program improvement. Providing these specific examples will hopefully assist leadership educators to obtain a glimpse of how programs via different contexts have come to fruition. Also, our hope is that these examples inspire you to "think outside the box" when defining and creating programs within the realms of leadership education.

The Role of Leadership Educators: Transforming Learning, pp. 117–128
Copyright © 2018 by Information Age Publishing

CO-CURRICULAR PROGRAMS

The National Clearinghouse of Leadership Programs (NCLP) has the most comprehensive list of co-curricular programs offered in higher education institutions. As discussed in Chapter 3, NCLP offers several professional development opportunities for leadership educators, most often those who work in co-curricular programming. Leadership programs offered in a co-curricular format vary greatly, thus we chose just a few to demonstrate how they might look in multiple contexts.

Discipline-Specific

The Florida Leadership Academy at the Heavener School of Business at the University of Florida is an excellent example of a discipline-specific co-curricular program (Florida Leadership Academy, 2017). The Florida Leadership Academy was created in 2004 and initially served 30 students but has since evolved to 100 students each year. This program specifically targets sophomore students who have taken an introduction to business class and have demonstrated leadership initiative in high school and during their first semester at the University of Florida. The Florida Leadership Academy is centered on Principled Leadership, which they define as a challenge to "reflect on your own experiences in the college and determine what motivates you" (The Florida Leadership Academy, 2017). This program encourages students to think about their role as future business leaders and prepares them to work in a global society. Participation in the program requires students to attend weekly 2-hour sessions, which include hearing speakers from various subfields within business, collaborating with mentors in small groups, and developing team building and networking skills. In addition to the weekly Friday sessions, students are also required to complete a community service project and actively engage with their mentor groups.

This business discipline-focused program is based on three pillars, which provide a foundation for student leadership development. These pillars include career development, personal and professional growth, and business ethics. Regarding career development, the Florida Leadership Academy focuses on acquiring knowledge and transferable skills and analyzing the behavior of leaders within organizations and connecting this learning to goals for future success. The personal and professional growth pillar focuses on developing critical thinking, problem-solving, and communication skills. The business ethics pillar connects with empowering future leaders to become positive role models through transparency, authenticity, and living to high ethical standards. The Florida Leadership

Academy has several characteristics of a distinctive program. This intentionally designed program aims to create a learning environment that is supportive yet challenging. Reflection is regularly incorporated, especially in application of knowledge, skills, and values learned from their business-focused courses in the context of leadership.

Launched in 2016, The Spelman Leadership Fellows is another example of a discipline-specific distinctive program. The Alliance Theatre in Atlanta, Georgia, partners with Spelman College to employ three rising senior students studying drama. After a 1-year internship, the Alliance Theatre will select one of the three interns to receive a 2-year, full-time fellowship in executive or artistic leadership. The lack of diversity in most nonprofit arts and culture institutions top leadership positions is apparent, and the Alliance Theatre wanted to take action in beginning to address this leadership challenge (Alliance Theatre, Spelman Leadership Fellows, 2017).

The Spelman Leadership Fellows program is co-curricular in nature because it is not a for-credit experience, but the interns' work with The Alliance Theatre directly connects with their coursework in application of knowledge, skills, and values. The community partner, Alliance Theatre, has intentionally designed the program as a potential pipeline in providing theatres across the country with a growing pool of highly qualified diverse candidates with professional experience at a top art center (Alliance Theatre, Spelman Leadership Fellows, 2017). The learning opportunities for the interns are reflective in nature and integrated with coursework because the internship is done in concert with their final year of their studies.

Interdisciplinary

The I-Programs at the University of Illinois at Urbana-Champaign are a series of day-long workshops offered multiple times each academic year. This workshop series was developed and are delivered by the Illinois Leadership Center, which is a partnership between academic affairs and student affairs. The I-Programs are co-curricular and interdisciplinary in nature; each program focuses on a particular aspect of leadership practice. The first I-Program, Insight, was offered in 2006, and the series has grown to seven I-Programs. From 2007 to 2016, 9,473 students attended I-Programs (Illinois Leadership Center, Annual Reports, 2017). These programs include:

- Petullo Insight: This program intends to help students focus on self-awareness and self-management skills. Students who participate will identify their personal values and personal leadership philosophy while exploring their personal strengths and social identities.

- Intersect: Intersect is designed to help students focus on interpersonal communication and team building. Students who participate will work with fellow students to accomplish team challenge goals.
- Ignite: This program focuses on skills necessary for effective group and organization development. Students who participate can expect to develop skills in leading change initiatives, learn about systems thinking, and coalition building. At Ignite, students will learn about organizational successes of past Illinois students and work to develop a plan for their own change initiative.
- Integrity: The Integrity program focuses on the skills necessary for interpersonal and organizational ethical leadership. Students who participate in Integrity are faced with ethical challenges and learn how to successfully navigate them with the help of skilled facilitators.
- Inclusion: Inclusion leadership program focuses on concepts such as equity, equality, diversity, inclusion, and bias. Students who participate will recognize the values of others and identify differing social identities in relation to leadership.
- Innovation: Focused on skills related to innovation, creativity, and diversity of idea in problem solving, students who participate in Innovation will develop skills in these areas and also an understanding of their dominant problem-solving style and its impact on organizations and people.
- Imprint: University of Illinois at Urbana-Champaign alumni serve as group facilitators for the Imprint program. This program focuses on skills necessary for displaying leadership during times of personal and professional transition. Students develop skills in managing themselves during times of change and learn how to develop and maintain the personal and professional networks necessary to sustain success in any environment.

The I-programs at the University of Illinois at Urbana-Champaign is an example of a distinctive program that is interdisciplinary and co-curricular in nature. These intentionally designed programs create learning environments where students can make meaning from their experiences, apply knowledge, skills, and values in various ways. At the end of each program, they conduct an assessment and regularly do curriculum revisions to ensure continuous program improvement.

ACADEMIC/CURRICULAR PROGRAMS

Jenkins (2012, 2013, 2016, 2017a) discussed instructional and assessment strategies in academic credit-bearing graduate- and undergraduate-level leadership courses. Participants in this study were recruited from organizational membership databases of several professional associations including the International Leadership Association (ILA), Association of Leadership Educators (ALE), NASPA Student Affairs Professionals in Higher Education, Student Leadership Programs Knowledge Community (NASPA SLPKC), and NCLP; the 2012 Leadership Educators Institute (LEI) attendee list; and a random sample of instructors drawn from the ILA Directory of Leadership Programs. This study was helpful in a number of respects, including tracing the academic origins of many leadership programs and courses. Most programs in the study were based in either schools of business (18.2%) or education (14.4%). See Table 7.1 for more specific information of leadership courses by school and college.

Table 7.1.   Leadership Courses by School/College

College	Frequency	%
Not indicated	266	23.8
Business or Management	203	18.2
Education	161	14.4
Academic Affairs, college-wide, no affiliated college	73	6.5
Arts & Sciences	61	5.5
Interdisciplinary Studies or Liberal Arts	49	4.4
Leadership	44	3.9
Social Sciences	38	3.4
Agriculture	38	3.3
STEM	35	3.1
Health & Human Services	31	2.8
Student Affairs	29	2.6
Other	28	2.5
Graduate school or studies	19	1.7
Adult or professional studies	16	1.4
Religiously affiliated, divinity, or clergy	10	0.9
Communication	9	0.8
Military	4	0.4
Honors	3	0.3
Total	1,117	100.0

Analyses conducted by department revealed that most courses were aggregated in either leadership (17.5%) or business (12.7%). Interestingly, 3.3% of programs reported offering credit-bearing courses through the division of student affairs. Table 7.2 provides more detail with regard to the distribution of leadership courses by academic department.

Table 7.2.   Leadership Courses by Academic Department

Department	Frequency	%
Not indicated	359	32.1
Leadership, Organizational Leadership, or Leadership Studies	196	17.5
Business (including Management)	142	12.7
Other	47	4.2
Educational Leadership, Admin, & Policy	39	3.5
Division of Student Affairs	37	3.3
Education (Non Educational Leadership)	35	3.1
Political Science, Public Policy, Admin, and Government	32	2.9
Academic Affairs (college-wide, Provost or President's office)	31	2.8
Academic "Center" or "Institute" for Leadership	29	2.6
Agricultural Education and Leadership	27	2.4
Behavioral Sciences, Psychology, Counseling, or Social Work	20	1.8
STEM	20	1.8
Communications	19	1.7
Interdisciplinary or Gen Studies	19	1.7
Public, Community, or Human and Health Sciences	18	1.6
Organizational Studies (not Organizational Leadership)	13	1.2
Humanities	10	.9
Higher Education Administration	9	.8
Theology, Divinity, or Clergy	5	.4
Liberal Arts	4	.4
Honors	3	.3
Adult or Professional Studies	2	.2
Student Affairs or College Student Personnel	1	.1
Total	1,117	100.0

Tables 7.1 and 7.2 provide an informative overview of where in the academy leadership programs tend to be situated. This can be helpful when

considering contextual factors affecting the development and execution a leadership program as to where other institutions situate leadership courses. There may be a college, department, or program you never thought about partnering with or approaching to offer academic/curricular-based leadership courses.

Discipline-Specific

Investigations conducted by the ILA (2016) and LLRC (2017) demonstrate the recent and historical growth of discipline-specific academic leadership programs. One interesting example of this increase is the emergence of more academic leadership programs in college of engineering. Although the relative number of engineering leadership programs is still small, the ILA (2016) data report six leadership programs focused specifically in the discipline of engineering, in which no such programs were listed in the directory in 2010. Health care is another discipline-specific context in which academic/curricular-based leadership programs are starting to emerge.

LLRC (2017) data revealed several academic/curricular leadership programs that were specific to health care (see table 7.3). These programs were mostly at a graduate level and ranged from a certificate to a PhD. Four programs offered one specific leadership course in health care to receive a concentration in Healthcare Leadership; these programs were not included in Table 7.3.

Table 7.3. Leadership Programs Focused in Health Care

Higher Education Institution	*Degree Offered*
Antioch University	PhD in Leadership and Change: Healthcare Concentration
Carlow University	MSN in Nursing Leadership and Education
Loyola University Chicago	MA in Healthcare Mission Leadership
Loyola University Chicago	Healthcare Ministry Leadership Certificate
Regis College	MS in Nursing Leadership/Clinical Research
Rockhurst University	MBA in Healthcare Leadership
University of Denver	MPS in Professional Studies in Healthcare Leadership
Wilmington University	MS in Nursing Leadership

Sources: ILA (2016); LLRC (2017).

Lewis University, a small, private institution in Illinois, offers a bachelor's, masters, and graduate certificate in Healthcare Leadership (Lewis University, Nursing, 2017). This program's mission is to prepare students for leadership roles within dynamic healthcare organizations. Their curriculum centers on preparing learners for a rapidly shifting healthcare policy and practice landscape. Innovative coursework that applies values-centered leadership to train leaders who are able to take on the challenges of providing effective health care is necessary. Coursework in this program includes healthcare management strategies and culminates with specific healthcare leadership coursework and practicum. This is an excellent example of a discipline-specific, academic/curricular-based leadership program that is offered at both undergraduate and graduate levels.

Interdisciplinary

Many academic leadership programs take an interdisciplinary approach to teaching. Kansas State University's interdisciplinary minor in the Staley School of Leadership Studies (K-State, Leadership, 2017) and Clarion University's (Clarion University, 2017) Minor in Leadership-Interdisciplinary Studies are two examples of leadership programs in such contexts. The former is at a large public institution and is more prescriptive in nature. The latter example is at a small private institution and provides various choices for students to select from. Despite these differences, both programs represent innovate ways of approaching leadership learning from more than one disciplinary orientation.

Kansas State University is a large, public, research-intensive institution. Leveraging Rost's (1991) definition of leadership as "… an influence relationship among leaders and followers who intend real changes that reflect their mutual purposes" (p. 102), this interdisciplinary minor intends to complement any academic major. The 16-credit minor provides a formal, structured learning experience for comprehensive leadership learning. It draws from various disciplines to provide a theoretical foundation focusing on personal leadership development and experiences. Kansas State University's minor is mainly prescriptive, meaning it requires 10 credit hours of specific courses and 6 credit hours of electives.

As a small, private institution, Clarion University, provides a leadership minor with an interdisciplinary track. This minor incorporates courses throughout the university. To complete this minor, students choose from a list of required and elective courses from across academic departments on campus. The flexibility in choosing from multiple required and elective courses makes the minor easily adapted to any disciplinary focus. The leadership minor, interdisciplinary track gives students exposure to a body of knowledge emphasizing leadership concepts and leadership skills from an interdisciplinary lens.

Both Kansas State University and Clarion University's interdisciplinary minors have characteristics of being a distinctive program. Although these two examples of minors approach interdisciplinary differently regarding curriculum, both are intentionally designed programs that have taken their institutional contexts into consideration. These programs value continuous program improvement, incorporate reflection, and apply learning throughout the curriculum.

INTEGRATED CURRICULUM

As discussed in Chapter 5, contexts matter when developing leadership programs. As Owen (2015) discusses, integration of learning and leadership learning is necessary to move past fragmented approaches to undergraduate and graduate education. Many integrated approaches to learning have been identified as high-impact practices (Kuh, 2008), such as civic engagement, capstone projects, and mentoring (Owen, 2015). Below we offer a few examples of leadership programs that create integrated leadership learning opportunities for students.

Discipline-Specific

Leadership programs focusing on a specific discipline while in an integrative learning structure are increasing. A singular disciplinary focus provides a specific context for students to apply their leadership learning. More colleges than ever are recognizing the benefit of integrated leadership programming within disciplines as a way to prepare students to be leaders in their specific industry. Whether this programming is through discipline-specific student organizations, workshops through the career center, or programs through the academic department, there is great benefit for offering leadership programming in this format. A 2014 *Journal of Leadership Studies* symposia explored this phenomenon through a "bird's eye view of leadership education across the disciplines" and examined the "curriculum, pedagogy, learning goals, assessment, and outcomes across a variety of academic areas where leadership education takes place" (Jenkins & Harvey, 2014, p. 83) including: (a) Social Sciences (Perruci, 2014); (b) Engineering (Kotnour, Hoekstra, Reilly, Knight, & Selter, 2014); (c) Student-Academic Affairs partnership (Buschlen & Guthrie, 2014); (d) Agriculture (Velez, Moore, Bruce, & Stephens, 2014), and (e) Liberal Arts (Peart, 2014).

The Gordon Undergraduate Engineering Leadership (GUEL) Program at Northeastern University is an undergraduate, co-curricular program that is focused in the engineering discipline (Northeastern, About Gordon Leadership Institute, 2017). GUEL is a program of The Gordon Institute of Engineering Leadership. GUEL's primary objective is to offer supplementary curriculum to make leadership development a focus of their cooperative education program. Connecting it to their cooperative education program allows this to be an integrative learning experience. As a reminder, cooperative education is combining classroom-based education with practical work experience and is also known as co-op.

While enrolled in Northeastern University's undergraduate engineering program, students are required to complete up to three 6-month co-op experiences. During their second or third co-op experience, students are invited to participate in GUEL and then self-select to participate in a series of workshops, culminating in a reflective presentation to program faculty. The workshops are split into an intensive two-part series followed by five self-directed modules. The intensive workshops introduce students to their own leadership practices and engineering leadership in the context of personal leadership style, power, influence, and situational leadership. Following the introductory workshops, the self-directed modules are intended to provide opportunities of learning within their co-op placement. Modules include topics on leadership characteristics, enhancing leadership skills, developing project management skills, and communicating your accomplishments. Culminating in a presentation to program faculty, GUEL participants reflect on their leadership learning and how it is applied to their co-op experiences and future career as an engineer. GUEL demonstrates characteristics of a distinctive program by being intentionally deigned, structuring reflection, and providing assessment on the application of knowledge, skills, and values.

Interdisciplinary

Allen and Shehane (2016) and Guthrie and Bovio (2014) describe the Undergraduate Certificate in Leadership Studies at Florida State University as a prime example of an academic/curricular-based integrated program, which is also interdisciplinary in nature. According to Guthrie and Bovio (2014), the Undergraduate Certificate in Leadership Studies is an 18-credit, interdisciplinary, and experiential program that prepares students for leadership in multiple contexts, including social change, theory to practice, experiential learning, and service-learning projects to frame leadership learning. The Certificate in Leadership Studies functions as a partnership between The Center for Leadership and Social Change in the Division of Student Affairs and the Department of Educational Leadership and Policy Studies in the College of Education. This integrated program has five core courses focused on leadership knowledge, skills, and values. The core courses include:

1. *LDR 2101: Leadership Theory and Practice* provides a theoretical foundation for general leadership and how an individual may participate in the leadership process.
2. *LDR 2162: Leadership in Groups and Communities* focuses on leadership in the context of groups and communities while integrating a service-learning experience.
3. *LDR 3215: Leadership and Change* provides understanding of change and transition theories and how one can participate and lead change efforts.
4. *LDR 3263: Leadership Experience* provides an opportunity for theory to be observed and practically applied through an internship, research project, or service-learning opportunity.
5. *LDR 4105: Leadership and Complexity* serves as a capstone experience and provides an opportunity to synthesize all material learned in previous core courses.

The sixth certificate course is the student's choice from a preapproved course list, which may be in their academic discipline or of personal interest to them. This allows students to apply theories and concepts learned in core certificate classes to other theoretical concepts. Each LDR course relies on various disciplines to inform leadership learning by providing both academic and practical ways of exploring leadership. Guthrie and Bovio (2014) provide an example of an LDR class that incorporates service learning: *LDR 2162: Leadership in Groups and Communities*. Although students spend ample time in the classroom learning leadership, social psychology theories related to intergroup and intragroup interactions, and group problem-solving and communication skills, students also practice these theories within their service-learning experiences. Drawing from various disciplines creates a strong leadership learning opportunity for students. Reflection and making meaning from experiences are critical aspects of leadership learning (Guthrie & Bertrand Jones, 2012). The inclusion of reflection throughout the certificate contributes to student development, which allows program participants to synthesize and make meaning of their leadership knowledge and experiences.

CONCLUSION

We acknowledge that only a few examples of leadership initiatives with characteristics of distinctive programs that situate themselves in various institutional contexts were offered here. Many programs deserve to be highlighted here. We hope that you search these other program examples out if none of the programs we offered fit the needs of your institution or specific context. The programs we provided here or examples you find will hopefully enable you to benchmark these established programs to create or enhance your own initiatives.

Exploring contexts and how multiple frameworks can work beautifully in concert can be helpful in reflecting on the complexities at each of our institutions. By providing examples in co-curricular, academic/curricular, interdisciplinary, discipline-specific, and interdisciplinary contexts, hopefully you are able to see the multiple dimensions of a leadership program and how intentionally designing programs can provide leadership learning opportunities for all students.

CHAPTER 8

ASSESSMENT IN LEADERSHIP EDUCATION

Until recently, little information existed with respect to leadership assessment. This void is starting to be addressed through scholarly collaborations in the *New Directions for Student Leadership* (2016), *Journal of Leadership Studies* (2012), and *The Leadership Quarterly* (2011). However, much more needs to be done in this area. We begin this chapter with an overview of the purpose of assessment in leadership education and proceed to essential tools and resources for doing assessment. The remainder of the chapter is organized by hierarchical tier. We move from individual-level to course/program-level assessment (including curricular design) and finally to institutional-level assessment. Each section includes examples of strategies used by leadership educators, their purpose, and tips for facilitating each assessment process. We source these examples in the International Leadership Association (ILA) Guiding Questions (2009) section on outcomes and assessment:

> … this topic's focus is on program evaluation, both formative and summative; institutional and program evaluation will be informed by assessment of student learning outcomes. Institutional evaluation informs organizational decision making about a program at the institutional level. Program evaluation focuses on the decision making related to program delivery, curriculum, and content related to a degree program, certificate program, and major or minor within another program. Learning outcomes assessment relates to gathering evidence and making judgments about the attitudes, knowledge, and skills students develop during the program. The assessment and

The Role of Leadership Educators: Transforming Learning, pp. 129–147
Copyright © 2018 by Information Age Publishing
All rights of reproduction in any form reserved.

evaluation processes and results at each level are linked to each other and to other underlying contextual frameworks, leadership content, teaching, and learning. (p. 27)

Accordingly, this chapter is meant to be an accessible guide for navigating the resources available for assessment purposes across leadership education contexts and as a reference that provides processes for doing so.

ASSESSMENT IN LEADERSHIP EDUCATION: THE WHY

Assessment is inextricably linked to learning and development; in this way, assessment is intrinsic to education (Ewell, 1988). Thus, it is imperative that leadership educators understand not only why assessment is vital to program sustainability but also what resources are available for assessment purposes, where to access them, and how to accurately assess their programs and services. In many cases, assessment is needed to justify resource allocation as well as demonstrate how the program being funded is contributing to student learning. As Owen (2011) states, "Most leadership educators have an awareness that assessment and evaluation are important processes for the design and delivery of leadership programs, the fostering of student learning, and for program advocacy at the institutional level and beyond" (p. 177). However, most assessment stops at what the experiences are and are even in forms of satisfaction. Indeed, we must shift the focus of "...assessment away from *what* experiences foster leadership learning (e.g., service-learning, workshops) to what about these experiences fosters growth and development across programs and influences student growth from entrance into college to graduation and beyond (to alumni)" (Inter-association Leadership Education Collaborative, 2016, p. 7). We must be able to prove that students are learning leadership.

According to Dugan (2012) and Goertzen (2009), higher education institutions are exerting increased pressure on leadership educators and leadership program administrators to demonstrate that student learning is occurring and to illustrate how learning extends across leadership programs (Roberts & Bailey, 2016). However, assessing the unseen and social construction of leadership is not easy. As in much of contemporary social science research, there is controversy about leadership paradigms and how knowledge is created and through what dimensions we understand it (Kellerman, 2012).

THE WHAT

According to Burns (1978), "Leadership is the most observed and misunderstood phenomena on the planet" (p. 3). As discussed, leadership is a social construct. Thus, how do we assess something that is always chang-ing, shifting, and evolving? Which leads to, *what* should we be assessing? The short answer is outcomes. Institutional and program evaluation will be informed by assessment of student learning outcomes (ILA Guiding Questions, 2009). Yet what are these outcomes? Owen (2011) argues that assessing student learning outcomes in leadership programs is multifac-eted and encompasses assessing leadership behaviors; traits, styles, and attributes; student needs and satisfaction; and attendance and participa-tion. Furthermore, these answers are equally important at the individual or student level as they are at program and institutional levels. According to Piatt and Woodruff (2016), there are varied types of outcomes, but most fit into the following categories:

1. Overall program effectiveness—reviewing the bigger picture to determine how the program impacts participants.
2. Individual student development—examining the growth of each student individually.
3. Student learning—outcomes that articulate the knowledge, skills, or attitudes students will attain.
4. Student satisfaction—identifying what aspects students enjoy within the programs.
5. Demographics and scope—quantitative outcomes such as enroll-ment numbers or participant characteristics that can provide insight into program impact.
6. Overall program effectiveness—reviewing the bigger picture to determine how the program impacts participants.
7. Individual student development—examining the growth of each student individually.
8. Student learning—outcomes that articulate the knowledge, skills, or attitudes students will attain. (p. 23)

THE HOW

"The work of leadership development is only as strong as educators' abili-ties to document student learning" (Dugan, 2012, p. 99). The good news is that, today, greater intentionality is found in assessing leadership programs and outcomes (Haber-Curran & Owen, 2013). Accordingly, the remainder of this chapter is organized as follows. In Table 8.1, we offer a comprehen-sive amalgamation of "best assessment practices" from across leadership education. We then describe a few seminal, holistic resources for doing assessment and provide some definitions of important assessment terms as a primer for delving into (a) individual-level assessment, where we describe direct and indirect measures (i.e., assessment strategies) that may be used to assess learning at the student level (e.g., grading or attainment of a co-curricular workshop); (b) program-level assessment, where we describe strategies for assessing the outcomes of program curricula (e.g., across multiple academic courses; sequencing); and (c) institutional-level assessment, where we provide examples of campus-wide efforts to evaluate the effectiveness of leadership programs.

Table 8.1. Assessment Practices in Leadership Education

Phase	Recommendations
Planning	• Include a timeline that ensures each phase receives appropriate consideration (Hynes, 2016): o Does the institution currently have an assessment calendar? o During what times of year does it make sense to implement each assessment phase? When will stakeholders need information necessary for decision making? o How long will it take to gather and analyze data? o When does resource allocation occur and what impact could this have on the timing of the assessment plan? • Establish collaborative capacity for programmatic assessment by involving others in the process (Andenoro et al., 2013; Piatt & Woodruff, 2016): o Who are the stakeholders and what skills do they have (e.g., are staff leadership educators or coordinating leadership programs)? o Who can contribute to the success of the program and its assessment processes (e.g., an institution's center for teaching excellence = course design; institutional research department = data)? o How can you intentionally delegate the work? o What are the goals of each of the stakeholders, and in what ways can the program assist them? o Are there areas of common interest? o In what ways can others be involved in your assessment strategies, data analysis, and the strategic planning? • Assess viable programmatic resources (Andenoro et al., 2013): Consider what financial resources and assessment materials (e.g., data sources) are available at each phase (see also Komives et al., 2011).

(Table continues on next page)

Table 8.1.   (Continued)

Phase	*Recommendations*
Outcome Formation	• What are the intended outcomes at the institutional, program, and student levels, and how will they be assessed and used to ensure accountability, continuous quality improvement, and result in changes in programs and services (ILA GQ; CAS SLPs)?
	o Identifiable leadership competencies and proficiencies and how they relate to a program's philosophical and theoretical perspectives (e.g., CAS SLPs)
	o How outcomes are related to conceptual, contextual, content, and delivery-related elements
	o What essential indicators will demonstrate that outcomes have been achieved (i.e., What is the assessment system? How are criteria for excellence incorporated? How will the by measured?).
Outcome Measurement and Reporting	• Surveys
	• Conceptual Framework: Consider organizational culture, institutional assessment priorities, staff knowledge and skills related to both leadership and assessment, and the student population you are working with (Roberts & Bailey, 2016).
	• Models: Is the program grounded in a formal leadership model designed to shape all leadership programs (e.g., the SCM) or an individual-level model (e.g., LID; HERI, 1996; Komives et al., 2006; Roberts & Bailey, 2016)?
	• Review other institutions' webpages and documentation for example models, mission and vision statements, and curricula.
Choosing Methods, Data Sources, and Levels of Assessment	• Determine strategies and targets (Piatt & Woodruff, 2016). Consider these points:
	o Collecting survey data at various levels:
	■ Institutional (e.g., CIRP, CSEQ, NSSE. MLQ)
	■ Program (e.g., CAS SAG, student leadership competencies, MSL, LABS-III, student needs or satisfaction surveys, portfolios, NACA Guide)
	■ Individual (EILS Inventory, MBTI, DiSC Classic, SCM, LPI, SRLS, StrengthsFinder, LBS, SEL, Motivation to Lead; see Chan & Drasgow, 2001; self-, peer, and instructor assessment)
	o Use various approaches (e.g., quantitative, qualitative, or action and critical; see Owen, 2011)
	• Determine needed levels of assessment, be they institutional, program, or individual (Owen, 2011)

(Table continues on next page)

Table 8.1.   (Continued)

Phase	Recommendations
Choosing Methods, Data Sources, and Levels of Assessment	• Consider (a) attendance and participation (tracking); (b) leadership traits, styles, attributes, behaviors, learning outcomes, and in groups and organizations; and (c) program effectiveness (i.e., benchmarking and national standards, cost analyses, comparing to national normative data)
Analyzing	• Analyze the data (Piatt & Woodruff, 2016): Consider: (a) what the data indicates and infers; (b) how results are interrelated; (c) what outcomes have or have not been reached and why; (d) what strategies were most and least effective, (e) the relevancy of identified outcomes, and; (f) the reliability and validity of selected methods.
Acting and Reporting	• Create a plan of action that addresses (Piatt & Woodruff, 2016): (a) which program components (e.g., courses, internships, workshops) or aspects should be sustained, revised, or eliminated; and (b) goals for the next assessment cycle (i.e., which outcomes, measures, and targets need refining).
	• Report data to important stakeholders and funding sources (e.g., administrators, alumni, employers, colleagues, community partners) in visually appealing formats (Piatt & Woodruff, 2016)

Note: CAS SLPs = Council for the Advancement of Standards in Higher Education: Student Leadership Programs (CAS, 2009); CAS SAG = CAS Self-Assessment Guide (CAS, 2009); CIRP = Cooperative Institutional Research Program; CSEQ = College Student Experience Questionnaire (CSEQ Assessment Program, 2007); DiSC = Dominance, Influence, Steadiness, and Conscientiousness; HERI: Higher Education Research Institution; EILS: Emotionality Intelligent Leadership for Students Inventory; ILA GQ = Intentional Leadership Association Guiding Questions; LABS-III (Wielkiewicz, 2002), see Sunn, Ho, Odom, and Perdue (2016); LBS: Leadership Behavior Scale (Podsakoff, MacKenzie, Moorman, & Fetter, 1990); LID: Leadership Identity Development Model; NACA Guide: National Association of Campus Activities Competency Guide for College Student Leaders; SCM = Social Change Model of Leadership Development; SEL = Self-Efficacy for Leadership scale (Murphy, 1992); SRLS: Socially Responsible Leadership Scale.

Resources

In this section, we provide coverage of the most widely used and accessible resources for assessing leadership education outcomes. Many of these resources were developed in collaborative efforts by members of the professional associations and informed by the publications addressed in Chapters 3 and 6.

ILA Guiding Questions

In Chapter 6, we reviewed this resource as a guide for intentionally designing leadership programs. We would be remiss not to discuss its utility for program assessment. Just as you might intentionally design a program by progressing through the five sections outlined in the ILA Guiding Questions—Context, Conceptual Framework, Content, Teaching and Learning, and Outcomes and Assessment—each section can be used as a lens for assessing and making revisions to leadership programs.

Council for the Advancement of Standards in Higher Education. Developed by the Council for the Advancement of Standards in Higher Education (CAS), whose mission is "to promote the improvement of programs and services to enhance the quality of student learning and development" (Council for the Advancement of Standards in Higher Education, 2015, p. 1), CAS Standards for Student Leadership Programs (CAS SLPS) were designed to be used to "help professionals provide comprehensive leadership programs and enhance students' learning opportunities" (Council for the Advancement of Standards in Higher Education, 2015, p. 3). It includes a contextual statement about the role of student leadership programs (which provides a comprehensive narrative of the development of leadership programs over the last 50 years) as well as standards and guidelines for student leadership programs in the following areas: (a) mission; (b) purpose; (c) organization; (d) human resources; (e) ethics; (f) policy; (g) access; (h) relations; (i) financial resources; (j) technology; (k) facilities and equipment; and (l) assessment and evaluation. Unlike the ILA Guiding Questions, which offer a series of interrogatives for contemplation in preparation for action, each area of the CAS SLPs includes prescriptive statements. For example, "Student Leadership Programs (SLP) must have a clearly articulated assessment plan to document achievement of stated goals and learning outcomes, demonstrate accountability, provide evidence of improvement, and describe resulting changes in programs and services" (Council for the Advancement of Standards in Higher Education, 2015, p. 19). The CAS SLPs prescribe relevant and desirable student learning and development outcomes from six domains (and offer related dimensions): (a) knowledge acquisition, integration, construction, and application; (b) cognitive complexity; (c) intrapersonal development; (d) interpersonal competence; (e) humanitarianism and civic engagement; and (f) practical competence. Furthermore, the CAS SLPs prescribe the advancement of student competencies in the categories of (a) foundations of leadership; (b) personal development; (c) interpersonal development; and (d) the development of groups, organizations, and systems. Relatedly, *The Handbook for Student Leadership Development* (Komives et al., 2011) provides several resources for aligning CAS competencies with specific learning outcomes, as does Owen (2015). In any event, the CAS SLPs may be used as an assessment checklist, but they do not offer variety or guidance for implementation.

The Handbook for Student Leadership Development. Komives et al. (2011) represents a continuation of efforts spearheaded by Roberts (1981) and sustained through a collaboration of seasoned and impassioned leadership educators through the National Clearinghouse for Leadership Programs (NCLP). It is inclusive of both curricular and co-curricular leadership programs and includes four key parts: (a) foundations of leadership education (i.e., leadership and student development theories); (b) program design (i.e., inclusive design, assessment and evaluation, and program funding); (c) program context (i.e., curricular and co-curricular models); and (d) program delivery (i.e., pedagogy, culture and identity, and emerging topics). We echo many of the sentiments in the *Handbook*'s "Assessment and Evaluation" chapter, including (a) issues and tensions in assessing leadership (i.e., the complexity within and interplay between the fields of leadership development and evaluation); (b) approaches to assessment (i.e., the necessity of an assessment cycle and developing an assessment plan); and (c) bountiful examples and resources for measuring student learning outcomes (which we have integrated in Table 8.1). Like the ILA Guiding Questions and CAS SLPs, the *Handbook* can be used as a guide to both design and evaluate a leadership program.

Individual-Level Assessment

Student learning assessment should not be confused with program evaluation (i.e., student satisfaction, effectiveness of teaching, and program mission/goal achievement) because such efforts are not a substitute for measures of student ability (Janke et al., 2016). Assessment "is the process of defining, selecting, designing, collecting, analyzing, interpreting, and using information to increase students' learning and development" (Erwin, 1991, p. 15). Thus, at the individual or student level, it is essential to define learning outcomes and integrate strategies for assessing each student's attainment of stated outcomes. Correspondingly, we begin this section by introducing the idea of direct and indirect measures of student learning and include descriptions of associated individual-level assessment strategies. In doing so, we offer examples of individual-level assessment, discuss the issue of grading, and end with an overview of a competency-based approach.

Direct and Indirect Measures of Student Learning

Making decisions about individual-level assessment involves critical considerations regarding the properties of evidence of student learning and includes authentic—direct and indirect—measures of that learning (Goertzen, 2013). To be authentic, assessment activities must "…closely simulate or actually replicate challenges faced by adults or professionals" (Wiggins & McTighe, 1998, p. 141). Per this distinction, outcomes deemed "authentic" are often highly valued due to their proximity to the learning outcome of interest (Ewell, 2002). Goertzen (2013) argues that the authentic assessment of learning will likely involve observable performance and provide opportunities for leadership educators to acquire evidence of student learning based on direct measures. However, indirect measures, commonly associated with reflective learning activities and based on making meaning and learning from experience (Kolb, 1984), are widely used in leadership education (Densten & Gray, 2001; Guthrie & Bertrand Jones, 2012; Harvey & Jenkins, 2014). Furthermore, there is merit to both measures. Correspondingly, Nobbe and Soria (2016) propose three primary sources of evidence of students' leadership development for which to assess: (a) students' self-reported outcomes; (b) instructors' assessment of students' development, and; (c) objective assessments of students' development in critical areas. Hence, we provide coverage of the most commonly used individual-level measures of student learning (i.e., assessment strategies) across Nobbe and Soria's (2016) three primary sources, comment on student grading in academic contexts, and then describe direct and indirect measure in more depth.

Assessment Strategies and Grading

One of the primary techniques by which we assess individual-level learning in academic/curricular leadership education is through course grades. Although much has been written about grading issues in higher education (e.g., Dweck, 1986; Svinicki & McKeachie, 2014), this scholarship may discount leadership education experiences in nonacademic settings. In a related study, Jenkins (2016) investigated the relationship between assessment strategy use and the learning goals leadership educators established in their courses. He found leadership educators value application-based learning goals above most others. However, foundational knowledge of the discipline does not appear to be a substantial learning goal in most leadership studies courses (Jenkins, 2016). Instructors who emphasize foundational knowledge in their courses tend to use exams and quizzes far more than those who value other outcomes (Jenkins, 2016). This is perhaps best explained by the historical emphasis of leadership studies on the development of learners' skills. Jenkins (2016) proposed that leadership educators who focus on their students becoming more proficient in the practice of leadership focus on course grades in activities that assess their ability to evaluate or work by themselves and demonstrate specific skills. Conversely, traditional assessment such as exams and quizzes do not appear as the assessment of choice for these types of outcomes.

Direct Measures of Student Learning

Direct measures of student learning include "… observable deployment of the ability in question" (Ewell, 2002, p. 21), such as tests, oral presentations, demonstrations, case studies, simulations, and feedback to demonstrate that learning or development has occurred (Palomba & Banta, 1999; Seemiller, 2013). Goertzen (2013) stresses, although direct measures of student learning may not be "authentic," they are widely perceived as being more credible than indirect measures. One way to address this divide is to assess valuable student learning artifacts, such as interviews, focus groups, and reflections with rubrics (Preston & Peck, 2016). Similarly, abilities might be assessed via rubrics, checklists, or expert panels, and values could be assessed through a reflection papers or group dialogues (Allen & Shehane, 2016). In any event, direct measures are largely derived from instructors' assessment of student development (Nobbe & Soria, 2016).

Indirect Measures of Student Learning

Indirect measures of learning "…capture how students 'feel' and often reflect the consequences of the learning experiences such as related behaviors (e.g., job placement, civic participation), or testimonies about the learning experience (e.g., self-report data about knowledge, skills, or attitudes gained)" (Goertzen, 2013, p. 56). Simply, student perceptions of what they are learning are important. As discussed in Chapter 4 in the leadership learning framework, leadership efficacy is an indirect measure of learning. By listening to students and understanding their experiences, leadership educators can "… gain insight into what they are learning, to what extent they are learning, how they interpret what they are learning, and how well they can articulate this learning to others" (Preston & Peck, 2016, p. 80). Correspondingly, indirect assessment can include reflections, interviews, inventories, and self-assessment (Seemiller, 2013).

Students' Self-Reported Outcomes: Measuring Student Experience. There is a long-established value of student experiential leadership learning outside the classroom (e.g., Keeling, 2004). Although programs provide meaningful learning experiences unto themselves (Preston & Peck, 2016), embedded reflection activities focused on student experiences external to leadership programs are cornerstones of most programs (Harvey & Jenkins, 2014) and are arguably critical components of successful leadership programs (see Chapter 6). Thus, approaches to assessment should consider methods for prompting students to identify and examine these experiences. When such experiences help students achieve leadership learning outcomes, assessment methods should be chosen based on their capability of documenting and evaluating those gains (Janke et al., 2016).

The most common and easily administered method for measuring student experiences, self-evaluation (Schellings & van Hout-Wolters, 2011), can be used to assess learning outcomes after any event, experience, internship, co-op, course, workshop, program, or leadership position (Hynes, 2016; Nobbe & Soria, 2016; Seemiller, 2016). Benefits of self-evaluation include providing good feedback to leadership educators and serving as a vehicle for self-reflection, which can be useful for future lifelong learning (Sitzmann, Ely, Brown, & Bauer, 2010). Leadership educators may develop their own self-evaluations or utilize preexisting ones (e.g., Student Leadership Competencies; Seemiller, 2013, 2016). Yet according to Seemiller (2016), there are drawbacks to self-reports such as social desirability bias, which can lead to an over-inflation of self-ratings (Spector, 2004) and the role of the blind self from Johari's Window (Luft & Ingham, 1955), in which students may not be aware of their true development to accurately report in a self-evaluation. The immediacy of the administration of self-evaluations may cause students to potentially overstate the impact the event had on their learning (Rosch & Schwartz, 2009). Consequently, students who do not see themselves as leaders may rate themselves lower in their learning than those who see themselves as leaders (Rosch & Schwartz, 2009).

Competency-Based Approach

Another strategy for individual-level assessment is through competency-based models (Seemiller, 2013, 2016). According to Seemiller (2013), leadership competencies are defined as the "... knowledge, values, abilities, and behaviors that help an individual contribute to or successfully engage in a role or task" (p. xv). Specifically, the competency model asks: What do students need to know, believe, and do in terms of effective leadership? When called on to engage in a leadership competency, do students utilize the competency proficiently? For a comprehensive report on how to administer and integrate the student leadership competencies approach campus-wide, see Seemiller (2016).

Program-Level Assessment

How do we know whether our leadership program—and specific parts (e.g., workshops and courses)—are providing opportunities for students to achieve and attain the stated learning outcomes? Furthermore, how do we make effective improvements? Two strategies for assessing leadership education at these levels are through formative (designed to assess student learning while it is happening to improve both teaching and learning) and summative (designed to assess student learning at the end of a specific educational program) assessment. Although some programs value one form of assessment over the other, many combine both formative and summative approaches (e.g., Lindsay, Foster, Jackson, & Hassan, 2009). To help leadership educators understand their options, we provide some brief examples of formative and summative assessments. It is important to note that culture and context are important factors to consider when assessing any leadership program. These constructs define an institution's values and, equally important, what is not valued. Moreover, context and—more aptly—culture often dictate how leadership is exhibited on campus (Roberts & Bailey, 2016). In the previous sections, we offered some resources such as the ILA Guiding Questions, which include advanced organizers for considering these topics. Although we do discuss the importance of assessing programmatic outcomes with institutional ones as well as consider the alignment of programmatic and institutional missions, our focus here is mainly curricular.

Formative

Program improvement refers to the formative aspects of assessment and evaluation (Southern Association of Colleges and Schools Commission on Colleges, 2015). Through a process of formative assessment, students may provide information about how well they are grasping concepts during the learning process, thereby providing information to allow leadership educators and program administrators to reshape programs and policies and adapt the curriculum to emergent student needs (Clark, 2012; Hattie & Timperley, 2007). Formative assessments take many forms, such as practice quizzes, one-minute papers, and various kinds of group work. However, to be truly formative, activities should consist of low-stakes, ungraded, and peer- or self-assessed activities (which can be applied to students' participation grades if applicable; Ives, 2014). According to Ives (2014), these formative assessment practices have many benefits, such as: (a) encouraging attendance; (b) allowing even the shyest students to earn points toward participation grades; (c) demonstrating the value to students of scaffolding formative into summative assessment; (d) allowing learners to demonstrate knowledge in multiple ways; (e) providing tangible evidence on students engaging and learning (or not); and (f) encouraging students to reflect on their own learning (particularly with self-assessment). For additional strategies for integrating formative assessment, please see Chapter 9.

Developmental Sequencing. Outcomes from formative assessment may be used to make decisions about developmental sequencing—how to organize the "pipeline" of students who progress through leadership programs (Keating, Rosch, & Burgoon, 2014). Still, how might leadership educators assess students' incoming capacity and place them in programs accordingly? Although some academic disciplines may require entrance exams for appropriate course placement (e.g., mathematics, music theory), the field of leadership studies may not be able to leverage such mechanisms (Harvey & Riggio, 2011). Although it is a common practice in mathematics that students begin in algebra and then progress from trigonometry to calculus, an equivalent process does not exist in leadership education (Avolio & Hannah, 2008; Murphy & Johnson, 2011). For example, should a student begin an educational program with coverage of essential leadership theory or instead with group dynamics (or neither)? Consequently, how do we make decisions about which courses or program components students should participate in before or after others?

One suggestion offered by Janke et al. (2016) is to have students complete reflection documentation related to specific leadership competencies (e.g., empowering others) over a sustained period of time. For example, this competency might be addressed through a series of assignments or activities embedded across an educational program or in several introductory experiences. Afterward students might review the series of assignments and perform a self-evaluation. According to Janke et al. (2016), this collection of tasks and subsequent critical analysis of them could then be assessed, possibly by a panel of faculty or other stakeholders, for growth and signs of competency attainment. In any event, further exploration is needed in this important area (Andenoro et al., 2013). We recommend the ideas and processes presented in this chapter as springboard for these important decisions.

Summative

Program accountability refers to the summative or "effectiveness" dimensions of assessment. Findings from summative assessments are typically used to make decisions about the contributions of a program (Erwin, 1991) or in administrative decisions about funding, placement, and (re)structuring. Thus, some programs measure student leadership learning and

skill development through specific leadership courses or activity completion (Blackwell, Cummins, Townsend, & Cummings, 2007; Brungardt
& Crawford, 1996). For example, Black and Earnest (2009) developed
a summative method for participants at the conclusion of a leadership
development program to determine the amount of knowledge retained.
Furthermore, we can use formative assessment activities to scaffold into
summative assessments by using formative assessment activities as vehicles
for student feedback about how the course is going and by using it to create
a reflective culture of assessment that is focused on learning rather than
solely on grades (Ives, 2014).

Curriculum

One of the most helpful resources we have come across for implementing program-level assessment of curriculum (i.e., instruction, assessment,
content) at both the course and program levels came from a conference
roundtable discussion hosted by three faculty members from Virginia Tech
and Kansas State University (Priest, Friedel, & O'Dell, 2012). The facilitators shared resources on assessing student learning outcomes at the course
and program levels (Staley School of Leadership Studies, 2017). Their
process was captured in a *NASPA Student Leadership Programs Newsletter:
Best Practices & Research Edition* article (Jenkins, O'Dell, & Priest, 2013).
In the article, the authors explain how, through a facility-initiated assessment process, they sought to answer the following questions: (a) What
are our students learning? and (b) How well are our students learning
what we are teaching? Guided by the program's mission, the assessment
team analyzed the learning outcomes in every core-course syllabus and
discussed how each was aligned with program-level outcomes and delivered
through course content, texts and readings, assignments, grading rubrics,
and assessment strategies (O'Dell, 2009). "Once all data and feedback is
gathered, an annual report of student learning is written and submitted
to the Office of Assessment ... and the process begins again!" (Jenkins,
O'Dell, & Priest, 2013, p. 18). To illustrate this procedure, we provide three
examples of the assessment processes described previously.

Curriculum Assessment. Nobbe and Soria (2016) suggest that assignments should be aligned with institutional student learning outcomes.
For example, "... a paper in which students investigate the complexity of
a social issue was designed to help students unpack the ambiguity sometimes found in novel, real-world social problems so as to enhance their
tolerance of ambiguity" (Nobbe & Soria, 2016, p. 98). Likewise, within
their institution's global capstone course, Nobbe and Soria (2016) provide
"... rubrics for each assignment to identify specific student learning

outcomes and instructors provide students with feedback about their proficiencies as they pertain to each learning outcome" (p. 98). Students could be asked to reflect on crucible moments in their leadership history (Northwestern Engineering News, 2011). These narratives could then be assessed by leadership educators using a rubric specifically developed to identify phases of the leader identity development model (Komives et al., 2005) or other relevant indicators of leadership development. This process could provide an institution insight into a cohort of students, which could aid instruction and continuous quality improvement of the leadership program (Janke et al., 2016). Finally, in a more hands-on approach, Nobbe and Soria (2016) administered the Intercultural Development Inventory (Hammer, 2010) in a global leadership capstone course associated with their institution's learning outcome focusing on effectively communicating across cultures and departments. After the inventory was complete, each instructor had an individualized feedback session with every student in his or her course. Consequently, students who participated in a feedback session saw a larger increase in their Developmental Orientation Scores on average than those who did not (Nobbe & Soria, 2016). Through these strategies, instructors can report individual- and course-level data regarding students' attainment of institutional student learning outcomes.

In their study of institutional-level assessment of leadership programs, Nobbe and Soria (2016) described a process for better understanding students' growth and development across a leadership minor (see also Haber-Curran & Tillapaugh, 2014). Their process included (a) a document analysis of 143 students' final leadership journey papers from four sections of a 1000-level course; and (b) interviews with 30 students to investigate their leadership development through the lens of self-authorship—"the internal capacity to define one's beliefs, identity, and social relations" (Baxter Magolda, 2008, p. 269)—to better understand students' interpersonal development (e.g., they were asked to share experiences they had working with others to accomplish a goal such as a preferred role; Nobbe & Soria, 2016). Using these methods, the researchers collected data about students' sense of confidence and voice, how they wrestled with ambiguities as they developed new understandings of nonpositional leadership, recognition of their own agency, and value related to working collaboratively with others to achieve common outcomes (Nobbe & Soria, 2016).

Long-Term Assessment

To understand the long-term effects of leadership education on student behaviors and learning outcomes, research is needed that follows students longitudinally in leadership programs (i.e., postgraduation; Day, 2011;

Janke et al., 2016; Riggio & Mumford, 2011). This may mean revising graduating student and alumni surveys to more carefully assess leadership competencies, such as success in motivating and inspiring others toward leadership roles. Also, qualitative approaches to assessment and evaluation may be useful, "such as interviews on use of leadership knowledge/ skills or stories describing leadership successes. In addition to input from graduates, it may be helpful to include that of employers, residency directors, and colleagues" (Janke et al., 2016, p. 11). Furthermore, studies of programs with differing approaches to leadership education, sequencing of curricula, distinctive pedagogies, learning communities, and environments might address this area of inquiry most directly (Andenoro et al., 2013).

Institutional-Level Assessment

Institutional-level assessment is no less imperative than any of the other levels. Yet little research has been done on the topic. The exemplar study, "Leadership Assessment from an Institutional Approach" (Nobbe & Soria, 2016), offers a model framework for institutional-level assessment. Nobbe and Soria (2016) describe in great detail how an institution: (a) engaged in a systematic process of assessment that began with intentionally situating leadership development within institutional student learning and development outcomes; (b) created a culture of assessment among curricular and co-curricular programs by involving staff, faculty, and students; and (c) collected data using multiple measures, angles, and methodologies to support overall assessment goals. Accordingly, Nobbe and Soria (2016) make the following recommendations for any program looking to embark on the institutional-level assessment process: (a) focus on student leadership outcomes, (b) develop valuable partnerships, (c) use existing data sources, and (d) align activities with institutional priorities.

Establish Leadership Outcomes

Begin with the end in mind by defining agreed-on student leadership learning outcomes (see Chapter 6). However, effective leadership educators remember that "leadership is complex—there is no single survey item or interview question that can be developed to measure students' leadership development (Nobbe & Soria, 2016, p. 103). Nevertheless, proceeding to establish leadership outcomes involves (a) linking curricular or co-curricular outcomes to institutional learning outcomes, (b) prioritizing course learning objectives, and (c) mapping outcomes to theoretical frameworks (e.g., the five practices of exemplary leadership from *The Leadership Challenge*; Nobbe & Soria, 2016).

Using Existing Data Sources

Institutions administer myriad surveys to collect data about their students' retention and persistence, engagement, and feelings about a range of programs and efforts. We suggest capitalizing on these existing data sources to measure constructs such as the student experience to gauge program effectiveness.

Some data sources such as the Multi-Institutional Survey of Leadership (MSL) assess leadership specifically. However, participation is optional, and unfortunately institutions are unlikely to participate. For example, although the most recent 2015 administration of the MSL garnered just over 100 participants, this number is far short of the more than 2,000 leadership programs worldwide (ILA Program Directory, 2017). Hynes (2016) argues that for a large university, the $3,750 participation cost may not be overwhelming; conversely, for a smaller school, this amount could equate to an entire year's programming budget. Moreover, Hynes (2016) and others have scrutinized the value of the MSL data—what they measure and how to use them effectively. Nonetheless, the MSL has been featured in several national reports and scores of peer-reviewed articles, theses, dissertations, and other publications (MSL Publications, 2017). Furthermore, information on the MSL website describes in detail the theoretical framework and how the instrument measures the following constructs: (a) authentic leadership; (b) relational leadership model; (c) emotionally intelligent leadership; (d) servant leadership, (e) leadership practices, and (f) transformational leadership (MSL Design, 2017).

According to Hynes (2016), national surveys to measure student leadership development are few and far between. Nonetheless, those that exist (e.g., the MSL) have contributed to the improvement of leadership programs and curriculum. Additionally, most institutionally administrated surveys do not group leadership data but rather have been pushed by publishers of leadership instruments such as the Multifactor Leadership Questionnaire (MLQ) and assessment instruments such as Clifton StrengthsFinder (Antonakis, Avolio, & Sivasubramaniam, 2003; Soria, Roberts, & Reinhard, 2015). "Although these studies have contributed to understanding of particular theories and models, they do not lend themselves easily to institutional use and impact" (Hynes, 2016, p. 70).

Align With Institutional Priorities

It is imperative for leadership educators to understand and consider institutional assessment priorities and values including and ranging across: (a) various units and divisions; (b) administration; (c) required reporting to the Board of Trustees or the state; and (d) external reports required for institutional accountability (e.g., institutional or professional accreditation; International Leadership Association, 2009; Roberts & Bailey, 2016). Accordingly, "if the environment relies heavily on quantitative data the plan will look very different than the plan at a school that needs to provide the qualitative data associated with individual learning experiences" (Roberts & Bailey, 2016, p. 15). Keeping this in mind, effective leadership educators understand how assessment fits with the context of their institutions. To this end, the following questions can be used to guide this process: (a) What is the institution's mission and espoused values? (b) What beliefs about leadership does the institution hold? (c) How do the identified outcomes relate to the mission of the program? and (d) In what ways can the assessment data contribute to demonstrating institutional effectiveness?

We speak from experience in noting that leadership program administrators would be wise to consider program outcomes alongside institutional strategic plans, mission, and vision statements. For example, part of the University of South Florida's (USF's) strategic plan included "Global research, community engagement, and public service" (University of South Florida, 2017). When tasked with revising their leadership studies minor, the USF team added a three-credit requirement in "global and organizational dimensions of leadership." In a more opportunistic approach, Morehouse College explicitly aligned programmatic documents with the institution's mission: "to produce academically superior, morally conscious leaders for the conditions and issues of today" (Morehouse College, n.d., para. 1). Similarly, program faculty in Nobbe and Soria's (2016) study linked student leadership learning outcomes to the following institutional-level outcomes: problem solving; understanding the role of creativity, innovation, discovery, and expression across disciplines; and skills for effective citizenship and life-long learning. Likewise, program staff "intentionally linked co-curricular leadership development programs to the student development outcomes of responsibility and accountability, self-awareness, resilience, appreciation of differences, and tolerance of ambiguity" (Nobbe & Soria, 2016, p. 95). In both instances, the investigated program followed a process of aligning outcomes with curricular components (e.g., workshops, academic courses) quite similar to the program-level matrices discussed.

CONCLUSION

The important work of leadership education begins and ends with assessment. As leadership educators, we must remember that assessment is an iterative process with several desired goals. Assessment needs to be intentionally designed and in alignment with institutional strategic aims, programs goals, learning objectives, and student experience. Assessment is intended to provide feedback and can be useful if results are reported and evaluated and changes to programmatic design and curricular are made accordingly. Acknowledging that learners' opinions are heard and taken seriously is key for future assessment engagement.

Beyond the resources and tools we highlighted in this chapter, the American Evaluation Association provides information and resources on evaluation as a field. This professional association offers broad assessment tools that can be tailored to your specific leadership program assessment needs. Whether it is an academic or co-curricular program, a single course, or a series of workshops, assessment is critical to the success of meeting program goals and students achieving the program's desired learning outcomes. Assessment does not need to be complicated. Frameworks and examples can help guide your efforts. However, assessment does need to be an important part of an overall leadership program design.

SECTION III

DELIVERING LEADERSHIP EDUCATION

In Chapter 6, we introduced experiential learning as a foundation for leadership education. Indeed, leadership education and experiential learning (Kolb, 1984) are inextricably linked (Allen & Hartman, 2009; Eich, 2008; Guthrie & Bertrand Jones, 2012; Guthrie & Thompson, 2010; Jenkins, 2013, 2017). Leadership is a process of learning in which individuals make sense of their experiences, uncover leadership within themselves, and work in communities of leadership practice with others (Antonacopoulou & Bento, 2004). In fact, hundreds of peer-reviewed publications offer theoretical frameworks, instructional and assessment applications, as well as examples of experiential learning in leadership education.

Building off Kolb's (1984) experiential model, we present the Leader and Follower Experiences as a Source of Transformational Learning model as a representation of the union between leadership education and experiential learning as well as a framework for the final section of this book (see Figure III). We echo Wisniewski's (2010) proposition that "the role of the leadership educator is not to deliver or transmit information" but instead "to actively engage the learners in constructing personal theories and philosophies of leadership by creating a learning environment that builds upon learners' existing knowledge and experiential base" (p. 65). Correspondingly, each source of transformational learning (i.e., instructional strategies) presented in Chapters 9-17 offers opportunities to facilitate leadership learning across all four stages of this model.

STAGE 1: EXPERIENCE AS A LEADERSHIP OR FOLLOWER

The first stage represents any experience or set of experiences that an individual might have in a leader or follower role. The experience could happen in the workplace, in a student organization, or while the student is volunteering at a local soup kitchen. Moreover, the individual doesn't have to be in a formal leadership role or position to have the experience, nor does the individual have to be an active participant (they could just as well be a passive observer). In fact, most experiences that contribute to leadership learning involve the individual in a follower role (Chaleff, 2009; Kellerman, 2008, 2012).

STAGE 2: CRITICAL REFLECTION

The second stage represents the process of critically reflecting on the experience or set of experiences from Stage 1. By critical reflection, we mean the iterative process of returning to the experience or set of experiences and reflecting on what one studied, thought, did, and felt, and an autonomous but still relatively structured and disciplined process of synthesizing lessons, conclusions, uncertainties, and questions (Harvey & Jenkins, 2014; Owen, 2016).

STAGE 3: EXPERIENTIAL ABSTRACTION

The third stage represents the meaning-making process—that is, the process by which the individual constructs meaning (e.g., knowledge, skill, value) from the critical reflection of their experiences as a leader or follower. By meaning making, we mean the set of assumptions that determine how an individual perceives and organizes his or her life experiences (Baxter Magolda, 2001; Kegan, 1994). See "Making Meaning Through Reflection" in Chapter 6 for additional explanation.

STAGE 4: METACOGNITIVE DISCOVERY
AND EXPLORATION

The fourth stage represents opportunities for the individual to experiment with new behaviors and skills while self-monitoring in the present. That is, the learner is practicing a heightened metacognition of leadership and followership.

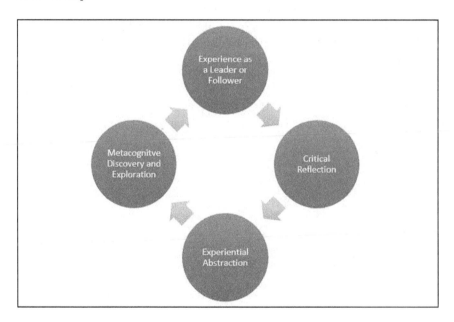

Figure III.   A model of leader and follower experiences as a source of transformational learning.

In addition to providing an array of instructional strategies to facilitate transformational leadership learning, this final section of the book aims to fill another gap in leadership education resources. Section III of this book will look at specific instructional strategies for delivering leadership education. Each chapter will be organized in the following manner:

1. An introduction and overview of the focused instructional strategy situated in the college teaching literature. This section will include examples and substrategies of the pedagogy.
2. Applications of the instructional strategy in leadership education as well as related leadership education literature.
3. Specific examples of the instructional strategy including in-class, co-curricular, and online activities, assignments, and related examples.
4. Finally, "Pedagogy to Practice" will provide summary points from the focused instructional strategy and a few ways to immediately put the instructional strategy into practice.

CHAPTER 9

LEADERSHIP EDUCATION AS A TRANSFORMATIVE PEDAGOGY

In this chapter, we introduce how the critical components of leadership education, including experiential and active learning, feedback and debriefing, and model facilitation, transcend all instructional and assessment strategies. We begin by exploring the experiential and active learning components of applied leadership learning, the reflective emphasis that pervades leadership education, and their associated frameworks. Correspondingly, feedback and debriefing relate directly to the process of experiential learning: learning from and making sense of experiences. Providing effective feedback and facilitating debriefings are essential skills for leadership educators. Finally, we discuss the role of leadership educators as leadership role models, where teaching is practiced as a type of leading. That is, leadership educators aren't just teaching content; they are also—through course design and teaching—role modeling the leadership we want students to exhibit. Taken together, these premises help frame leadership education as a transformative pedagogy for students, instructors, and programs.

LEADERSHIP: AN APPLIED DISCIPLINE

When asked *why* we teach leadership—or the classic "leadership for what?"—our response is that we want our students to have the skills to

The Role of Leadership Educators: Transforming Learning, pp. 153–171
Copyright © 2018 by Information Age Publishing

create positive, sustainable change. Leadership is an activity and a process; it is something in which we engage in, not force onto someone. In any event, leadership is something we *do*. Furthermore, the varied outcomes of leadership education are all intended to be practically applied by students. Subsequently, it is no surprise that leadership educators use active and experiential learning approaches (Eich, 2008; Guthrie & Bertrand Jones, 2012; Moore, Boyd, & Dooley, 2010).

Recent qualitative research on the experiences and identities of leadership educators confirms that leadership educators aren't often prescribed into the practice (Jenkins, 2017b; Seemiller & Priest, 2015, 2017). On the contrary, leadership educators describe serendipitously finding their way to leadership education, often as "autobiographical work" resulting from early impressions or experiences leading others, working with bad leaders, and curiosities about the process of leadership development and terminology. Moreover, leadership educators tend to seek out opportunities to teach leadership and make lasting impacts on their students (Jenkins, 2017b). It is no surprise that the leadership classroom has become a social laboratory for good teaching, learning, and facilitating these practices through teaching. In his work on creating significant learning experiences for college students, Fink (2013) describes good courses as those that: (a) challenge students to significant kinds of learning; (b) use active forms of learning; (c) have teachers who care—about the subject, their students, and teaching and learning; (d) have teachers who interact appropriately with students; and (e) have an explicit system of feedback, assessment, and grading. Fink (2013) goes on to explain that his list simply reflects his view that,

> If someone's teaching successfully meets these criteria, its impact is going to be good, no matter what else is bad about it…even if a teacher is not a great lecturer or well organized. Conversely, if someone's teaching does not meet these five criteria, that teaching is poor, no matter what else is good about it. (p. 33)

Similarly, Shulman (2005) described effective educators not as charismatic figures but instead as ordinary teachers in challenging disciplines who feel a responsibility for their students' learning. This type of responsibility for student learning—the kind of teaching that should be within the grasp of any faculty member— "…is not magic, it's pedagogy" (Shulman, 2005, p. 25). Finally, similarities abound between Fink's list and the classic *Seven Principles for Good Practice in Undergraduate Education* offered by Chickering and Gamson (1987) include: (a) encourages contact between students and faculty; (b) develops reciprocity and cooperation among students; (c) encourages active learning; (d) gives prompt feedback; (e) emphasizes time on task; (f) communicates high expectations, and (e) respects diverse talents and ways of learning.

Arguably, leadership educators have more opportunities to apply the practices suggested by Fink (2013), Chickering and Gamson (1987), and others compared with their peers in other parts of the academy due to the applied nature of leadership education. That is, leadership education is grounded in learning from individual experience as a leader, follower, or both. However, "experience" isn't limited to the individual. Instead, leadership education encourages learning from others' experiences through class discussion, observation, case studies, and guest speakers, as well as provides opportunities for reflection and meaning making of these experiences. These align nicely with the leadership learning framework we presented in Chapter 4.

LEADERSHIP LEARNING AS EXPERIENTIAL AND ACTIVE INTEGRATION

In many cases, leadership learning is experiential because it is crafted to emphasize the central role that experience plays in the learning process (Kolb, 1984). This is further demonstrated in our *Leader and Follower Experiences as a Source of Transformational Learning* model introduced in the Section III Introduction. The word "experience" comes from Middle English of the 1300s and stems from the Latin *experiēns*, a past participle of *experīrī*, which means to try, test, or see (Online Etymology Dictionary, 2017). The historical development of this word contributed over the next 100 years to observation as the source of knowledge. Actual observation is "an event which has affected one," from Old French *esperience*. This means "experiment, proof, or experience," and the Latin *experiential*, meaning, knowledge gained by repeated trials (Online Etymology Dictionary, 2017). Correspondingly, experiential learning is the "...process through which a learner constructs knowledge, skill, and value from direct experience" (Luckmann, 1996, p. 6).

In our experience, when leadership educators are asked, "What is teaching leadership like?", they related it to a series of experiments that, when done well, are a series of dynamic "on-your-toes" experiences. Yet these experiences range from individual to small groups, challenges and interactions, and immersion in the content presented. Emphasis is placed on preparing students to engage in potentially transformative opportunities and encouraging them to open themselves up to those experiences as part of the bigger framework (Jenkins, 2017b). Similarly, active learning means involving students in doing things and thinking about the things they are doing (Bonwell & Eison, 1991). "Doing" refers to activities such as debates, simulations, guided design, group problem solving, and case studies. Thinking refers to reflections about the meaning of what students learn or about the learning process (Fink, 2003). Thus, through experiential learning, "knowledge results from the combination of grasping and transforming experience" (Kolb, 1984, p. 41). The utilization of active and experiential learning techniques to promote leadership development in the classroom has demonstrated effectiveness through many techniques (e.g., Moore, Boyd, & Dooley, 2010).

According to Bonwell and Eison (1991), activities such as role-playing, simulation, debate, and cases studies are specific teaching activities rather than general teaching strategies because collectively they offer students experiences that have profound psychological, social, and intellectual dimensions. These activities provide clear alternatives to teaching as just supplying information. For example, in one leadership course, Burbach, Matkin, and Fritz (2004) uncovered that student engagement in active learning techniques led to gains in students' critical thinking abilities. For the purposes of their investigation, critical thinking was defined as a purposeful, self-regulatory judgment that results in interpretation, analysis, evaluation, and inference, as well as an explanation of the evidential conceptual methodological, criteriological, or contextual considerations on which that judgment was based (Facione, 1990)—in other words, gains in cognition, decision making, and metacognition. Such active learning strategies include out-of-class service projects, instructor-mediated reaction journals, group projects involving contextual scenarios, case studies, role-playing activities, Socratic questioning, and student presentations. This example and many like it add credence to the proposition of leadership education as a transformative pedagogy when the activities of leadership learning are experiential and active.

Integration

At this point, one might reasonably inquire as to how active and experiential learning became commonplace pedagogical practice in leadership education. The answer starts with how we define "leadership education." Narrowly, we define leadership education as the collection of learning activities and educational environments intended to foster and enhance leadership abilities (Brungardt, 1996). Pragmatically, leadership education is the pedagogical practice of facilitating leadership learning to build human capacity and is informed by leadership theory and research. It values and is inclusive of both curricular and co-curricular educational contexts (Andenoro et al., 2013). Courses, retreats, and co-curricular workshops are typical leadership education program curriculum delivery methods (Eich, 2007). Holistically, these instructional techniques can be different from those found in most academic disciplines; they focus on the students' subjective experiences more directly than the content imparted.

Thus, in practice, it is critical for leadership educators to develop lessons that impact a student's ability to *see* and *experience* leadership (Buschlen, 2009). Case in point—group projects may be viewed by students as just another "group project." However, if the task is accomplished by an explanation of how this project can also be an exercise in leadership, then more productive outcomes may be attained (Buschlen, 2009). Students must realize that the lessons of leadership—that is, the outcomes of leadership education and pedagogy—transcend the final grade and might aid in enhancing their leadership knowledge, skills, and values. Research supports, and we believe, that integration of leadership learning content and process helps students come to this realization, thereby transforming them through leadership pedagogy.

Teaching Leadership Through Transformative Pedagogy

Leadership is a relational process (Komives et al., 2013). Like many other applied social sciences, there are observable processes that can be studied, understood, and applied to a variety of contexts. Furthermore, students who participate in leadership education should experience multiple interventions and repeated exposure to varied perspectives with the intent of solving complex, real-world issues. Yet this art is not easily understood, and thus formal training with simulations and other experiential and active learning strategies are needed to help bridge the gap between the real world and the classroom (Hughes, Ginnet, & Curphy, 2012). Nonetheless, the leadership educator's responsibility is to help students identify the core knowledge and practices of leadership and make meaning of them in their own lives and the world around them (Owen, Dugan, Berwager, & Lott, 2006). Indeed, leadership has been studied extensively from scholars across disciplines using an array of quantitative, qualitative, and mixed methodologies. Collectively, research findings on leadership provide a far more nuanced and detailed view of this phenomenon than the ones often presented in popular media. The results also provide a valid and reliable empirical basis for further study (Northouse, 2015). B. M. Bass (1990) cited more than 7,500 research studies on leadership and described the mounting theoretical, conceptual, and methodological evidence discovered about leadership as an antidote for the arguments made by those who complain about the unknowing, elusive, mysterious nature of leadership. Yet leadership is not as mysterious as previously conceived. In fact, as leadership educators, we can work to successfully enlighten our students by effectively teaching leadership theories and behaviors, thereby solving the preconceived unknown.

In a theoretical analysis of leadership education, Billsberry (2009) posited that leadership is socially constructed. Thus, it can be viewed in a multitude of ways. Accordingly, disparity exists among the theoretical frameworks, curriculum, influences, and assessment strategies in leadership education. Indeed, because learning leadership and developing leadership skills may be different from learning other content in a traditional classroom setting, leadership education may require a unique pedagogy to facilitate learning (Eich, 2008; Komives et al., 2013; Wren, 1994). The word *pedagogy* has roots in the Greek *paidagōgeō*, which literally translates to "lead the child" (Online Etymology Dictionary, 2017). Thus, the emphasis on leadership as the foundation of successful pedagogy means that educators should conceptualize pedagogy as larger than teaching strategies, where educators serve as leaders themselves in helping students learn and grow (Rosch & Anthony, 2012).

Successful pedagogies encompass three distinct components: (a) the implementation of effective instructional strategies; (b) environmental/classroom management techniques; and (c) program design (Marzano, 2007). Accordingly, any critical considerations of leadership learning experiences reflect intentional design (Jenkins & Allen, in press). Thus, leadership educators who maximize their potential in developing students' leadership capacity must first be intentional in constructing their course or program around a set of desired educational outcomes. Leadership educators must then identify the pedagogy and experiences necessary for the actualization of these outcomes and couple them with relevant student and leadership development theories. Next, leadership educators should strategically sequence these learning activities, apply effective strategies for the delivery of material to a diverse student population, and establish a robust set of assessment activities to measure student learning and development (Harper, 2011). Finally, leadership educators should use assessment information to understand the incoming developmental readiness of students in their courses and programs to construct strategies for building their leader identities, leadership capacity (Rosch & Anthony, 2012), and leadership efficacy. Although programs constructed without this framework may still be successful, we advocate for this approach as one that maximizes instructional efficiency.

As a result of our differential teaching and learning contexts, leadership educators may institute different ways of teaching leadership theories and content to students, but some common elements may be present across programs (Eich, 2008). In fact, many different reasons undergird faculty members' selection of specific instructional strategies. For example, some instructional strategies are better suited for small courses, whereas others can be equally effective in large courses. Likewise, some instructional strate-gies may be better suited for introductory courses, whereas other strategies might be used pragmatically to teach advanced undergraduate courses. All sources of learning have benefits and drawbacks, and each has its time and place in a leadership development initiative (Allen & Hartman, 2009).

The challenge for leadership educators is to make intentional decisions that best facilitate students' ability to positively impact their "leadership for what?" Middlebrooks and Allen (2008) recognize two key pedagogical challenges facing this process. The first is a lack of connection and involve-ment in community issues. This challenge entails how leadership educators can help students become leaders in their communities or engaged in a specific issue—their "leadership for what?" The second, referred to as *Con-necting the Dots: Activity and Insight*, describes pedagogy that only provides the classroom portion of leadership education. This challenge entails how we might get students to be able to practice what has been learned in real time where leadership is messy, consuming, and lacking clear solutions. Specifically, how do we better connect the dots between co-curricular and curricular experiences? Through transformative pedagogy, students learn about themselves and leading while engaging in leadership processes, simultaneously reflecting on and applying their new learning in collab-orative action. Effective leadership pedagogy guides leadership educators in creating conditions for students to overcome these challenges as well as complete activities and assignments designed to encourage reflection and meaning making. Transformational learning is the result of these processes.

FEEDBACK AND DEBRIEFING

To transform learning in leadership education, we must facilitate the con-nection between students' experiences—whether they are from learning activities or assignments or their own experiences external to our lead-ership programs—and related components to the leadership learning framework. Two principal strategies for facilitating this transformation and bridging students' experiences with leadership learning are feedback and debriefing. Through feedback, we can offer scenarios with the types of obstacles students of leadership are likely to encounter and suggest ways to overcome them (Ericsson & Pool, 2016). Through debriefing, we support students in their learning processes by providing structured opportuni-ties for meaning making. In the following subsections, we will explore additional strategies for using feedback and debriefing to facilitate trans-formative learning.

Feedback

Feedback, the process by which individuals learn about past actions, is both a core leadership competency (Larsen, 1998) and, we believe, an integral component of leadership education. In leadership education and development, feedback is generally considered most effective in multisource applications and may take many forms, including 360-degree feedback and executive coaching, mentoring and networking, as well as job assignments and action learning (Day, 2001). Accordingly, throughout Part III of this text, you will see feedback reviewed in its many forms. For example, feedback may come from an instructor or an individual's peers. Feedback may also be coupled with debriefing as a strategy for providing feedback on an activity that just occurred in the classroom or following service learning (Shappell & Barbato, 2010). Here we will discuss some basic strategies for providing feedback and facilitating debriefings in leadership education contexts. Applications associated with specific instructional strategies will be offered in later chapters.

When used early and often, feedback can be a truly transformational instructional strategy. "Through effective feedback processes, we can learn about our strengths and weaknesses in a number of leadership skills" (Conger, 1992, p. 50). However, to be effective, feedback processes need to connect to the ways in which people actually learn. These processes should "...create the *want* to learn, provide abundant opportunities to *learn by doing*, provide a great deal of useful *feedback* to learners, and take account of the fact that learning does not happen instantly, but needs time for *digestion*" (Race, 1993, p. 63, italics original). Accordingly, we suggest beginning leadership education experiences (e.g., courses, workshops) with feedback as a topic of focus. Through role modeling feedback processes (e.g., drawing attention to your own practices) and providing opportunities for students to practice giving and receiving feedback (e.g., through the use of rubrics, peer review, one-on-one discussions, interactive logs with instructor responses, one-minute-papers, individual reading/writing conferences, and group debriefs), students' understanding of feedback processes improves (Fayne, 2009; Larsen, 1998). Role modeling proactive participation in feedback processes illustrates how students can exert agency by relinquishing power in leadership environments. This is a unique consideration in multisource feedback techniques and the key to facilitating one's own learning (Hafford-Letchfield & Bourn, 2011). With this in mind, we can help students become more conscious users of feedback processes and develop an affinity toward feedback-seeking habits.

De Villiers (2013) suggested two types of feedback for individuals who lead organizations: organizational and educational. Organizational feedback refers to honest performance and behavioral appraisals. Organizational feedback is generally not readily available from the learner's colleagues because they fear repercussions and lack the skills to provide feedback (de Villiers, 2013). According to de Villiers (2013), "peers and colleagues hence provide 'nice' feedback which may lack in truthfulness, platitudes which lack in specificity or is ambiguous" (p. 67). This "nice" feedback is not developmental and deprives the learner of crucial information they need to improve (Boyatzis & Kolb, 1969; Goleman, Boyatzis, & McKee, 2002). Challenging and providing feedback to leaders can be difficult tasks for followers. Chaleff (2009) suggests that followers can build courage to challenge leaders by practicing providing critical feedback. However, to do so, the follower must prepare leaders for feedback by prefacing feedback with a defusing statement or linking feedback to outcomes the leader desires (Chaleff, 2009). Followers must find a way to give feedback so that the leader will listen. Chaleff (2009) suggests directing negative feedback toward specific behaviors or policy, utilizing "I" statements whenever possible, or indirectly challenging leaders by posing questions regarding policy or behavior, which can stimulate dialogue rather than incite debate.

Educational feedback, as conceptualized by Hattie and Timperley (2007), is the "information provided by an agent (e.g., teacher, peer, book, parent, self, experience) regarding aspects of one's performance or understanding" (p. 81). This typically happens after instruction is completed, and it seeks to deliver skills and knowledge or even to cultivate particular attitudes (Hattie & Timperley, 2007). In the educational environment, feedback interventions are all events, including interactions of either person through verbal or written format that provides feedback to the learner. As Race (2010) adds, the feedback interventions may be formative (developmental) or summative (additive). These feedback interventions may be provided by lecturers, student peers in collective feedback, team or group members, interviews with practitioners or experts in the field, computer-generated feedback in response to online assignments, or other means (Brown, Rust, & Gibbs, 1994). For example, the Center for Creative Leadership incorporates feedback-intensive experiences in its programming that are concerned with helping a person to see significant patterns of behavior, understand the attitudes and motivations underlying these patterns, reassess what makes the person more or less effective relative to the goals he or she wants to attain, and evaluate alternative ways of meeting these goals (McCauley, Moxley, & Van Velsor, 1998). By using these strategies, learners can incorporate organizational and educational feedback processes as leadership abilities, transforming the way they interact in leadership settings.

Feedback From Practice and Peers

Beyond multisource feedback, the leadership and management education literature appears to organize feedback into two general categories: (a) practice feedback; and (b) peer feedback.

Practice Feedback. To create a culture of feedback, you must provide opportunities for practice. Doing so supports the notion that what we do in our classroom environment mirrors how we intend our students to act in their organizations. Respectively, opportunities for practice can be joined with any active learning strategy, particularly those that include a student-led or student-facilitated component. Yet there are many challenges inherent in ensuring meaningful practice and feedback (Hess, 2007). These include providing feedback to all students and allowing every student the chance to practice skills necessary to elicit a substantial skill set. In most academic settings, the opportunity for students to practice skills and receive feedback on their performance tends to be limited to involvement in brief role plays or simulations and to whatever applications students might attempt outside the classroom. Hess (2007) offered a strategy that keeps the practice within the classroom, where the classroom becomes the setting for each student's experience. Hess (2007) found that students who were provided a significant opportunity to lead a two-week team project and received detailed feedback on their effectiveness in that role experienced enhanced learning by integrating a greater emphasis of the transfer phase (i.e., taking into account past experiences to influence current learning). According to Hess (2007), this practice opportunity is of optimal complexity and sufficient duration is required to exercise a broad range of leadership skills, from providing direction and support to managing conflict and achieving consensus.

However, with any new skill, students should be provided with instructions and criteria for giving and receiving feedback. Any course seeking to achieve enhanced skill development through greater emphasis on learning transfer must consider issues of quality, of both the practice opportunity and feedback provided. Holmer (2001) recommended having students prepare for leading in-class teams, review rules for giving feedback, and then practice framing feedback statements. Similarly, Rubin (2006) concluded that effective feedback should be concrete, specific, descriptive, balanced, nonthreatening, and constructive.

Peer Feedback. Although we primarily suggest that leadership educators model feedback processes, a secondary strategy involves creating opportunities for peer feedback. Using students as the primary source of developmental feedback is consistent with recommendations from Falchikov and Goldfinch (2000) and Macpherson (1999). The evidence they offer suggests that sufficient practice and clear methodology leads students to offer peer feedback that is highly congruent with faculty member feedback. Effective leadership educators can find prospects for peer feedback in any activity, through peer review of written assignments, or immediately following student-led presentations. An important guideline associated with effective peer-feedback facilitation is structure. Specifically, students must know what they are being evaluated for in order for the feedback exercises to be productive.

Consider beginning a class meeting with the following prompt: "Take a minute to reflect on your experience in this class thus far. How have you applied what you've learned in class and from our readings in your leadership approach?" Then, after a minute, ask students to hand their paper to the nearest student. Next, ask students to provide constructive written feedback to their partner. Finally, have students discuss the feedback in pairs and then debrief as a group. Students are often pleasantly surprised by what this activity empowers them to consider, and how constructively critical they are with the feedback they can offer peers.

As alluded to earlier, one of the best ways to create a culture of feedback is to incorporate it into student-led activities and assignments. Rubrics are another great example of a tool for students to practice giving and receiving feedback.

Example

Chapter Review Discussion Facilitation

Facilitate a brief but provocative discussion on the week's assigned readings, write a one page review/outline of the most salient elements of the reading assignment (this will be distributed to your classmates), and utilize the following to supplement your dialogue:

1. A short (no more than 7 minutes, but could be as short as 30 seconds) video, movie clip, etc., that is closely connected to or demonstrates components/concepts from the week's readings. You must prepare at least two discussion questions related to the video you choose.

2. An example related to the reading and from your own experience.

3. An example from the week's reading assignment that resonated with you.

4. Select a case study from our text *A Day in the Life of a College Student Leader* that relates directly to the assigned chapter. Present the scenario to the class in a creative way and answer all discussion questions posed in the text. Then, show the class how you would approach/solve the scenario by applying a theory, method, model, etc., from the assigned chapter in *Exploring Leadership*. Finally, illustrate how you might handle a similar situation at [your institution].

(Example continues on next page)

Example (Continued)

Note: The entire event should last no longer than 30 minutes. Your facilitated discussion will be graded based on your use of visuals, creativity, organization, enthusiasm, and most importantly, your ability to engage your peers in discussion. You may **not** use PowerPoint. Chapter Reviews are essential as assigned readings are used as a base for classroom work. Your review/outline should be typed and you should bring enough copies for the instructor and your classmates. **You will be assessed on your ability to facilitate discussion, not present information.** Expectation for your timeline:

- 0:00 – 0:10: Re-introduce/-orient your peers to the assigned chapter and show your media (five-point deduction for exceeding the 10-minute mark)
- 0:10 – 0:20: co-facilitate a class discussion (with the instructor) on the chapter (this section includes the examples as noted above). You should be prepared with at least two discussion questions (again, no "yes/no" responses) and ready for the following:
  - o   How you would respond to your questions.
  - o   How your peers might respond to your questions.
- 0:20 – 0:30: facilitate discussion around your chosen case study from *A Day in the Life of a College Student Leader* as noted above.

The rubric, provided to each student not involved in the presentation, includes the following questions:

1. How effectively did the facilitator(s) introduce the key concepts from the assigned chapter?
2. Was the summary provided clear, concise, and to the point?
3. How effective was the facilitator in engaging and facilitating discussion of their summary discussion questions?
4. How focused and connected to relevant content was the video?
5. How effectively did the facilitator ask interesting discussion questions and engage the class is focused discussion about the video?
6. How relevant was the case study selected by the facilitator?
7. How engaging was the facilitator's approach to facilitating the case study and debriefing through discussion questions?
8. Overall, how effectively did the facilitator lead a productive and educational discussion?

Additionally, based on a suggestion from Brené Brown's *Daring Greatly* (2015):

9. What are three things the facilitator did well (i.e., strengths)?
10. What is one area where the facilitator could improve?
11. Finally, how could the facilitator leverage one of their strengths from #1 to address the area of improvement in #2?

By providing this type of structure, peer-feedback sessions are given time, content, and contextual boundaries for their feedback, resulting in discussions and dialogues that are focused, critical, and creative. Despite these recommendations, leadership educators should play an active role in both the practice- and peer-feedback processes. In peer-feedback processes specifically, that role can be in the debriefing activities, which the next section thoroughly details.

Debriefing

Debriefing is the processing phase of the learning experience from which learners are encouraged to contextualize their feedback experiences (Dennehy, Sims, & Collins, 1998). The debriefing process consists of using skillful questioning techniques and is a structured part of building reflective practice (R. Gardner, 2013). Debriefing is commonly used following simulations or experiential learning both in and out of the classroom and has roots in and applications to the armed services, the aviation industry, as well as the fields of education, psychology, medical education (specifically nursing), and business (R. Gardner, 2013). To fully comprehend the value and utility of debriefing, we must mention Kolb's (1984) conceptual four-stage framework of experiential learning again (see Chapter 6 and ask you to review the Leader and Follower Experiences as a Source of Transformational Learning model from the Introduction of Section III). The debriefing process transforms students from passive recipients of information to learners who observe and experience phenomena in their environments (concrete experience), write about, reflect on, and discuss what has been experienced (reflective observation), think about how their experiences and those of other students relate to concepts and theories considered in their coursework (abstract conceptualization), and use the new knowledge productively (active experimentation; J. Walker, 2005). Through focused and guided reflective observations (Kolb, 1984), debriefing allows the facilitator to call slow down and help participants reflect on their own thoughts, feelings, actions, decisions, behaviors, and role in the group; connect information gained from the experience, instruction, or reflection; and get to the point of discussing what was learned (Hammel, 1986). It includes probing and open-ended questions presented after an event that help elicit feedback and is crucial to making meetings, activities, and workshop experiences meaningful and lasting (Lunken, 1993). The instructor can guide participants to deeply introspect and create their own interpretations of events to maximize learning experiences. "It is not the 'real' challenges presented by the situation that counts, but those that the person is aware of" (Csikszentmihalyi, 1990, p. 75). Debriefing increases this type of awareness.

As a general rule, debriefing guides should take a cooperative (i.e., not authoritative) role and describe the agenda for the debriefing session, including how it reflects Kolb's framework (Dennehy, Sims, & Collins, 1998; Thiagarajan, 1992). To these ends, J. Walker (2005) offered the following debriefing steps to integrate Kolb's framework:

- Students objectively describe an event or activity that happened during the experiential learning experience and articulate how they were feeling during the experience (Concrete Experience)

- Educators and other students offer alternative perspectives on the described experience (Reflective Observation)
- Students connect prior lectures, readings, and reports to the experience (Abstract Conceptualization)
- Students use what is learned from the discussion to prepare for future experiential learning activities (Active Experimentation)

Thus, the product of the debriefing session is an articulated sensing of "meaning," where students can freely organize, compare, classify, evaluate, summarize, or analyze an experience and construct personal meanings that reveal their misunderstandings, oversimplifications, and personal theories (Raths, 1987).

Perhaps one of the best resources we have encountered for debriefing came from a workshop at the 2010 Leadership Educators Institute. For 90 minutes, two facilitators from Emporia State University guided participants through six phases of focused debriefing. We present them below as an exemplary outline for facilitating a debrief session in most leadership education contexts (Shively & Relph, 2010).

Example

Six Phases of Debriefing

Phase 1: How Do You Feel?

This phase gives the participants an opportunity to get strong feelings and emotions off their chest. It makes it easier for them to be more objective during the later phases. Begin this phase with a broad question that invites the participants to get in touch with their feelings about the activity and its outcomes. Encourage them to share these feelings, listening actively to one another in a nonjudgmental fashion. Additional probing questions:

- What was your initial reaction(s) of the activity?
- Was the activity frustrating?
- What are your thoughts on the activity?
- How well did the group cope with this challenge?

Phase 2: What Happened?

In this phase, collect data about what happened during the activity. Encourage the participants to compare and contrast their recollections and to draw general conclusions during the next phase. Begin this phase with a broad question that asks the participants to recall important events from the training activity and/or create and post a chronological list of events. Ask questions about specific events or use some of the following probing questions:

(Example continues on next page)

Example (Continued)

- Tell me how the activity went?
- Tell me about how your group handled the activity?
- How well did you think the group worked together?
- What could have been done differently?
- How successful was the group? Were there struggles?
- How long did it take? Could you have finished faster?

Phase 3: What Did You Learn?

In this phase, encourage the participants to generate and test different hypotheses. Ask the participants to come up with principles based on the activity and discuss them. Begin this phase by presenting a principle and asking the participants for data that supports or rejects it. Then invite the participants to offer other principles based on their experiences. Additional probing questions:

- What skills did it take for the group to be successful?
- What are the strengths and weaknesses of the group?
- What's one thing you learned about another person in your group?
- What's one thing you learned about yourself?
- What communication strategies worked best?
- Did you trust your group members?
- What does our group need in order to trust each other to work more effectively?
- How did the group come up with its best ideas?

Phase 4: How Does This Relate to the Real World?

In this phase, discuss the relevance of the activity to the participants' real-world experiences.

Begin with a broad question about the relationship between the experiential learning activity and events in the workplace. Suggest that the activity is a metaphor and ask participants to offer real-world analogies.

Phase 5: What If?

In this phase, encourage the participants to apply their insights to new contexts. Use alternative scenarios to speculate on how people's behaviors would change. Begin this phase with a change scenario and ask the participants to speculate on how it would have affected the processes and the outcomes of the activity. Then invite the participants to offer their own scenarios and discuss them. Conclude this phase by asking, "How could you have accomplished the goal of the activity in a different way?"

(Example continues on next page)

Example (Continued)

Phase 6: What Next?

In this phase, ask the participants to undertake action planning. Ask them to apply their insights from the experiential activity to the real world. Begin this phase by asking the participants to suggest strategies for use in future rounds of the activity. Then ask the participants how they will change their real-world behavior as a result of the insights gained from the activity. Additional probing questions:

1. What do you think you've learned from this activity which can be applied in future activities?

2. What did each group member learn about him/her self as a group member and how will this help in the future?

3. What lessons did the group learn from this exercise that could be applied to future situations?

Other Debriefing Strategies. It is important to note that not all debriefing must occur through facilitated discussion of large or small groups. The Example lists several alternative debriefing strategies described by Shively and Relph (2010), Raths (1987), and others.

Example

Think pair share: Each person thinks about the experience and then pairs up with someone next to them to discuss their thoughts and then everyone has the opportunity to share with the larger group.

Write it, share it: This is an opportunity for each person to write out his or her thoughts and then share it with the larger group. This allows the participants to take a minute to articulate what they want to say before they share it. This allows some to feel more comfortable sharing what they have written down.

Post-it®: The facilitator chooses topics for the group to reflect on and posts the main topics around the room; topics could include the six phases of debriefing. Each person uses sticky notes to reflect on each topic; once they have written down their reflection, they take their Post-it® and stick it under the topic. The facilitator then reads the thoughts from the Post-it® notes to debrief the activity and/or start a deeper discussion.

Honest and Anonymous: Students write down on a piece of paper their thoughts and reactions and then wad it up and throw them all over the room. Then a student or facilitator picks one up at a time, reads it aloud, and then discuss as a group. This technique is best used for debriefing sensitive or heated discussions, where it would be more beneficial for it to be anonymous.

(Example continues on next page)

Example (Continued)

Around the room: Everyone shares about the experience as you go around the circle or everyone shares one word (or 2 or 3 words) about the experience. Technique provides everyone to share their thoughts.

Metaphors: This technique is used to help students describe what they are feeling based on another experience. Metaphors are used to allow students to communicate about an experience and apply it to something that is not exactly related in order to suggest a similarity in what they have learned.

Paint-a-Picture: This technique is used to help students describe what they are feeling through a variety of mediums; paint, clay, pipe cleaners, Popsicle sticks, and recycled materials. Paint-a-picture allows students to communicate how they feel or what they learned about an experience through an alternative method. Students describe their thoughts and perspectives to something they have created.

Finally, the skills of the debriefer are important to ensure the best possible learning. Lack of preparation and guidance could lead the learner to negatively transfer a mistake into their practice, focus only on the negative, or develop fixations (Dennehy, Sims, & Collins, 1998). As you fine tune your debriefing skills, be aware of participants' level of response, personal impact of the experience, level of self-awareness, ability to verbalize feelings and thoughts, and level of comfort with sharing (Hammel, 1986).

THE LEADERSHIP EDUCATOR AS A ROLE MODEL

One of the five most important high-impact practices for college teaching identified by Fink (2013) is to be a leader to your students. Fink explains that good leaders motivate and enable others to do something important well. Accordingly, skilled leadership educators invite their students to participate in leadership learning by motivating them with modeled leadership behaviors. The role of the leadership educator is not to simply transmit information, "but rather to actively engage the learners in constructing personal theories and philosophies of leadership by creating a learning environment that builds upon learners' existing knowledge and experiential base" (Wisniewski, 2010, p. 65). In this way, leadership educators describe modeling leadership through the way they teach and facilitate learning in the classroom; they see teaching as a type of leading (Jenkins, 2017b). According to Jenkins's (2017b) study exploring the experiences of becoming and being a leadership educator, leadership educators felt they had to be "teacher leaders" because they either had impactful role models who they sought to emulate as part of the leadership and teaching processes and/or they were modeling the leadership they wanted students to exhibit.

According to Harding's (2011) study, leadership educators reported feeling obligated to model effective leadership whenever they engaged with students. In the classroom and online (Jenkins, 2016), the practice of engagement is facilitated most often through discussion-based pedagogies that model inclusive behaviors, emphasize the use of empowerment in the classroom (Cross, 2002), and are consistent with being inclusive as a means of understanding how different groups or individuals might approach issues from different perspectives, maintain attitudes that respect differences, and value equity and involvement. How leadership educators teach and, more specifically, how they facilitate learning through discussion exemplify how they want students to facilitate leadership and change when they return to their organizations.

In an organization, being inclusive can mean having the skills that develop members' talents and readily involves them, listening with empathy, and communicating with civility. Accordingly, "empowering environments are learning climates," in which people expect successes yet know they can learn from failures or mistakes. Equally, "it is important to establish organizational environments that empower others to do and be their best" (Komives et al., 2013, pp. 94–95). Similarly, effective positional leaders recognize the power and ability to be effective comes from the members of their group—their participants (Kouzes & Posner, 2012). As leadership educators, being inclusive embraces having the skills to develop the talents of one's students so they can be readily involved. In this way, "inclusiveness breeds new leadership and creates a positive cycle that sustains the quality of an organization over time" (Komives, Lucas, & McMahon, 2007, p. 86). Correspondingly, effective leadership educators empower students to be active contributors, adding their perspective and insight to the teaching and learning processes. Likewise, hoarding power in leadership (or in the classroom) risks negative responses from others that contradict positive group goals and objectives.

One of the best pedagogical examples of modeling these behaviors comes from the "Creating Learning Communities" section of the *Instructor's Guide for Exploring Leadership: For College Students Who Want to Make a Difference*, 2nd ed. (Owen, Komives, Lucas, & McMahon, 2007). The heart of the approach is captured in Owen et al. (2007), as the authors suggest during the first class meeting, "It might be helpful to ask students to jot down ideas about what it would take to make this the best class or program they have ever had" (p. 7). In its purest sense, beginning a semester-long course by setting course expectations together, establishing ground rules for things like discussion, and openly discussing acceptable and disruptive behaviors creates an environment that both models and empowers inclusivity. Moreover, it implicitly and explicitly creates dynamics where instructors shape environments they intend students will replicate in their own organizations. With respect to outcomes and results, multiple occasions and one-on-one conversations support that students learn from these practices. Although students often experience or report dissonance from their first leadership courses, it is clear that students see the value and aim to implement the practice.

Example

Empowering Students to Take Ownership in Learning			
Best Class Ever		Worst Class Ever	
What the Teacher Did	What the Student Did	What the Teacher Did	What the Student Did

Beginning a leadership class by asking them to discuss this table (adapted from Weimer, 2013) empowers students to take ownership in their own learning process. In fact, in one class meeting, a student made a profound connection to this model. He suggested that the teacher was "the leader" and the students were "the followers," and that if the purpose of the class was to learn leadership, we'd have to work together through this dynamic. The teachable moment occurred when he corrected his own suggestion, offering that, "Hey, we're all leaders and followers in this class!"

CONCLUSION

Leadership education is transformative because, when done correctly, leadership educators alter our students' ways of thinking about and practicing leadership. When done well, leadership education is active. Equally, it is experiential: students' knowledge and skills are gained from reflecting on experiences in educational programs and other contexts. This reflective practice should include opportunities for feedback and for meaning making through guided debriefing. Through this process, leadership is transformed for the learner, turning knowledge to experience and experience to meaning.

CHAPTER 10

DISCUSSION

Leadership Education's
Signature Pedagogy

In this chapter, we introduce leadership education's signature pedagogy: discussion. But what is a signature pedagogy? Shulman (2005) defines a signature pedagogy as the instructional strategy that is most frequently used to prepare members of a particular profession. The author implicitly defines what constitutes knowledge in a field and a field's epistemology—how things become known. Furthermore, Shulman (2005) defines how knowledge is analyzed, criticized, accepted, or discarded, as well as how to inform students on thinking, performing, and acting with integrity. Examples of signature pedagogies included the Socratic method in law school as well as confirmation labs in physics (Lattery, 2009) and biological sciences (Bauer-Dantoin, 2009). Yet many scholars argue that leadership studies transcend the disciplines and prepare students for all professions (e.g., Doh, 2003; Harvey & Riggio, 2011; Wren, Riggio, & Genovese, 2009; Zimmerman-Oster & Burkhardt, 1999). Shulman (2005) explains that effective signature pedagogies (a) incorporate active student participation; (b) make students feel deeply engaged; (c) promote a learning environment where students feel visible (making it hard for students to disappear and become anonymous); (d) tend to be interactive, meaning students are accountable to their teacher as well as fellow students; and (e) breed

The Role of Leadership Educators: Transforming Learning, pp. 173–187
Copyright © 2018 by Information Age Publishing

accountability of performance and interaction, as well as remove the cloak of invisibility, leading to a much higher affectivity in class.

Arguably, because leadership development workshops, classic team-building seminars, and other interactive activities represent the earliest forms of leadership education, leadership educators have consistently demonstrated these types of techniques. To confirm this hypothesis, Jenkins (2012, 2013) explored the instructional strategies used most frequently by instructors across the country who taught undergraduate academic-bearing face-to-face leadership studies courses. He found that leadership educators used varying forms of class discussion, including interactive lecture/discussion and small-group discussion, more than any other instructional strategy surveyed. In a series of follow-up studies including quantitative and qualitative inquiries, Jenkins (2017a) found that discussion-based pedagogies were also the signature pedagogies of graduate and online leadership education.

Accordingly, this chapter begins with an overview of discussion-based pedagogies from the college teaching literature. Then we will look at specific applications of discussion-based pedagogy in leadership education. Finally, we provide examples from face-to-face and technology-enhanced leadership education contexts.

DISCUSSION-BASED PEDAGOGY

The discussion method refers to the process of the pedagogy, that is, the method of an instructor facilitating a structured, preplanned discussion to lead students through the process of analyzing a piece of material. Correspondingly, much of the literature on classroom discussion describes the process "as much a method of instruction as ... a curriculum outcome. As a method [discussion] provides an approach for teaching content, while as an outcome or goal of instruction it emphasizes that students become competent discussants" (Larson, 1997, p. 207). Accordingly, discussion method teaching can center around any number of devices that motivate analysis and is often discipline-specific (e.g., a floor plan in architecture, a new theoretical model or approach, a patient's chart in medicine, a poem in literature, a newspaper article in political science, and a statistical table in economics).

Apart from asynchronous online teaching, spoken language is the central medium by which instructors teach (Cazden, 2001; Dudley-Marling, 2013) and, arguably, the primary means by which students learn because communication makes reflection the process that individuals can relate new knowledge and content to what they already known (Cazden, 2001). Furthermore, scholars have argued, "From Socrates to

Dewey to Habermas, educative dialogue has represented a forum for learners to develop understanding by listening, reflecting, proposing, and incorporating alternative views" (Michaels, O'Connor, & Resnick, 2008, p. 284). Instructional developers suggest that when compared with the traditional lecture method, discussion elicits higher level reflective thinking, problem solving, and retention of information (Ewens, 2000). However, according to a comprehensive literature review of discussion pedagogy in postsecondary education, most educators have been reluctant to abandon lecture in favor of discussion. Thus, discussion in the classroom is rare; when instructors do provide opportunities for it, few students tend to participate (Dudley-Marling, 2013). The important distinction, however, lies in whether the instructor is truly engaging in discussion. It is unclear whether instructors are performing discussion as described by the high-quality literature of the field or are instead disguising some other mode of teaching (e.g., lecturing) in the language of "discussion." The former is different from conversation and other forms of group talk because of its "concern with the development of knowledge, understanding, or judgment among those taking part" (Brookfield & Preskill, 2005, p. 17). Discussion focused on open-ended questions, where the conversation focuses on a topic or topics that are maintained, extended, or developed, are far more engaging (Haroutunian-Gordon, 1991). Instructors who facilitate these interactions but do not dominate them or insist on "correct" answers. From Dillon's (1994) perspective, instructors who facilitate these interactions but do not dominate them or insist on "correct" answers are anathema to true discussion (Dudley-Marling, 2013).

Even so, opportunities to participate in class discussions differ across disciplines (Dudley-Marling, 2013). Cross (2002) contends that there is nothing wrong with discussion if it is used with the conscious and expressed purpose of promoting learning—the purpose is the key:

> Class discussion covers a wide range of learning sins and virtues. Some teachers use class discussion to promote learning; others use it to fill class time. Some discussion is carefully planned; some occurs by default. Some challenges and engages students; some bores. Some is task-oriented; some lacks any focus. Some is learner-centered; most is teacher-centered. And some discussion consists largely of questions and answers with a call for "right answers," while some is more like a conversation, challenging analysis and higher-level thinking skills. (pp. 8–9)

Similarly, Christensen (1987), professor emeritus of the Harvard Business School and widely considered a master of the teaching by discussion method, asserts:

Class discussion is especially effective when educational objectives focus on qualities of mind (curiosity, judgment, wisdom), qualities of person (character, sensitivity, integrity, responsibility), and the ability to apply general concepts and knowledge to specific situations, discussion puts students in an active learning mode, challenges them to accept substantial responsibility for their own education, and gives them first-hand appreciation of, and experience with, the application of knowledge to practice. (p. 3)

Equally, Mercer and Howe (2012) conclude, "When teachers actively engage students in reflective discussions of what they are studying, this helps them learn, develops their understanding and prepares them well for independent learning" (p. 14). Brookfield and Preskill (2005) contend that discussion transforms students into "cocreators of knowledge" (p. 22). In the context of dialogue, "the group constructs and discloses deeper meaning, enriching understanding for all participants" (Eeds & Wells, 1991, p. 134). In addition, discussion may lead to more interest in "interdisciplinary and connected learning" (Cox & Richlin, 1993, p. 3). Given these findings, the benefits of adopting a discussion-based approach to pedagogy in any field, but particularly leadership education, are clear.

Advocates for discussion-based pedagogy argue its inherently democratic nature (Redfield, 2000), ability to actively involve students in the learning experience (Rocca, 2010), emphasis on active learning (Cross, 2002), and impact on the development of problem-solving (Gilmore & Schall, 1996) and critical thinking skills (Robinson & Schaible, 1993). Researchers also find that discussion motivates students to learn, engages students in higher level thinking, increases class morale, provides feedback to teachers, and envelops more positive student attitudes toward instruction (Barnes & Ellner, 1983; Crone, 2001; Dudley-Marling, 2013). Likewise, Hardman and Mroz (1999) conclude that discussion gives students a means to draw on the knowledge and experience they bring to their courses, giving them more responsibility and control over their learning. In general, many postsecondary scholars and practitioners view discussion as an alternative to lecture, which is criticized for encouraging passive acceptance of factual information rather than promoting deep engagement with ideas (Steen, Bader, & Kubrin, 1999).

DISCUSSION-BASED PEDAGOGY IN LEADERSHIP EDUCATION

Discussion-based pedagogy is the most widely used instructional strategy in leadership education, regardless of academic level or modality (Jenkins, 2012, 2013. 2016, 2017a). Whether it is through instructor-facilitated class discussion, interactive lecture/discussion, small-group discussion, or instructor-led, student-led, or shared instructor- and student-led online discussion boards, discussion pedagogy transcends undergraduate and graduate leadership education (Jenkins, 2016, 2017a). Respectively, recent research suggests that high-quality leadership programs must incorporate student-centered experiential learning (e.g., meaningful discussion), and to be effective, leadership must be taught through learner-centered pedagogies (Eich, 2008, 2012), meaning the pedagogy lends itself to the learner being responsible for contributing to his or her own learning by engaging in discussions. To dig in deeper with this instructional strategy, we will discuss constructing brave learning spaces and practicing discussion, and we will provide several examples of discussion-based pedagogy in leadership education.

Constructing Brave Learning Spaces

One responsibility of a leadership educator is to create a space for students to engage in discussion where they are able to experiment and reflect. As introduced in Chapter 6, brave spaces move beyond the safe space conceptualization and ask students to engage in understanding across difference in both productive and creative ways (Arao & Clemens, 2013). Brave spaces start with discussing expectations of respect within the group and go on to include awareness and ownership of one's intentions and impact, engagement in controversy with civility (Higher Education Research Institute, 1996), upholding of a respectful environment while understanding respect looks different in various cultures, and encouraging students struggle with the uncomfortable (Arao & Clemens, 2013). Often facilitators begin a potentially challenging conversation with the understanding of challenge by choice, allowing individuals to disengage if they feel unsafe. This practice is creating a safe space, where brave space challenges participants to reflect on why they may want to disengage and, if possible, lean into the discomfort for the benefit of the individual and group growth (Arao & Clemens, 2013).

The primary goal of the leadership educator is to empower students in the task of making meaning from content and their experiences, and this requires communication and contemplation of what we know and what we are exposed to. Communication and contemplation occur in both external (social) and internal (reflective) settings. In these spaces, learners must deliberate, ruminate, and consider many possibilities to determine what they think is correct, decide what the ideas or events represent, and work together to solve problems (Brierton, 2011). In this way, using discussion-based pedagogy in an intentionally constructed brave space can support all students to engage fully in their learning.

Practicing Discussion in Leadership Education

In considering how to incorporate and apply discussion-based pedagogies in leadership education, we return to how leadership is a process and requires engagement. According to Kasulis (1982), a class discussion has three dimensions: (a) content (what the class is about); (b) process (how the class is functioning); and (c) people (who is involved in the process). Thus, the content is the purpose of the class. How a purpose is achieved (the process) is just as important as the outcome (Komives et al., 2013). How goals are accomplished and how others are involved in the process matter greatly in leadership. In effective leadership education, how the class is functioning during a discussion is just as important as the teaching and learning goals established by the instructor. Instructors can role model this approach by seeking to understand the people in the process and actively valuing and engaging diversity in views, approaches, styles, and aspects of individuality, such as gender or culture, which add multiple perspectives to a group's activity and fosters inclusivity. How we talk about people in the organization, how we refer to them (colleagues vs. subordinates or participants vs. followers), and how the organization is structured are indicators of inclusive environments (Hesselbein, 2002).

Equally important is the role of student participation during discussion plays in leadership development. Here are some practical tips for facilitating discussion-based pedagogy in your leadership course:

- Start early, practice often. Set and discuss expectations with your students just like you would in an initial meeting with collaborators, team members, or in preparation for strategic planning (see e.g., Owen, Komives, Lucas, & McMahon, 2007; Weimer, 2013). Also, consider a dialogue early in the semester—and perhaps even a similar check-in later on—where you openly discuss what good discussion looks like as well as what good participation looks like in that model. Be intentional to identify the roles of the students and the instructor in your model; remember, good discussion pedagogy, like leadership, is an activity.

- Show, don't tell. "The role of the leadership educator is not to deliver or transmit information," suggests Wisniewski (2010), "but …to actively engage the learners in constructing personal theories and philosophies of leadership by creating a learning environment that builds upon learners' existing knowledge and experiential base" (p. 65). Make time to empower your students to contribute and add their perspective and insight to the teaching and learning processes.

- Focus on listening. Eich (2008) identified meaningful discussions as student-centered and experiential learning opportunities. Meaningful discussions improve communication skills through listening to others and telling their own thoughts.
- Be clear and consistent. Consider requiring students to facilitate discussions on topics versus giving passive presentations. Make sure to develop a clear rubric and require student facilitators to do less than 50% of the talking during their time limit.
- Read the room. Finally, if you want discussion to be an effective pedagogy for teaching leadership, make sure to consider the environment as well as the physical layout of your classroom. If a small class size is not practical, then invoke smaller groups within a larger class that might have similar effects (Odom, 2015). If your classroom is set up lecture style, then reorganize the chairs into a circle or square and sit with your students.

Discussion Methods in Leadership Education

In this final section of the chapter, we will offer some examples of discussion-based pedagogy in leadership education contexts such as case-in-point and peer-facilitated discussion. However, attempting any discussion-based pedagogy without first setting participation expectations for your students and yourself is setting yourself up for failure. A review of the leadership education assessment literature suggests that leadership educators place a high value on class participation and attendance (Jenkins, 2017a). We suspect this finding is associated with leadership educators' affinity for discussion-based pedagogy. According to Dudley-Marling (2013), the impact on student participation and engagement is one of the most beneficial components of employing discussion pedagogy. Specifically, more frequent student participation leads to improved learning outcomes, increased student motivation, and engagement in "higher levels of thinking, including interpretation, analysis, and synthesis" (Rocca, 2010, p. 188). While reviewing various leadership course syllabi in preparation for this book, we came across the following simple, straightforward attendance and participation statement on several syllabi: "Points cannot be earned when you are not in attendance." Although this seems simple, setting the expectation for participation and engagement—in both writing and early conversations with your students—in any educational program cannot be overstated.

Correspondingly, we offer an engagement rubric for leadership education contexts, which, according to Almagno (2017), moves students from passive to active learners or seekers of knowledge. This rubric may be used to evaluate students' participation and engagement in class discussions. However, it is critical to keep in mind that ways of engaging vary across cultures. We do not offer this rubric up for leadership educators to blindly apply these criteria to students. Although these indicators are a good place to start, inclusive leadership educators will filter these standards through the lens of multiculturalism and adapt this framework for use with students from diverse backgrounds.

Example

Engagement	Preparation (Outside of Session)	Participation (in Session)
Fully engaged student	Completed assigned readings and/or exercises with a full effort. Reflected and sought out related material.	Attends and is consistently attentive. Thoughtfully listens and advances the discussion by providing examples from their own or others' experiences. Offers research, media, and so on related to the topic.
Occasionally engaged student	Completed most of the assigned readings and/or exercises with a mixed effort. May have reflected or sought out related material.	Attends class but is occasionally attentive and is seldom distracted by technology. Sometimes offers examples.
Needs guidance to be engaged, student	May or may not have completed assigned readings and/or exercises, reflected, or sought out related material.	Attends inconsistently, is often distracted by technology, and participates only when prompted.
Disengaged student	Neither read nor completed exercises.	Attends inconsistently and when in class is distracted by technology.

Questioning

An essential component of high-quality discussions is questioning (Brierton, 2011). An instructor's questions should guide and focus the discussion but be flexible enough to allow for appropriate tangents. Instructors need to carefully choose questions that do not allow for rapid-fire responses, which can devolve into class recitation. Good questions feed discussions like kindling fuels fires—their purpose is to entice and engage students into a thoughtful discussion, one that allows them to ask questions of each other and the class. Questions like these create a setting for social constructivism, where students are able to share in meaning-making and more complex thinking (Wilen, 2004). In general, low-quality questions elicit low-quality responses, and high-quality questions are more likely to elicit high-quality responses. However, the quality of the question does not guarantee the quality of response (Mills, Rice, Berliner, & Rousseau, 1980). Instructor's questions should not be exclusively dependent on rote memory to answer. Conversely, not all questions need to be at higher cognitive levels to receive higher order thinking answers. Students can and will provide deep answers to shallow questions and vice versa. In general, varying the question levels is good for discussion, and it is important to examine the specific audience and purpose or intention of the lesson. Often questions begin in a simpler fashion and gain complexity as the discussion progresses (Wilen, 2004). Simply stated, if the purpose is to achieve higher order thinking skills, then questions of higher levels need to be asked.

Student-Facilitated Discussion Versus Traditional Class Presentations

A myriad of positive outcomes of discussion are associated with student learning. Dudley-Marling (2013) offers these outcomes:

- improved ability to deal with problems
- supported learning
- deeper understanding of content
- heightened creation of new meanings
- enhanced critical thinking
- enhanced oral and written communication
- enhanced learning
- improved achievement

Subsequently, we suggest altering the traditional student-led presentation to a discussion-based model. There are many reasons for this suggestion, including past experiences leaving most presentation-heavy class meetings frustrated with the lack of engagement by presenters' peers. Thus, although we may have explicitly assigned student presenters to prepare and ask discussion questions, we had not provided much structure around expectations for delivery and facilitation. Here we offer a brief syllabus statement that offers guidance in student-led facilitation rather than presentation formats.

Example

Syllabus Statement for Group Presentation

*Note: You will be assessed on your ability to facilitate a discussion, not present information. Although this is not a presentation, you should plan on being prepared as if it were. Expectation for your timeline:

- 1–5 minutes: Reintroduce/reorient your peers to the article/topic (5-point deduction for exceeding the 5-minute mark)
- 5–20 minutes: Cofacilitate a class discussion (with the instructor) on the article. Be prepared with at least five discussion questions (again, no "yes/no" responses) and ready for the following:
  o   How you would respond to your questions?
  o   How your peers might respond to your questions?
  o   How you will keep the discussion going if your peers to not provide the answers you had hoped for?

Discussant

In a similar peer-led approach, the discussant method empowers a student or group of students to design course-related activities and questions for their peers and facilitate associated discussion. Goertzen, McRay, and Klaus (2016) offer an online "module discussant" approach where students post activities and questions in a discussion board and facilitate discussion there. We have used a similar approach in blended/hybrid courses, where half of the students attend face to face and the other half attend virtually (e.g., Google Hangouts, Adobe Connect). Accordingly, students begin their discussant role online (in this example, they summarize a research article related to group dynamics, provide open-ended discussion questions, and moderate the ensuing dialogue) and continue it in the classroom a week later—physically or virtually—with a 20-minute facilitated discussion on their topic. Students are also required to integrate ideas presented by their peers online into the in-class component.

This method "stimulates students to think more deeply about the connections between leadership theory, research, and practice, and to allow for substantive peer-to-peer interaction, laying the foundation for a rich *community of inquiry*" (Goertzen, McRay, & Klaus, 2016, p. 153). Students who engaged in this method reported greater satisfaction (compared with instructor-led discussions) and engagement with course material. Recommendations for future use include intentional pairing of student discussants, integrating peer feedback at each stage of the assignment, greater instructor interaction with discussants during their facilitation week, and helping students with self-discipline and time management leading up to and during their discussant weeks.

Discussion Boards

Technology-enhanced discussion boards are available within most learning management systems (LMSs). Systems such as Blackboard, Canvas, Sakai, and others usually include subsystems with a twofold purpose of content presentation and facilitation of discussion (student-student and student-instructor) through interactive technologies (Rovai, 2006). Keeping in mind that the identifying characteristic of constructivist learning environments online is social interaction, most often in technology-enhanced environments, this interaction is manifested via online discussions (Rovai, 2006). However, facilitating online discussion is not without its challenges. Case in point: What typically happens when you assign a discussion board assignment and ask students to respond to their peers before a set deadline? If you are like most instructors your answer is along the lines of, "...with the exception of one or two students who post days before the deadline and complain that 'there's no one to respond to,' most students post within the final 12 hours of a deadline." The frequency increases as you get closer to the deadline. We came across a model that solves this issue—Online Threaded Discussions—and the following provides an example (Dolisso, 2011).

Example

Online Threaded Discussion Model

- What is it?
    - o Asynchronous, web-based discussion that takes place in an online environment under a number of different topics (i.e., "threads"; Kirk & Orr, 2003).
    - o An initial message and subsequent posted responses that are sequentially linked to the initial message.
    - o A form of conversation in which people express ideas, elaborate arguments, and answer questions of other group members.

Online Threaded Discussion Model

- Benefits
    - o Improving higher order thinking (Kirk & Orr, 2003; Meyer & Marsick, 2003).
    - o Meeting constructivist curricular objectives (Weasenforth, Biesenbach-Lucas, & Meloni, 2002).
    - o Helping students become participatory citizens (Larson & Keiper, 2002).
    - o Building online learning communities (Edelstein & Edwards, 2002).
    - o Improving students' writing skills (Jordan, 2001).

(Example continues on next page)

Example (Continued)

Online Threaded Discussion Model

- Benefits

  o   Facilitating student collaboration (Miller & Benz, 2008).

  o   Promoting active and group learning (Kirk & Orr, 2003).

- Process:

  o   Please read case study X and/or watch video clip and follow the steps given below to engage in the discussion.

  o   Step 1, week 1: Formulate and post your response to the case after reading the case/watching the case video clip. This has to be your intuitive and original response as to how you would handle or respond to that situation (one or two paragraphs long).

  o   Step 2, week 2: Review your peers' first posts and formulate your second responses to this case and post it. Did your response change in anyway? Why or Why not?

  o   Step 3: Students are encouraged to carry on discussion beyond the two required posts if the topic interests them, but they are not required to make more than two posts.

In addition to the structure in the example, consider the following recommendations for using discussion boards in your leadership course offered by D. N. Smith (2015): (a) develop a discussion board grading rubric; (b) share example posts (and what type of grade examples would have received); (c) encourage students to participate in nongraded discussion boards early; (d) privately email students who post either late or incomplete responses; (e) subdivide larger classes into smaller discussion groups; and (f) restrict students' ability to read others' posts until their responses are submitted. In line with these recommendations, we offer the following syllabus statement as an example.

Example

Syllabus Statement for Online Discussion Boards

The course is designed around the discussion and application of personal reflection and assigned readings. Completing the assigned readings will prepare you and your classmates for effective online and intellectual discussion as well as interconnectedness to the theories and concepts imbedded therein. Thus, in addition to the assignments, you will be asked to post and respond to your peers on various questions. The format for posting/responding to these assignments will be as follows:

(Example continues on next page)

Example (Continued)

1. A due date for posting answers to assigned questions will be given. Students must post answers by the date indicated and will not be able to view other students' answers. This first post is referred to as the Individual Post and is worth 2 points.

2. Once the due date has passed, students will be able to view other students' responses.

3. Students will then respond to other students' answers by answering the following questions (this post is referred to as the Response Post and is worth 2 more points):

   a. Based on your peers' answers, would you have changed any of your original answers? If so, why and how?

   b. What new perspectives did you come across that you had not previously thought about?

   c. Are there any answers that you disagree with? If so, why and how? Respond directly to that student and begin a dialogue!

Posting Guidelines: The goal is creating new understandings of the material and new insights about leadership. Below are the criteria I use. Please use a professional tone and writing style. Informality and a bit of humor is fine, with prudence.

Note: You may be asking, how much participation is enough? The rubric below will help you answer this question. Basically, the more you contribute, and the more substantive your contributions, the more points you will earn. If you participate meaningfully during each unit, you will likely receive full credit. Posts consisting of "I agree" or "Me too" or "How lame" will not gain you lots of points. Meaningful comments, tied into class topics and/or your real life experiences are far more likely to gain you points. I will post questions in each unit to spark conversation. You are at liberty to share insights, thoughts, observations, and media (popular and scholarly) items of interest. Being bold enough to find things outside the boundaries of our class and sharing them will serve you well.

- 1.5–2.0 points–Participant has contributed ideas, insights and pertinent questions with careful reference to texts but in their own words, expanded our collective thinking or strengthened other ideas in discussion. The contributions are original, well explained and written, and may be humorous. They may also refer us to relevant additional resources such as websites, articles, authors, ideas, etc., and/or apply ideas to their experiences or other prior knowledge in a manner that adds to our knowledge and understanding of the material.

- 1.0–1.5 points–Participants' contributions are clear, to the point but offers fewer new ideas, poses fewer meaningful questions, and offers fewer helpful responses than the A contributor. The contributions may not be as well written and may prompt fewer responses from others.

Syllabus Statement for Online Discussion Boards

- 0.5–1.0 points–Participant contributes ideas, responses and questions to the conversation, but the contributions are less clear or unoriginal. The point of the contributions may be unclear. Peers may not be moved to respond.

- 0.5 or less points–Participants' contributions do not add to the discussion or analysis in a meaningful way or miss the point entirely. The contribution may be so poorly worded as to be uninterpretable.

(Example continues on next page)

Example (Continued)

- Responses (if you need clarification before responding to someone, just ask before offering your response) should also follow the criteria above. Here are some hints:

- 1.0–2.0 points–Excellent responses make connections among various points made by others leading to new understandings, point out critical issues neglected in initial posting and suggest redirection of thought, or fully respond to a question and/or raise yet another new question either of which takes the discussion forward another step.

- 0.5–1.0 points–Competent responses answer fully, competently, and with some insight but with less critical thought than above.

- 0.5 or less points–OK, did it but didn't add much or unclear/incomplete.

PEDAGOGY TO PRACTICE

In summary, we offer highlights of reflection as a leadership education pedagogy and putting this instructional strategy into practice, which has the potential to transform leadership learning.

Pedagogy Overview

- Class discussion helps students develop critical thinking skills, active learning, and problem-solving techniques.
- Using the discussion pedagogy, educators need to allow for questions that will elicit high- or low-level responses. This is dependent on your learning objectives for a particular concept or reading but is essential for discussions to be productive.
- Educators need to make sure they are actively engaged with students in the discussion and are focused on listening to their thoughts and perspectives.
- Student participation is integral to classroom discussion. Consider encouraging your students to facilitate class discussions and create a list of shared expectations (instructor and students) to create a shared learning space.

Transforming Leadership Learning Through Discussion

- Creating spaces for students to experiment, reflect, and converse about turbulent issues, social justice, and identities is essential for leadership educators.

- Leadership educators must thoughtfully consider and prepare before implementing discussion activities. Articulating expectations, anticipating and preparing for difficulties, and practicing facilitation can benefit leadership educators to positively implement discussion in their work.
- Engagement rubrics allows for leadership educators to evaluate the participation and engagement of their students, but need to be developed with a lens of multiculturalism to use with students from diverse backgrounds.
- Online threaded discussion provides an active opportunity for learning leadership, but specific guidelines and expectations are necessary when implementing discussion boards.

CHAPTER 11

CASE STUDY METHODS FOR LEADERSHIP EDUCATION

In this chapter, we explore various case study methods for teaching leadership. Emerging from the case study method of teaching from the Harvard Business School, the "case study" is an instructional strategy used to bring experiences learners may not be able to access to the learning environment, stimulating the application of research techniques, decision-making skills, and critical thinking analysis (Herreid, 2011). Case studies are also valuable for bridging the gap between theory and application (Bonwell & Eison, 1991; Erskine, Leenders, & Mauffette-Leenders, 1998) and working through the challenges of making tough decisions. The case study method was used by chemistry faculty in the 1940s via didactic lecture and later in the 1960s by the Medical College of McMaster University in Canada, where students met in small groups with a facilitator and together diagnosed patients' ailments. Acknowledging this common thread, we classify these approaches and others as variants of the initial Harvard model of student engagement by teaching in context. Simply stated, "Case studies are stories with an educational message" (Herreid, 2007, p. xiv).

Accordingly, this chapter begins with an overview of the various case study methods from the college teaching literature. Then we will explore case study methods for teaching leadership. Finally, we provide some examples of case study methods, including activities and assignments, in leadership education contexts.

The Role of Leadership Educators: Transforming Learning, pp. 189–203
Copyright © 2018 by Information Age Publishing

CASE STUDY METHODS

The case study refers to a written description of a problem or situation for analysis. In many instances, case studies are stories about situations (including characters, issues, and environmental factors), with a set of facts, arranged in chronological order, specifically crafted to promote engaged discussion and focused analysis. The student's role begins by reading and analyzing the case, identifying the objectives and goals of key characters, and putting him or herself in each character's shoes. Accordingly, this first-person analysis incorporates the evaluation of resources, constituencies, and limitations; the nature and sources of conflicts and behaviors; and decision making (and the implications of each decision). Additionally, students should apply relevant theoretical paradigms and constructs, reciprocally reinforcing theory from practice and practice from theory (McDade, 1995). Although a case study is most often analyzed through facilitated in-class discussion, a case can also be the foundation for simulations, role-plays, written exercises, and a wide variety of other pedagogical methods. Likewise, case studies vary in their utility for much of the same reasons as any other group of instructional strategies.

Considering this variance, learning outcomes associated with case study methods may be quite different from those of traditional lectures or small-group discussions. Specifically, the learning outcomes associated with the case methods are not typically knowledge acquisition but instead critical thinking processes that have been modeled for students by the instructor or their peers and in which they have actively participated (McDade, 1995). Further, instructors who plan to use case study methods prepare differently. For example, they might prepare an outline of questions to facilitate discussion, analysis, and application, as opposed to an outline of statements for a lecture. The result of these preparatory differences is a classroom experience that differs greatly from a traditional question-and-answer session and instead develops through a progression of thinking, goes beyond the specific story, includes the students and instructor in dialogue, and allows students to generalize to similar situations and experiences (Herreid, 2011; McDade, 1995). At this point, it may be helpful to explore a few of the most common case study methods, beginning first with three in-class approaches—lecture, discussion, and small group—and concluding with two distinct approaches associated with the use of an individual case—dialogue and direct.

In the lecture method of the case study, the instructor takes on the role of the storyteller. Herreid (2011) argued that this is the weakest way to enhance learning using cases because the lecture cases are still lectures, albeit more interesting and entertaining than typical lectures. Yet lecture materials are often not retained in most students' minds for long. The discussion method is conducted by an instructor who calls on students to discuss the case at hand, intending for critical thoughts and analysis to emerge via discourse. As stylistic choices, the discussion method can be conducted as a cross-examination, debates, symposia, trials, or public hearings. However, a limitation of this method is that only one or a few students are engaged in the discussion at any moment while the rest of the class is passively attending (Herreid, 2011). A third approach, the small-group method, is completed in a group that is small enough to deeply engage in discussion. This method promotes collaborative and cooperative learning (Johnson, Johnson, & Smith, 2006), is more effective than lecture methods (Johnson & Johnson, 1989), and is especially effective in promoting diversity of opinion, respect for divergent views, and for improving the expression of ideas. Additionally, the small-group method provides opportunities for students to teach other students—an approach Svinicki and McKeachie (2011) coined as the most effective method of teaching resulting in the greatest retention (Herreid, 2011).

Another range of utility exists within the use of individual cases. Here, we will discuss the dialogue and direct case methods to illustrate this point. In the dialogue method, the instructor directs students to create a dialogue between two "experts" on a controversial topic (Herreid, 2007). Then the experts (e.g., Kerry and Dave) hold opposing views on a question, such as climate change. Kerry and Dave have at least 20 exchanges, 20 from Kerry and 20 from Dave. The exchanges should be substantive, intelligible, and referenced; the students must be able to use course content to justify any claims the discussants make. Finally, at the end of the dialogue, the students should declare their own position on the topic and their reasons for it. In the direct case method, a case is provided to the entire class, but students work on it alone (Cliff & Wright, 1996). In this classic method, the case includes a brief scenario with a series of questions. In some disciplines (e.g., anatomy and physiology), there is only one correct answer for each question, and the purpose of the case is to emphasize factual information, whereas in other disciplines (e.g., ethics), there may be multiple interpretations, and the purpose of the case is to promote discussion.

CASE STUDY METHODS IN LEADERSHIP EDUCATION

When we use the case study method to teach leadership, there are multiple ways to frame case studies. Although the educational message is often related to leadership decision-making processes, it does not always need to be leader-centric. Instead, case studies can and should be focused on the process of leadership, where either the process is the primary focus or being relational in nature is the central focus. The case study method is a popular and an effective instructional strategy in leadership education because the nature of our discipline is social, behavioral, and relational—it is almost always about the interaction of and relationships between and among people. Yet the method is often criticized for excluding student experiences (Cova, Kassis, & Lanou, 1993; McCarthy & McCarthy, 2006), being nonrealistic (McCarthy & McCarthy, 2006), and lacking student participation in the narrative (Cunliffe, 2002). Similarly, drawbacks might surface when an instructor introduces an inaccessible case study; that is, a case where the context, characters, or situation in the case are so disparate from students' reality that they are unable to relate and therefore little learning occurs. Effective leadership educators construct cases that are both representative of the learning outcomes and are framed in accessible ways for students. Considering leadership content and lived experiences of students can maximize the effectiveness of case study methods in leadership learning. For example, consider providing scenarios and decision-making dilemmas in contexts relevant to the student experience, such as cases from Marshall and Hornak's (2008) *A Day in the Life of a College Student Leader: Case Studies for Undergraduate Leaders*, which contains a considerable among of case studies in undergraduate students' contexts, including Greek life, living/learning communities, athletics, residence halls, and student organizations. Other approaches to improve case-based instruction involve creating live cases out of news items (McWilliams & Nahavandi, 2006), increasing the role of narrative in learning (Goodrich, Irvine, & Boccher-Lattimore, 2005), and using creative writing techniques to analyze and evaluate cases in organizational ethics (Atkinson, 2008). Additionally, in a "reverse case study" method, students encode theory into their own cases; design the setting, plot, characters, conflict, and conclusion; and swap cases for analysis and decoding. In the following subsections, we explore and provide example applications and assignments for many of the aforementioned case study methods.

Individual and Direct Case Methods in Leadership Education

The most common case study method in leadership education is the individual or direct approach, where the instructor assigns a case study for students to read, analyze, and then engage in discussion. Many leadership textbooks and their course or instructor's guides (e.g., Bolman & Deal, 2013; DuBrin, 2015; Northouse 2016; Scott & Davis, 2007) include myriad case studies associated with the leadership theories, models, and concepts presented in each chapter. Presented alongside each case study are a series of questions designed to connect theory to practice for student learners. As a general approach, we often assign a case study or two—or allow students to pick from several if there are more than two to choose from in each chapter or unit—along with other readings and respond to questions to provide an alternative and complimentary method of learning from their own experiences. In class, the facilitation is simple and direct, but feel free to use a variation of think-pair-share by having students share their responses to the questions with a partner before moving into small groups or sharing with the rest of the class.

Case in Point

This challenging approach popularized by Heifetz (1994) and Parks (2005) combines the seminar, simulation, presentation of ideas and perspectives (through lecture, reading, and film), discussion and dialogue, clinical-therapeutic practice, coaching, the laboratory, the art studio, writing as a form of disciplined reflection, and the case study method. Case in point is a reflective, immersive, and ideally reflexive exercise. This method uses the actions and behaviors of the individuals participating, as well as focusing on the group they are working with. Parks (2005) particularly stresses the case-in-point method as a powerful pedagogical tool that gives students multiple situations, concepts, and images to work with as they think about experiences that they may not have had (Garvin, 2003; Parks, 2005). This experiential framework, borrowed from John Dewey, draws on practical experience but is usually somewhat removed from the actual, immediate experience of the student.

According to Parks (2005), in the search for a methodology to teach further below the neck—the default settings that people act from in a crisis—case-in-point teaching and learning seeks to make optimal use of the student's own past and immediate experience. In case-in-point teaching, what occurs in the classroom is an occasion for learning and practicing leadership within a social group. Correspondingly, the class is recognized as a social system inexorably composed of several different factions and impacted by multiple forces. Here, the student's responsibility is to make progress as well as understand and practice leadership. Likewise, it is the instructor's responsibility to offer ideas and frameworks but then wait for a case to emerge in the process of the class, using the explicit and underlying issues that surface, connecting them to the course content. Additionally, the instructor must reflect to the class as it is happening, asking, "How can I use what is happening in class right now to illustrate the content I want the class to learn?" Put another way, the instructor must imagine that any length of time (e.g., the most recent 10 minutes of class) was a case. Then the instructor works to use it to illustrate the themes, concept, or skill they are trying to present—the challenge is to create and facilitate a live encounter between the experience of the learner and the idea (Parks, 2005).

The case-in-point method assists leadership educators with two key elements of leadership development. First, this specific instructional strategy more realistically prepares participants to have stamina and resilience to work with others in the difficulties of change to practice adaptability. Second, it requires educators to generate an increased awareness of themselves, their impact, and the systems of which they are a part.

To further explain this approach, Heifetz (1994) uses the metaphor of a dance floor and a balcony. The dance floor is where the action is taking place, and the balcony is where the observers can read the larger pattern of what is going on below and figure out how to intervene in ways that will improve the experience for everyone. Applying this metaphor, the instructor remains the facilitator but is also practicing leadership—skillfully allowing enough disequilibrium to help the group move from unexamined assumptions about leadership to understanding and acting in tune with the art and practice of leadership (Parks, 2005).

Parks addressed the issue of transferability of this approach by echoing the sentiments of Shulman (2005) and Fink (2013). Educators from a variety of backgrounds can employ this method because they each bring a different style and set of talents to the work, and because they share: (a) a curiosity about how to practice a quality of leadership education that can more adequately address change on behalf of the common good; (b) and informed respect for the process of human growth and development, and (c) a willingness to take on a mode of working that challenges both their own and others' assumptions about how teaching and learning take place.

Multimedia

The case study is most often constructed as a written case. However, with the advent of YouTube and the emergence of TED talks, among other media outlets, cases might include videos or video clips, Twitter, or other social media feeds. More formalized collections such as Stanford's Leadership in Focus, which is a collection of case vignettes, videos, and other resources intended to enhance leadership development, may also be worthwhile sources for leadership education cases. Cases may also come from popular television shows or movies (Smith, 2009) and may be accessed via Netflix, Hulu, and other video streaming services.

Multimedia allow leadership educators to teach leadership theory in new and inventive ways, which capture students' attention (Raffo, 2013), provides a catalyst for thoughtful discussion (Graham, Sincoff, Baker, & Ackerman, 2003), and generates dialogue to demystify difficult or complex points (J. R. Williams, 2006). For example, Raffo (2013) suggests using the video "Leadership Lessons From Dancing Guy" (Sivers, 2010) to teach the concept of followership. In this video, a lone dancer in a large outdoor music amphitheater gets a crowd to join him. The scene and narration provide a humorous learning tool to further stimulate students' thinking about followership from the postindustrial paradigm. Raffo (2013) recommends following the video with a class discussion, activities, and guided reflections, thus demonstrating how case studies can be paired with other instructional strategies.

Discussion Boards

As discussed earlier in this chapter and introduced in Chapter 10, in-class case discussions are facilitated by instructors through active questioning, directly challenging students, and building on previous relevant contributions from a variety of sources. Facilitating the case method online—through discussion boards—offers a more emergent and arguably thoughtful instructional design. Based on information collected during conversations with various business faculty, Rollag (2010) proposed that discussion board, case-based learning is more effective because (a) students can take time to formulate and edit their responses and are able to contribute more than once (because discussions typically transpire over several days); and (b) the online forum is less stress-inducing, allowing for a larger number of students who have access to appropriate technology to engage in the conversation and demonstrate mastery of the course content. Additionally, discussion boards produce an archive of the conversation for faculty and students to revisit. Although asynchronous case discussions can be convenient, it takes time and knowledge of the discussion board system to adequately construct, facilitate, wrap up, and assess discussions. Frequently, however, instructors who employ these methods reported struggling to build personal connections with students and the inability to rely on visual cues present in the face-to-face classroom. We offer this instructional strategy, recognizing that any instructors who choose to employ it should also consider and proactively prepare to plan around its shortcomings, both those inherent to the medium as well as those represented by their specific students' ability to engage in this manner.

Competition-Based

One of the unique features of the case study method is the organic and constructive nature of the analysis. Whereas some cases may have generally agreed-on solutions, many hold their value in offering myriad resolutions for discussion. One popular method for capitalizing on this feature is to promote competition, with respect to case analysis, among students (Atkinson, 2014).

To illustrate this approach, we reimagined a semester-long virtual team assignment to include a case study competition, similar in many aspects to the International Leadership Association (ILA) Student Case Competition, in which students from different institutions must explore and provide a solution for a particular case in leadership. The competition allows student teams to vie against one another in a contest, where teams analyze a real-world case involving contemporary leadership issues. During the semester, students collaborate in established teams, mostly virtually, to prepare and evaluate their peer teams' Case Study Brief, Presentation Showcase, and Final Presentation. Each phase integrates group work as well as the application, synthesis, integration, evaluation, and creation of knowledge. Accordingly, the stated learning objectives for this activity were: (a) develop a deeper understanding and appreciation of the complexity of leadership in practice in various contexts; (b) apply leadership theory and research to a real-world scenario; (c) gain experience in presenting ideas and leadership analyses in a professional setting; and (d) engage in case study dialogue and constructive criticism to strengthen the case analysis. We include details of this example below (for a similar activity, see Bailey, Sass, Swiercz, Seal, & Kayes, 2005).

Example

Case Study Competition		
Round One—Case Study Brief: **Teams will**	**WEIGHT**	**CONSIDER THIS…**
Grasp of the issues, feasibility of recommendations	50%	Does the team have an understanding of all the facets? Do they correctly identify the problems before recommending solutions? Are solutions feasible?
Demonstrated relationship between theory and practice	20%	Does the case demonstrate an understanding of human behavior, leadership theories, and the ability to apply them?
Awareness of the complex nature of leadership	20%	Does the team understand what is possible and what is not? Do they have knowledge of the limitations and the responsibilities of leaders?
Well organized, well supported	10%	Is the document professionally and academically sound?
Round Two—Presentation Showcase: Team members should build on their cases using instructor and peer feedback. Each team must prepare a digital presentation according to the guidelines below:		

(Example continues on next page)

Case Study Competition (Continued)

CRITERIA	WEIGHT	CONSIDER THIS...
Organization, well presented	20%	Is the presentation self-explanatory? Does it include all salient points?
Articulation, persuasiveness, comprehensiveness	50%	Are your peers thoughtful about the problems, understand the feasibility of, and believe in their recommendations? Understand leadership in organizations?
Team participation and response to questions	30%	Is there evidence that all team members have contributed? Do all team members fully understand the case, their analysis, and recommendations?

Round Three—Final Presentations: Final Presentations will include comprehensive material from the term. Accordingly, each team should build on case analysis, using the material from their term for further learning and supporting material. Please see below for specific instructions.

The Final Presentation allows teams to formally present their case, incorporating all they have gathered from their instructor and other teams. The Final Presentation will be 15 minutes for each team, in addition to 5 minutes of questions from the instructor and at least one representative from each of the other teams. Student teams should have a strong, prepared presentation on their analysis of the situation, from start to finish.

Round Three Evaluation Criteria

CRITERIA	WEIGHT	CONSIDER THIS...
Articulation, persuasiveness, and comprehensiveness	50%	Are the students thoughtful about the problems, understand the feasibility of, and believe in their recommendations? Understand leadership in organizations?
CRITERIA	WEIGHT	CONSIDER THIS...
Team participation and response to questions	50%	Is there evidence that all team members have contributed? Do all team members fully understand the case, their analysis, and recommendations?
Team participation and response to questions	50%	Is there evidence that all team members have contributed? Do all team members fully understand the case, their analysis, and recommendations?

Case Preparation: In preparing their submissions, teams may explore any public information source that would be accessible by any scholar, student, or professional consulting group. Teams may consult books or articles, textbooks, search libraries, use the Internet, and so forth.

Assistance: Teams may be advised by faculty or other; however, advisers, coaches, or other individuals may not contribute to any of the team's products (i.e., case brief, poster, and presentation). Teams are free to receive verbal feedback on initial drafts and practice presentations.

Interviews as Case Studies

Other widely used instructional strategies in leadership education are interviews where students observe or interview an individual leading others effectively or ineffectively and report their findings to the instructor/class. In this strategy, students interview a leader in their context, and the interview becomes the case. The assignment, grounded in constructivist (Bush, 2006) and social learning (Bandura, 1977) theories, allows students to learn to deconstruct the complexities of leadership while applying leadership theory to practice. Through this process, students have opportunities to reflect on how they construct, define, and make meaning of the practice of leadership (D. N. Smith & Roebuck, 2009). An example of this appears in the *Instructor's Guide for Exploring Leadership: For College Students Who Want to Make a Difference*, 2nd edition (Owen et al., 2007).

Example

Leadership Interview Paper

Option #1- Students will identify a person who is part of an organization working to make social change. Try to meet face to face with interviewee; if this is not an option, technology-enhanced options (Google Hangout, Skype, FaceTime) are encouraged. Formulate your questions in advance. Areas to cover include:

o   Basic biographical information and information about any organizational affiliation.

o   Brief history of how they worked to address the social issue at hand. What successes or changes have they seen?

o   What pressing problems are they still facing?

o   What other individuals or organizations have they partnered in change efforts?

o   What suggestions would they have for college students interested in having an impact on the issue? How do they define leadership? Service? Do they see them as connected?

o   What other resources (organizations, websites, readings) do they recommend?

o   Write a paper connecting insights gained from your interview with the elements of the Relational Leadership Model (Komives et al., 2013).

We have modified this assignment over the years to:

Option #2- Interview someone who you believe is a good or even a great leader. Choose a leader who is not a student, a relative, or your immediate supervisor. Find out their philosophy of leadership and how they apply it. Additional, suggested questions are available on our Blackboard page. Your task is to write a 3- to 5-page paper that includes the following:

o   A summary of each of your "interviewee's" answers to your questions.

o   Your reactions to each of your interviewee's responses, including how they impact your impressions of their leadership effectiveness and how you might change your own leadership behaviors accordingly.

o   A summary of what you learned from the interview.

In our experiences, students appreciate having some suggested interview questions to guide their interviews. This idea emerged after noticing some serious missed opportunities from students (e.g., they interviewed great leaders but asked them nonleadership or superfluous questions). Others have suggested limiting students from interviewing family members, close friends, and fellow undergraduates (if applicable). Other practical suggestions include asking students to submit the name and background of leader they intend to interview early enough in the semester for instructors to give feedback on those choices, keeping a database of the interviewees, and considering using the interview data for a qualitative research study (D. N. Smith & Roebuck, 2009) when appropriate consent and approvals are in place.

Guest Speakers and Panels as Case Studies

Due to the dialogical nature of leadership and leadership education (Berkovich, 2014), guest speakers and panels, in which students listen to a guest speaker(s) or lecturer(s) discuss their personal leadership experiences, are widely used in leadership education (Jenkins, 2012, 2013, 2016, 2017a). These forms of case study methods improve students' knowledge through exposure to the topic of leadership (Conger, 1992) and are observer-oriented (Jenkins, 2012, 2013). These activities may be less inclusive and experiential, yet students report favoring lectures on the topic of leadership, observing effective leaders, watching films about leadership, and listening to stories about leadership (Allen & Hartman, 2009). Leveraging these learner affinities toward case study pedagogies can be an effective means of attaining leadership learning objectives.

Just like with the interview assignments, practical suggestions have emerged from frequent leadership educator use of this pedagogy. Just as you would review a book, article, or video, prior to assigning it, effective leadership educators thoroughly research speakers and panelists. For example, a leadership educator we know once brought in a panel of female colleagues from across the Chicago metro area to talk about women's leadership. Although this instructor had thought out representing three generational groups (i.e., someone in her 50s, someone in her 40s, and someone in her 30s), what they didn't know was that one was divorced, the other two were single, none had children, and all three had perceived they had sacrificed their personal lives for their career. This singular perspective is not the only story the instructor meant to offer. As advice, we suggest digging deeper and taking time to understand the perspectives of invited guests rather than making immediate assumptions.

Other suggestions relate to the panel's focus on intentionality, specifically regarding who is invited, what they are invited to talk about, the topics being discussed, how the prospective panelists "do leadership," and how relevant and representative the panelists' work is to students' contexts. The key is to construct and provide a bridge to students' own lives.

Stories and Storytelling

Stories are students listening to the narratives of others, and storytelling is when students engage in sharing their own personal narratives. In both stories and storytelling, highlighting various aspects of leadership can be a powerful pedagogical method in leadership education. As we discussed in Chapter 2, creating personal narratives and sharing them as educators are influential on our identity as leadership educators. Using this same framework as an instructional strategy for students can be just as powerful for leadership learning. Discussing the power of stories and storytelling can help students understand how important stories and storytelling are in leadership.

Example

Six Stories You Need to Know How to Tell

Read Chapter 1: "The Six Stories You Need to Know How to Tell" from Simmons and Lipman's (2006) *The Story Factor.* Then respond to the following:

1. Which type of story do you think is most effective? Why?

2. Choose one of the six types of stories—Who I Am; Why I Am Here; My Vision; Teaching; Values in Action; or "I Know What You Are Thinking"—and compose your own based on personal experiences. Be prepared to share your story in class.

In a related example from a module focused on "Developing a Multicultural Mindset," Torrez (2013) had students watch the TED Talk "The Danger of a Single Story" as a framework for discussing social identity. This varies from our media-based example above of "dancing guy," in that the video showcases a keynote speaker versus a specific scene and narrator. However, similar to the prior example, this module also ends with discussion questions.

Current and Local Events

Because leadership is an applied discipline, we can find examples of individuals engaging in the process of leadership all around us. Whether we choose to use the president of our institution, the student body collectively advocating for needs, local community activists, or our national and international political scenes, we have plenty of examples to use as case studies. For example, the "*New York Times* in Leadership" offers "teachers, scholars, practitioners and students the opportunity to connect and discuss real-world leadership examples through various platforms, online and offline" (The *New York Times* in Leadership, 2017, para. 1). To capitalize on this, consider beginning class meetings with a discussion of current events from your campus, local, national, or international news sources. These conversations can improve students' understanding of course content, illustrate real-world application of concepts and theories (Auster & Wylie, 2006), and provide opportunities to talk about the world and reality while also learning culturally shared ways of understanding leadership (Merriam & Caffarella, 1999).

Another variation of the current event and case study pairing is the "live case" offered by McWilliams and Nahavandi (2006). In this model, students select a current event that involves a current societal issue or problem (they suggest ethical violations as a topic) and write a case about it. Students then present their case to their peers and facilitate a debate about the challenges and issues outlined in their case as well as the actions that could or should have been taken. This activity has been shown to allow for the application of concepts, create emotional engagement in the case, is relevant, holds students accountable for their position, and creates a setting that encourages students to think critically (McWilliams & Nahavandi, 2006).

Finally, consider the following advice from two experienced leadership educators gathered from interviews from Jenkins' (2017b) study.

Example

LE1: So, like last night, and things come to me at the spur of the moment ellipses I had this slide which was what are the differences between character and virtues and moral and ethics and values, really kind of bland and then like, "lets us talk about Bill Clinton in the second term, talk about Bill." And I kind of got provocative with them and they kind of got in to the topic and I said, "Let's talk about ISIS." From your average Syrian without much vision, is ISIS a moral organization, are they behaving morally? And so we got in to this provocative discussion and it just turned up the heat on, "let us talk about Catholicism and where has it failed along the way" so I might kind of turn up the heat and by being more provocative on the topic and talk it like bringing up, "let us talk about Abraham Lincoln in the eyes of the Southern slave holder" and so I kind of went there last night and people really got in to the conversation, the room lit up, right, and some of it is an art, kind of what I am going to introduce in the moment and what is happening in the room. Well, what I try not to do, and I've said this already, is just go to the same ones over and over, I want it to always feel what is going to happen next?

(Example continues on next page)

Example (Continued)

> LE2: Sometimes I will give them case studies and give them all different roles to play. For example, you know how Ohio State's tradition of jumping in the lake during the Michigan game? We had a great discussion on sort of social responsibility that was great. So, we had some case studies around we sort of tricked them into the conversation but I had a grad student help me with that class and so we wrote some case studies around that sort of student safety/tradition type things ... but after that we did that discussion it was the day of the jump you know that we did that. So, they were leaving our class, our class ended at five and they were literally like going to get ready for the jump. So, we knew we have got to capitalize on this, this is going to be a great conversation around ethical leadership and social responsibility. And the next day one of the students came and told us that she had been to the lake and she jumped in and there was a girl like off on the side and she was shivering, I mean it is cold and November and she looked kind of disoriented and she was like hovering in a ball and so the girl that was walking by who was in our class thought to herself; am I going to walk by this girl or am I going to think about what I was taught in the class today and am I going to help her. And she like helped her and took her into a warm classroom, she was intoxicated and so she really needed help and kind of nursed her back to health. I think she even ended up taking her to the hospital I am not sure. But it was interesting that she was like I don't know if I hadn't had that discussion if I had just been in party mode and like not even give her a second look.

Reverse Case Study

Atkinson (2014) offers an example of the "reverse case study" method. In this example, students are sorted into teams and challenged to use creative writing techniques to encode theory into their cases. After teams drafted their case studies, they were exchanged among groups to then be analyzed. It is important to note that Wasserman (1994) suggested using creative writing in case preparation for teachers, and Laditka and Houck (2006) suggested using student-developed cases in learning. However, Atkinson (2008) further suggested using creative writing techniques in student-developed cases to enhance the method and overall student experience. A case-based instructional method that uses some creative writing techniques suggested by Atkinson (2008) entails setting, plot, characters, conflict, and conclusion. By combining these creative writing metaphors with leadership theory, students would achieve what Ward (2001) called "conceptual combination" and "creative cognition," which involves merging disparate concepts to create something new and thereby enhancing creativity. In short, you should prepare students for the creative writing endeavors they're expected to live out.

PEDAGOGY TO PRACTICE

Case study pedagogy can be a powerful vehicle for leadership learning. In summary, we provide a few points highlighting case study as a leadership education pedagogy and how to potentially put this instructional strategy into practice, which can transform leadership learning.

Pedagogy Overview

- Case study has multiple meanings: it is an activity and a pedagogy, an individual, group, and community activity; it can be in person or online, about a person in the room or a historical figure; it can involve hearing a person's story or a student telling their own. This broad array of connotations presents educators with an assortment of opportunities to apply case study to their work.
- Most often a case study is a story about a situation (including characters, issues, and environmental factors), with a set of facts, arranged in chronological order, specifically crafted to promote engaged discussion and focused analysis.
- Individual and direct case studies help individual students see themselves, the world around them, and their place in it differently by filtering their own learning through constructed conditions.
- Case study competitions, interviews, guest speakers and panels, stories and storytelling, and using current events are all ways case studies are used as an instructional strategy.

Transforming Leadership Learning Through Case Study Methods

- Interviews as cases give students the opportunity to see leadership and leading through someone else's leader identity and critically deconstruct their own leading to ultimately reformulate relationships toward greater effectiveness.
- Guest speakers and panels as cases demonstrate the wide array of leadership identities and leading attitudes and behaviors which can lead to important self-reflection and introspection.
- Current events provide excellent content for case study examples in leadership education. With a leadership learning framework, current events connect application of leadership content to situations occurring daily.
- Case-in-point method applies active experiential learning by using the moments happening in the classroom to dissect human intention, interaction, and development to learn about leadership.

CHAPTER 12

REFLECTION AS
LEADERSHIP PEDAGOGY

Active learning involves *experiential learning* (through observing and doing) and *reflection* on what and how one is learning (Fink, 2013). Reflection, the process whereby we construct and make meaning of our experiences, has a central role in applied learning (Ash & Clayton, 2009). As pedagogy, reflection comes in many forms, such as keeping a diary or journal, stream-of-conscious writing, or generating a summary of activities (Ash & Clayton, 2009). Although often misunderstood or seen as unnecessary, reflection "can easily be associated with 'touchy-feely' introspection, too subjective to evaluate in a meaningful way and lacking in the rigor required for substantive academic work" (Ash & Clayton, 2009, p. 27). When designed with intentionality, reflection can promote significant learning, including problem-solving skills, higher order reasoning, integrative thinking, goal clarification, openness to new ideas, adoption of new perspectives, and systemic thinking (Conrad & Hedin, 1990; Eyler & Giles, 1999). Structured reflection can also serve as both a program outcome and a learning outcome (Volpe White & Guthrie, 2016), which is important to note.

Effective and intentionally designed reflection-based pedagogy emphasizes the link between reflection and action. That is, a metacognitive process of continuous intertwining of thinking and doing—thought and action—and the relationship between them (Ash & Clayton, 2009; Schon, 1983). According to Ash and Clayton (2009), when understood this way, reflection becomes "critical reflection." Critical reflection generates learning,

The Role of Leadership Educators: Transforming Learning, pp. 205–217
Copyright © 2018 by Information Age Publishing
All rights of reproduction in any form reserved.

deepens learning, and documents learning. Performing these tasks requires the structure and guidance of a skilled facilitator—it is not enough to just tell students, "it is now time to reflect" (Welch, 1999, p. 1). In fact, many students struggle with forced reflections (White, 2012). Instead, begin with the end in mind (Covey, 1989; Wiggins & McTighe, 1998) by identifying the desired learning outcomes and then intentionally selecting reflection-based pedagogies to meet them. Accordingly, the next section describes the application of reflection-based pedagogies, as well as applied examples, in leadership education contexts. We decided to combine these two sections—reflection-based pedagogy generally and applications in leadership education specifically—in this chapter because of the inextricable link between leadership development and reflection (Densten & Gray, 2001) as well as intentional coverage of content.

As you read about these reflective instructional strategies, consider Ash and Clayton's (2009) *Questions to Guide the Design of Reflection Strategies and Mechanisms*:

1. When and how often will reflection occur? (Before, during, and after the experience, or, will students reflect iteratively such that reflection builds on itself over time?);
2. Where will reflection occur? (In or outside class?);
3. Who will facilitate and/or participate in reflection? (e.g., instructors, members of the community/workplace, peers);
4. How will feedback be provided and/or reflection products graded? (What is the relationship between the amount of feedback, the level of expected outcomes, the reflection products, and the overall grade?);
5. What mediums will be used for the activity (e.g., written assignments, worksheets, photos, media, games, drawings, discussion boards, in-class discussion, out-of-class reflection sessions, concept maps);
6. What prompts will be used to guide the activity?;
7. What products will demonstrate the learning the activity generates? (e.g., essays, journals, PowerPoint, poster, or oral presentations); and
8. What criteria will be used to assess the learning?

REFLECTION IN LEADERSHIP EDUCATION

Regardless of whether an educational program contains a specific experiential component, leadership is inherently an experiential pedagogy. As such, leadership educators should build reflection into courses, create opportunities to reflect with students, set clear expectations regarding structure and assessment, and provide feedback on reflections (Guthrie & Thompson, 2010). By creating environments that support and value reflection, educators embody this pedagogy. As Volpe White and Guthrie (2016) clearly state, "Reflection is essential to applying leadership learning to students' lives" (p. 70).

The capacity to reflect relates directly to how effectively individuals can learn from their personal experiences (Boud, Keogh, & Walker, 1985). To be fair, reflection opportunities come in many forms within the leadership classroom and curriculum. These can be written reflection activities in the form of journals, essays about readings, verbal reflection in reaction to class discussions, questions posed, and current events to programs that formally engage students in completing vision- and goal-setting activities and other projects to personalize the concepts to the individual (Eich, 2008). Among these reflection-based pedagogies are two broad learning and developmental outcomes for students: (a) learning more about oneself (e.g., developing future visions and goals, gaining a sense of purposefulness; and becoming better able to make decisions aligned with one's goals, values, and identity), and (b) developing a meaningful leadership philosophy or framework to help systematize and analyze one's thoughts and actions and to grow as a leader. Conger (1992) explains that these techniques are "based, generally, on the assumption that leaders are individuals who are deeply in touch with their personal dreams and talents and who will act to fulfill them," as well as, "induce reflection on behaviors, personal values, and desires" (pp. 45–46). Reflective opportunities that guide the meaning-making process also assist in the growth of students' identity and cognitive and moral development (Jones & Abes, 2004; Strain, 2005; Wang & Rodgers, 2006). Correspondingly, we will cover in depth reflective activities that pair opportunities for student exploration of experience with practice or action (i.e., experimentation).

Personal Reflection, Self-Development, and Self-Awareness

One of the chief findings from the leadership education literature is the link between leadership development and reflection-based activities that provide opportunities for exploration of individual development and awareness (Densten & Gray, 2001; Murry, 1992). This connects to the meta-cognition aspect of the leadership learning framework (see Chapter 4). Reflection-based activities unlock many key developmental opportunities in a learner's experience and have been shown to improve critical thinking, promote growth in self-awareness and self-actualization, stimulate the development of new knowledge, increase student learning, and foster meaningful personal insights more than lecture and reading assignments alone (Burbach, Matkin, & Fritz, 2004; Buschlen & Guthrie, 2014). Moreover, reflection-based activities provide a meaningful way for leaders to gain a genuine understanding of themselves; their perceptions of experiences and events; their relationships; their feelings, needs, expectations, and values; and self-care and balance in their leadership roles (Densten & Gray, 2001; Eich, 2008; Hughes, Ginnett, & Curphy, 1999; White, 2014). In considering each of these vital leadership learning outcomes, reflection represents "an essential facet of leadership education" (Buschlen & Guthrie, 2014, p. 61). Furthermore, reflection is important for leadership development because it can provide leaders with a variety of insights into how to frame problems differently, to look at situations from multiple perspectives, or to better understand followers (Densten & Gray, 2001). Conversely, avoiding self-development and reflection could allow students to forget developmental activities that entail both uncomfortable emotional and cognitively complex ways to view leadership (Allen & Hartman, 2009).

A popular individual reflection-based pedagogy used to curate self-development and challenge participants to focus on topics such as goals, personal mission, and experiences is the "Individual" or "Personal Development Plan" (Allen & Hartman, 2009). This activity is a process through which students learn more about themselves, develop future visions and goals, and become more purposefully authentic. They practice making congruent decisions through the preparation of a meaningful leadership philosophy, model, or framework to analyze their own thoughts and actions and take personal responsibility in their life and leadership (Eich, 2008). While popular in practice (e.g., Owen, Komives, Lucas, & McMahon, 2007), this pedagogy lacks an extensive literature base (Allen & Hartman, 2009). Equally, these activities are easy to assign, but students often fall victim to poor implementation and a lack of follow-through. Unless they are linked to organizational systems, return on investment is unlikely. To combat this, effective educators help students evaluate how their interests and motivation toward leadership development may be aided or hindered through self-development opportunities. For example, challenge your students to consider self-selecting activities and matching their learning styles and levels of preparation (Allen & Hartman, 2009).

As an example of this sequence, we have included an activity from an introductory leadership class (adapted from Owen et al., 2007). This sequence can be used with anything in-between—that is, in this example, the "in-between" is the duration of the course—such as a project, service learning, study abroad, or other structured and time-bound leadership development experience (Buschlen & Guthrie, 2014; Preston & Peck, 2016).

Example

Who Am I?

This three-page paper should include your own personal mission statement. It should be written to provide insight about the real you. Answering the question "Who am I?" is the first step in becoming a great leader! For example, what is your purpose in life? What values are important to you and what do you stand for? What do you want to be and do in your life (your life goals)? What attributes and capabilities are important to you? What experiences have influenced your development? What is your theory of leadership and what role will leadership play in life? The paper should be written to give insight into the real you. Answering these questions is the first step to becoming an effective leader!

Leadership Action Plan

This assignment will allow you to reflect on what you learned about yourself during the semester in relation to your capacity to demonstrate leadership. In addition to reflecting on what you learned about your leadership capacity, reflect on what you see as your leadership strengths and weaknesses and how you will take advantage of both in the future. Briefly describe the leadership philosophy you have developed throughout this class. Has it changed since the beginning of class and what you wrote about in your "Who Am I"? If so, how? Describe two action steps you can take to continue to develop your leadership in the future.

Critical Reflection in Leadership Education

The teaching of leadership is conducive to student-driven learning, where contemporary theory is linked to practical experience (Densten & Gray, 2001). Consequently, a common challenge when discussing leadership theories is connecting these theories to students' lives in a relevant way. Underpinning theories may only make sense through practice, but practice makes sense only through reflection as enhanced by theory (Raelin, 1997). We suggest navigating the bridge between theory and reflection through the use of critical reflection; an "iterative process of returning to what one has studied, thought, experienced, done, and felt, and an autonomous but still relatively structured and disciplined process of synthesizing lessons, conclusions, uncertainties, and questions" (Harvey & Jenkins, 2014, p. 79). According to Harvey and Jenkins (2014), critical reflection serves to help integrate the academic study and experiential learning of leadership, stimulate individual growth, and enable students to enhance their leadership ability through evaluating the significance of their experiences from a leadership perspective. Our "Leader and Follower Experiences as a Source of Transformational Learning Model" reinforces this construct and process.

Moreover, critical reflection involves "a commitment to questioning assumptions and taken-for-granteds embodied in both theory and professional practice" (Reynolds, 1999, p. 538). The capacity to reflect relates

directly to how effectively individuals can learn from their personal experiences (Boud et al., 1985). Owen (2016) purports critical reflection goes
beyond critical thinking, requiring examination of power dynamics. Effective leadership programs are structured to induce students' adoption and
adaptation of critical perspectives in leadership, whether their own or
those of others (Harvey & Jenkins, 2014). In an example of this approach,
Owen (2016) describes a situation where critical reflection questions students to contemplate who is represented in the organization and who is
enacting formal and informal power. "Critical reflection invites students to
consider who benefits and who is silenced by service and leadership efforts"
(Owen, 2016, p. 39). Reflection can stimulate the dialectic energy of the
knowledge-experience interaction: theories may only come alive and make
sense through practice, but practice leads to purposeful learning in large
part through reflection as enhanced by theory (Raelin, 1997). Through
critical reflection, students can explore whether organizational members
have a voice in creating an organization's goals or programmatic priorities
(Owen, 2016).

Accordingly, the role of the effective leadership educator is to actively
engage learners in critical reflection within learning environments, using
processes that build on learners' existing knowledge and experiential
background. To do so, educators challenge students to integrate personal
experiences and reconstruct theories and philosophies of leadership, act
on new ideas, and challenge conventional thinking in both theory and
practice (Reynolds, 1999; Wisniewski, 2010). For example, students could
be required to reassess the influence they use in leadership situations to
achieve their desired results (Jenkins & Cutchens, 2011). However, experience is more than just the events themselves; it also involves the perceptions
of these events.

Leaders actively shape and construct their experiences by selectively
attending to particular situations. These perceptual sets are affected by
feelings, needs, prior experience, and expectations (Hughes, Ginnett, &
Curphy, 1999). Often leaders are unaware of their perceptual sets and
biases. Thus, an important function of leadership education is to provide
opportunities for student reflection so that students gain understanding of
how they perceive and interpret their observations. Reflecting on personal
perceptions and biases can be challenging but essential. Engaging students
on their hidden or unknown identities and experiences, providing feedback, and sharing with others what they might not be aware of is helpful
for changing potential biases and unproductive perceptions in the future.

Further, critical reflection is important for leadership development
because it can provide leaders with a variety of insights into how to
frame problems differently, look at situations from multiple perspectives,
or better understand followers (Densten & Gray, 2001). One approach

for facilitating this process is to empower students to seek out multiple forums for reflection beyond individual or written reflection. According to White (2014), students found great value in reflecting with a supervisor, family member, friend, mentor, faculty member, or coach. Thus, the use of critical reflection enables students to enhance their leadership ability through evaluating the significance of their experiences from a leadership perspective.

Yet engaging in critical reflection can create discomfort and dissonance (Dewey, 1933; Reynolds, 1999). This discomfort and dissonance comes from the potential discussion of the "systemic and institutionalized nature of oppression" (Owen, 2016, p. 39). As Fink (2013) and others assert, discomfort often means students are thinking in depth and consequently expanding their learning. Moreover, when reflection is absent, there is greater risk of making poor decisions and bad judgments (Brookfield, 1995). Student and leadership development must include a dynamic environment of strategic events with a heavy reliance on theoretical application of leadership knowledge with appropriate reflection (Hughes, Ginnett, & Curphy, 2006; Komives, 1996). We understand that creating these dynamic environments is a tall order, but as leadership educators, it is critical to work toward this type of learning environment. For example, without reflection, leaders may be convinced by past successes of their invincibility and fail to consider other viewpoints, with possibly disastrous consequences (Densten & Gray, 2001). Similarly, leaders may avoid reflecting on a course of action because such reflection might challenge their favorable perceptions of themselves (Conger, 1992). Keeping this in mind, we offer the following individual reflection-based pedagogical strategies.

Journaling

One of the most popular methods for facilitating reflection is through journaling. A journal is a sequential, dated chronicle of events and ideas, which includes the personal responses and reflections of the writer (or writers) on those events and ideas (Stevens & Cooper, 2009). Further, a journal has six defining attributes: It is written, dated, informal, flexible, private, and archival. Journals promote reflection on and learning from experience while reflection gives an individual an increased power of control (Dewey, 1933). It is not enough just to have an experience; reflection directs that experience to learning and deeper insights. Accordingly, reflective journaling activates students to reflect critically about their readings, experiences, and issues addressed in class, as well as examine hidden personal assumptions that influence personal responses and actions, and engage in creative and "out-of-comfort-zone" thinking. Journal writers can actively experiment with the ideas that motivate their actions and thus approach new experiences with fresh insights and the possibility for new learning (Kolb, 1984). As suggested by Guthrie and Bertrand Jones (2012), here are some specific journaling activities tailored for leadership education.

Example

Concept Maps: Students list key elements needed for a leadership project. Using the list, they create a concept map of the items, cluster like things, and identify relationships among the items.

Vocabulary: Students receive a list of key leadership vocabulary; they describe occurrences where they have encountered these ideas in their leadership experiences. This activity helps students to label their experience and connect the events to leadership.

Three-part journal: Students divide their journal entry into three parts, including (1) description of the activities, (2) analysis of how the activities relate to leadership, and (3) application to their personal or professional life.

Self-assessment: In the context of a leadership activity, students ask themselves: What kind of leader am I? What have I learned about leadership? How did I learn it? (Guthrie & Bertrand Jones, 2012, p. 58)

With any journaling activities, including the example above, we suggest maintaining informality, including allowing students a safe space to write that is free of the constraints and expectations of conventional grammar or spelling. Thus, a good journal entry is judged more by its willingness to take risks, voice confusions, and explore undeveloped ideas (or even projects), and the degree to which it furthers the development of voice and the ability to take the perspective of others. Nonetheless, the effectiveness of journaling activities depends on how the reflection assignment supports, reinforces, and helps students meet course objectives and learning outcomes. Finally, when students respond in writing to readings outside of class, usually in a "learning journal," they retain more and are more active during class discussion (the #1 pedagogy in the leadership classroom). Thus, having students keep learning journals addresses concerns that students are not doing the course readings and increases involvement (Brost & Bradley, 2006).

Grading Reflective Journals

One of the most popular questions we receive about reflective journals is whether to grade it and, if so, how? In their compelling book, *Journal*

Keeping: How to Use Reflective Writing for Learning, Teaching, Professional Insight and Positive Change, Stevens and Cooper (2009) contend that, to encourage students to probe deeply and critically reflect, we must create safety in expressing their beliefs and assumptions. One way to create a safe environment is to not read the journal at all—just check it for completion not content. Students often want feedback, and to get students' attention about journal writing, instructors need to actively engage with them. For example, by pointing out concepts they connected and commenting on aspects of their experiences that stand out, the instructor shows that he or she is actively engaged. Grading their work is another way to get students' attention about journal writing. If you choose to evaluate students' journals, consider providing preset criteria that answers the student question: "How is this going to be graded?" To answer this oft-posed question, Stevens and Cooper (2009) provide the following five-point assessment criteria, which is readily adaptable to leadership education contexts:

> 5 = Thoughts and feelings are purposeful and insightful. The content is either detailed or approached philosophically. The unique voice of the learner is present and sustained. Significant risks in thought may be evident. Readers can follow the entry easily.
>
> 4 = The thoughts and feelings expressed are purposeful— either insightful and general, or detailed and conventional. The expression is clear, easy to follow, and appropriate for the context.
>
> 3 = Thoughts and feelings are present but not always clearly connected to the purpose for language use. Language and thinking may be very conventional and lack development. Readers can follow the writer, but may need to work a bit to do so. The language is generally appropriate for the context.
>
> 2 = Thoughts and feelings are not consistent or connected but are related to the purpose and context. The content and expressions do no anticpate the audience. The writer knows what is meant but does not lead the reader through the intended meaning.
>
> 1 = The content is very confusing or even conflicting. It maybe only tangentially related to the intended purpose.

Additional Reflection-Based Pedagogies

The remaining parts of this chapter include information on various reflection-based pedagogies that may be used with large and small groups, technology-enhanced strategies, and example activities.

Reflection-Based Pedagogies for Groups

Group reflection is defined as a source of learning that often occurs after an activity or event within the context of a learning activity. The purpose is to help participants make connections and capture learning (Allen & Hartman, 2008). It can be difficult to separate group reflection as a single pedagogy because the interactive activities central to undergraduate leadership education almost always include a follow-up session of discussion questions and reflection. Please refer to Chapter 13 about more specifics in team-based learning, which provides information on facilitating group educational activities.

Reflective Discussion

Because learning is relational, dialogue and listening are essential elements for the reflective process (Guthrie & Bertrand Jones, 2012). As such, intentional engagement with peers, staff, or faculty encourages students to reflect on their own experiences, thoughts, or opinions. Hatcher and Bringle (1997) offer the following suggestions for structured discussions that we have tailored to leadership education:

- *Examples*. Educators ask students to cite examples of their experience that illustrate a leadership theory or concept. The group discussion allows the students to learn from each other.
- *Weekly dialogues*. Students participate in weekly structured dialogue about leadership with other student leaders either face to face or electronically.
- *Minute papers*. Students write for 1 minute about a leadership topic. The papers are then exchanged and discussed with peers.
- *Values clarification*. Students are asked to describe their feelings about leadership, describe their actions related to leadership, describe their thoughts about leadership, and describe the contradictions they experience related to leadership. (pp. 58–59)

Multimethod

Despite being less common than written reflections, students may benefit from reflection activities that engage them in discussion or creative activities (Odom, 2015; Roberts, 2008). Like debriefing (see Chapter 9), reflection can be captured in processes that range from photos to poetry, videos, games, drawing, and concept maps. To illustrate this, we offer the following example.

Example

Metaphor: Creating metaphors allows students to envision objects, persons, or concepts from a different viewpoint (Stevens & Cooper, 2009). Metaphor development may be an isolated exercise (e.g., as a vehicle for formulating and expressing a concept or theory of leadership) or a theme developed throughout the course of an experience (e.g., if you take students on a service trip, have them reflect periodically on how their experience is like the changing of seasons or the growth of a tree; Singh, 2010).

Example prompt: "Meaningful reflection is like…"

Dialogue: Dialogue in journaling is about creating a conversation between people, ideas or things. The dialogue format allows the student to distance him or herself from the subject, making them "the other" and thus allowing them to be objectified. "When we objectify an experience, a relationship, our feelings, our worries, and our obligations, we gain some control and we can look at them from a different perspective to understand them anew" (Steven & Cooper, 2009, p. 89). Consider having students dialogue with (a) significant or historical leaders; (b) current or future leaders of their organizations; (c) course topics (e.g., a leadership theory or model); (d) issues in their lives (e.g., ego, self-esteem, etc.); (e) objects or feelings; (f) contradictions or conflicts in thinking; (g) opposing points of view (e.g. supporters of and the opposition to gay marriage); (h) barriers or obstacles of their own progress; or (i) an inner mentor/voice. Here is an example from the 2012 ILA Global Conference (Espinola, Wells, & Jenkins, 2012):

Josie (J): Well, here we are again. Why won't you leave me alone?!

Procrastination (P): Josie, you know you love me—we're like besties!

J: No, really I am sick of you being part of my life. I need to get it together.

P: But we've always worked so well under the pressure. I think I keep you sharp.

J: I'm pretty sure you are limiting my potential. If I had more time to think and plan, I could do even more and with higher quality. I just need to invest more during my down time.

P: You'll never shake me. Together forever—I'm how you roll!

J: No, you're how I used to roll. From now on, I am going to do whatever it takes to avoid you, so I can minimize my stress and maximize my success!

Power sentences: As an alternative to the questions at the end of a chapter, ask students to select a set number of sentences from an assigned reading that made an impact on them—"power sentences." After each sentence, they must journal for a brief paragraph (2–3 sentences) about why the sentence stood out or had special meaning to them, how it applies to their life, and understanding of specific course concepts.

Technology-Enhanced Reflection

Although many of the aforementioned reflection-based pedagogies are transferable to distance learning modalities—almost anything a student might write in a journal could be typed into a digital applet—additional structure may be required. Specifically, like discussion-based pedagogies, the instructor must make clear the forum for which the reflection will be facilitated. Also consider whether the content students are providing is appropriate for public consumption or whether it should be shared only with the instructor. For example, consider posting guided questions on a learning management system-based discussion board focused around course materials-reinforced learning outcomes, requiring students to integrate applied experiences at internship or community service sites with theoretical concepts (Guthrie & McCracken, 2010b). In another example, Guthrie and McCracken (2010b) had students in an internship course write each time they were at their placements, and students in a service learning course write an entry for every 4 hours of community service. Students in their courses reported that maintaining written journals was a means of reflecting especially beneficial to their learning.

PEDAGOGY TO PRACTICE

In summary, we provide a few points highlighting reflection as a leadership education pedagogy and putting this instructional strategy into practice, which has the potential in transforming leadership learning.

Pedagogy Overview

- Active, experiential learning is incomplete without reflective activities to help participants make meaning of their learning experiences.
- Reflection is defined as the process whereby we construct and make meaning of our experience. Critical reflection encourages students to question assumptions and biases and observe and reflect critically on their experiences and/or observations.
- Reflection as a pedagogy has not only been described in the scholarly literature as improving learning gains for students across a wide array of metrics, but it also can be a source of feedback for instructors to make meaningful shifts in their approach to teaching.
- Reflection can range from formal and structured to informal and improvisational. The most important factors to consider when constructing reflective experiences include intent, connections to content, and clear guidelines for students.
- Almost any reflective activity can be modified to be effective among distance learners, or among local learners in novel ways, by leveraging advances in learning technologies.

Transforming Leadership Learning Through Reflection

- Reflection activities allow students to gain insight into perceptual sets and biases, encouraging a broadening of self-awareness in their leadership development.
- The role of the leadership educator is to actively engage learners in critical reflection through a learning environment and process that builds on learners' existing knowledge and experiential base.
- Reflection comes in many forms within the leadership classroom and curriculum:

  - o Written reflection activities in the form of journals
  - o Essays about readings
  - o Verbal reflection in reaction to class discussions
  - o Questions posed by students
  - o Current, local, and national events
  - o Programs that formally engage students in completing vision and goal-setting activities and other projects to personalize the concepts to the individual.

- Group reflection exercises allow students to develop authentic perspectives on their own leadership learning as well as empathize with the successes and challenges of those around them. Individual reflection exercises may facilitate students' development of agency, capacity, and efficacy in leadership by clarifying their own thoughts, feelings, and values around leading.
- Often leaders are unaware of their perceptual sets and biases. Thus, an important function of leadership education is to provide opportunities for student reflection so that students gain an understanding of how they perceive and interpret their observations.

CHAPTER 13

TEAM-BASED LEARNING

It's All About Process

This chapter focuses on team-based learning (TBL) as a pedagogy for teaching leadership. We begin by outlining TBL and provide methodical recommendations for facilitating this type of learning, regardless of content. Then we will look at applications of TBL in leadership education, including teambuilding, feedback and assessment procedures, as well as virtual teams. An essential theme of this chapter is TBL's focus on the process over outcome. In other words, TBL's priority rests squarely on providing facilitated structure around how student teams will function and learn to collaborate, which trumps any project or presentation you might assign. This emphasis places value on the notion that dysfunctional teams cannot produce high-quality leadership. As leadership educators, we have a responsibility to ensure our student teams recognize how to function at a high level.

TBL

TBL is defined as a structured and systematic instructional strategy in which small groups work together to produce a common product (Michaelsen, Knight, & Fink, 2004) in preparation for the teamwork they are likely to encounter in the workplace (Humphreys, Greenan, & McIlveen, 1997; Thomas & Busby, 2003). This approach fosters an educational atmosphere

The Role of Leadership Educators: Transforming Learning, pp. 219–232
Copyright © 2018 by Information Age Publishing

of interdependence—ensuring participants within learning groups develop a sense of responsibility for one another's learning. Accordingly, TBL qualifies as cooperative learning, where students succeed or fail together, work interactively, have a goal to learn, help other students in their group, and learn how to cooperate effectively while the teacher holds them accountable. In this cooperative learning model, student team members are expected to hold each other accountable as well. Additionally, accountability includes preparing for class (e.g., completing readings or assignments) as well as a shared responsibility for team members' learning during in-class group work or activities.

Together these dynamics create conditions for discussion, clarify ideas, and foster learning, critical thinking, experimentation, and sense of ownership of information (Gokhale, 1995). Furthermore, team-based group discussions may encourage students to confront counterarguments, motivating them to think beyond their own perspectives and improve respect for diversity (Cooper, Robinson, & McKinney, 1993; Slavin, 1983). In fact, there is considerable scholarly and empirical support for gains in students learning when working in groups compared with individualized activities (Chiriac & Granstrom, 2012; Slavin, 1996).

The primary learning objective of TBL is to teach beyond content delivery, with intense focus on providing students opportunities to apply course concepts to resolve issues. Moreover, TBL is designed to allow students to leverage the marriage of conceptual and processual knowledge (Michaelsen & Sweet, 2008). Effective group assignments promote both learning and team development processes. Yet in many educational environments, the only aspects of process assessed are team dynamics—sometimes about initial ground rules agreed on by the team and thus formative and summative (Brooks & Ammons, 2003; Siciliano, 1999)—and time on task (Willcoxson, 2006). Although team dynamics and task completion efficiency are important, effective leadership instructors also pay attention to how teams develop, team competence in locating and accessing resources and information, scheduling, accountability, and group goals (Daft & Noe, 2001; Leon & Tai, 2004). Team-based pedagogy seeks to drive instructors' and leaners' attention to these facets of leadership.

According to Michaelsen and Sweet's (2011) examination of the relationship between best practices of evidence-based teaching and the principles that constitute TBL, four practical elements overlap: (a) strategically formed and permanent teams; (b) ensuring readiness to participate; (c) application activities promoting critical thinking and team development; and (d) peer evaluation. To illustrate these elements, we share the course structure from a graduate management course titled, *Leadership & Teams*. In this course, students were randomly assigned to teams during the first day of class and remained in these teams for the duration of the term. Throughout the semester, students took a variety of self- and team assessments and were required to delegate tasks for multiple assignments, culminating in a team-facilitated activity and discussion with the entire class near the end of the term. Individual reflection and peer evaluations were also required. Each of the four elements that Michaelsen and Sweet (2011) offered was attended to in this course. In accordance with this example, the following subsection provides a course blueprint for intentionally structuring TBL, which includes setting expectations, forming the groups, outlining the grading system, and providing opportunities for group development.

Setting Expectations

We recommend embarking on any TBL experience by offering reasons that you have decided to use TBL and what it means for the way class will function (Michaelsen & Sweet, 2008). Effective leadership educators are certain to review learning objectives, express the importance of student accountability for individual and group work, and articulate formal expectations. Students will appreciate this transparency (Chriac & Granstrom, 2012). Finally, detail the grading system. Although these may seem like topics you can describe in the syllabus, research suggests (e.g., Chiriac & Granstrom, 2012; Naumann & Bennett, 2002; Sinclair, 2003) that many students' sources of anxiety and frustration associated with group work are lack of clarity, a sense of unfairness around the grading system, and whether —and in what way—self- or peer assessment would be used (Willcoxson, 2006). Michaelsen and Sweet (2011) suggest setting two pivotal expectations to alleviate these concerns: (a) a high level of individual accountability for preclass preparation and class attendance, and devoting time and energy to group assignments (i.e., counting individual scores on the readiness assurance tests and basing part of the grade on a peer evaluation); and (b) ensuring that team assignments will be done in class and be based on thinking, discussing, and deciding, making it highly unlikely that one or two less motivated teammates members can put the entire group at risk.

Forming Groups

Effective TBL is more likely to occur when all groups have the chance to develop into learning teams (Michaelsen & Sweet, 2008). In doing so, consider optimal group sizes of three to four students. Conscientious leadership educators strive to ensure that each group has adequate resources and balanced skill sets to employ when completing assigned tasks (i.e., fair distribution of various subject-relevant knowledge and experiences), that there is both equity and diversity among group members, and that any member coalitions that might interfere with group development are avoided (Chriac & Granstrom, 2012; Fink, 2013; Kelly, 2009; Michaelsen & Sweet, 2008).

Provide Opportunities for Group Development Early and Often

Classroom leadership is essential to successful TBL: "An instructor must be able to understand, model, and lead group processes, which includes the roles all team members will play and the dynamic of team members within those roles" (Barbour, 2006, pp. 32–33). When done well, TBL is combined with knowledge of the group development process (Barbour, 2006; McKendall, 2000). At the same time, students must hold one another accountable and be actively engaged in their learning (Haberyan, 2007). Returning to our focus on the process rather than the product, effective leadership educators prepare students for work in group settings, teaching them how to plan, communicate, and perform as a team (Chriac & Granstrom, 2012). Interdependence among group members can exist only when individuals perceive that they can reach their goals with their group members, are cooperatively linked to reach their goals, and promote each other's efforts to achieve the goals (Johnson, Johnson, & Smith, 2007). Correspondingly, accountability is key to the success of the group and helps to prevent some group members from exerting less effort than others (Onwuegbuzie, Collins, & Jiao, 2009) or reduced individual effort resulting from too much dependence on other group members.

Teambuilding

Perhaps no component of TBL is more integral than the use of application activities designed to promote team development or "teambuilding." Teambuilding emphasizes members working together in a spirit of cooperation and generally has one or more of the following goals: (a) setting team goals and priorities; (b) analyzing and allocating how work is performed; (c) examining how a group is working—that is, examining processes such as norms, decision making, and communication; and (d) examining relationships among people doing the work (Moorehead & Griffin, 2010). We suggest beginning the teambuilding process by providing activities such as icebreakers, where students can get to know their group members. The most fundamental aspect of designing team assignments that promote learning and team development is ensuring that they truly require group interaction (Michaelsen & Sweet, 2008). Allen and Hartman (2008) extend these recommendations by suggesting that we provide opportunities where student teams and their members can interact, dialogue, and develop norms as well as reflect on these experiences as a guide to becoming a leader in a collaborative environment. Subsequently, tasks requiring students to investigate, critique, play collaborative games, apply course concepts to decision making, involve complex issues, and allow teams to share their products in simple forms generate higher levels of interaction than requiring students to write a longer paper (Kennette & Hanzuk, 2017). This is because students will focus on producing a lengthy paper by dividing the work up individually instead of interacting and discussing course material (Michaelsen & Sweet, 2008).

Offer Feedback and Support

In their study of students' experiences in high- and low-quality group work, Chiriac and Granstrom (2012) found rich evidence to support the claim that students and groups need wholehearted support as well as frequent and timely feedback to help the group and its members learn. Accordingly, students prefer instructors who structure group work, consults during the group work phases, and intervene when a conflict arises (Barbour, 2006; Borredon, Deffayet, Baker, & Kolb, 2011). Additionally, students prefer a democratic versus laissez-faire or authoritarian style of leadership, implying that the instructor "read" the group's needs and is accessible for consultation—the physical and mental presence of the teacher seems to be of great importance to the students (Chiriac & Granstrom, 2012). Even so, the instructor must be an arranger and supporter in this role, not a controller (Howe et al., 2007).

Course/Experience Ending

The team project should be meaningful and relevant and allow for some type of presentation of each group's final product. Concurrently, the instructor must integrate appropriate levels and types of assessment and evaluation (Meyers, 1997). Feedback from the instructor as well as immediate feedback from the group on organization, completeness, clarity, audience participation, and delivery are both important forms of evaluation (McKendall, 2000; Webb, 1985). It is also appropriate to allow for both formative and summative feedback from their team members about their contributions to the team as well as its successes and challenges

(Michaelsen & Sweet, 2011). Accordingly, "whereas members of a group feel mostly accountable to an outside authority, team members also feel accountable to each other, and peer evaluation is a mechanism by which the teacher can stimulate that experience in one's students" (Michaelsen & Sweet, 2011, p. 48).

TBL IN LEADERSHIP EDUCATION

TBL is a significant component of leadership education programs and may be present in service-learning initiatives, in-class activities, group projects, and presentations. Jenkins (2017a) found that leadership educators attached the most overall weight in undergraduate students' course grades to group projects and presentations (and second-most in graduate leadership courses behind major writing projects or term papers). Yet even with so much at stake, announce a group project at any point in a semester, and you'll hear groans reminiscent of past experiences in student groups ranging from social loafing (Albanese & Van Fleet, 1985; Joyce, 1999; Sheppard & Taylor, 1999) and disputes to the classic, "I ended up doing all the work" (Kennette & Hanzuk, 2017). Working with others and often in a team-based setting is a distinction of leadership education. We have an opportunity and responsibility to ensure that our student working teams are more efficient, relational, process-oriented, and prepared.

There may be instances in which an instructor did not discuss the nature of group dynamics or what it means to be a good lab partner, or he or she allowed individuals in the working group to have a conversation about collective expectations, norms, and/or delegation of work. We suspect, and the scholarship supports, that these activities have the potential for positive impact on group processes throughout the duration of team members' work together, but seldom are they encouraged. As leadership educators, it is our responsibility to "differentiate between working *in* a group and working *as* a group" (Chiriac & Granstrom, 2012, p. 345). Further, the benefits of working on group tasks are not an effect of cooperation but rather social facilitation, which is when individuals perform better when they know that others are observing them. However, this is when they are not working *as* a group, just working *in* a group (Chiriac & Granstrom, 2012). Again, this is where leadership educators have a responsibility to intervene skillfully.

Our advice is to take the following approach—focus on the process, not the product. We are not saying you should be ambiguous in setting expectations for group work or that rubrics aren't important—they are. Student teams need a goal, task, or mission to accomplish. Yet in many cases, the product is less important than the process. That is, the learning that occurs through the group work, interactions, journeying through Tuckman's

(1965) group development stages, reflective activities, and debriefing this work may far outweigh the group's product. In fact, we would argue that without going through the motions of teambuilding and developmental activities, there are no opportunities to journey beyond the initial forming of the team.

Facilitating Group Process in Leadership Education

In the previous sections, we outlined the steps needed to facilitate an intentional TBL process. We believe, as leadership educators, we have a responsibility to build on this process and provide clear expectations and guidelines. The following recommendations are an amalgamation of team-based exercises/activities from our experiences and the literature (e.g., Dyer, 2007)—including student perceptions and suggestions—to promote group cohesiveness and development in TBL. We begin with the example activity below, which provides a structured forum for getting students to think about their past group work experiences and sets the stage for an optimum experience. Then we build on the steps offered in the section above as they relate to leadership education contexts.

Example

The Best Team

Begin the activity by having each student think about the best team they have ever been on and to write down a description of why it was the best. Then ask students to:

1. Share their descriptions with their team members.

2. Take their descriptions and write 5–10 characteristics of that best team they've ever been on (i.e., what made it the best?) onto sticky notes.

3. Bring their sticky notes to the board and decide, as a team, on a collective list that integrates their peers' ideas. It could be a Top 10, Top 15, "rules teams should live by," whatever they want, but they must ensure that the list in inclusive <u>and</u> no team member feels their ideas were left out.

4. Debrief this exercise by having the team identify ways to maximize the "best team" characteristics.

Setting and Sharing: Realistic Priorities, Expectations, Goals, Roles, and Processes

Just like in the natural world, students assigned to teams arrive with differential levels of priority or commitment. For example, some students assign more or less value to the assignment and are willing and able to

provide respective levels of time and energy (Dyer, 2007). This can critically hamper TBL processes, teams, and members (Kreie, Headrick, &
Steiner, 2007; Tan, Ivy, Sharan, & Lee, 2007; Weeks & Kelsey, 2007). To
address this challenge, we recommend providing a structured assignment,
group discussion, or technology-enhanced forum (e.g., discussion board,
group page, or Google document), where students must share the amount
of time—and the reasons why—they are able and willing to commit over
the duration of the team's lifespan. This is often referred to as a "team
contract" (Bailey et al., 2005; McKendall, 2000; Sargent, Allen, Frahm, &
Morris, 2009) and may also be derived through collaborative construction
of a Gantt Chart, which is a bar chart that illustrates project management
(Cook & Olson, 2006). Consider including the following prompts for
further dialogue around individual expectations offered by Dyer (2007):
(a) What worries you most or is your biggest concern about working on
this team? (b) How would this team function if everything went just as you
hoped? (c) What do you expect to be the barriers to effective team functioning? (d) What will likely prevent the team from achieving its goals? and (e)
What actions do you think must be taken to ensure the positive outcomes?

Next, we suggest shifting students' focus to clarifying goals, roles, and
assigned tasks (McKendall, 2000; Siciliano, 1999) and, finally, to responsibilities and tasks. As a primer for process-related discussions, encourage
and provide resources to enhance group communication and meeting efficiency, as well as suggestions for handling competition and conflict. For
example, Barbour (2006) assigned *How to Make Meetings Work* (Doyle &
Straus, 1976) to students who spent the semester in teams to help develop
meeting and group skills. Dyer (2007) offered the following prompts to
make collective decisions around group process: (a) How will we make decisions? (b) What will be our basic method for work? (c) How do we make sure
that everyone gets a chance to discuss issues or raise concerns? (d) How
will we resolve differences? (e) How will we ensure the completion of work?
and (f) How will we change things that are not producing results? Consider
strongly encouraging student teams to meet outside of class—or, in the case
of virtual teams, via conference call or group video (e.g., Google Hangouts)—and ask that meeting minutes are recorded. Again, these activities
may take the form of written assignments (as long as they are shared with
group members), group discussions, or in technology-enhanced forums.

Getting to Know You

Create opportunities for team members to get to know one another
and discuss individual differences (McKendall, 2000). The previously indi-

cated dialogues related to expectations and priorities are helpful but are also limited in scope mostly to group tasks and processes. Instead, consider assigning students to complete self-assessments (e.g., Myers-Briggs Inventory, StrengthsFinder), providing structured exercises where they analyze and reflect on their results, and use the products of their analyses and reflections as a primer for group dialogue around individual learning styles, preferences, behaviors, values, strengths, weaknesses, and other salient characteristics (Barbour, 2006; Clinebell & Stecher, 2003; Hogan & Champagne, 1979; McKendall, 2000). Begin these activities by sharing your own inventory results and implications for teamwork (for more activities related specifically to inventories, self-assessments, and personality tests, see Chapter 15).

Collaboration and Problem Solving

Give students practice activities and problems that enable team development. For example, McKendall (2000) suggests problems that involve ranking tasks and require a consensus solution. Another popular activity is the Jungle Survival Situation (Lafferty & Smith, 1987), where students have to decide what essential items to bring along in a deserted jungle hut or the "Populating a New Planet" activity (Kouzes & Posner, 2014a, 2014b), where Earth is facing full destruction and students must decide which 10 individuals—out of a possible 30—they will take on a spaceship to populate a new planet. Additionally, McKendall (2000) suggests the prisoner's dilemma exercise (Pfeiffer & Jones, 1972) to illustrate the cooperation versus competition mindset.

Reflecting

To improve trajectory along the stages of group development, team members need opportunities to discuss and reflect openly with one another. In fact, we argue, and other scholars agree, creating a conversational space for these kinds of discussions is essential (A. C. Baker, 2009). The opportunity for teams of students to engage in reflective conversations and explore different experiences and perspectives is directly related to learning and improving performance (Baker, 2009; Kayes, Kayes, & Kolb, 2005). Thus, we suggest regular check-ins for student teams. In these check-ins, consider structured reflective exercises such as one-minute papers related to group development, challenges, strengths, tensions, and so on, and then proceed to a team discussion where members share thoughts from their papers. If additional structure is needed, consider using a team evaluation model where members assess themselves to indicate where improvement is needed (McKendall, 2000).

Feedback as a Form of Reflection. If reflective exercises do not provide ample opportunities for feedback about individual member performance, create structured exercises that do. Per Chapter 9, introducing feedback early in a team's lifespan establishes a culture where feedback is a valued part of the process. For example, letting students practice designing feedback (e.g., specific, problem-based, owned, validating, immediate) statements for situations related to punctuality and attendance, communicative behaviors, or accountability (Holmer, 2001) enhances the feedback culture and builds skill among students. The Collegiate Leadership Competition suggests an activity like this during initial team practices. In the activity, students are empowered to "Create a Culture of Feedback" through determining as a group how team members would like to give and receive feedback (College Leadership Competition: Coaches, 2017). Because a large part of students' learning from participation in the CLC comes from feedback and debriefing sessions, collaboratively developing these norms is a powerful exercise with lasting effects.

Assessment and Evaluation

Although we have stressed the importance of the process, the product or task given to the groups should be challenging and perceived by students as authentic and important (Fink, 2013). For tasks, we suggest application exercises requiring students to engage in high-quality intragroup dialogue and culminate in a media-enhanced group presentations, facilitated discussions, workshops, or training sessions intended to last a significant portion of a class period. The task could also require logistical steps, such as identifying a problem on campus (e.g., inadequate lighting), gathering information (e.g., crime statistics), meeting with stakeholders (e.g., students, campus administrators), and presenting to decision makers (e.g., student government; McKendall, 2000). Conversely, having groups co-write a lengthy document is not a good group assignment because it does not promote a high level of interaction (Fink, 2013; Michaelsen & Sweet, 2008).

Grading

Deciding how to appropriately grade team projects in light of the potential for social loafing further complicates educators' ability to maximize team learning experiences (Isaacs, 2002) and reward systems have become a topic of investigation (Sinclair, 2003). McKendall (2000) suggested a balance in grading between collective and individual performance. Fink

(2013) recommended a grading system with three components: (a) individually graded tasks; (b) group tasks; and (c) peer evaluation. Individual and group tasks as well as their grading mechanisms can be determined by the instructor or the class. For peer evaluation, we suggest the following:

- Ask students to summatively assess, at the end of the course, the contribution of their fellow students in areas such as task and relationship behavior, dependability, and free riding (Paswan & Gollakota, 2004).
- Use serial assessments where students rate themselves and others on the extent to which they met deadlines, contributed their fair share to the workload, completed the tasks assigned them, and demonstrated positive attitudes (Brooks & Ammons, 2003).
- Allow audience members to evaluate the importance of the chosen project, the processes used to solve it, and the outcomes produced. McKendall (2000) suggests that teams should also complete an evaluation of their performance and the instructor should do the same (see e.g., Wilcoxson, 2006). Then the instructor should meet with the group, compare ratings, and dialogue about any inconsistencies.

Debriefing

In Chapter 9, we discussed debriefing in-depth, but below we offer some additional lessons we have learned over the years debriefing teams.

Example

Debriefing Group Process in Leadership Education

During our first few years as adjunct faculty we developed from applauding after a group project was presented by students to asking brief questions about the content of their presentation or project to focusing the time immediately following a group's presentation on the group's process. Why? Because they've already presented the information, task, product, etc. Nothing we say or do is going to change what happened in the 10, 20, or 30 minutes they were presenting nor will it integrate important topics that were left out or essential conclusions or arguments we had expected would be included. What we can learn, however, is how the group worked together.

For example, consider asking the group whether there were any challenges related to the group process. Expect to hear that finding a common time to meet was challenging and that everyone is "so busy." Follow up by asking them what they did as a group to mitigate that challenge. How did they choose to communicate as a group? In our experiences, students use GroupMe (group texts), Twitter, and Facebook messenger as their primary modes of communication. Contrary to what we, as leadership educators use, E-mail was not the first thing students checked.

(Example continues on next page)

Example (Continued)

Debriefing Group Process in Leadership Education

What else might you ask and learn from a group project debriefing session? I often ask the following questions after fishing for any challenges the group may have had:

- What went well? Why?

- Did anyone emerge as a leader of the group? How so? (This one can be very telling and reveal quite a bit about the group process and how they were organized—or not—during their lifespan.)

Virtual Team-Based Learning

We conclude our review of team-based learning with a brief discussion of "virtual TBL." Although leadership educators value group work in traditional, face-to-face learning environments, this does not appear to be the case in online learning environments. Earlier, we referred to Jenkins's (2017a) study that compared the instructional and assessment strategy use of more than 1,000 leadership educators around the world. He found that group projects/presentations were the primarily (undergraduate) and secondarily (graduate) heaviest weighted assessment strategies in face-to-face courses. In comparison, this category dropped precipitously to #12 (undergraduate) and #9 (graduate) among fully online courses. In blended courses, group projects were valued more closely as face-to-face courses as first among undergraduate courses and third for graduate coursework. All other factors remaining the same (e.g., course type or subject matter), why are instructors sometimes hesitant to include group work in their fully online classes? Are aspiring leaders who take online classes less expected to work in virtual teams? Of course not. Arguably, the anxiety associated with facilitating such learning in online classes may be the catalyst.

Facilitating virtual TBL requires additional considerations around how to best prepare our students for success in their virtual teams. According to the "Virtual Leadership Competency Framework" offered by Endersby, Phelps, and Jenkins (2017), the integration of technology centers on four key considerations that affect group members' ability to collaborate in virtual settings: (a) adaptive facilitation; (b) understanding technological amplifications of power; (c) recognition of integrated social-technical processes; and (d) nuanced understanding of technology. Accordingly, we suggest the following:

- Expose students to the benefits and drawbacks of virtual meetings to accomplish different team objectives (Schaefer & Erskine, 2012).

- Offer appropriate technological platforms through an LMS, Google suite, other or free or university-licensed interfaces—as well as video, audio, e-mail, etc.,—to accommodate and enhance virtual collaboration based on team needs (Endersby, Phelps, & Jenkins, 2017). Provide students opportunities to practice using technological tools and provide user guides or YouTube tutorials for any tool you suggest.
- Allow students to make decisions about communication technology choices and experience the consequences of those decisions (Schaefer & Erskine, 2012).

When making technological choices, it is important to consider how technology affects power and social processes. For example, a tech-savvy team member may have a clear advantage over others, particularly if a member's audio or video is inhibited by technological challenges. Equally, technological inhibitors can negatively affect members' ability to contribute, thus quashing collaborative opportunities.

One thing is clear, the process in virtual TBL is as, if not more important, than in face-to-face teams. Consider the recommendations in the subsections above (i.e., setting expectations, forming the groups, providing opportunities for group development, feedback, and support). For example, McKendall (2000) suggest videotaping a team meeting to evaluate communication patterns (e.g., who talks most, who interrupts most, who takes up the most space, who solicits opinions most, etc.). This suggestion can be transformed for virtual environments by recording a virtual team meeting with Screencast-O-Matic or having students analyze the text in a conversation that occurred in a message-based format (e.g., GroupMe, Facebook Messenger, iMessenger). Although it may take some creative liberties on the part of the instructor, transplanting each recommendation to the virtual environment is critical for successful TBL.

PEDAGOGY TO PRACTICE

Team-based learning can be an influential approach to preparing leadership learners to successfully work with others. Here we offer a few points highlighting team-based learning as an instructional strategy and how to transform leadership learning using this pedagogy in leadership education.

Pedagogy Overview

- Team-based learning creates an educational atmosphere of interdependence—ensuring participants within learning groups develop a sense that they are responsible for one another's learning.

- Encourage students to create team contracts that meet the learning objectives of the structured assignment, discussion board, or technology forum. This will help students clarify goals, expectations, and roles.
- Team-based learning in digital spaces may require additional proactive planning, careful monitoring, and creative feedback mechanisms that leverage the very tools we expect students themselves to master.
- To assess and evaluate student learning have them engage in varying activities such as: high levels of intragroup dialogue, a media-enhanced group presentation, facilitated discussion, workshop, or training that lasts a significant portion of the program.

Transforming Leadership Learning Through TBL

- Effective leadership instructors carefully craft team-based expectations, activities, feedback processes, and grading schemes to reflect TBL's emphasis on social processes.
- Leadership educators who confront and challenge students' resistance to working in groups and teams role model leadership and empower students to overcome detrimental behavioral patterns collaboratively.
- Virtual team-based learning requires leadership educators to be mindful of setting up online learning environments in which: students are exposed to the benefits and drawbacks of virtual meetings, offer appropriate technological platforms and tools (include tutorials), and allow students to make decisions on their use of communication technology and learn from those decisions.
- Intentionally structured reflection is critical for leadership learning when using team-based pedagogy. Students need to have an opportunity to make meaning of their experiences as a team collectively and to give each team member appropriate feedback.

CHAPTER 14

SERVICE-LEARNING AS LEADERSHIP PEDAGOGY

This chapter explores integrating service-learning and community engagement with teaching leadership. Although incorporating service-learning in leadership programs is not a new concept, they can be challenging to combine effectively. We begin this chapter by defining service-learning as well as discussing strategies for implementation, including critical considerations every educator would be well advised to reflect on when using this pedagogy. Finally, we review the intersections of leadership and service-learning, applying them to leadership education. Service-learning is rich pedagogy that benefits leadership learning when implemented correctly.

SERVICE-LEARNING

Service -learning is defined as "a form of experiential education in which students engage in activities that address human and community needs together with structured opportunities intentionally designed to promote student learning and development" (Jacoby, 1996, p. 5). The beauty of Jacoby's definition is its inclusion of both co-curricular and academic/curricular learning opportunities. Both engage students in intentionally designed student learning. Academic/curricular-based service-learning experiences are those done within a structured classroom setting, connect to specific academic content, and earn academic credit. Co-curricular

The Role of Leadership Educators: Transforming Learning, pp. 233–248
Copyright © 2018 by Information Age Publishing
233

service-learning opportunities vary in community engagement depth, but all include intentional design of opportunities, connect service to learning, and incorporate refection exercises. In this chapter, we use service-learning to refer to both co-curricular and academic/curricular-based community service intentionally connected to learning. However, for our purposes, most terminology and examples will be based in academic/curricular contexts. Building on Jacoby's (1996) definition, service-learning is facilitated through active service and community engagement within the context of specific course structures, field seminars, and workshops, which can be offered face to face, online, or through hybrid experiences (Guthrie & McCracken, 2010a; Guthrie, 2016). When done well, these learning opportunities are linked to continuous critical reflection (Jones & Abes, 2004; Stanton, Giles & Cruz, 1999). Service-learning dates back to the work of Jane Addams (1910) and John Dewey (1933). Service-learning, as we now recognize it, has its beginnings in the United States in the early 1970s, when educators and community activists identified that active, structured activities would provide deeper, stronger, and more relevant learning opportunities for students (Stanton et al., 1999).

Kuh (2008) discussed service-learning as a high-impact educational practice in higher education. He outlined the importance of giving students opportunities to have direct and practical exposure to organizational challenges and social issues that reflect in-class learning. Learning at community service sites can then be reciprocally connected to classroom content via structured reflection to make meaning. To these ends, Kuh (2008) advised:

> service-learning ... requires students to work with their peers beyond the classroom and test what they are learning in unfamiliar situations. As a result, students better understand themselves in relation to others and the larger world, and they acquire the intellectual tools and ethical grounding to act with confidence for the betterment of the human condition. (p. 17)

Service-learning is a high-impact practice that provides students the opportunity to learn about themselves, as well as see theory put into practice. The content they are learning in their class comes alive.

From a sample of 3,450 first-year students, Astin and Sax (1998) found that undergraduates who participated in community service while in college experienced enhanced life skill development, academic development, and sense of civic responsibility. Their findings revealed that most undergraduate community service work was performed in co-curricular contexts facilitated by student affairs administrators, specifically in student activities. Astin, Vogelgesang, Ikeda, and Yee (2000) furthered this research by focusing on academic/curricular service-learning. Data was collected from 22,236 undergraduate students, from which 30% participated in academic/curricular-based service and 46% participated in other forms of community service (in co-curricular programs, through off-campus organizations, or on their own). This study also included case studies, group interviews, and classroom observations. Astin et al. (2000) reported that engaging in academic/curricular-based service-learning add considerable benefits to students' academic outcomes across a range of metrics. Self-effectiveness, or feeling like one is making a difference, was also reported as having a significant impact: "Better than four service-learning students in five felt that their service 'made a difference' and that they were learning from their service experience" (Astin et al., 2000, p. iii). From these and other studies, we strongly suspect students can anticipate a wide range and great depth of learning gains from well-constructed service-learning opportunities. We now focus on how effective and intentional leadership educators can craft maximally didactic service experiences.

Intentionally Developing Service-Learning Opportunities

Creating high-quality service-learning opportunities is essential to achieve positive learning outcomes. Astin et al. (2000) suggested three factors in creating positive service-learning experiences, each of which we review briefly. The first factor is students' degree of interest in the subject matter, which allowed the service experience to enhance the learned course material. Situating service-learning opportunities with discipline-specific contexts is encouraged.

Another factor of a positive service-learning experience is "whether the professor encourages class discussion..." (Astin et al., 2000, p. iii). Community service can be unpredictable and often confusing because of the complexities presented to students in various situations. Providing space for students to discuss with peers is critical for a positive and reflective service-learning experience. The Astin et al. (2000) findings support the essential nature of peer discussion in general, as well as focused and intentional discussions about the service experience. These opportunities to discuss and make meaning from academic content, service experiences, and the connection between the two are influential in the overall experience.

Finally, the more the educator intentionally links course material with the community service experience, the more students will be able to leverage those connections when making meaning of their experiences. Educators who develop service-learning opportunities often design them solely through their disciplinary lens. Effective service-learning educators clearly recognize connections between academic content and the community service experience. However, students don't always make those connections as readily (Hatcher & Bringle, 1997). "Students in applied learning pedagogies may have a vague sense of the impact their experiences have had on them but not be fully aware of the nature of their own learning, its sources, or its significance" (Ash & Clayton, 2009, p. 26). One way that educators can help students make meaning from their experiences and make connections to their academic content is through reflective exercises.

Reflection

Making meaning from service-learning experiences is critical for intentionally developing such programs. Although the prime goal of reflection is to improve student learning from a service experience, consistent reflective activities can also provide feedback to assess student learning and improve the overall teaching. Reflection in service-learning activities encourages clarification of values and supports students' personal development (Hatcher & Bringle, 1997), which may influence future career paths. Reflection is reviewed extensively in Chapters 4, 6, and 12.

Comprehensive Action Plan for Service-Learning (CAPSL)

CAPSL was created by Bringle and Hatcher (1996) with the purpose of implementing and institutionalizing service-learning in higher education. CAPSL was developed from a 3-year study with 44 institutions that participated in a Campus Compact Project on Integrating Service with Academic Study. Although there are multiple stakeholders in service-learning, CAPSL focuses on four main constituencies: institution, faculty, students, and community. Each of the four constituencies has recommended activities, tasks, and associated outcomes suggested by CAPSL. These activities, tasks, and outcomes include (Bringle & Hatcher, 1996):

- Planning (initial preparation)
- Awareness (of the general nature of service-learning)
- Prototype (creating concrete examples)
- Resources (gathering various assets to design activities)
- Expansion (of ideas, relationships, and resources to this point)
- Recognition (efforts should be recognized and celebrated)
- Monitoring (documenting implementation plans)
- Evaluation (program outcomes and student learning outcomes)

- Research (for public dissemination and contribution to knowledge)
- Institutionalization (growth and maturity of program assist in acceptance)

A starting point with CAPSL is creating a common understanding of what service-learning is at your institution. Bringle and Hatcher (1996) recommend, "it is important in planning a service-learning program to know the nature of the student climate and culture, including student attitudes toward voluntary service activities (individual or through student groups) and student attitudes toward service-learning courses" (p. 233). The community partner needs to help guide by identifying community service activities at both a community level (macrolevel) and a particular course (microlevel). CAPSL is an excellent resource for designing and implementing service-learning programs.

Service-Learning as Counternormative

Howard (1998) refers to service-learning as a "counter-normative" pedagogy, one that "qualitatively changes the norms and relationships of the teaching-learning process" (p. 22). Counternormative means acting against dynamics that have become the standard (Howard, 1998). Embracing this aspect of service-learning is vital in intentionally designing service-learning opportunities. Clayton and Ash (2004) describe the importance of shifting perspectives when developing and delivering service-learning opportunities. Perspective shifting causes both conceptual and functional dimensions of service-learning to occur and results in changing the overall understanding of how educators engage in teaching service-learning.

Clayton and Ash (2004) discuss the importance of supporting faculty and students in shifting their perspective in relation to service-learning opportunities. They offer steps in supporting drastic shifts in both conceptual and practical dimensions. First is to identify characteristics that make service-learning counternormative to previous experiences. Next is to categorize those differences and define the shifts in each category. The step that requires the most reflection is identifying ways shifted perspectives influence practices. Understanding how developing new skills and adopting new attitudes can impact new behaviors is essential in this step. The final step is actively supporting faculty and students making these shifts in perspective and practice while honoring the difficulty in the process and attending to specific situations that may arise.

CRITICAL CONSIDERATION IN SERVICE-LEARNING

When developing and delivering service-learning opportunities, especially those linked to teaching leadership, several important elements should be taken into consideration. Institutional support of faculty providing service-learning courses, communication of these opportunities to students, and the quantity and quality of relationships with community partners all impact the success or failure of service-learning initiatives. Bringle and Hatcher (2000) stress the importance of understanding the institutionalization of service-learning in higher education as critical in successful development and implementation of such courses. Institutionalization of service-learning may be experienced differently for faculty and students. For faculty, support in curriculum development; inclusion of service-learning in faculty promotion, tenure, recognition, and rewards; faculty development activities; and encouragement of service-learning scholarship demonstrate institutional support. Among students, scholarships, wide offerings of service-learning courses, co-curricular transcripts to document community service engagement, and overall student culture represent institutionalization of service-learning (Bringle & Hatcher, 2000). In addition to how an institution supports service-learning, other aspects that should be taken into consideration include the challenges associated with service-learning and more recent challenges to traditional service-learning strategies. We confront these challenges in the following sections.

Challenges of Service-Learning

Speck (2001) identified three challenges faculty often face when trying to develop service-learning courses. These challenges include initial miscalculations of the time and resources it takes to implement effectively, objection by students to service being required, and student resistance because service is seen as indoctrination into a certain way of thinking. To provide high-quality service-learning opportunities, it takes more time and resources to build community partnerships than it would appear to a casual observer. Additionally, instructional strategies to intentionally connect academic material with service experiences require significant care and attention. Although it may be perceived that these investments steal focus from traditional ways of teaching course content, we believe, and the research cited earlier in this chapter demonstrates, the consequences of ignoring the gains obtained by service-learning pedagogy are more dire than the cost of crafting such experiences.

Another often encountered challenge of service-learning is the potential objection of community service being required in a course. Although academic courses have various requirements, mandating community service can be seen as forcing volunteerism onto students, which is by definition not voluntary. Schnaubelt and Watson (1999) contend, "One could argue that forcing a student to do algebra homework also violates one's personal freedom. This imposition, however, may lead to greater freedom (i.e., a better job, etc.). In a sense, some impositions lead to greater freedoms" (pp. 12–13).

A final challenge we wish to confront is resistance to community service as "a liberal infusion of power, privilege, and social justice" (Mendizabal & Guthrie, in press, p. xxx). Speck (2001) phrased this phenomenon as indoctrination to particular political views. Recently, The National Association of Scholars (2017) specifically called for a return to "Civics Education" and described it as a shift back to focusing on policy, law, and other systems-based situations rather than centralizing social issues and the broader social contexts in which service-learning is situated (Mendizabal & Guthrie, in press). This final challenge is discussed further in the next section as a critical consideration in implementing service-learning to be inclusive of diverse student populations and shifting focus from student learning to community need. These three challenges, among others, are issues that effective service-learning educators consider when planning, executing, and assessing service-learning pedagogies.

Challenging Traditional Service-Learning Pedagogy

Recently, contentious issues that challenge traditional service-learning paradigms have emerged (Mitchell, Donahue, & Young-Law, 2012; Stoecker, 2016). Mitchell et al. (2012) called for closer examinations of service-learning implementation, contending that traditional service-learning has become a "pedagogy of whiteness" (p. 612), which reinforces race-based privilege in the United States and norms of color-blindness, as well as lacks historical understanding of social inequities. When blind to biases and historically marginalizing societal practices, service-learning has limited community impact, and White students remain unchallenged on issues of racism, isolate students of color, reinforce stereotypes, and miss transformative opportunities. When service-learning lacks a critical race focus, socially constructed mechanisms of whiteness, power, privilege, and oppression are reinforced (Mitchell et al., 2012). Providing time and space for students engaged in service-learning to examine their own identity development, even in the context of and response to their service experience, enhances student learning.

Stoecker (2016) also challenged traditional service-learning strategies, claiming that higher education often uses vulnerable community members as social research subjects and community agencies as social laboratories by leveraging academic privilege for personal gain. Research publications, lines on curriculum vitae and resumes, and fundraising opportunities become the primary concern over altruism and social change. Stoecker (2016) argued that student development and learning will not cease even if we prioritize community development over student learning in service-learning pedagogy. This idea of placing the needs of community ahead of teaching is another example of counternormative service-learning, as discussed earlier in this chapter. Given our review of service-learning as a pedagogy, now we detail how service-learning can be effectively infused with a leadership education context.

SERVICE-LEARNING IN LEADERSHIP EDUCATION

Scholars suggest that co-curricular involvement, interaction with diverse peers, and student involvement promote leadership development (Astin, 1993; Pascarella & Terenzini, 2005). Yet until recently, little scholarship existed focusing on undergraduate leadership development activities and service-learning. Pascarella, Palmer, Moye, and Pierson (2001) found that college students involved in experiences discussing diversity, which often occur in service-learning, had significant gains in critical thinking skills, which is essential to processes of leadership.

According to Scharff (2009), service-learning is a pedagogy designed to transform students by combining social activism with academics and is commonly evaluated as a model pedagogy for leadership development for university students. Leadership and service-learning theories and practices share similar elements that make service-learning an appropriate instructional strategy for leadership educators (Wagner & Pigza, 2016). These intersections and tensions are discussed below.

Brief Overview of Empirical Studies

Despite the limited number of empirical studies conducted regarding service-learning's influence on the development of leadership knowledge, skills, and values, a careful overview of the extant literature helps situate our theoretical understanding and practical suggestions in the best of what we know. Findings from the Astin et al. (2000) study of 22,236 undergraduate students across three in-depth institutional case studies demonstrated community service's significant positive effects on 11 outcome measures, including proficiency in leadership activities, self-rated leadership ability, and interpersonal skills.

In an empirical study conducted by Webster, Bruce, and Hoover (2006), students who engaged in service-learning activities reported significant gains in academic, social, and personal growth. Similarly, utilizing a grounded theory methodology, Stenta (2001) found that students in a service-based undergraduate leadership program personalized nearly every aspect of their experience. by connecting leadership with others, tending to the common good, understanding difference, realizing the relationship of interconnectedness of complex issues, and understanding social change movements.

Service-learning pedagogy develops and reinforces linkages between theory and service as well as connects participants with the community in a structured and direct manner (Hoover & Webster, 2004). Through these experiences, participants develop an understanding of how to specifically help communities and enhance their own theoretical learning (Webster, Bruce, & Hoover, 2006). For instance, Seemiller (2006) asserts that participation in *The Social Change Project* (a service-learning project) encourages students to recognize the need for leadership in creating effective social change, which supports active utilization of these same leadership concepts in the future.

Service-learning pedagogy has also been effective in outcomes that reach beyond social activism and personal growth. Sessa, Matos, and Hopkins (2009) emphasized service-learning pedagogy and leadership theories in an experimental undergraduate course. Students in the study found situational leadership theories, team leadership theories, and leadership principles most relevant to their experiences. According Sessa et al. (2009), students learned about themselves personally as individuals, leaders, team members, and community members. Civically, students learned how to apply leadership theories, work in teams, and about the community as a system. In terms of depth of learning, as evaluated using Bloom's (1956) taxonomy, students were able to identify, describe, and apply concepts, and, to some extent, to analyze and synthesize them. These findings suggest that using service-learning to teach students about both the theory and practice of leadership is a viable approach (Sessa et al., 2009).

Congruency and Tension: Intersections of Service-Learning and Leadership

Wagner and Pigza (2016) outlined five intersections of service-learning and leadership, as well as the tensions they create. These include intentionality, role of failure, participation, prerequisites of agency, and learning across cultures. See Table 14.1 for more information on how these aspects intersect and represent tension.

Table 14.1.   Intersecting Elements of Service-Learning and Leadership

Common Elements	Congruency	Tension
Intentionality	Intention to contribute to social good	Good intentions do not always guarantee good outcomes
Role of failure	Potential to create influential learning opportunities	Student learning might come at the expense of community
Participation	Developing and implementing projects are valued	Community members are often not consulted in the design phase
Prerequisites of agency	Common messages of anyone can engage in leadership and anyone can serve	Lack of recognition that learning of community needs to comes first before serving
Learning across cultures	Social perspective taking in leadership learning and community service-learning opportunities are valued	Can be emotional for community member interactions and risky for community members to be stereotyped

Source: Wagner and Pigza (2016).

Awareness, attention, and intention regarding these tensions when engaging in leadership and service-learning experiences are pivotal in developing successful service-learning opportunities. Next, we offer specific service-learning projects that can be implemented for individuals, groups, and across distance learning contexts.

TYPES OF SERVICE-LEARNING PROJECTS

In this section, we discuss group, individual, and online service-learning projects. Although each of these types of service-learning projects could be further discussed in terms of their potential for activism and advocacy, political and civic engagement, as well as charitable and philanthropic aspects, we purposefully kept these descriptions at a level of detail sufficiently broad to promote their generalizability for various educational contexts.

Group Service-Learning Projects

As discussed in Chapter 13, team-based learning is a fitting pedagogy for leadership education programs. Michaelsen, Knight, and Fink (2004) defined team-based learning as a structured instructional strategy in which small groups work together to produce a common product. Group service-learning projects combine team-based and service-learning instructional strategies. In the context of service-learning, the product is engagement in community work. Often times academic/curricular-based opportunities use group service-learning projects. When developing and supporting group service-learning projects, effective leadership educators consider opportunities to leverage already established groups, design new group formulations, and the impact of community needs where a predetermined number of individuals develop group placement.

Example

Students and Individuals Living in a Shelter Collectively Create Art

At the University of Illinois at Urbana-Champaign, a registered student organization worked with a local homeless shelter to create art together. Students involved in this co-curricular service-learning opportunity came from various disciplines (art education to social work to finance majors), but all were interested in some aspect of community arts. The student organization approached the local shelter with their idea of providing art lessons, as a creative outlet, for those staying at the shelter. Over a three-month period students provided art lessons and painting supplies for interested individuals staying at the shelter. Collectively they created incredible paintings and with the shelter's help decided to pursue turning the art into book. Working closely with the shelter, proceeds from the book sales went back to the shelter to fund future art programs. Individuals in this student organization took lead on different aspects of the project and met weekly as a group to further learn about community arts and capitalizing on community assets, reflect on what they were learning, and discuss logistics of the project.

Individual Service-Learning Projects

Simply put, individual service-learning projects are those accomplished independently. These individualized learning opportunities can be influential in developing leadership competencies; knowledge, values, abilities, and behaviors that contribute to successfully completing a task or role (Seemiller, 2013). Seemiller's (2013) student leadership competency model includes 60 competencies across eight conceptual categories. Conceptual categories include learning and reasoning, self-awareness and development, group dynamics, interpersonal interaction, civic responsibility, communication, strategic planning, and personal behavior (Seemiller, 2013). Additionally, Seemiller (2016) provided a five-step model for designing service-learning opportunities using this leadership competency-based approach. Competency-focused leadership educators should consider using this model to create individual service-learning projects or guide students through processes to create projects themselves. Seemiller's (2016) five steps include:

1. Selecting leadership competencies (either you want the student to learn or the student wants to learn).
2. Choosing an appropriate service-learning project (specific project should align with learning outcomes).
3. Consulting with community partners (collaborative work to identify projects that fulfill community needs or enhance community assets).
4. Action and reflection (engage in service with structured reflection to make meaning).
5. Assessing (evaluate learning, development, and impact on community).

Intentionally designing an individual service-learning opportunity offers more meaningful contributions to student leadership development rather than haphazardly integrating service-learning because it is broadly beneficial.

Example

The Moellership Program through the Center for Leadership and Social Change at Florida State University provides undergraduate and graduate students the opportunity to focus 8–12 weeks of their summer on service at a non-profit agency. Students receive a stipend of up to $4,000 for participation in the program. Past examples of individual projects include serving at a camp for children with chronic illnesses in North Carolina, engaging in bicycle advocacy in Washington, D.C., implementing a reading curriculum in South Africa, caring for people with HIV/AIDS in Spain, designing a poultry production project in Tanzania, and promoting sustainability in Brazil (Moellership Program, 2017). Students involved in the Moellership Program do not receive any course credit, but are required to attend bi-weekly meetings. These meetings focus on connecting their service experiences to leadership knowledge, skills, and values, making meaning from experiences, exploring multiple critical perspectives of service, and identity development.

Online Service-Learning

Online service-learning is a fairly new combination of pedagogies that provides novel opportunities for leadership education (Guthrie, 2016). The potential of integrating service-learning in leadership education in a virtual environment expands the possibilities of teaching, learning, and serving in a global community. Educators might shy away from integrating leadership and service-learning pedagogies in a completely virtual environment because of the lack of scholarship available and educators' lack of experience with intersecting these complex pedagogies. Not fully understanding how a traditionally face-to-face course content or community service might translate to a virtual space causes educators to be cautious in creating such opportunities (Guthrie, 2016).

Vital to the success of academic/curricular online service-learning courses is the integration of service-learning, leadership, and experientially based learning, which are situated in local communities. Intentional design of such learning opportunities can transform the way leadership learning occurs. Guthrie (2016) offers four considerations for instructors when contemplating developing and delivering online service-learning course in a leadership education framework:

- Build virtual environments that allow for continuous interaction, communication, and relationship building. For example, requiring engagement between students, faculty, and community service contacts through various reflection methods such as discussion board posts, blogging, or social media interaction such as Twitter.
- Create instructional strategies that nurture both autonomy and collaboration. This is a delicate balance to achieve, but for example, create a course around individual service experiences, but require reflections to focus on how their individual experiences apply to the collective, especially in leading others in making positive change.
- Develop, implement, and require various opportunities for critical reflection and inquiry. An example is to provide multiple ways for students to reflect critically. We all reflect differently, so providing different ways of reflecting will not only promote reflection, but also critical inquiry.
- Support primary leadership learning goals, as well as secondary skills, such as mastering navigation of websites and use of hardware and software (Guthrie & McCracken, 2010), through universally accepted platforms.

Example

Students and Individuals Living in a Shelter Collectively Create Art

EXL 361 is a completely online service-learning course which examines community engagement from a positive social action framework, exploring a range of leadership styles, and students' capacities to enact broad change.

Course learning objectives include:

1. Recognition of various historical models of leadership in social change.

2. Development of core personal values and an ethical framework that can be applied to civic engagement and leadership issues.

(Example continues on next page)

Example (Continued)

Students and Individuals Living in a Shelter Collectively Create Art

Course learning objectives include:

3. Identification of strategies for social influence/social change in others and self.

4. Reflection on the relationship between the individual and society within contemporary American context.

5. Enhancement of overall service-learning comprehension by participating in the reflective learning process.

Course assignments combine creating and completing individual service experiences, and reflecting on those experiences in futuristic and collective frameworks. These assignments serve as assessment for student learning.

1. Service Action Plan includes a description of the proposed service project and a description of three personal learning objectives. The personal learning objectives is what the student hopes to gain from the service experiences and should include activities that will assist in learning, supportive resources, and plans to assess their own learning.

2. Service Participation towards Social Change is the actual required service totaling 40 hours.

3. Reading Responses/Discussion Board Participation is engagement through online discussion of reading material and reflection on service experiences.

4. Reflection Journal is aimed at exploring the sociological implications of issues arising with service experiences. A total of 20 entries are required that outline the specific situation in 2-3 sentences and then the rest should focus on making meaning.

5. Addams and Carnegie Reflective Essay compares and contrasts how Jane Addams and Andrew Carnegie differed in purpose and methods of social change, with reflection of what student is seeing incommunity service experience.

6. The Women of Brewster Place Reflective Essay reflects on the book by Gloria Naylor (1982). This reflection essay requires students to discuss how two women they selected from the story demonstrated leadership and created social change. Additionally, students need to connect this to their individual community service project.

7. Final Action Project Reflection Paper synthesizes the course readings, individual service experience, personal learning objectives developed in the service action plan, and connects it to collective social change and leadership.

Resources will assist leadership educators in development and implementation of online service-learning courses. Minnesota Campus Compact's Center for Digital Civic Engagement (CDCE, Service-Learning in Online Courses, 2017) provides an excellent list of resources. This site provides links to scholarship in online service-learning, sample syllabi, and access to best practices. This site also offers connections to other educators doing this work.

PEDAGOGY TO PRACTICE

We would like to offer a few points highlighting service-learning as a leadership education pedagogy and how putting this instructional strategy into practice has the potential in transforming leadership learning.

Pedagogy Overview

- Service-learning can profoundly impact students' educational experiences by bringing together student identities, group dynamics, and community needs.
- Reflection is vital to successful service-learning programs because students need structured activities to make meaning from their experiences and connect it to course content.
- In the realm of higher education research, high-quality short-term and longitudinal studies on student learning demonstrate the wide breadth and deep gains associated with service-learning along dimensions of cognitive development, behavioral proficiency, and relational efficacy.
- The CAPSL created by Bringle and Hatcher (1996) provides insightful steps in implementing and institutionalizing service-learning in higher education.
- Instructors who seek to employ service-learning pedagogy should carefully consider the personal and institutional resources needed to construct meaningful experiences; although the gains are great, the costs are also high, especially among underresourced programs.

Transforming Leadership Learning Through Service-Learning

- Five intersections of service-learning and leadership offered by Wagner and Pigza (2016) provide congruency and tensions. Leadership educators need to keep these in mind when using service-learning as a leadership pedagogy. These intersections include intentionality, role of failure, participation, prerequisites of agency, and learning across cultures.

- Effective leadership educators consider incorporating various types of service-learning projects—individual, group, and distance—to maximize student learning and service to the surrounding community.
- Considering leadership competencies associated with the intersection of service-learning and leadership education are a worthwhile place to start infusing content and process.
- Practical recommendations for service-learning initiatives in leadership education, as well as examples of successful programs are offered to guide and inspire.

CHAPTER 15

SELF-ASSESSMENT, PEER-ASSESSMENT, AND OBSERVATION INSTRUMENTS

This chapter explores the use of self-assessment techniques, peer assessments, and observation instruments as pedagogy in leadership education. Each of these instructional strategies shares an evaluative approach, whether it is the assessment of one's self or others. In with each tool, the learner must practice mindfulness to reflect on his or her own or others' behaviors. Accordingly, there is strong support for representing assessment as a tool for learning (Dochy & McDowell, 1997). Studies have shown associations between using these instructional strategies and enhanced development of crucial leadership skills, such as responsibility, judgement, autonomy, critical thinking, and self-regulation (Kılıç, 2016). Moreover, the interpretation of assessment of student learning as solely something that happens when a process of learning is outdated (Dochy, Segers, & Sluijsmans, 1999). Thus, we suggest integrating a variety of these strategies throughout your educational program to engage students in the learning process and encourage them to take responsibility for their own learning (Kılıç, 2016). To those ends, we begin with a brief overview of each strategy, review its use in instructional contexts, and conclude with specific applications in leadership education.

The Role of Leadership Educators: Transforming Learning, pp. 249–266
Copyright © 2018 by Information Age Publishing

SELF-ASSESSMENT

Self-assessment refers to the involvement of learners in making judgments about their own learning, particularly about their achievements and the outcomes of learning (Boud & Falchikov, 1989). Research suggests using self-assessment as an instructional strategy to promote skill building, responsibility for one's own learning, and problem-solving capacities (Sluijsmans, Dochy, & Moerkerke, 1999). In short, students need to learn about themselves (Csongor, 1992). Fittingly, Csongor (1992) argues, "we can place more responsibility on students' shoulders for the evaluation of their own performance, attitude, and behavior" (p. 636). Examples of this sentiment from across higher education include (a) portfolios where students report on their own learning through the completion of assignments such as sharing preconceptions about teaching and learning, comparing goals, creating a community of learners, generating student explanations and improving communication, group quizzes, challenging thinking dispositions, posttest evaluations and collaborative assessing (Keith, 1996); (b) audio or video-recording oneself performing a desired skill (Anderson & Freiberg, 1995); and (c) reflective journaling about one's learning (McNamara & Deane, 1995). A fortunate by-product of these instructional strategies includes many students performing self-evaluation without being prompted (Csongor, 1992). Relatedly, when provided opportunities to engage in self-assessment within a subject, students' ability to accurately self-assess improves (Boud, Lawson, & Thompson, 2013).

Self-Assessment Instruments

One of the most frequently used instructional strategies for facilitating self-assessment among students are structured self-assessments or instruments, more commonly referred to as personality tests, questionnaires, and inventories (e.g., Hendrix, 1978). For consistency, we will refer to this collection of instructional strategies as "assessment instruments." There are many reasons to use assessment instruments as an instructional strategy. Given their representation in popular culture, students are already familiar with many of them. Thousands of them are available online, appearing on Buzzfeed, Facebook, and other popular websites such as HumanMetrics and Queendom. Additionally, they are simple, having two things in common: they ask us questions about ourselves and they tell us about ourselves (Thorson, 2014). Finally, research suggests that assessment instruments (a) help us achieve identity; (b) provide enjoyable feedback confirming our views of ourselves; (c) and help justify our behavior (Gollwitzer & Kirchhof, 1998; Swann, 2012; Thorson, 2014). Among the plethora of assessment instruments, a select few are used widely among leadership educators. Correspondingly, although you may use any assessment instrument alongside intentionality and defined learning objectives, we offer coverage of some of the most prevalent ones later in this chapter.

Peer Assessment Instruments

Peer assessments, or appraisal activities where students evaluate their peers and make observations of one another along established metrics (Bright et al., 2016), offer a variety of benefits in supplementing an educator's task of evaluating students. A primary benefit that occurs when students are asked to assume partial ownership of the educative process is enhanced engagement. Furthermore, assessing peers fosters mutual accountability among students and a greater commitment to learning (Bryant & Carless, 2010; Cestone, Levine, & Lane, 2008). If expected to submit peer evaluations, students may play close attention to, prepare for, and seriously consider work executed by their peers to compose representative evaluations of their efforts. Learning benefits are greater still when students are graded on their own assessments of peers (Michaelsen, Parmelee, McMahon, & Levine, 2008). As a secondary benefit, students working in groups have unique perspectives from which to evaluate the relative contributions of other group members (Malone, 2011). Hence, "peer-assessment is an arrangement for learners to consider and specify the level, value, or quality of a product or performance of other equal-status learners" (Topping, 2009, pp. 20–21). When assessing peers, students may simply provide performance feedback to each other, or they may determine a portion of others' grades (Gueldenzoph & May, 2002). Students may also design and administer their own assessments (Topping, 2009). This instructional strategy is one of the most developed meta-practices—a pedagogical element that is used across various teaching strategies or pedagogical systems (Bright et al., 2016)—in the constructivist repertoire education (Black & William, 1998; Harlen & James, 1997; Price, O'Donovan, & Rust, 2007). When used as an instructional strategy, peer assessment can increase variety and interest, activity and interactivity, identification and bonding, self-confidence, and empathy with others (Topping, 2009).

Observation Instruments

An observation instrument is an organized, objective system for observing, coding, arranging, and analyzing the behavior of an individual or group of individuals (Martin, 1977). Most widely used in teacher education, observation instruments have been used to evaluate specific teacher competencies, such as classroom talk (Mercer, 2010) and project-based learning (Stearns, Maorgan, Capraro, & Capraro, 2012), as well as subject-specific strategies, such as English reading (Gertsen, Baker, Haager, & Graves, 2005), content- and language-integrated learning (De Graaff, Jan Koopman, Anikina, & Westhoff, 2007), English language arts (Grossman et al., 2010), and mathematical instruction (Matsumura, Garnier, Slater, & Boston, 2008). By breaking up the continuous stream of observable behaviors (e.g., teacher-student), such instruments provide a rubric for recording interactions between and among individuals (Martin, 1977). However, Martin (1977) argues that the instrument categories "must be objective, relevant, parsimonious, efficient, reliable, and valid" (p. 45). Restated differently, to ensure that the behaviors recorded are directly observable and prepare the way for reliable coding across a number of independent observers, the behavioral categories must possess the status of observable, intervening variables, not hypothetical constructs (Martin, 1977).

ASSESSMENT AND OBSERVATION IN LEADERSHIP EDUCATION

The remainder of this chapter will include a variety of examples of the tools introduced above (i.e., assessment instruments, peer-assessments, and observation instruments) in leadership education contexts. In doing so, we provide an overview of the most commonly used assessment instruments (e.g., the Leadership Practice Inventory, 360-degree feedback), offer a tool for assessing skill development, and outline an exemplar observation instrument assignment. It is important to add that many of these tools can be combined. For example, pairing forms of self- and peer assessment provides opportunities for students to (a) enhance their performance by realizing their own gaps and reducing their mistakes (Kılıç, 2016); (b) promote self-awareness by means of feedback from multiple perspectives (Saito & Fujita, 2004); and (c) gain insight about their own performance through evaluating the performance or outcomes of others (Bostock, 2001). Additionally, self- and peer assessments could be used as part of co-assessment, enabling instructor and students to work together in constructive ways, but ultimately giving the instructor the final decision about the process or product (Somervell, 1993). For example, Roberts (2008) suggests pairing a self-assessment of individual factors (e.g., personality) and a 360-degree feedback on leadership ability from a student's superiors, peers, or subordinates (Foster & Law, 2006). In doing so, students compare and contrast sets of information and ultimately become more aware of their own limitations in self-assessment and how these limitations impact others (Roberts, 2008). We suggest that you consider the potential for multisource feedback through pairing and/or sequencing the instructional strategies and examples offered in this chapter in your educational programs.

Self-Assessment in Leadership Education

Self-assessment is inextricably linked to reflection (see Chapter 10) as a tool for connecting experience to meaning. Through the process of self-assessment, leadership students become more self-aware and engaged in their own learning. As such, this has a compounding benefit as many students leaving our educational programs for the workforce will be led by individuals with large spans of control, working in cultures that expect a high degree of independence, and the ability to be self-directed in learning (Dungan & Mundhenk, 2006). Reassuringly, feedback from self-assessment has been linked to gains in student transitions into professional life (Larsen, 1998; Taylor, 2014).

In an effort to explore specifically the effects of using self-assessments with leadership students, Dungan and Mundhenk (2006) took an action research approach that included leadership and management students from three different universities who engaged varied forms of self-assessment. Through content analysis of students papers and survey instruments, five major but overlapping themes related to student use of self-assessment emerged, including: (a) opportunities to reflect which in turn provided opportunities for new understandings and meaning making that students described as transformative; (b) motivation for greater achievement as a result of knowing they had to write and discuss their own performance; (c) accountability for the quality of their work and personal responsibility as a result of the opportunities to reflect; (d) becoming reflective learners and deeper understanding of the learning process; and (e) honesty and self-criticism of their own performance (Dungan & Mundhenk, 2006). Attendant to these findings, we offer the following leadership education self-assessment activities, each of which could be integrated and applied to an Individual Leadership Development Plan (see Chapter 12):

- Provide opportunities for students to assess their own work. Variations include establishing agreed upon criteria at the beginning of an educational program to assignment- and task-specific self-assessment.
- Guide students through a self-assessment of their leadership journey. For example, students might reflect upon their placement on the in the six stages of the Leadership Identity Development (LID)

model—Awareness, Exploration/Engagement, Leadership Identified, Leadership Differentiated, Generativity, and Integration/Synthesis (Komives et al., 2005)—and identify what experiences and lessons they need to transition between LID stages (Komives et al., 2006)

- Have students create a learning plan to develop agency and efficacy around their own learning needs. Then have students reflect across an educational program (e.g., one-minute papers) on the progress they are making with their plans. This activity intentionally displaces authority away from the professor and onto the student (Dungan & Mundhenk, 2006).

- Have students complete an assessment instrument and reflect on their results. We offer detailed coverage of this strategy in the following section.

Self-Assessment Instruments in Leadership Education

Popular in practice, leadership educators use a variety of assessment instruments to connect course material to the learning experience and invite introspective discussion (Allen & Hartman, 2008; Jenkins, 2012, 2013, 2016, 2017a). Moreover, studies demonstrate myriad benefits of assessment instruments, such as the positive impact on group and community values (Buschlen, 2009). The two most common assessment formats are: (a) normative (e.g., Likert-type), where individuals indicate their degree of agreement regarding how accurately items describe their behaviors; and (b) forced choice, where individuals are required to select from a set of statements matched regarding social desirability (Harland, 2003). In either format, participants have varied perceptions of accuracy, usefulness, control, and respectfulness (Alexander & Beggs, 1986; Gilliland, 1993; Harland, 2003; Rosse, Miller, & Stecher, 1994). In any event, we advise that instructors take the time to research the trustworthiness and credibility of any instrument they employ.

Any assessment pedagogy benefits greatly from serious consideration of how instructors intend to facilitate students' use of their results. Intentionality is critical; simply offering an assessment instrument is not an instructional strategy, nor is it pedagogy. Effective leadership educators approach these—and any learning activities— by purposefully constructing learning outcomes and strategically sequencing activities (Harper, 2011). For example, as an activity to accompany Chapter 4 of *Exploring Leadership: For College Students Who Want to Make a Difference* (Komives et al., 2007)—"Understanding Yourself"—Owen et al. (2007) use the Myers-Briggs Type Indicator (MBTI) assessment instrument as a way of examining individual differences related to values, beliefs, ethics, and character. Through this exploration of personal characteristics, students examine aspects of themselves, including self-concept, self-esteem, identity, values, and personality traits, which in turn lead to a common framework to discuss individuality among their peers. The *Instructor's Guide for Exploring Leadership* (Owen et al., 2007) offers the following prompt as a primer for this activity: "Write a reflection paper describing why you think your type description is or is not reflective of you" (p. 44). This written reflection could be completed as a short in-class writing activity or students could complete the writing exercise prior as homework; then provide an opportunity for students to share their reflections with peers and discuss individual differences. In summary, assessment instruments are best used as a primer, with complimentary experiential learning such as TBL (Clinebell & Stecher, 2003) or role play (Jenkins & Cutchens, 2012).

Widely Used Self-Assessment Instruments in Leadership Education

We have already remarked on the ubiquity of assessment instruments in popular culture, however; effective leadership educators cultivate a repertoire of tools that are appropriate for their students, outcomes, and educational contexts. We are not in the position to make these decisions on your behalf, yet we can offer the follow examples from our own experiences.

- Behavioral assessment instruments: Leadership Practices Inventory (LPI) (Posner, 2004), which is based on Kouzes and Posner's classic work, *The Leadership Challenge* (1995) and more recently, *The Student Leadership Challenge* (2014).
- Trait-based assessment tools: StrengthsFinder 2.0 (Asplund, Lopez, Hodges, & Harter, 2007; Rath, 2007), which is based on the Gallup Organization's research into human performance.
- Assessments of personality: These include various versions of the Myers Briggs Type Indicator (Myers Briggs, 2017) as well as other tests to measure Emotional Intelligence (Shankman, Allen, & Miguel, 2015).
- Popular leadership textbooks with assessments: *Leadership: Theory and Practice* (Northouse, 2016), *Leadership: Research Findings, Practice, and Skills* (DuBrin, 2016), *Crucibles of Leadership: How to Learn from Experience to Become a Great Leader* (Thomas, 2008), and *Leaders and the Leadership Process: Readings, Self-Assessments, and Applications* (Pierce & Newstrom, 2008) include assessment instruments on a variety of leadership-specific topics (e.g., "Leadership Trait

Questionnaire," "Least Preferred Co-Worker," "The Leadership Archetype Questionnaire") within and at the end of each chapter. The popular management textbook, *Developing Management Skills* (Whetten & Cameron, 2015), contains more than 30 self-assessments for students, including assessments of learning styles, emotional intelligence, stress management, time management, self-awareness, and communication styles.

At this point, a careful treatment of some of these recommendations may help those unfamiliar make decisions about their utility.

Leadership Practices Inventory. The Leadership Practices Inventory (LPI) is an assessment instrument developed by Kouzes and Posner (2013) to assess the behaviors of leaders, developed using a variety of managers and employees in public and private sector organizations. Results from the LPI provide ratings along scales associated with Kouzes and Posner's (2017) "Five Practices of Exemplary Leadership" from their bestselling book, *The Leadership Challenge*: (a) model the way; (b) enable others to act; (c) encourage the heart; (d) challenge the process; and (e) inspire a shared vision. The LPI has undergone intense scrutiny for reliability and validity (Carless, 2001), as well as gender effects (Posner & Brodsky, 1994) and cultural implications (Zagorsek, Stough, & Jaklic, 2006). A related *Student LPI* was later developed (Kouzes & Posner, 2003) and underwent rigorous psychometric testing (Posner, 2015b). The LPI has been used in a variety of disciplines, including the leadership practices of nurses (Tourangeau & McGilton, 2004), law enforcement (Vito & Higgins, 2010), and volunteers (Posner, 2015a). Instructor resources are plentiful for the LPI, including the *Leadership Practices Inventory: Workbook* (2012b), for use along with the assessment instrument, to analyze and make meaning of results; and *The Leadership Challenge Workbook* (2012c), a companion workbook for more detailed explanations of the five practices. For the Student LPI, *The Student Leadership Challenge: Facilitation and Activity Guide* (Kouzes, Posner, High, & Morgan, 2013) and *The Student Leadership Challenge: Activities Book* (Kouzes, Posner, High, & Morgan, 2013a), each contains a considerable number of experiential learning activities appropriate for leadership education programs, as well as the companion *The Student Leadership Challenge: Student Workbook and Personal Leadership Journal* (Kouzes, Posnner, High, & Morgan, 2013b), which includes complimentary workbook pages and structured reflection exercises.

StrengthsFinder®. The Clifton StrengthsFinder® online assessment focuses on areas of individuals' greatest potential for building unique strengths (Asplund, Lopez, Hodges, & Harter, 2009). It has been routinely validated (Asplund, Lopoez, Hodges, & Harter, 2007) and administered to more than 16 million individuals worldwide (Gallup, 2017). Strengths-Finder® helps individuals identify their "top fve strengths"—the fve most prominent personal characteristics from a list of 34 natural talent themes (Soria & Stubblefield, 2015). Talent themes are naturally recurring patterns of thoughts, feelings, and behaviors that, when refined with knowledge and skill, can be developed into strengths (Hodges & Harter, 2005).

As part of a growing trend, more than 500 colleges and universities have integrated "strengths-based" programming to boost student engagement and retention by identifying and applying students' individual talents to various aspects of student life (Bowers & Lopez, 2010; Lopez & Louis, 2009; StrengthsQuest, 2017). Based on the conceptual framework of positive psychology (Aspinwall & Staudinger, 2003; Buckingham & Clifton, 2001; Peterson & Seligman, 2004; Rath, 2007), strengths-based programming fosters individuals' potential as opposed to remediating their deficits (Keyes & Haidt, 2003), elevates individuals' emotional well-being (Seligman, 2002), promotes awareness of individuals' strengths (Peterson & Seligman, 2004), and increases personal confidence, resulting in greater recognition of leadership ability (K. D. Anderson, 2004). As a result, applications for leadership programs abound.

For example, students who were asked to reflect on their experiences with strengths-based programming reported improved interpersonal understanding and relationships, such as noticing talents and strengths in others, communicating better with others, higher self-worth, and greater authenticity (K. D. Anderson, 2004). Strategic strengths-based leadership educators combine programming with Rath and Conchie's (2009) *Strengths Based Leadership: Great Leaders, Teams, and Why People Follow*, which provides specific approaches for leading with an individual's top five strengths and enables them to plot the strengths of a team based on the four domains of leadership strength explained in the book: (a) strategic thinking; (b) influencing; (c) relationship building; and (d) executing.

Capitalizing on this application, Komives et al. (2013) replaced the MBTI for StrengthsFinder® in the third edition of their widely used *Exploring Leadership: For College Students Who Want to Make a Difference* (Komives et al., 2006). The companion, *Exploring Leadership, Facilitation and Activity Guide: For College Students Who Want to Make a Difference* and *Student Workbook* (Wagner & Ostick, 2013), includes more than a dozen activities to intentionally integrate students' StrengthsFinder® results and apply them to various leadership topics, including self-knowledge, diversity, and reflection. One such activity, "Understanding Your Talents" (Wagner & Ostick, 2013, pp. 76–77), provides the following prompts to build learners' capacity for using talents effectively through intentional practice:

1. What does this talent mean to you?
2. How would you describe this talent to someone else in your own words?
3. When was the last time you used this talent?
4. What is a goal you have for yourself?
5. How can you use this talent to help you reach your goal?
6. What are three ways in which you can practice using this talent in the next week?

We have included an adaptation of the activity "Talents in Action" from Wagner and Ostick (2013) in Chapter 15.

MBTI. The MBTI has become a popular tool in education (DiTiberio, 1998). Like the LPI and StrengthsFinder®, the MBTI personality inventory can be used to understand individual differences in how people behave as well as assist in team building and the development of communication skills (Goby & Lewis, 2000). Myers and McCaulley first used the MBTI as a means to enhance team effectiveness in 1974 (Myers, McCaulley, Quenk, & Hammer, 1998). According to the *MBTI Manual*, "the basic assumptions underlying using the MBTI with teams remain the same.... Knowledge of individual differences will help teams identify the particular talents and gifts that each member brings to his or her task; and this knowledge can help reduce conflict by reframing potential sources of misunderstanding as natural individual differences" (p. 348). Based on Jungian psychological theory, the MBTI assesses psychological type in terms of four dichotomous dimensions: (a) preferred modes of perception, either Sensing (S) or Intuition (N); (b) preferred means of judgment, either Thinking (T) or Feeling (F); (c) source of energy, either Extraversion (E) or Introversion (I); and (d) orientation to the outside world, either Judging (J) or Perceiving (P) (Clinebell & Stecher, 2003). Together, scores on the four dimensions result in 16 different possible personality types. For information related to reliability and validity of the MBTI, please see Gardner and Martinko (1996) and Myers et al. (1998).

Needs Assessments

Although leadership education varies widely, leadership educators may—like their peers in management development programs (see Rothwell & Kazanas, 1993)—conduct needs assessments (e.g., personality tests) prior to undertaking developmental activities (Fletcher, 1993; Greene, 1999; Starkey, 1992). According to Cacioppe (1998) and McClure and Werther (1993), needs assessments in a developmental context may be used to evaluate self-knowledge or self-awareness, identify strengths and weaknesses (Stanton & Matthews, 1995), ascertain learning or leadership styles (Allen & Hartman, 2009), and enhance team effectiveness (Kamen, 1997). Moreover, understanding the relationship between one's personality inclinations and day-to-day organizational behaviors may be critical for designing and applying successful individual development efforts (Berr, Church, & Waclawski, 2000).

A truly innovative approach involves students making their own assessments. For example, Harrington (1995) suggests three different methods for facilitating self-assessment as an instructional strategy: (a) students are provided a list of abilities with definitions and directions to indicate which areas they feel they are best or strongest; (b) a Likert scale to a group of designated abilities (e.g., "In comparison to my peers, my ability to influence others is excellent, above average, average, below average, or poor); and (c) students provide different examples of each ability's application and rate it from high to low.

Peer Assessment in Leadership Education

The use of peer assessments in leadership education varies widely in practice (Bright et al., 2016). Yet in many cases, the ability to develop and convey feedback for others is a crucial leadership skill (Cameron & Caza, 2005; DeRue & Wellman, 2009; Goleman, Boyatzis & McKee, 2013; Kouzes & Posner, 1995). Hence, developing these skills in leadership education contexts is essential. Moreover, effective and efficient feedback skill development provides many benefits for student leadership learning, such as (a) promoting the culture of and providing feedback; (b) enabling creativity, innovation, and self-awareness by establishing an egalitarian setting, which frees students to share meaningful perspectives with one another (Baker & Baker, 2012; Mayo, Kakarika, Pastor, & Brutus, 2012); (c) building community through requiring students to both influence and be influenced (Putzel, 2007); and (d) improvements in writing and group work (O'Donnell & Topping, 1998; Topping, 2009). To enable these abilities, effective leadership educators integrate peer assessments where students evaluate and provide detailed feedback to other students in team-based learning (TBL; as discussed in Chapter 13), during and following class presentations, attendance, learning of specific content, or other class deliverables (Bright et al., 2016).

It is important to note that students may experience a range of reactions and emotions when giving feedback to their peers (Bright et al., 2016). Moreover, many students are initially hesitant about sharing corrective feedback and being objective with one another early in a class. However, with practice, they may gain confidence and the ability to be honest with and empower their peers (Hanrahan & Isaacs, 2001; Kılıç, 2016; Putzel, 2007). As mentioned in Chapter 9, establishing a culture of feedback early in the semester creates learning environments where students are more comfortable sharing feedback associated with peer assessment and are more engaged (Bright et al., 2016). Below we offer two specific examples of peer-assessment interventions in leadership education contexts—peer evaluations and the 360-degree feedback tool.

Peer Evaluations

As described in Chapter 13, peer evaluations can be developmental learning activities for student teams. Michaelsen and Sweet (2008) go so far as to claim, "without peer evaluation, it [a class design] is not TBL" (p. 2). Indeed, TBL proponents claim that the motivational power of peer accountability is a primary influencer of student learning. Some instructors may rely solely on quantitative instruments, whereas others require teammates to deliver qualitative feedback throughout a term. Although the former is often presented through rubrics, the latter adds a level of sophistication to grading, empowering students to confront each other during projects (Buschlen, 2009). According to Buschlen (2009), this added measure of accountability enhanced students' leadership and interpersonal skills and developed students' delegation, conflict negotiation, and evaluation, as well as the realization of accountability. Lessons like these transcend the classroom, transforming students into more accountable leaders.

360-Degree Feedback

Much has been written about the benefits of the 360-degree feedback tool for leadership development (e.g., Alimo-Metcalfe, 1998; Day, Fleenor, Atwater, Sturm, & McKee, 2014; Markham, Markham, & Smith, 2015). Bass and Avolio (1996) found improvements in managers who attended a leadership training program after receiving 360-degree feedback. Alimo-Metcalfe's (1998) review of the 360-feedback literature noted, "individuals whose performance was originally rated low by their staff, were rated higher when rated again, several months later. This suggests that these individuals had modified their behaviors in the direction of perceived greater effectiveness by their staff" (p. 38). Toegel and Conger (2003) suggest specific guidelines for designing 360-degree assessments for the developmental needs of an individual, which we believe constitute an appropriate approach for use in leadership education classrooms: (a) organize the assessment around competencies or learning outcomes related to class content; (b) organize raters according to their level (e.g., peer-students, co-workers, faculty, staff, etc.); (c) provide opportunities for both quantitative and qualitative feedbac; and (d) educate students on how to analyze and reflect on received feedback and how to construct a personal development plan. Finally, if adapted for use across courses or programs, the "best class ever" activity from Chapter 9 can be a form and a model of 360-degree feedback. Although the initial activity is used to garner student buy-in and ownership of the course, we suggest providing opportunities for "mid-semester check-ins" with students, during which they can discuss topics related to class or challenges they are facing as leaders. According to Jenkins and Sowcik (2014), students who took part in this adaptation reported higher levels of interest in the course and greater facilitation of learning in their end-of-year evaluations. In addition, they specifically provided written comments in these evaluations about the importance of feedback in their classroom learning.

Observation Instruments in Leadership Education

Depending on what you want your leadership students to be able to do (e.g., lead members of a team), self-assessment may need to be coupled with observational instruments (i.e., observation of peers, instructors, bosses). Furthermore, assessments may need to occur in situations or contexts of increasing complexity or over time. For example, it may be helpful to "move from paper-based scenarios, to personal analysis of past instances with team leadership, to observed, authentic cases in early experiential settings, to focused skill assessments while working in a team" (Janke et al., 2016, p. 10). Subsequently, the scope and duration of leadership roles as well as the skills, competencies, and behaviors being developed, will vary.

In most leadership education settings, the instructor's responsibility is to ensure that students "do" leadership (Janke et al., 2016). As students practice leadership roles, skills, or behaviors, the competencies being developed must be assessed. For example, if students are to gain experience inspiring a shared vision, student learning might be assessed through a real-time log or a personal journal (e.g., lists of efforts to implement Kouzes & Ponser's "Inspire a Shared Vision" construct; Dellow & Jenkins, 2014). Learning experiences could also be documented after the activity through reflective journals, requiring students to move beyond describing contributions and including critical analyses and/or evidence of their influence (Janke et al., 2016). With these examples in mind, we explain the association between mindfulness and observation instruments, wherein we offer detailed examples from Dellow and Jenkins' (2014) example, as well as offer an additional exercise from the Collegiate Leadership Competition (CLC) to evaluate and develop skills-based competencies.

Observation Instruments and Mindfulness

When applied in an observational capacity, mindfulness can contribute positively to leadership effectiveness. We define mindfulness as being actively open and attentive to the present. In this instructional strategy, students develop through reflection on how they can improve their leadership skills. Additionally, this strategy reflects aspects of motivation and ability, two components that signal students' developmental readiness for more focused leadership development (Reichard & Walker, 2016). Anchored by a belief in the values of assessments across contexts, complexities, and frequencies, Dellow and Jenkins's (2014) pedagogical process helps students identify specific leadership skills in their supervisors using a case study approach (see Chapter 11 for a complete discussion of case study pedagogy). Through a series of observations, reflections, and personal logs, students became more mindful and aware of their own as well as others' leadership capacity.

Utilizing Observational Instruments to Enhance Case Studies

In the previous example, Dellow and Jenkins (2014) paired the LPI (but you could easily use other assessment instruments or any theoretical framework pragmatic to your course objectives or outcomes) with an observation instrument. Fortunately, each practice in the LPI is defined by observable behaviors that might be considered skills. Additionally, the practices provided an excellent theoretical lens to identify specific behaviors that might be considered "necessary, but not sufficient" for effective leadership. For the assignment, students completed a semester long case study, which acted as a vehicle toward student mindfulness of the presence or absence of the LPI behavioral indicators. In the case study, students were asked to focus attention on specific supervisor behaviors to better understand how theoretical concepts manifested under practical circumstances. In doing so, an observation instrument to provide examples of skills and behaviors characteristic of each of the practices described in *The Leadership Challenge* was developed. One of the behaviors listed was "Model the Way." Accordingly, the leadership practice section of the observation instrument was "During this observation period did they: Set an example for you and others, 'walked the talk?'" The choices to help students think about frequency were: (a) Did not observe during this period; (b) Observed occasionally; (c) Observed frequently; and (d) Observed most of the time.

Students were encouraged to consider frequency broadly, not attempt to measure it with discrete units of time (e.g., minutes, hours, days, etc.). The semester-long course assignment required three case study segments, and students tended to see and discuss different leadership practices over the course of the semester (unless there was a dominant behavior across time). After each case study portion of each segment, reflections followed.

Example

Syllabus Description for Case Study Assignment

One of the major tenets of this course is the Five Practices of Exemplary Leadership from our textbook *The Leadership Challenge.* To explore the five practices in more depth, you will need to read the textbook and also complete a leadership case study and personal leadership log that includes your personal observations and reflections of the five practices in action. To do so, you will be asked to select a person in a leadership/management/supervision position with whom you either work or are able to know well enough to obtain relevant information. The purpose of the case study is to observe that individual, unobtrusively, and describe his/her actions in terms of the different leadership concepts that will be studied in this course. The assignment has three parts:

Segment #1:

Case study section (3–5 pages)

Position description for the observee:

What is the position of the person you are observing and what is your understanding of the primary responsibilities of that person? How would you describe some criteria of effectiveness for that position? What is the background of that person? What kind of positions and experiences did he/she have prior to the current positions?

In Segment #1, you will be looking for the leadership practices described in any of the readings and the five practices of exemplary leadership. Initially you may want to use the Leadership Behaviors of Kouzes and Posner Observation Scale as a tool to focus your observations.

Leadership log section (2–3 pages)

Using the leadership log guidelines provided, you will provide more of a "critical self-reflection" on your reaction to the theories, ideas, and general observations about your own leadership journey.

Segment #2:

Case study section (3–5 pages)

You will continue to observe the behavior of your subject using the K&P Scale, but also add ideas from the Wren text, chapters from the DuBrin text, articles we have read, and any other theories or perspectives we have studied or other leadership practices that you personally believe important and have not been addressed.

Leadership log section (2–3 pages)

Continue with your critical self-reflection of your leadership journey.

(Example continues on next page)

Example

> **Syllabus Description for Case Study Assignment**
>
> Segment #3:
>
> Critical reflection of the exercise (4–6 pages)
>
> What does it all mean to you? Looking back over the three observations during the semester, what sticks out in your mind about what you observed, or didn't observe? What practices did you observe most? What practices did you observe the least?

Skill Building With Skill Sheets

Authentically developing leadership skills among students in realms such as negotiation, conflict management, problem solving, and ethical decision making is critical if we hope to develop well-rounded individuals prepared to engage in leading others (Allen, Jenkins, & Krizanovic, in press). Accordingly, leadership educators who focus on skill building narrowly, as opposed to integrating conceptual understanding (e.g., knowledge) or incorporating personal growth (e.g., identity development), invest tremendous time and energy in practice, coaching, and providing feedback. Consider this: proficient skill development (e.g., playing soccer, cooking, firefighting, becoming a black belt in karate, flying a plane, or administering CPR) requires deliberate practice. A place like the kitchen for a chef or a stage for a performer, where people can practice with an opportunity to rehearse, receive coaching and feedback and hone skills beyond their current ability, is also needed in leadership education (Ericsson, Prietula & Cokely, 2007). There is much to learn about these developmental processes from the expertise literature. Adapting Ericsson and Pool's (2016) elements of deliberate practice, we offer leadership educators the following suggestions for deliberate leadership practice: (a) emphasize the need for objective criteria upon which superior leaders can be judged; (b) require an instructor who can provide practice activities designed to help students improve their performance; (c) develop skills that others have figured out how to do and for which effective training techniques exist; (d) require a practice regimen; (e) take students out of their "ability comfort zones" ; (f) define specific goals; and (g) integrate feedback and modifications of efforts in response to feedback. Effective leadership educators are those who seek to develop expertise in their students and draw on practical recommendations, intentional pedagogy, and meaningful feedback to satisfy their learning objectives.

In designing learning experiences that lead to expertise, the CLC developed video tutorials, learning materials, and teaching tips as well as processes for activities such as negotiation, conflict management, presentation skills, ethical decision making, and problem solving. Most salient to this chapter, we direct attention to the skill sheets (Brennan & Braslow, 1995) developed by the CLC, which leadership educators can use to assess performance. According to Allen, Jenkins, and Krizanovic (2017), skill sheets are used in the following manner: (a) students are taught a relevant process (e.g., a simple decision-making model) and commit the process to memory and then are given a skill sheet that further outlines what "model" behavior looks like; (b) the leadership educator models the process for students so they can critique and evaluate performance; (c) students are placed in activities where they have a chance to "practice" leading the decision-making process; and (d) after the activity, students receive feedback (coaching) from their instructor and peers on their performance. In this example, skill sheets are used as observational instruments or rubrics to evaluate students' leadership performance. Opportunities to enhance this specific activity include peer observations or inviting other faculty or community members to volunteer in the evaluations. We encourage leadership instructors to consider how skill sheets may improve student learning while also assessing their appropriateness for their contexts.

PEDAGOGY TO PRACTICE

Assessments and instruments are often used as an instructional strategy in leadership education. In summary, we offer highlights of using assessments and instruments as a leadership education pedagogy, as well as how to put these strategies into practice, which can transform leadership learning.

Pedagogy Overview

- Assessments and instruments can be used to bring the learning-feedback cycle to life, involving students in their own learning, reflections on that learning, and integration of meaning to make learning actionable.
- Self-assessments are greatly represented in popular culture. Literally thousands are available online. However, many are not based on research, so be cautious in selection of self-assessments as an instructional strategy.
- By providing students with a structured observation experience, educators can facilitate opportunities for students to be mindful of the presence or absence of specific behaviors.

Transforming Leadership Learning Through Assessments and Observations

- Focusing on recommendations from expertise and human performance scholarship represents one of many starting points for leadership instructors who seek to incorporate instruments and assessments into leadership learning experiences.
- By focusing students' attention on a theoretical framework of leadership with observation instruments, theory informs practices in a real way. Nonetheless, the specific theory and the specific instrumentation are not as important as the use of an observation instrument and a log as a vehicle for critical self-reflection.
- When approached with mindfulness, assessment- and feedback-based pedagogy can move beyond paper surveys and into practical and applied leadership and management settings.
- Widely used assessment instruments in leadership education include the LPI), StrengthsFinder®, and MBTI.

CHAPTER 16

ROLE-PLAY, SIMULATION, AND GAMES AS LEADERSHIP PEDAGOGY

Role-play, simulation, and games are widely considered effective active learning instructional strategies to promote student engagement (Booth, 1993; Cherney, 2008; R. Stevens, 2015). Arguably, the primary advantage of these instructional strategies is that "students are active participants rather than passive observers" (Svinicki & McKeachie, 2014, p. 210). Moreover, these strategies are effective in achieving a broad range of learning outcomes (Rao & Stupans, 2012), including knowledge acquisition (Eitington, 2001; Lauber, 2007; Taylor, 1999; Van Ments, 1994), communication skill development (Nestel & Tierney, 2007), and emotional development (Roberts, Wiskin, & Roalfe, 2008). This introductory section will define and briefly describe each strategy's utility across educational contexts. The following sections will look at applications and examples of role-play, simulation, and games in leadership education contexts.

ROLE-PLAY

Role-play—where learners act out or improvise assigned roles (based on their conceptions) in case scenarios or unstructured situations (McKeachie, 1986)—is an effective active learning strategy that encourages participation

The Role of Leadership Educators: Transforming Learning, pp. 267–279
Copyright © 2018 by Information Age Publishing

among passive learners, enhances their motivation to learn, promotes retention of material, encourages working in groups, and can potentially generate student enthusiasm and interest (Beidatsch & Broomhall 2010; Bonwell & Eison, 1991; Frederick 2000). Moreover, role-play allows students to practice what they have learned, provides an experiential basis for discussion, and offers opportunities for students to develop an increased awareness of their own feelings and the feelings of others. Furthermore, role-play is utilized in a broad range of disciplines to address learning across cognitive, psychomotor, and affective domains (Rao & Stupans, 2012). For example, role-play has been used in counselor education programs to develop skills in managing emotional reactivity with clients, foster teamwork in aviation (Beard, Salas, & Prince, 1995), and emphasize the social-technical aspects of software engineering in computer programs (Tyson & Janine, 2006).

Role-plays and simulations may be part of a stand-alone activity, span the duration of one or more class meetings, or, in the case of "Role-Play Simulations," run through the term. For example, role-plays may entail situations that could never happen, such as Aristotle debating Nietzsche on the nature of good and evil in the world (DeNeve & Heppner, 1997), or in-depth scenarios, such as Seven Revolutions where students work through the entire policy process of a particular law and are assigned roles in all three branches of the U.S. government, to interest groups, and the press corps (Center for Strategic & International Studies/Seven-Revolutions, 2017). In any event, they should be used with purpose and intentionality.

SIMULATION

Simulations are activities that replicate complex problems or issues and require decision making. Although similar to role-play in several ways, simulations tend to be more structured events with guiding principles, specific rules, and facilitative relationships; generally require more class time; and are defined more precisely than role-plays (Bonwell & Eison, 1991; DeNeve & Heppner, 1997). Simulations can take several hours or even several days to accomplish (Bonwell & Eison, 1991). As with many other instructional strategies covered in this book, the success of a simulation depends on the skills of the facilitator and the structure of the activities.

Simulations challenge students to demonstrate a skill when it is not feasible to use a real-world setting (Palomba & Banta, 1999), and they can provide valuable evidence of student attainment that is both direct and authentic (Ewell, 2002). Most simulations are experiential in nature (Curry & Moutinho, 1992; Drew & Davidson, 1993; Faria & Dickinson, 1994; Keys & Wolfe, 1990) and provide the participant with rapid feedback about performance, which has the power to draw in participants (Drew & Davidson, 1993; Faria & Dickinson, 1994; Keys & Wolfe, 1990). In addition, some suggest that competition (Curry & Moutinho, 1992) and teamwork (Faria & Dickinson, 1994) are the most engaging aspects of a simulation. At times simulations provide realistic representations of real-world situations and deliver participants with a more global view of their organization (Faria & Dickinson, 1994; Keys & Wolfe, 1990; Van Velsor, Ruderman, & Phillips, 1989).

GAMES

Educational games involve students actively participating in some sort of competition or achievement in relationship to a goal—they should teach and be fun (Svinicki & McKeachie, 2014). Many games are also simulations. For example, they might model some real-life problem or situation or involve large-scale simulations, where participants play the roles of individuals or groups in some interpersonal, political, or social situation (e.g., business games, international politics, etc.; Svinicki & McKeachie, 2014), with one key factor: The participant is able to interact with the simulation, making decisions or performing actions that lead to different situations or contexts (Gredler, 1992). This process encourages the participants to reflect about their behavior, improving their skills of communication, decision making, and strategic planning, among others (Hunsaker, 2007). In many instances, games provide opportunities for students to learn from the experience of play (Lopes, Fialho, Cunha, & Niveiros, 2013) and assist students to consider diverse viewpoints (Svinicki & McKeachie, 2014).

ROLE-PLAY, SIMULATION, AND GAMES IN LEADERSHIP EDUCATION

The literature offers substantial support for the use of active learning strategies such as role-playing, games, simulation, debate, and case studies in both the leadership education scholarship (e.g., Allen, 2008; Gibson, 2003; Sogurno, 2003) and in the general college teaching research (e.g., Bonwell & Eison, 1991; Fink, 2013; Svinicki & McKeachie, 2014). Among their virtues, they offer students learning experiences along cognitive, social, emotional, and intellectual dimensions (Guthrie, Phelps, & Downey, 2011). In the remaining sections of this chapter, we provide specific examples for the application of role-play, simulation, and games in leadership education. Our examples include varied in-class and technology-enhanced activities for a range of applications. Finally, in between the simulations and games sections, we offer a list of best practices for facilitating in-class simulations and role-plays.

Role-Play in Leadership Education

Role-play activities provide opportunities for learners to engage in a variety of leadership situations and take on roles that students are unlikely to encounter elsewhere. Perhaps one of the most effective applications for each strategy is providing students opportunities to practice varying leadership styles, skills, behaviors, situations, dispositions, and attitudes while exerting some control of the practical consequences. For example, students may play roles of positional authority, such as a CEO, boss, president, or principal—statuses that are often far beyond the reach of a traditional undergraduate—or perhaps more supportive, followership roles (Sogurno, 2003; Tabak & Lebron, 2017). Role-play can also be used to demonstrate leadership styles such as autocratic, democratic, and laissez-faire (Sogurno, 2003); various points of view around a particular problem, concern, or issue (e.g., interest groups, law makers, citizens); and can potentially demonstrate to students how racial, religious, or socioeconomic backgrounds can shape one's lived and leadership experiences (Frederick 2000; Kornfeld 1990). In doing so, learners relate new and potentially unfamiliar roles and behaviors to practical situations, prompting meaning making, stronger retention of information, and more permanent learning. Additionally, role-play is an effective instructional strategy for specific cases and scenarios, such as the transition to supervisor, supervision of marginal employees, difficult conversations, conflict negotiation, disciplinary actions, and problem solving (Sogurno, 2003).

Effective leadership educators find myriad opportunities and applications for role-play in leadership education contexts. Fortunately, rich data support the use of role-play as a learner-centered pedagogical approach to facilitate deeper and more active engagement with leadership content (Tabak & Lebron, 2017). For example, in her meta-analysis of role-play in leadership training and education, Sogurno (2003) found that role-playing is less about "memorization or teacher-centered pedagogical approaches, but more concerned with active participation and sensitization of learners to new roles and behaviors … [therefore] … it opens up more possibilities of associating enacted roles and behaviors to real-life situations thereby making sense of learning" (p. 355). Moreover, "in an epistemological sense, role-playing facilitates retention of information and enhances, new and a more permanent learning" (Sogurno, 2003, p. 356). To demonstrate the utility of role-play, the following subsections include some examples of role-play use in leadership education and are organized by purpose and intentionality versus instructional strategy.

Inclusion

Role-plays such as "Inclusive Conversations" (Owen et al., 2007) offer students the chance to exercise behaviors related to understanding diversity of social identities and leading across difference, which can also be used to talk about being process-oriented. In the role-play, students are asked to solve a problem, such as a relevant campus issue through dialogue. However, each member of the group is given a nametag with a symbol designating how he or she is to be treated by other members (sheets explaining each treatment and excluding their own treatment are provided to students). For example, "*Star*: This person is liked by everyone but doesn't think the same way as everyone else. S/he comes up with a lot of ideas but usually the rest of the group just ignores them" (Owen et al., 2007, p. 37). As with any role-play, debriefing and reflection is essential to help students make meaning from what they experienced (see Chapters 9 and 12 for more information on debriefing and reflection).

Situational Leadership II

One of our favorite role-play activities uses a fictitious AmeriCorps service project as a scenario for teaching Blanchard's (1985) Situational Leadership II (SLII) model (see also Tremble, n.d.). In this "match-mismatch" role-play, students form groups of eight. The first four members of the group represent the four developmental levels of member followers: (a) the "enthusiastic beginner" (low competence/high commitment), (b) the "disillusioned learner" (low competence/low commitment), (c) the "reluctant contributor" (high competence/low commitment), and (d) the "peak performer" (high competence/high commitment). The remaining four group members represent the four related supervisory styles: (a) high directive/low supportive; (b) high directive/high supportive; (c) low directive/high supportive; and (d) low directive/low supportive. To enact the role-play, the facilitator sets eight chairs in a wagon wheel formation—the team leaders sit at the hub with their backs facing each other's backs, and the team members sit in chairs along the outer rim facing the team leaders. Group members then examine the scenario—again, an AmeriCorps service project (i.e., where the leaders are pitching a tree planting project along a local riverbed)—and get into character. The role-play begins with the first four combinations of members and leaders engaging in conversation based

on their role descriptions (e.g., the "reluctant contributor" and a high direc-
tive/low supportive leader). Allow for four 3-minute rounds so that each
team member has a chance to meet with each leader type. Then debrief the
activity (see Chapter 9 for our earlier conversation on debriefing).

Simulation in Leadership Education

Simulations are important sources of learning (Allen, 2008). According
to Haro and Turgut (2012), among the instructional strategies that foster
students' leadership experiences and in turn provide a better understanding of content, simulations are probably the most effective (Gopinath &
Sawyer, 1999; Zantow, Knowlton, & Sharp, 2005). This is because simulation allows students to make decisions through problem solving (Keys &
Wolfe, 1990), gain exposure to complex decision making under conditions
that approximate real life, and learn from their own mistakes and the
mistakes of others (Haro & Turgut, 2012). Moreover, rather than passively
learning about terms used to describe complex social and technical dynamics, students have opportunities to witness these dynamics unfold firsthand
among their peers. This notion is exemplified by a student's comment from
Allen's (2008) study of the popular ethics simulation *StarPower*: "it brings
individuals in touch with their true ethical values and beliefs. It is easy
to say you believe one thing, but actually behaving that way is altogether
another issue" (p. 146). Accordingly, simulations are effective in teaching both adaptive and technical skills (Heifetz & Linsky, 2004) required
by leaders (Haro & Turgut, 2012). Hence, in the following subsections,
we offer some examples—in-person and technology-enhanced—for using
simulation in leadership education contexts.

Classroom as Organization

In the Classroom-as-Organization (CAO) design, the class evolves as
an organizational system in which students direct their peers, much as
managers do in a business (A. R. Cohen, 1976; W. L. Gardner & Larson,
1988; Putzel, 2007). According to Bright et al. (2016), this meta-practice
takes Dewey's (1938) "learning by doing" to an extreme, treating every
aspect of the class experience as data to be examined in light of organizational theory (Putzel, 2010). In doing so, the CAO approach is constructive,
making extensive use of students to design the curriculum (Bright et al.,
2016). For example, the instructor may delegate students to facilitate in-
class activities, generate performance measures, and assess peers (Putzel,
2007; Romme & Putzel, 2003).

In another example of CAO—"The Organization Simulation"—from the Instructor's Site for the popular organizational theory text *Reframing Organizations* (Bolman & Deal, 2013), Bolman (2014) borrows from the work of Barry Oshry's (1996) *Seeing Systems*. In the 60- to 75-minute simulation, students are assigned to different roles in a three-tier firm whose business is designing slogans, as well as a client group that wants to buy said slogans. The simulation comes in three versions—Private sector, Education, and Public sector—and incorporates a variety of organizational dynamics, particularly around power and structure.

Computer Simulated

The advantages of using computer-based simulations for educational purposes include providing a structured environment to train practical skills and foster participants' complex problem solving and decisions making while engaging players in activities but allowing for experimentation within fictitious situations to enhance student engagement and motivation (Kiili & Lainema, 2008; Lean, Moizer, Towler, & Abbey, 2006; Salas, Wildman, & Piccolo, 2009; Tennyson & Breuer, 2002). Moreover, computer-based simulations offer participants—and the roles they play within the simulator—informational content designed to reflect what people encounter in specific, real-world environments with the added advantage of making mistakes without adverse consequences. Simulations may be enhanced to facilitate the development of leadership behavior by involving peers to provide feedback during decision-making processes (Hunsaker, 2007) or through simulations offering feedback on decisions and outcomes in real-time (Laurillard, 1996). With all of these benefits, computer-based simulations have been used as an effective pedagogical approach to teach a variety of leadership and business concepts ranging from strategic management and accounting to marketing (Aldrich, 2004; Bodoff & Forster, 2005; R. C. Mitchell, 2004; Prensky, 2001; Sparling, 2002; Springer & Borthick, 2004). For a comprehensive list of leadership and business simulations and games, see North-Samardzic (2014). We describe an exemplar computer simulated activity for team-based leadership below.

Mount Everest. Recently, Harvard Business Publishing has expanded their computer-simulated offerings to include individual, multiparticipant, and team-based simulations on topics including entrepreneurship, finance, marketing, negotiation, operations management, organizational behavior, and strategy development (Harvard Business Publishing, 2017). Winner of the 16th Annual MITX Interactive Award in eLearning, the largest awards competition in the country for interactive and web innovations, the leadership and team simulation "Everest V2" (Roberto & Edmondson, 2011) uses the dramatic context of a Mount Everest expedition to reinforce student learning in group dynamics and leadership. In the six-round, 90-minute web-based simulation, students are assigned to one of five roles as part of a team attempting to summit the mountain. Players experience varied challenges related to weather, health, supplies, and hiking speed and must make tough decisions to reach the summit successfully. According to Beaudry (2016), the content provides opportunities for students to learn about the role of an individual with a specific organization, including how values, learning styles, motivation, and decision making can affect individual success and organizational dynamics; "the team," including team concepts such as team development and effectiveness, communication, power and influence, conflict management, as well as leadership styles; and "the organization," including organizational concepts theories such as culture and change management (McShane & Von Glinow, 2009).

In the following list, we have included a list of best practices for facilitating simulations and role-plays in your educational programs (adapted from Freeman & Capper, 1998; Jenkins & Cutchens, 2012; Joyner & Young, 2006; Pescuric & Byham, 1996; Rao & Stupans, 2012; Taylor, 1999).

Example

Best Practices in Using Simulations and Role-Plays

1. Consider the purpose and type of the role or simulation.

- Review the activity or case in advance to evaluate quality, depth, and time needed to facilitate.

- Assess the size of the group needed to act out the required roles.

2. Be prepared.

- Consider what content knowledge students need to know prior to participating in the activity.

- Consider props and backgrounds (e.g., a PowerPoint slide with a full screen photo of the scene) to contextualize the situation and enable student to visualize their roles.

3. Select players strategically and buy some time.

- Ask for volunteers who enjoy role-play, improvisation, feel comfortable, etc. Selecting players strategically is important for the success of role-plays.

- Allow an appropriate amount of time (usually 5–10 minutes will do) for role-players to read the information related to their role and get in character. Just like any pedagogical approach, role-playing succeeds only when students are motivated, enthusiastic, and take their roles seriously (Sogurno, 2003).

- Have something for those not "playing" while role players are preparing (e.g., assessment instrument, reading, presentation on core knowledge, etc.).

(Example continues on next page)

Example (Continued)

Best Practices in Using Simulations and Role-Plays

4. Facilitate.

- Don't expect students to do everything.

- Although it is "role-play," this is not an acting class. Provide some direction, guidelines, prompts, ideas, etc.

- Scripts are okay.

- Set the scene (Backgrounds can be fun! Props too!).

5. Debrief and provide feedback.

- Like any active learning approach, intentionality is key. Capture your students' attention by emphasizing the relevance of role-play tasks through structured and reflective debriefing (Rao & Stupans, 2012).

- Provide a structured environment where students receive peer and instructor feedback on their performance (e.g., identify one strength, one weakness, and one "missed opportunity"; McEnrue, 2002).

Games in Leadership Education

Games are activities to interactively engage students in a prescribed setting and are constrained by a set of rules and procedures (e.g., Jeopardy, Who Wants to Be a Millionaire, Family Feud, etc.). Additionally, they may include traditional "tabletop" (Robinson & Robinson, 1994) and "red bead" varieties (Deming, 1986), as well as classic system simulations like the Beer (Senge, 1990) and more complex interactive environments such as the "training factory" (Haapsalo & Hyvonen, 2001). Furthermore, we can find games in virtual and simulated worlds—that have reached levels of sophistication not previously possible—such as "Second Life" (Svinicki & McKeachie, 2014). Although it may be unlikely for students to pursue careers involving work in virtual worlds, what happens under technologically simulated conditions can have an impact on leadership development (Jang & Ryu, 2011; Jenkins et al., 2015; Reeves & Malone, 2007; Reeves, Malone, & O'Driscoll, 2008).

Lewis and Maylor (2007) argue that students need to directly experience what it is like to be part of a system, particularly when educational programs represent a student's first exposure to particular leadership challenges. Pertaining specifically to leadership skills, Carucci (2009) explains how games accelerate leadership learning and are more effective and creative than traditional lectures for preparing leaders to take on new challenges.

Correspondingly, gaming promotes experiential learning by providing a shared concrete experience (Kolb, 1984) that many argue allows students to explore theory and practice more critically (Haapasalo & Hyvonen, 2001; McKenney, 1962, 1967; McKenney & Dill, 1966). To be of maximum utility, we offer examples of games based on physical environments as well as those that take place in virtual worlds.

The Prisoner's Dilemma

"The prisoner's dilemma is an important paradigm that illustrates the conflict between social incentives to cooperate and private incentives to defect" (Holt & Capra, 2000, p. 229). As an exemplar activity for demonstrating the importance of cooperation, students are pitted against one another to defect for maximum profits. Gibson (2003) has used the *Prisoner's Dilemma* (Pfeiffer & Jones, 1974) to teach ethics, Gallos (2013) suggests using it to explore the beliefs and methodologies of the Human Resources frame in *Reframing Organizations* (Bolman & Deal, 2013), and we have used it to teach the concept of leadership as a partnership (DuBrin, 2012). In practice, Gibson (2003) found games and specifically game theory an important tool that students found to be challenging and enjoyable. Further, Gibson (2003) suggests that games are pedagogically useful because they raise awareness, spark challenges, have normative implications, and are descriptive.

The Collegiate Leadership Competition

In Chapter 15, we introduced the Collegiate Leadership Competition (CLC) skill sheets as a tool for peer assessment. Games are one of the signature activities in which CLC competitors engaged. As recently as 2016, students competed in a massive adaptation of the classic blindfolded obstacle course. In this teambuilding game, all members—except one—must be blindfolded and proceed through the obstacle course with only instructions from the lone "sighted" team leader without touching any of the obstacles. In 2017, students had to solve both an Escape Room-style series of puzzles (in one activity) and build a "Pringles® Ringle" in another. In the Pringles® Ringle activity, teams were provided 45 minutes to plan and build a freestanding, upright, and closed structure resembling the shape of a circle using at least 100 Pringles. It is critical to note that students are evaluated on both results (i.e., how quickly and accurately they completed the task) and process (e.g., inclusion, empowerment, decision making, strategy, ethics, etc.). Effective games also include a feedback process, where learners and facilitators reflect on the experience and collectively make meaning of the activities.

World of Warcraft

One of the most well-known examples of a game-based virtual world is World of Warcraft, a massively multiplayer online roleplaying game (MMORPG) that peaked in 2010 with just over 12 million paying subscribers (Statista/WoW, 2017). Players advance in the game through completing tasks individually or in groups. As game play progresses, users rely on working together to complete more difficult tasks to received more significant rewards (Guthrie et al., 2011). Formed groups can range from 2- to 40-person teams working collaboratively toward a singular goal. Through these group interactions, individuals enhance their leadership skills (Guthrie et al., 2011). For teams to be successful, group leaders must develop and demonstrate certain leadership skills, including technical knowledge, problem solving, environment knowledge, organizational skills, instructional skills, and facilitation (Guthrie et al., 2011; Jenkins et al., 2015).

The following example from one of our student's experiences in the virtual world game World of Warcraft (WOW) was published in *Leadership Education 2050: Changing the Spaces and Faces of Experience* (Jenkins et al., 2015):

> While teaching a course at the University of South Florida, one of the authors had an undergraduate student who stayed after class to explain his predicament about an upcoming assignment. The student explained that he could not reflect on an organizational issue he had experienced because he was not a part of an organization and had not held a leadership position prior. A few more minutes of dialogue between the student and instructor uncovered the time the student spent playing WOW. And, that the student was not a passive gamer, but instead had organized a clan of virtual warriors, created a virtual web-space where issues were vetted, goals set, and conflicts handled. Ironically enough, the student was experiencing much of the same challenges and successes of his peers in non-virtual organizations. (p. 132)

In an exploration of the in-game experiences of MMORPG players and offline leadership, Jang and Ryu (2011) found that these types of games are capable of providing social activities, interacting with others, and creating a sense of community. As a result, these communities (e.g., a guild or clan of virtual warriors) help players build their leadership experience (Jang & Ryu, 2011). Relatedly, coordinating the community as a clan or guild master includes responsibilities such as managing constructed hierarchies, daily operations, scheduling events, maintaining membership, enforcing codes of ethics, mediating disputes between players, and managing the overall direction of the guild (Hettrick, 2012; D. Williams et al., 2006), all of which have implications for leadership learning. In a related study, Reeves and Malone (2007) compared the leadership traits exhibited in MMORPGs to the four core capabilities for effective leadership, including sense making, relating, visioning, and inventing. Evidence of all four capabilities was included in their findings on varying levels and importance. As they explained, "This is evidence that good leaders are good leaders, regardless of context. This means that games are at least an important source of practice for the real world (and vice versa)" (Reeves & Malone, 2007, p. 10).

For leadership educators, most MMORPGs and related video games provide little, if any, opportunities for structured facilitation. Yet as Jenkins et al. (2015) explain, "the physical places and virtual spaces *where* we work are more so interchangeable than ever before. As a result, the truths about where leadership happens and experience is gained have changed" (p. 127). Consequently, we recommend enabling students of leadership to write and reflect about experiences in virtual as well as physical places and spaces. For a more structured technology-enhanced application, consider altering a role-play so that students are assigned roles within one or multiple organizations and provided with scenarios that require communication only through virtual channels (e.g., e-mail, text, and instant messaging).

PEDAGOGY TO PRACTICE

Role-playing, games, and simulation exercises all have a place in leadership education. In summary, we provide a few highlights of the pedagogy and how putting this instructional strategy into practice can transform leadership learning.

Pedagogy Overview

- Role-play allows students to take on personal characteristics in ways they might not normally, creating opportunities for expansive perspective-taking.
- Role-play helps encourage participation amongst passive learners, promotes retention of material, promotes working in groups, and helps generate student enthusiasm and interest.

- Simulation activities give students opportunities to find ways of leading under conditions that replicate those in other arenas without having to contend with the consequences of costly mistakes.
- Games, which can provide levity, also challenge students to meet goals and obtain objectives while considering individual and group gains and losses.

Transforming Leadership Learning Through Role-Play, Simulations, and Games

- Role-play, simulations, and games only become pedagogy when they are infused with explicit leadership learning outcomes at the outset and are reinforced with effective debriefing and reflective discussions at the conclusion.
- Use role-plays—by assigning students to play the roles of any important content knowledge, theory, model, behavior, trait, approach, historical figure, or leader/follower role—to allow for deeper learning and engagement in material.
- Effective leadership educators carefully attend to the experiences of their students under these otherwise artificially imposed conditions and actively seek to help students apply leadership learning in practically meaningful ways.

CHAPTER 17

LEADERSHIP AS ART

Leaders need to true be artisans who have vision and can see the world for what it could be not what it currently is. Leadership education has the unique opportunity to use art to encourage creativity and innovation. More recently, the integration of arts in college teaching is becoming more present. Disciplines such as allied health and the medical professions (Lake, Jackson, & Hardman, 2015; Ousager & Johannessen, 2010; Perry et al., 2011), literacy and language arts (Dover, 2016), and social work and social care (Hafford-Letchfield et al., 2008) have integrated arts-based pedagogies in their curricula. Due to this integration, we begin this chapter not by introducing the myriad art-based instructional strategies available to college educators, but instead by describing the relationship between experiential leadership education and arts-based pedagogy. Next, we introduce a framework for teaching leadership with art that is informed by the extant literature. The remaining sections of this chapter include examples of arts-based leadership education interventions from our experiences and the literature.

TRANSFORMING LEADERSHIP EDUCATION THROUGH ARTS

Arts-based leadership education is situated within the framework of experiential learning as knowledge creation through the transformation of experience (Kolb, 1984). Arts-based leadership education has developed through the application of arts-based methodologies (S. S. Taylor, 2008;

The Role of Leadership Educators: Transforming Learning, pp. 281–299
Copyright © 2018 by Information Age Publishing
281

S. S. Taylor & Ladkin, 2009) and drawn from concepts originating in arts sociology, investigating the arts for self-configuration and development (DeNora, 2003; Lincoln, 2005). According to Sutherland (2013), the underpinning theory is that "participants involved in arts-based education learn experientially by transforming aesthetic experiences to develop non-rational, non-logical capabilities and self-knowledge that constitute and cultivate experiential knowing, aesthetic awareness and, in general, the so called soft issues of managing and leading" (p. 27). S. S. Taylor and Ladkin (2009) refer to this outcome as "skills transfer," reasoning that artistic endeavors allow "participants to reveal inner thoughts and feelings that may not be accessible through more conventional developmental modes" (p. 56). Consequently, the literature is filled with detailed examples and underlying theories supporting art-based leadership development in a variety of contexts and an array of mediums. For a comprehensive literature review of arts-based management education, see Katz-Buonincontro (2015).

The value of art-based leadership education is present in a variety of applications ranging from integration (Sutherland, 2013) and intervention (Romanowska, Larsson, & Theorell, 2013) to creation (e.g., Wicks & Rippin, 2010) and interpretation (e.g., Purg & Walravens, 2015); utilizing music (e.g., Emiliani & Emiliani, 2013), literature (e.g., Loughman & Finley, 2010), and theater (Soumerai & Mazer, 2006), as well as many other art forms. One of the most prevalent themes in the leadership scholarship addresses the application of leadership *as* art. Springborg (2010) offers the following definition from his experiences of working with art and leadership: "Art is an arrangement of conditions intended to make us perceive some part of the world more directly through our senses— and less through our concepts and ideas about this part of the world" (p. 245). Springborg (2010) further explains the aesthetic function of art: it "puts us in a situation where we get the chance to examine our felt sense of some part of our experience" (p. 245). This process is facilitated "through arranging elements belonging to the medium specific for the art form to which the artwork belongs" (Springborg, 2010, p. 245), and this arrangement awakens us to new and different possibilities. For example, arrangements of leadership elements (knowledge, skills, abilities, attitudes, behaviors, etc.) may be surprising, intriguing, provocative, aesthetically pleasing, or in some other way capture our attention and place it in our senses. This, in turn, provides us with new information about an element of our experience, such as information about how we perceive it, and this new information may, like Kolb's (1984) "Experiential Learning Cycle," change our understanding about the respective element of our experience. This proposition is summarized by S. S. Ladkin and Taylor (2010), who posit that our complex world "cannot be fully understood solely by reference to scientific forms of logic and sense-making. The arts, and art-based practices, provide different ways of both describing and relating to that complexity, thereby offering novel ways of responding" (p. 235). This celebration of the arts connects to what we already know about leadership—they are expressions of our essential humanity; both art and leadership are "humanities" in the literal sense.

Leadership Development From the Art Experience

The art experience has been documented as influential toward participants' leadership development. To illustrate this phenomenon, E. Rodgers, Bradley, and Ward (2010) drew from their experiences as both students and teachers of art to describe how participation in the arts (both visual and performing) can offer fertile ground for developing leadership. They argue, "Conductors, directors, painters, sculptors, and other artists must begin to view themselves as leaders, and they must pass these leadership qualities along to others as well" (E. Rodgers et al., 2010, p. 91). Accordingly, each author shares a personal story that associates leadership and the arts: (a) The Musical Experience: Learning to Listen; (b) The Theatrical Experience: Learning to Direct; and (c) The Painterly Experience: Learning Audacity. In their narratives, they attribute the arts as leadership cultivators and argue that musical, theatrical, and other artistic expressions contribute the following leadership characteristics and principles to leadership education: (a) creative environment; (b) collaboration and continuous evaluation; (c) multitasking and adaptability; (d) audacity and the ability to perform; (e) self-discipline, self-authorship, and self-reflection; and (f) vulnerability. Accordingly, E. Rodgers et al. (2010) contend:

> When the arts are undertaken deliberately, they offer training in the "art" of leadership. All artists are leaders, and all leaders are artists. By adopting and cultivating methods of creative leadership such as collaboration and evaluation, adaptability and audacity, those who operate in an environment where both the problem and the solution are complex and obscure will be better equipped to face the challenges of leadership and help others translate aspirations into reality. (p. 96)

Thus, art as leadership is equally about the experience of creating or being a part of its creation or making sense out of the experience and its aesthetic properties. Likewise, the use of the arts to stimulate, engage, and enable deeper levels of understanding self and others may be the necessary foundation for more complex discovery, analysis, and decision making. Leaders can perform with greater clarity and more confidence when taking principled actions grounded in their values through heightened identity awareness and adaptability, thereby enhancing their leadership meta-competencies (J. McCarthy, O'Connell, & Hall, 2005) in using the arts as a platform and vehicle for discovery and learning. Per De Pree (1987), leadership is an art. Arguably, leaders today need to truly be artisans who see the world not only as it is but as it could be. To echo J. F. McCarthy (2015), "We are hopeful that the continued integration of the arts in leadership studies will bring tone, depth, color, texture, and form to shaping holistic, self-aware, and adaptable leaders who will meet the challenge with dignity, grace, empathy, and beauty" (p. 31). Integrating the arts with leadership studies can be a productive and meaningful way to open and expand mind-sets, stimulate creativity, and bring broader perspectives on human behavior, thus better preparing our learners for their current and future leadership challenges (J. F. McCarthy, 2015). Many institutions and organizations have recognized the critical need for the arts to spark innovation, re-onceptualize leadership, and bring hope toward the challenge of leading positive change in our world (Adler, 2006).

Arts-Based Education in Leadership Studies: Constructivist and Interpretivist Pedagogy

A clear distinction between constructivist and interpretivist pedagogies emerged from the literature on arts-based leadership education. Correspondingly, our framework for providing coverage of arts-based instructional strategies in leadership education includes two components. The first is constructivist, which is a view that learning is an active process in which learners construct their own understanding and knowledge of the world through action and reflection. The second is interpretivist, which is a view that learning comes from the content of works that are ultimate arbiters of meaning rather than the relative knowledge learners bring.

We believe, and the scholarship supports the notion, that art is not only a method of individual expression; it can also be a method for emphasizing and understanding others' experiences (Leonard, Hafford-Letchfield, & Couchman, 201). In the constructivist realm, for example, students may be asked to "create a metaphor that describes their beliefs about leadership" (Owen et al., 2007, p. 28) out of tinker toys, Legos®, Play-Doh, or a flip chart and markers (or other art supplies if preferred). While in the interpretivist realm, students may be asked to identify the five bases of power in the *Pirates of the Caribbean* (J. R. Williams, 2006) or *Harry Potter* series (Rosser, 2007), interpret the impact of the art of far-reaching social movements, or associate varied musical pieces to emotional intelligence and work environments (Lynn, 2002). These two pedagogical viewpoints provide the leadership educator with distinct approaches for integrating the arts in their teaching.

Constructivist

The process of creating or conceiving art as leadership pedagogy relates to constructivist teaching and learning design. According to Gagnon and Collay (2006), the images that students have of constructivist teaching are "memories of teachers who explored what students knew, engaged students in learning, expected students to think for themselves, and supported students as they made meaning of their learning" (p. xiv). Such teaching often occurs in performing arts, and those experiences stand out powerfully in memory. Moreover, constructivist learning design offers teachers an image of how to organize student learning and thinking that is consistent with this remembered experience (Gagnon & Collay, 2006). Correspondingly, Springborg (2010) attributes the process of conceiving art to sense-making and argues:

> When conceiving a work of art, the artist is engaged in the process of artistic appreciation of his material. He/she is aware of the direct, personal, sensed experience the material provokes or initiates in him/her, and how this experience changes when the material is changed. (p. 248)

You don't see to draw, you draw to see—it's the same for leadership; you don't learn to lead, you lead to learn (S. S. Taylor, 2015). This idea of leading to learn draws on a practice of leadership that is based on exploration or what artists call being open (S. S. Taylor, 2012, 2015). According to S. S. Taylor (2015), a leader that is "open" is a public learner; we see them learning and sharing that learning in real time, and in that way we can watch them lead to learn. Respectively, the arts provide a balance to the dominance of the analytic approaches to our organizational worlds. There is an old saying that you can only manage what you can measure. The arts can help us to work with what we cannot measure, and the way to do that is by leading to learn (S. S. Taylor, 2015). Examples we have used include having students take a picture of something reflective of their greatest leadership strength and then share a photo gallery or slide show with their classmates, acting out a mythological story and then re-creating the scenario effectively, writing poems about one's True Color (see Lowry, 1990), and flash mob dancing. In the following subsections, we provide examples and related literature of constructivist arts-based pedagogy in leadership education.

Making

"The very making of art can foster a deeper experience of personal presence and connection" (S. S. Taylor & Ladkin, 2009, p. 56). In line with this thinking, Katz-Buonincontro's (2015) research on studio arts-based management education suggests that exercises such as collage, drawing, and sculpture can be used to develop creativity and empathy. We agree and include the suggestion of capturing these experiences through the use of digital tools such as graphic design software (e.g., Adobe Photoshop, CorelDRAW), presentation software (e.g., Prezi, PowerPoint, Keynote), or tools built into popular word processors (e.g., Microsoft Word's "SmartArt," Canva). Fittingly, we offer the following examples where individuals create, draw, build, or construct as part of the learning process.

Drawing. The use of intentional drawing activities in leadership education has been shown to develop new perceptions of one's leadership practice (Katz-Buonincontro, Phillips, & Arnold, 2013) and provide opportunities for students to explore and discuss their evolving leadership identities (Arnold, 2012). For example, the following activity, adapted from Wagner and Ostick (2013), uses the StrengthsFinder® assessment instrument (see Chapter 15) as an advanced organizer to help students understand the concept of theme dynamics (i.e., the dynamics among the 34 talents and, more specifically, students' "top 5"). To prepare for the activity, students should be given a worksheet with the instructions indicated below, a separate sheet of paper to draw their "talents in action," and an assorted variety of drawing utensils (e.g., color pencils, crayons, markers). We have witnessed students creating amazing works of arts representative of their "talents in action," such as elaborate illustrated flowcharts, stick figures, word clouds, poetry, and nature scenes.

Example

Talents in Action

Two people with any of the same talents in their "top 5" could still behave differently. This is due in part to the different contexts within which people are raised. It is also because each of your "top 5" interacts with the other four, influencing your behavior in a variety of different ways. Consider the ways in which your "top 5" interact with one another and draw or create a visual representation of your "talents in action." Here are some prompting questions to get you started:

1. How do your talents interact with one another?

2. How do these interactions show up in your day-to-day behavior?

3. Are there times when some talents show up more than others?

4. What do your talents allow you to do?

Caricature. In this activity, students are challenged to imagine leadership constructs as individual caricatures. To begin the activity, assign individual or small groups of students different combinations of leadership traits, styles, behaviors, theories, concepts, and/or models, along with a position (e.g., CEO; you can also have students pull the combinations from a hat), and ask them to depict an individual through a visual representation of the unique combination with art supplies (e.g., flipchart paper and drawing utensils). The activity concludes with students sharing their drawings, full-group discussions, and debriefing. Through this activity, participants have opportunities to explore leadership constructs in greater depth, examine stereotypes, and challenge assumptions.

Systematizing. For this activity, which focuses on developing the understanding of organizational systems, students can make the product with any medium, including digital tools. We have used this activity in a graduate leadership theory course where Heifetz, Linsky, and Grashow's (2009) *The Practice of Adaptive Leadership* and Hughes, Ginnett, and Curphy's (2012) *Leadership: Enhancing the Lessons of Experience* are the primary texts. Students are asked to diagnose the system.

Example

Diagnose the System

Thinking about the readings in *The Practice of Adaptive Leadership* (Heifetz, Linsky, & Grashow, 2009), which focus on systemic thinking as well as the various complexities posited on page 488 of Hughes, Ginnett, and Curphy (2012), sketch a model of your organization that resembles the cogs/gears of a machine. Try and illustrate how each component interacts with the other. Finally, in a short paragraph, describe how a problem would go through this machine.

In a similar example, Imagination Lab's Serious Play method enables people to use Legos® to build organizational strategy (Burgi, Jacobs, & Roos, 2005; Roos, Victor, & Statler, 2004).

Doll Making

Wicks and Rippin (2010) invited participants to create leadership touchstones, or dolls, as a way of learning about leadership and themselves as leaders. Drawing from therapeutic and psychoanalytic perspectives, the researcher facilitators noted participants explored the dolls' power to provoke, unsettle, and evoke strong reactions on the part of their makers and demonstrate how these dynamics played out in our inquiry. For example, one student from the study made a "two-faced doll," with one side representing her boss and the other side representing herself. According to Wicks and Rippin (2010), the student's "'revelation' which she understandably finds 'a bit hard to explain' is that she sees a 'distorted image' of herself" that is, "a 'reflection of ourselves within ourselves' which, like the half-distorted, dual faces of her doll, reveals as much as it masks" (p. 268). From this doll-making experience, the researchers concluded that, like art, leadership "can most constructively engage with the human condition when it is able to hold, not collapse, our experience of the uncanny, the abject, and the other—including the 'other' within the 'self'—within the complexities of organizational life" (Wicks & Rippin, 2010, p. 261).

Music

According to J. L. Hall (2010), "Music affords students a 'personal experience,' one that educators can use to stimulate thought and reflection. Reflection then leads to action—action that ultimately leads to student learning" (p. 109). For example, Purg and Walravens (2015) piloted an experience where students conducted a choir. Because of their interactions with the chorus singers, participants described becoming more aware of their listening habits, better understanding the importance of right communication, and realizing the importance of an emotional relationship. Similarly, Sutherland (2013) applied the conducting experience in a master chorale class workshop for MBA students, finding the "aesthetic workspace ... deroutinizing activities" leading to "aesthetic reflexivity" and ultimately resulted in "memories with momentum" or the ability for participants to retain leadership concepts and skills longer (p. 38). However, Parush and Koivunen (2014) argue that these workshops (directing a choir) present managers with a variety of contradictory demands, and that the capacity to tolerate contradictions and paradoxes is itself construed as an essential virtue of the "creative" managerial self. They purport that more research into the paradoxes and double binds encapsulated in the art and management discourse is needed and that double binds may be paralyzing in some contexts and inspiring in others.

Theater

Innovative theater-based curricula have also been used to teach leadership (e.g., Catani & Lambri, 2009; Meisiek, 2004; Mirvis, 2005). Examples range from improvisational theater (e.g., Gagnon, Vough, & Nickerson, 2012) to classical acting and role-play (see Chapter 15). For example, J. F. McCarthy (2015) used live stage plays in a management course to engage students more fully in their own learning and help teach lessons in conflict, power, and leadership. Similarly, Soumerai and Mazer (2006) developed theatrical tributes to inspirational historical figures (e.g., Anne Frank, Martin Luther King, Jr., and the Dalai Lama) and had students participate in these productions to learn about the lives of these figures and share their stories with large numbers of their peers. The researchers discovered that students and faculty found the activity to be engaging, provocative, relevant, and valuable (J. F. McCarthy & Carr, 2015).

In this tradition, we offer the example activity "Leadership Theater," which can be altered for most leadership models. In this group project, students are asked to conduct a play and presentation that demonstrates one of the four frames from *Reframing Organizations* (Bolman & Deal, 2013)—structural, human resource, symbolic, or political—that illustrates how the frame is applied in a real-world setting. Student groups creatively formulate a challenging situation for a leader and conduct a play that shows how an effective leader would act in that situation as well as how the frame the situation occurred in affected the leader's decisions. Through this group project, students synthesized knowledge from across the term and constructed their own meaning through theater.

Improvisational Theater and Skits. Improvisational (improv) skits have been shown to improve creative thinking and problem solving (Pruetipibultham & Mclean, 2013), strengthen individual and collective empathy (in and out of the classroom; Katz-Buonincontro, 2015), and foster difficult discussions (Meisiek, 2004). According to Katz-Buonincontro (2015), these kinds of interactions help students think and act with spontaneity and understand the nature of complex emotional reactions in the workplace (Feinstein, Mann, & Corsun, 2002), resulting in the desire to act in new ways (Meisiek, 2004; Mirvis, 2005).

Huffaker and West (2005) introduce five tenants of improv that translate well to learning collaborative leadership in the classroom. These tenants include being present (being in the moment rather than focusing on certain outcomes), being fit and well (having a high level of confidence and competence and a willingness to take risks with a positive attitude), listening (focusing wholly on others), having a willingness to change (enables use of information gained through listening to be adaptable and flexible to new developments), and accepting offers ("in improv lingo, an offer is anything you can do something with"; Huffaker & West, 2005, p. 856). These general tenants of improv directly apply to skills needed to be a successful leader and can be practiced in leadership educational settings.

For example, early in the semester (and sometimes the first day of class), we facilitate a variation of the "Paper Bag Skits" icebreaker (St. Cloud University, 2012). In the activity, students are split into small groups and given paper bags filled with assorted props (e.g., plastic insects, hats, fake money, a detective badge, a clown's nose, etc.) and provided a scenario relative to something on campus (e.g., "scenes from the dining hall"). The object is to present a skit using all the props provided. Give your students a few minutes to plan and rehearse before they perform the skit. After students perform, debrief and facilitate a discussion about how the improvisational nature of the activity relates to leader and follower roles.

Storytelling, Poetry, and Spoken Word

The process of constructing a story and storytelling has been shown to emphasize the act of meaning making through narrative and in turn influence and shape leadership identity (Polkinghorne, 1996), build trust and empathy, and, when used in cross-cultural settings, enable learners to bridge cultural gaps and find common understanding (Grisham, 2006). Similarly, poetry exercises can help students bridge the dichotomy between their work and personal identities. For example, Van Buskirk and London (2008) designed a "Poetry Gallery" workshop, where participants circulate around a room individually reading 75 to 100 poems, followed by a process where they select and then share a poem with others. Next, participants compose their own poems and share them. This is a powerful tool for individuals not only to make meaning from their experiences but have the opportunity to share it with others.

Example

Narrative-Building Activity

This activity can either be used in a curricular or co-curricular setting where a group collectively builds a narrative. The facilitator starts with a prompt in which each participant then adds in order to build a story. This story is recorded either by writing, audio, or video recording. Once each participant has contributed to the narrative, a brief review of the story built reminds the group of how the story evolved. The narrative then becomes a platform for critical analysis of leadership, may provide an opportunity for problem solving. This activity can be used with a specific leadership theory, current event, or problem in mind. It is up to the facilitator to start with an appropriate prompt and then to debrief the story, process, and make connections to students' overall leadership learning.

Additionally we offer an example for integrating storytelling in your curriculum in Chapter 11: "Six Stories You Need to Know How to Tell." This activity could be altered for distance learning or as a culminating project where students perform a rehearsed version of their story. Here we offer two examples for technology-enhanced storytelling.

Video Journal Projects. In this group project, students are asked to produce a documentary that demonstrates at least one major leadership theory or construct (e.g., traits, power and influence). Students may get video footage from individuals on campus or in their own organizations and communities. Through this instructional strategy, students are empowered to illustrate leadership theories and constructs that are applied in practical settings. Through this activity, students identified their own values and beliefs and reflected on how those values and beliefs affected their role as a leader; learned to observe and utilize emotional intelligence when interacting with other students, role models, and future colleagues; gained an increased appreciation for leadership styles, practices, and potential; and learned to practice continued self-reflection and self-evaluation of their own leadership styles and practices.

My Frame Digital Storytelling. For this activity, students are asked to record a 5-minute YouTube video that describes a specific example of one of Bolman and Deal's (2013) organizational frames and illustrates how the frame is applied in a real-world setting. The video must include mixed mediums such as artwork, short video clips, pictures, text, and so on. Specifically, the video should follow the "digital storytelling" format (see Robin, 2008). Students are also provided the following exercise.

Example

My Frame Digital Storytelling

The video must describe how an organization functioned within your frame and could be part of an organization you have been a member of, a television show, movie, book, and so on. Specifically, your job is to creatively formulate or illustrate a challenging situation for a leader within your assigned frame, show your audience how an effective leader would act in that situation, and demonstrate how the frame in which the situation occurred within affected the leader's decisions.

Example within the Political Frame: A leader is faced with an employee who is consistently late to work, delaying projects, and making customers angry. Your video would creatively—through the digital storytelling format—demonstrate how a leader would handle this employee in the political frame to make them more productive. You may also wish to contrast effective behavior by illustrating ineffective leadership behaviors within the political frame, then contrasting it with a leader who does it the right way. So, you might show how a politically savvy leader might function in the political frame versus how a leader that dismisses the political climate might function. (Remember, your only restraint/constraint is the Digital Storytelling format. Whatever else you choose to create in your video is up to you.)

Mixed Media and Three-Dimensional Art

It is often claimed that a picture is worth a thousand words. As such, visual and artistic representations of leadership concepts as well as individual leadership journeys or goals through collages, sculptures, or photo captioning (for example) offer a brilliant alternative for class presentations (e.g., Katz-Buonincontro et al., 2013; Palus & Horth, 2012). In this tradition, we often use some form of art expression (i.e., visual or pictorial representation) as a culminating project. Early on, the project took a vague form: "Find a fun or interesting way to tell us what the most significant thing you learned this semester. A poem, picture book, PowerPoint, musical expression—however you want to get your point across. Your final project will be your final leadership expression that we will all want to remember." During the final class meeting of the semester, students would perform or "show and tell" their art pieces. What ended up happening was a montage of beautifully written poems, collages, oil paintings, digital stories, and sculptures. The assignment emerged over the years, culminating with these two unforgettable expressions: (a) a performed guitar composition—with lyrics—on Tuckman's stages of group development; and (b) a 10-minute play with papier-mâché puppets of class members and the instructor (Jenkins still has his papier-mâché head in his office). This project can also be used in online modalities with impressive results, including recorded interpretive dance, raps, skits, digital stories, animations, more collages, and plenty of mixed media. The online version of this assignment has emerged in structure over the years.

Example

Leadership in Art Expression: Syllabus Description

A leader's job is to understand the diversity of people's gifts, talents, ideas and skills. The art of leadership lies in polishing and liberating and enabling those gifts (De Pree, 1987). For this assignment, you are to select a meaningful theory, concept, or term from the course that either peaked your interest or you felt a personal connection with. For example, you could choose Emotional Intelligence, SLII, or Charismatic Leadership. *What was the reason for this interest or connection?* Your task is to create a visual art form representation—with a one-paragraph explanation—through one or more of the following mediums that expresses your chosen theory, concept, or term and your connection to it in a creative way:

- Microsoft Moviemaker, iMovie, YouTube, or another viewable video/movie
- Digital Storytelling
- Other art-based program such as Adobe Illustrator, Photoshop, etc., that can be converted to a file that all class members can view. If you are not sure please ask!
- Create an art piece and take a picture or movie of it and use one of the mediums above.
- Slide Presentation (e.g., PowerPoint, Prezi, Keynote; no more than four slides and MUST include personalized audio/video)
- Google Image or other picture (or clip art) with a creative/humorous caption (and MUST include personalized audio/video)

Constructivist-Interpretivist

Willis (1995) offered an alternative constructivist-interpretivist instruc-tional design model with the seven primary constructivist values of collaboration, personal autonomy, generativity, reflectivity, active engage-ment, personal relevance, and pluralism. This model has the following characteristics: (a) the design process is recursive, nonlinear, and sometimes chaotic; (b) planning is organic, developmental, reflective, and collabora-tive; (c) objectives emerge from design and development work; (d) experts may not exist; (e) instruction emphasizes learning in meaningful contexts (the goal is personal understanding within meaningful contexts); (f) forma-tive evaluation is critical; and (g) subjective data may be the most valuable. To illustrate this model, the following subsections provide examples and related literature of constructivist-interpretivist arts-based pedagogy in leadership education.

Visual Arts

The interpretation of the visual arts can be a powerful leadership peda-gogy. In a strategy referred to by Adler (2015) as strategic or aesthetic reflection, leaders use images from the *Leadership Insight* journal (Adler, 2010a, 2010b), which includes "paintings and wisdom from many of the world's most insightful leaders" (Adler, 2015, p. 49). Through this process, "executives re-remember the meta-reason that had originally led them to choose their profession and industry—to heal people—and thus why the organization had to succeed" (Adler, 2015, p. 49). According to Adler (2015), "Reflecting on the visual imagery of the paintings quickly takes managers beyond the dehydrated language and minimal aspirations of economics, accounting, and finance and allows them to go beyond day-to-day reality and return to possibility" (p. 49). Similarly, Purg and Walravens (2015) found that students who analyzed leadership through the metaphor of visual arts became better observers, realized the power of the metaphor (in speaking), become more aware of their own leadership style through art styles, and could talk about their own style.

Visual Metaphor Cards and a Visit to the Art Museum

The output of artistic endeavors allows participants to reveal inner thoughts and feelings that may not be accessible through more conven-tional developmental modes (S. S. Taylor & Ladkin, 2009). Art offers a specific illustration that is meant to have each observer connect to it in his or her own particular way and thus has divergent generalizability (S. S. Taylor & Ladkin, 2009). Visual metaphor cards such as The Center for Creative Leadership's Visual Explorer™ 216-card set and facilitator's guide (Palus & Horth, 2012) offer instructors a tool for facilitating creative conversations and deep dialogues using a wide variety of images on almost any leadership topic (Center for Creative Leadership, 2017). For example, individuals might select an image that best captures their understanding of leadership generally, a specific leadership theory or concept, or how they see themselves as a leader. In a related example, individuals are asked to choose an image that best captures a complex problem or issue they are trying to address, and then they discuss what the image says about the issue as a group (McCauley & Van Velsor, 2004). In line with the constructivist-interpretivist framework, the individual who selected the image may see one thing, whereas others may see something else. The resulting dialogue helps everyone see the issue from new perspectives and delve into the implicit ways in which individuals perceive situations (S. S. Taylor & Ladkin, 2009).

In a similar example, Ricke-Kiely and Matthias (2013) suggest taking students on a trip to a local art museum and facilitating the following pedagogical process while viewing works of art: (a) Impression (What were your first impressions as you viewed the piece of art? Did you get the impression of leadership in this painting?); (b) Description (How many perspectives are there in the picture?); (c) Interpretation (Please describe your experience "describing and interpreting" this painting); (d) Storytelling (After you heard the story of the characters, did your impressions of leadership in the painting change? How do these ideas inform your leadership practice?); and (e) New Impression (As you studied the picture, did you find your first impressions about the situation were correct?).

Film and Television

"Arts-based methods can enable participants to apprehend the 'essence' of a concept, situation, or tacit knowledge in a particular way, revealing depths and connections that more propositional and linear developmental orientations cannot" (S. S. Taylor & Ladkin, 2009, p. 56). Accordingly, film has been used widely in leadership education (see Billsberry, 2013) as a visual experience, which resonates with the purpose of using symbols to analyze themes prevalent in leadership theory and experience (Katz-Buonincontro, 2015). For example, the instructor's guide that accompanies the classic organizational theory text *Reframing Organizations* (Bolman & Deal, 2013) includes dozens of suggestions and activities, integrating motion pictures such as *12 Angry Men* to explore interpersonal and group dynamics, *Lord of the Flies* and *Flight of the Phoenix* as examples of group dynamics in crisis situations, *Inside Out* as a lens for teaching Emotional Intelligence, and *The Hudsucker Proxy, Margin Call, Moneyball, Office Space, Antz, Modern Times, Disclosure, 9 to 5, Broadcast News, Brazil 97, M*A*S*H, Lean on Me,* and *Wall Street* as diverse depictions of organizations with a wide range of structural concerns (Gallos, 2013). In the same way, Purg and Walravens (2015) used film interpretation to help students become more aware of different leadership styles; reflect on their own style; challenge assumptions about life, management, and leadership; and focus on the ethical and moral issues of management and leadership. Finally, through viewing episodes of the television series *The Office* or *Orange Is the New Black* and writing in reflective journals, students could connect the leadership scenarios shown in the episodes to those they may experience in their own life (Wimmer, Meyers, Porter, & Shaw, 2012). For additional information on entertainment media for teaching leadership, see McMahon and Bramhall (2004) and Rosser (2007).

Finally, if you plan to use any entertainment media, consider using the following teaching tips adapted from McMahon and Bramhall's (2004) "Activity Planning Template":

- Determine the intent of the entertainment media.
- Identify the medium to use (e.g., movie, television show, TED talk) and make sure you have noted the timestamp and length of the clip you intend to use (if applicable).
- Frame the experience of watching the media with a discussion or overview of related content. Instruct students to notate specific behaviors, traits, communication (verbal and nonverbal), relevant to the selected content and learning objectives.
- Watch the media.
- Process the media-watching experiencing through debriefing (see Chapter 9).

Music

Music offers a unique framework for helping learners understand leadership concepts (B. Hall, 2008). For example, jazz—particularly its improvisational elements—has been used to demonstrate spontaneous thinking connected to creative and innovative thinking as well as problem solving in fast-paced and rapidly changed work environments (Katz-Bunononcinco, 2015). Relatedly, individual jazz musicians and ensembles have been used as an example of organizations (Boughon, Weick, & Binkhorst, 1977; De Pree, 1992). Wagner and Ostick (2013) illustrate this concept in their activity "Orchestra versus Improv Jazz," where students watch and listen to video music clips from a jazz ensemble and classical orchestra. While watching, students are instructed to take notes about anything they notice that is related to leadership and then share their thoughts with classmates. The clips are played again, and students are asked to "consider each as a metaphor for leadership approaches in other settings, like student organizations" (Wagner & Ostick, 2013, p. 27).

Emiliani and Emiliani (2013) used music as a framework to better explain the concept of lean leadership to senior managers. Specifically, the researchers associated timing and synchronization of a production system with that of a symphony and the lean process and music with "takt time" (the rate of customer demand). One of their senior managers in their study reported, "To me, it was like looking at a symphony. Everybody knew their instruments and their music. They knew when to come in and when not to come in" (Emiliani & Emiliani, 2013, p. 409). Similarly, takt time relates to the time signature in a music score, which tells musicians the beats per measure (Emiliani & Emiliani, 2013).

In another example of teaching leadership with music, B. Hall (2008) drew from Zull's (2002) biological explanation of the ability of music to influence the human brain—sensing, integrating, and acting—and aspects of popular culture as a method for introducing leadership concepts (i.e., transformational approach and emotional intelligence) and developing students' leadership style (see also Andenoro & Ward, 2008; B. Hall, 2008; J. R. Williams, 2006). For example, B. Hall (2008) associates the expression of the lyrics "Yo, whatever happened to the values of humanity" from the Black Eyed Peas' "Where Is the Love" with the vision component of transformational leadership (i.e., articulating idealized goals and examining shortcomings in status quo to help followers reach their accomplishments).

Relatedly, McMahon and Bramhall (2004) suggest using "music to show differences in how leadership is conceptualized by asking the following questions: How is leadership like classical music? Jazz? Country music? Rap? Hip hop? Pop?" (p. 69). For example, Kao (1997) uses "Take Five" by the Dave Brubeck Quartet as an exemplar of why artistry and constancy are both important in leadership and organizations. One without the other is incomplete (McMahon & Hall, 2004). Hence, "people sense what is happening in their environment, then integrate what is happening into images and thoughts, and finally take action in various forms" (B. Hall, 2008, p. 48). Correspondingly, through teaching with music, students hear the lyrics and instruments (sensing), create images and thoughts from this experience (integrating), and then take action based on the complete experience. Consequently, teaching leadership with music influences learners' emotions, attitudes, and perspectives that individuals portray in life, creating personal connections that draw on previous meaningful experiences (B. Hall, 2008; Zull, 2002).

Literature

Like film, literature is ripe with examples of which leadership educators can harvest for their courses. For example, Fraiberg (2010) utilized Melville's *Bartelby, the Scrivener* to teach impossibility in business contexts, and Loughman and Finley (2010) utilized *Beowulf* to teach charismatic leadership. Furthermore, Shushok and Moore, (2010) utilized the so-called "great texts" of literature, philosophy, and politics (e.g., Aristotle, Shakespeare, Austen) to teach ethics, virtue, and deception. In this tradition, Kellerman's (2010) *Leadership: Essential Selections on Power, Authority, and Influence* offers a bountiful collection of excerpts from classical texts (e.g., Plato's *The Republic*), historical documents (e.g., Thomas Paine's *Common Sense*), literature (e.g., Betty Friedan's *The Feminine Mystique*), and great speeches (e.g., Nelson Mandela's "I Am Prepared to Die").

As a strategy for teaching the history of leadership through the lens of theory, we recommend using Kellerman's (2010) text—or another similar text (e.g., McMahon, 2010; Wren, 1995)—and a culminating term paper. In this assignment, students are asked to select one of each of the different types (e.g., literature, speeches) from Kellerman's text and apply their knowledge of the leadership theories and approaches discussed throughout the term and discuss how the leader in each selection applies a variety of one or more of them. Guiding questions include: (a) How does the leader use the theory or theories? (i.e., for the literature selections, you might discuss how the theory was portrayed through their dialogue); (b) What parts of leadership theory or approach are evident in the leaders' actions, words, behavior, writings, and so on? (c) What is unique, peculiar, humorous, and so on about how the leader chooses to utilize certain leadership theories/approaches? (d) What might have been different if the leader used a different style, approach, or theory of leadership? Culturally inclusive leadership educators may also seek partnerships with their colleagues in other academic units to identify significant literary works from writers of color and from across nationalities, ethnicities, gender identities, and sexual orientations to infuse a wider array of literary examples for students.

Radio and Podcasts

Like literature, radio and podcasts offer an alternative art form for consumption. For example, as a lens for introducing the concepts of charisma and audacity, students could listen to Winston Churchill's speeches made over the radio (Rodgers, Bradley, & Ward, 2010). Wagner, Ostick, and Komives (2014) suggest enabling students to create their own values statement through an activity based on the National Public Radio series *This I Believe* (a storytelling series where ordinary and famous people discuss their beliefs in eloquent and brief stories). Once students have heard the audio essays, they are prompted to write five values that are important to them. The activity concludes with a debrief and a discussion about values and beliefs. This activity could easily be replicated with podcasts, webcasts, and video blogs.

Teaching Tips

Finally, we recommend the following teaching tips adapted from Katz-Buonincontro (2015) and B. Hall (2008) for facilitating any art-based activity in your educational program:

1. Choose art activities that are intentionally aligned with students' situational factors (e.g., developmental readiness, age), course content, and learning outcomes/objectives. Remember, simply doing art is not pedagogy.
2. Consider when the art activity should be introduced and integrated in relation to the sequence of your educational program.
3. Use a variety of art mediums. For example, when using music, select from different time periods and be mindful of your audience (i.e., don't stereotype). Also, be aware of important historical, current, and social events associated with the music and musicians (each can influence students' perceptions or images of the music—positively or negatively).
4. Prepare the necessary art materials (e.g., lyric sheets for music activities; drawing utensils) and make certain you have the proper facilities and equipment (e.g., pottery kiln, audio visual).
5. Consider what kinds of data you might collect from the artistic process or resulting works of art.
6. Debrief and reflect on what worked well and what needs improvement.

PEDAGOGY TO PRACTICE

Leaders are arguably artisans who are skilled at visioning and seeing situations for what they could be not just as they are. We believe art can be a transformative pedagogy for leadership education. Here we highlight a few points of art as an instructional strategy and how leadership educators can use this pedagogy to transform leadership learning.

Pedagogy Overview

- There are various ways of incorporating art into learning including but not limited to making (creating various art forms), viewing (listening and watching), and participating (actively engaging with a group).
- Art may capture the attention of individuals who might not take in and digest information well in a more traditional setting, for example, visual and tactile learners.
- Arts-based education can be constructivist (learners construct their own understanding and knowledge) or interpretivist (learning comes from the content of works).
- Art is an opportunity to engage the campus and local community in education—museum visits, theatrical productions, concerts. Performance art, not to mention public art, is a whole other way to assess the values, perspectives, and ideals of a community or culture.

Transforming Leadership Learning Through Art

- Art and artistry can be helpful to leadership learners from both content and process perspectives:
  - o As content, art created by others can be filtered through a leadership lens to help student make sense of art, contextualize leadership, and widen their perspectives on both.
  - o As a process, artistic and creative activities provide students with practical opportunities to refine leadership practices, artistic skills, and develop along humanistic dimensions.
- Inclusive leadership educators should form partnerships with their colleagues in other academic units to identify significant literary, film, theatre, and musical works from writers of color and from across nationalities, ethnicities, gender identities, and sexual orientations to infuse a wider array of literary examples for students.
- Sometimes students can be intimidated by art-based pedagogies because they may feel like they are not creative enough. Leadership educators should encourage students that there is not a right or wrong way to work with art.
- Effective leadership educators apply artistic ways of knowing, being, and doing to their approach to instruction.

REFERENCES

Adams, M., Bell, L. A., & Griffin, P. (Eds.). (2007). *Teaching for diversity and social justice* (2nd ed.). New York, NY: Routledge.

Addams, J. (1910). *Twenty years at Hull-House.* New York, NY: Macmillan.

Adler, N. J. (2006). The arts and leadership: Now that we can do anything, what will we do? *Academy of Management Learning and Education, 5*(4), 466–499.

Adler, N. J. (2010a). Going beyond the dehydrated language of management: Leadership insight. *Journal of Business Strategy, 31*(4), 90–99.

Adler, N. J. (2010b). *Leadership insight.* Milton Park, UK: Routledge.

Adler, N. J. (2015). Finding beauty in a fractured world: Art inspires leaders—Leaders change the world. *Academy of Management Review, 40*(3), 480–494.

ACPA: College Student Educators International, & NASPA: Student Affairs Administrators in Higher Education. (2015). *ACPA/NASPA professional competency areas for student affairs practitioners* (2nd ed.). Washington, DC: Authors.

Adler, N. J. (2015). Finding beauty in a fractured world: Art inspires leaders—Leaders change the world. *Academy of Management Review, 40*(3), 480–494.

Albanese, R., & Van Fleet, D. (1985). Rational behavior in groups: The free-riding tendency. *Academy of Management Review, 10,* 244–255.

Aldrich, C. (2004). *Simulations and the future of learning: An innovative (and perhaps revolutionary) approach to elearning.* San Francisco, CA: Pfeiffer Publishing.

Alexander, C., & Beggs, J. (1986). Disguising personal inventories: A situated identity strategy. *Social Psychology Quarterly, 49,* 192–200.

Alimo-Metcalfe, B. (1998), 360 degree feedback and leadership development. *International. Journal of Selection and Assessment, 6,* 35–44.

Allen, K. E., & Cherry, C. (2000). *Systemic leadership: Enriching the meaning of our work.* Lanham, MD: University Press of America.

Allen, S. J. (2008). Simulations as a source of learning: Using *Star Power* to teach ethical leadership and management. *Journal of Leadership Education, 7*(1), 140–149.

Allen, S. J., & Hartman, N. S. (2008). Leadership development: An exploration of sources of learning. *SAM Advanced Management Journal, 73*(1), 10.

Allen, S. J., & Hartman, N. S. (2009). Sources of learning in student leadership development programming. *Journal of Leadership Studies, 3*(3), 6–16.

Allen, S., Jenkins, D., & Krizanovic, B. (in press). Exploring deliberate practice & the use of skill sheets in the collegiate leadership competition. *Journal of Leadership Education.*

Allen, S. J., & Shehane, M. R. (2016). Exploring the language of leadership learning and education In D. M. Roberts & K. J. Bailey (Eds.), *New directions for sdent leadership no. 151: assessing student leadership* (pp. 35–49). San Francisco, CA: Jossey-Bass.

Almagno, S. (2017, March 17). Participation points: Making student engagement visible. *Faculty Focus.* Retrieved from http://www.facultyfocus.com/articles/effective-teaching-strategies/participation-points-making-student-engagement-visible/

American Council on Education. (1937). *The student personnel point of view.* Washington, DC: Author.

Andenoro, A., & Ward, S. (2008). Infusion of popular culture: A catalytic approach to developing critical thinking in undergraduate leadership students. *Journal of Business & Leadership: Research, Practice and Teaching, 4*(2), 85–94.

Andenoro, A. C., Allen, S. J., Haber-Curran, P., Jenkins, D. M., Sowcik, M., Dugan, J. P., & Osteen, L. (2013). *National leadership education research agenda 2013-2018: Providing strategic direction for the field of leadership education.* Retrieved from http://leadershipeducators.org/ResearchAgenda.

Anderson, J. B., & Freiberg, H. J. (1995). Using self-assessment as a reflective tool to enhance the student teaching experience. *Teacher Education Quarterly, 22,* 77–91.

Anderson, K. D. (2004). The nature of teacher leadership in schools as reciprocal influences between teacher leaders and principals. *School Effectiveness and School Improvement, 15*(1), 97–113.

Antonacopoulou, E. P., & Bento, R. F. (2004). Methods of "learning leadership": Taught and experiential. *Leadership in Organizations: Current Issues and Key Trends,* pp. 81–102.

Antonakis, J., Avolio, B., & Sivasubramaniam, N. (2003). Context and leadership: An examination of the nine-factor full-range leadership theory using the Multifactor Leadership Questionnaire. *The Leadership Quarterly, 14,* 261–295.

Arao, B., & Clemens, K. (2013). From safe space to brave space: A new way to frame dialogue around diversity and social justice. In L. Landreman (Ed.), *The art of effective facilitation: Reflections from social justice educators* (pp. 135–150). Terre Haute, IN: Stylus.

Arnold, N. W. (2012). Photo-elicitation and critical geography as bridging-building: Lessons from an educational leadership classroom. In C. Boske (Ed.), *Educational leadership: Building bridges among ideas, schools, and nations* (pp. 161–185). Charlotte, NC: Information Age Publishing.

Ash, S. L., & Clayton, P. H. (2004). The articulated learning: An approach to guided reflection and assessment. *Innovative Higher Education, 29*(2), 137–154.

Ash, S. L., & Clayton, P. H. (2009). Generating, deepening, and documenting learning: The power of critical reflection in applied learning. *Journal of Applied Learning in Higher Education, 1*(1), 25–48.

Aspinwall, L. G., & Staudinger, U. M. (Eds.). (2003). *A psychology of human strengths: Fundamental questions and future directions for positive psychology.* Washington, DC: American Psychological Association.

Asplund, J., Lopez, S. J., Hodges, T., & Harter, J. (2007, February). *The Clifton StrengthsFinder® 2.0 technical report: Development and validation.* Retrieved from https://strengths.gallup.com/private/Resources/CSFTechnicalReport031005.pdf

Asplund, J., Lopez, S. J., Hodges, T., & Harter, J. (2009). *The Clifton StrengthsFinder® 2.0 technical report: Development and validation* [technical report]. Lincoln, NE: Gallup.

Association of American Colleges and Universities. (2012). *A crucible moment: College learning & democracy's future.* Washington, DC: Association of American Colleges and Universities.

Association of American Colleges & Universities. (2017). Integrative learning. Retrieved from https://www.aacu.org/resources/integrative-learning

Astin, A. W. (1984). Student involvement: A developmental theory for higher education. *Journal of College Student Development, 40*(5), 518–529.

Astin, A. W. (1993). *What matters in college? Four critical years revisited.* San Francisco, CA: Jossey-Bass.

Astin, A. W., & Astin, H. S. (2000). *Leadership reconsidered: Engaging higher education in social change.* Battle Creek, MI: W.K. Kellogg Foundation.

Astin, A. W., & Sax, L. J. (1998). How undergraduates are affected by service participation. *Journal of College Student Development, 39*(3), 251–263.

Astin, A. W., Vogelgesang, L. J., Ikeda, E. K., & Yee, J. A. (2000). *How service learning affects students.* Los Angeles, CA: Higher Education Research Institute.

Astin, H. S., & Leland, C. (1991). *Women of influence, women of vision: A cross-cultural study of leaders and social change.* San Francisco, CA: Jossey-Bass.

Atkinson, T. (2008). Using creative writing techniques to enhance the case study method in research integrity and ethics courses. *Journal of Academic Ethics, 6*(1), 33–50.

Atkinson, T. T. (2014). The "reverse case study": Enhancing creativity in case-based instruction in leadership studies. *Journal of Leadership Education, 13*(3), 118–128. Retrieved from http://www.journalofleadershiped.org/attachments/article/345/13_3atkinson221.pdf

Auster, E. R., & Wylie, K. K. (2006, April). Creating active learning in the classroom: A systematic approach. *Journal of Management Education, 30*(2), 333–353.

Avolio, B. (2008). *Leadership development in the balance: Made/born* (2nd ed.) Mahwah, NJ: Lawrence Erlbaum Associates.

Avolio, B. J., & Hannah, S. T. (2008). Developmental readiness: Accelerating leadership development. *Consulting Psychology Journal: Practice and Research, 60*(4), 331–347.

Ayman, R., Adams, S., Fisher, B., & Hartman, E. (2003). Leadership development in higher education institutions: A present and future perspective. In S. E. Murphy & R. E. Riggio (Eds.), *The future of leadership development* (pp. 201–222). Mahwah, NJ: Lawrence Erlbaum Associates.

Bailey, J., Sass, M., Swiercz, P. M., Seal, C., & Kayes, D. C. (2005). Teaching with and through teams: Student-written, instructor-facilitated case writing and the signatory code. *Journal of Management Education, 29*(1), 39–59.

Baker, A. C. (2009). *Catalytic conversations: Organizational communication and innovation.* Armonk, NY: M. E. Sharpe.

Baker, D. F., & Baker, S. J. (2012). To "catch the sparkling glow": A canvas for creativity in the management classroom. *Academy of Management Learning & Education, 11*(4), 704–721.

Bandura, A. (1977). *Social learning theory.* Englewood Cliffs, NJ: Prentice-Hall.

Barbour, J. (2006). Team building and problem-based learning in the leadership classroom: Findings from a two-year study. *Journal of Leadership Education, 5*(2), 28–40.

Barnes, C. P., & Ellner, C. L. (1983). *The present perspective.* In C. L. Ellner & C. P. Barnes (Eds.), *Studies of college teaching: Experimental results, theoretical interpretations, and new perspectives* (pp. 13–27). Lexington, MA: Lexington Books.

Barr, R. B., & Tagg, J. (1995). From teaching to learning: A new paradigm for undergraduate education. *Change: The magazine of higher learning, 27*(6), 12–26.

Bass, B. M. (1990). From transactional to transformational leadership: Learning to share the vision. *Organizational Dynamics, 18*(3), 19–31.

Bass, B. M., & Avolio, B. J. (1996). *Multifactor leadership questionnaire.* Menlo Park, CA; Mind Garden.

Bass, R., & Eynon, B. (2016). *Open and integrative: Designing liberal education for the new digital ecosystem.* Washington, DC: Association of American Colleges and Universities.

Bauer-Dantoin, A. (2009). The evolution of scientific teaching within the biological sciences. In R. A. R. Gurung, N. L. Chick, & A. Haynie (Eds.), *Exploring signature pedagogies: Approaches to teaching disciplinary habits of mind* (pp. 224–243). Sterling, VA: Stylus.

Baxter Magolda, M. B. (2001). *Making their own way: Narratives for transforming higher education to promote self-development.* Sterling, VA: Stylus.

Baxter Magolda, M. B. (2008). Three elements of self-authorship. *Journal of College Student Development, 49*(4), 269–284.

Baxter Magolda, M. B., & King, P. M. (2004). *Learning partnerships: Theory and models of practice to educate for self-authorship.* Sterling, VA: Stylus.

Beard, R. L., Salas, E., & Prince, C. (1995). Enhancing transfer of training: Using role-play to foster teamwork in the cockpit. *The International Journal of Aviation Psychology, 5*(2), 131–143.

Beaudry, S. L. (2016). Summiting Mount Everest: An experiential learning application for organizational behavior. *Developments in Business Simulation and Experiential Learning, 43*, 23–26.

Becher, T. (1989). *Academic tribes and territories: Intellectual enquiry and the cultures of disciplines*. Buckingham, UK: Open University Press.

Beidatsch, C., & Broomhall, S. (2010). Is this the past? The place of role-play exercises in undergraduate history teaching. *Journal of University Teaching & Learning Practice*, *7*(1), 1–20.

Berkovich, I. (2014). A socio-ecological framework of social justice leadership in education. *Journal of Educational Administration*, *52*(3), 282–309.

Berr, S., Church, A., & Waclawski, J. (2000). The right relationship is everything: Linking personality preferences to managerial behaviors. *Human Resource Development Quarterly*, *11*(2), 133–137.

Bertrand Jones, T., Guthrie, K. L., & Osteen, L. K. (2016). Critical domains of culturally relevant leadership learning: A call to transform leadership programs. In K. L. Guthrie, T. Bertrand Jones, & L. Osteen (Eds.), *New directions for student leadership, No. 152: Developing culturally relevant leadership learning* (pp. 9–22). San Francisco, CA: Jossey-Bass.

Biemiller, A., & Meichenbaum, D. (1992). The nature and nurture of the self-directed learner. *Educational Leadership*, *50*, 75–80.

Billsberry, J. (2009). The social construction of leadership education. *Journal of Leadership Education*, *8*(2), 1–9. Retrieved from http://www.leadershipeducators.org/resources/Documents/jole/2009_fall/Billsberry.pdf

Billsberry, J. (2013). From persona non grata to mainstream: The use of film in management teaching as an example of how the discipline of management education is changing. *Journal of Management Education*, *37*, 299–304.

Birkelund, R. (2000). Ethics and education. *Nursing Ethics*, *7*(6), 473–480. Black, A. M., & Earnest, G. W. (2009). Measuring the outcomes of leadership development programs. *Journal of Leadership & Organizational Studies*, *16*(2), 184–196.

Black, P., & William, D. (1998). Assessment and classroom learning. *Assessment in Education: Principles, Policy & Practice*, *5*(1), 7–74.

Blackburn, R. T., & Conrad, C. F. (1986). The new revisionists and the history of U.S. higher education. *Higher Education*, *15*(3), 211–230.

Blackwell, C., Cummins, R., Townsend, C. D., & Cummings, S. (2007). Assessing perceived student leadership skill development in an academic leadership development program. *Journal of Leadership Education*, *6*(1), 39–58.

Blanchard, K. H. (1985). *SLII: A situational approach to managing people*. Escondido, CA: Blanchard Training and Development.

Bloom, B. S. (1956). *Taxonomy of educational objectives: The classification of educational goals, by a committee of college and university examiners*. New York: Longman.

Bodoff, D., & Forster, P. (2005). A virtual market for teaching electronic market concepts in information systems education. *Journal of Information Systems Education*, *16*(1), 93–103.

Bolman, L. (2014). *The organization simulation*. Retrieved from http://www.leebolman.com/organization_simulation.htm

Bolman, L. G., & Deal, T. E. (2013). *Reframing organizations: Artistry, choice, and leadership* (5th ed.). San Francisco, CA: Josey-Bass.

Bonwell, C. C., & Eison, J. A. (1991). *Active learning: Creating excitement in the classroom.* Washington, DC: George Washington University ERIC Clearinghouse on Higher Education.

Booth, A. (1993). Learning history in university: Student views on teaching and assessment. *Studies in Higher Education, 18*(2), 227–235.

Bordas, J. (2013). *Salsa, soul, and spirit: Leadership for a multicultural age.* Oakland, CA: Berrett-Koehler.

Bordas, J. (2012). *The power of Latino leadership: Culture, inclusion, and contribution.* Oakland, CA: Berrett-Koehler.

Borkowski, J., Carr, M., & Pressley, M. (1987). "Spontaneous" strategy use: Perspectives from metacognitive theory. *Intelligence, 11*, 61–75.

Borredon, L., Deffayet, S., Baker, A. C., & Kolb, D. (2011). Enhancing deep learning: Lessons from the introduction of learning teams in management education in France. *Journal of Management Education, 35*(3), 324–350.

Bostock, S. (2001). Student peer assessment. Higher education academy. Retrieved from https://www.cs.auckland.ac.nz/courses/compsci747s2c/lectures/paul/Student_peer_assessment_-_Stephen_Bostock.pdf

Boud, D., & Falchikov, N. (1989). Quantitative studies of self-assessment in higher education: A critical analysis of findings. *Higher Education, 18*, 529–549.

Boud, D., Keogh, R., & Walker, D. (1985). Promoting reflection in learning: A model. *Reflection: Turning Experience into Learning*, pp. 18–40.

Boud, D., Lawson, R., & Thompson, D. G. (2013). Does student engagement in self-assessment calibrate their judgement over time? *Assessment & Evaluation in Higher Education, 38*(8), 941–956.

Boughon, M., Weick, K., & Binkhorst, D. (1977). Cognition in organizations: An analysis of the Utrecht Jazz Orchestra. *Administrative Science Quarterly, 22*, 606–639.

Bowers, K. M., & Lopez, S. J. (2010). Capitalizing on personal strengths in college. *Journal of College & Character, 11*(1), 1–11.

Boyatzis, R. E., & Kolb, A. (1969). *Feedback and self-directed behavior change.* Unpublished working paper. Cambridge, MA: Sloan School of Management, Massachusetts Institute of Technology.

Brennan, R. T., & Braslow, A. (1995). Skill mastery in cardiopulmonary resuscitation training classes. *The American Journal of Emergency Medicine, 13*(5), 505–508.

Bridges, W. (2009). *Managing transitions: Making the most of change* (2nd ed.). Boston, MA: De Capo Press.

Brierton, S. B. (2011). *Higher order thinking skills as demonstrated in synchronous and asynchronous online college discussion posts.* Raleigh, NC: North Carolina State University.

Bright, D. S., Caza, A., Turesky, E. F., Putzel, R., Nelson, E., & Lutchfield, R. (2016). Constructivist meta-practices: When students design activities, lead others, and assess peers. *Journal of Leadership Education, 15*(4), 75–99.

Bringle, R. G., & Hatcher, J. A. (1996). Implementing service learning in higher education. *Journal of Higher Education, 67*(2), 221–239.

Bringle, R. G., & Hatcher, J. A. (2000). Institutionalization of service learning in higher education. *Journal of Higher Education, 71*(3), 273–290.

Brookfield, S. (1995). Adult learning: An overview. *International Encyclopedia of Education, 10*, 375–380.

Brookfield, S. D., & Preskill, S. (2005). *Discussion as a way of teaching: Tools for democratic classrooms* (2nd ed.). San Francisco, CA: Jossey-Bass.

Brooks, C. M., & Ammons, J. L. (2003). Free riding in group projects and the effects of timing, frequency, and specificity of criteria in peer assessments. *Journal of Education for Business, 78*(5), 268–272.

Brost, B. D., & Bradley, K. A. (2006). Student compliance with assigned reading: A case study. *Journal of Scholarship of Teaching and Learning, 6*(2), 101–111.

Brost, B., & Bradley, K. (2012). Student compliance with assigned reading: A case study. *Journal of the Scholarship of Teaching and Learning, 6*(2), 101–111.

Brown, B. (2015). *Daring greatly: How the courage to be vulnerable transforms the way we live, love, parent, and lead.* New York, NY: Avery.

Brown, P. C., Roediger, H. L., & McDaniel, M. A. (2014). *Make it stick.* Boston, MA: Harvard University Press.

Brown, S., Rust, C., & Gibbs, G. (1994). *Strategies for diversifying assessment.* Oxford, UK: Oxford Centre for Staff Development.

Brungardt, C. L. (1996). The making of leaders: A review of the research in leadership development and education. *The Journal of Leadership Studies, 3*(3), 81–95.

Brungardt, C. L. (1998). The new fact of leadership: Implications for training educational leaders. *On the Horizon, 6*(1), 7–8.

Brungardt, C. L., & Crawford, C. B. (1996). A comprehensive approach to assessing leadership students and programs: Preliminary findings. *Journal of Leadership & Organizational Studies, 3*(1), 37–28.

Brungardt, C. L., Greenleaf, J. P., Brungardt, C. J., & Arensdorf, J. (2006). Majoring in leadership: A review of undergraduate leadership degree programs. *Journal of Leadership Education, 5*(1), 4–25.

Bryant, D. A., & Carless, D. R. (2010). Peer assessment in a test-dominated setting: Empowering, boring or facilitating examination preparation? *Educational Research for Policy and Practice, 9*(1), 3–15.

Buckingham, M., & Clifton, D. O. (2001). *Now, discover your strengths.* New York, NY: Free Press.

Burbach, M. E., Matkin, G. S., & Fritz, S. M. (2004). Teaching critical thinking in an introductory leadership course utilizing active learning strategies: A confirmatory study. *College Student Journal, 38*(3), 482–493.

Burgi, P. T., Jacobs, C. D., & Roos, J. (2005). From metaphor to practice in the crafting of strategy. *Journal of Management Inquiry, 14*(1), 78–94.

Burkhardt, J. C., & Zimmerman-Oster, K. (1999). How does the richest, most widely educated nation prepare leaders for its future? *Proteus, 16*(2), 9.

Burns, J. M. (1978). *Leadership.* New York, NY: Harper & Row.

Buschlen, E. (2009). *Can college students learn to lead? An examination of a collegiate leadership course using the social change model of leadership* (Doctoral dissertation). Available from ProQuest Dissertations and Theses database. (Publication No. AAT 3351998).

Buschlen, E., & Dvorak, R. (2011). The social change model as pedagogy: Examining undergraduate leadership growth. *Journal of Leadership Education*, *10*(2), 38–56.

Buschlen, E., & Guthrie, K. L. (2014). Seamless leadership learning in curricular and cocurricular facets of university life: A pragmatic approach to praxis. *Journal of Leadership Studies*, *7*(4), 58–63.

Bush, G. (2006). Learning about learning: From theories to trends. *Teacher Librarian*, *34*(2), 14–18.

Cacioppe, R. (1998). An integrated model and approach for the design of effective leadership development programs. *Leadership and Organization Development Journal*, *19*, 44–53.

Cameron, K. S., & Caza, A. (2005). Developing strategies and skills for responsible leadership. In J. P. Doh & S. A. Stumpf (Eds.), *Handbook on responsible leadership and governance in global business* (pp. 87–111). Northampton, MA: Edward Elgar.

Carless, S. A. (2001). Assessing the discriminant validity of the Leadership Practices Inventory. *Journal of Occupational and Organizational Psychology*, *74*(2), 233–239.

Carucci, R. (2009). Companies rehearse a very different future: Connecting leadership capability and strategy execution through simulation. *Global Business and Organizational Excellence*, *28*, 26–38.

Catani, M., & Lambri, L. (2009). The use of psychodrama in the training of vocational teachers. *Vocational Education: Research & Reality*, *17*, 118–131.

Cazden, C. B. (2001). *Classroom discourse: The language of teaching and learning* (2nd ed.). Portsmouth, NH: Heinemann.

Center for Creative Leadership. (2017). Leadership development. Retrieved from https://www.ccl.org/

Cestone, C. M., Levine, R. E., & Lane, D. R. (2008). Peer assessment and evaluation in team-based learning. In L. Michaelsen, M. Sweet, & D. X. Parmelee (Eds.), *New directions for teaching and learning, no. 116: Team-based learning: Small group learning's next big step* (pp. 69–78). San Francisco, CA: Jossey-Bass.

Chaleff, I. (2009). *The courageous follower: Standing up to and for our leaders*. San Francisco, CA: Berrett-Koehler.

Chan, K. Y., & Drasgow, F. (2001). Toward a theory of individual differences and leadership: Understanding the motivation to lead. *Journal of Applied Psychology*, *86*(3), 481.

Cherney, I. D. (2008). The effects of active learning on students' memories for course content. *Active Learning in Higher Education*, *9*(2), 152–171.

Chickering, A. W., & Gamson, Z. F. (1987). Seven principles for good practice in undergraduate education. *AAHE Bulletin*, *39*(7), 3–7.

Chiriac, E. H., & Granstrom, K. (2012). Teachers' leadership and students' experience of group work. *Teachers and Teaching*, *18*(3), 345–363.

Christensen, C. R. (1987). *Teaching and the case method*. Boston, MA: Harvard Business School.

Chunoo, V., & Osteen, L. (2016). Purpose, mission, and context: The call for educating future leaders. In K. L. Guthrie & L. Osteen (Eds.), *New directions for higher education, No. 174: Reclaiming higher education's purpose in leadership development* (pp. 9–20). San Francisco, CA: Jossey-Bass.

CSIS. (2017). Seven revolutions: An ongoing research effort to identify and analyze the most important trends shaping our world out to the year 2035. Retrieved from https://www.csis.org/programs/seven-revolutions

Clark, I. (2012). Formative assessment: Assessment is for self-regulated learning. *Educational Psychology Review, 24*(2), 205–249.

Clayton, P. H., & Ash, S. L. (2004). Shifts in perspective: Capitalizing on the counter-normative nature of service learning. *Michigan Journal of Community Service Learning, 11*(1), 59–71.

Cliff, W. H., & Wright, A. W. (1996). Directed case study method for teaching human anatomy and physiology. *Advances in Physiology Education, 270*(6), S19–S28.

CliftonStrengths for Students. (2017). Develop engaged & thriving students, on campus and beyond. Retrieved from http://www.strengthsquest.com/home.aspx

Clinebell, S., & Stecher, M. (2003). Teaching teams to be teams: An exercise using the Myers-Briggs® Type Indicator and the Five-Factor Personality Traits. *Journal of Management Education, 27*(3), 362–383.

Cohen, A. M. (1998). *The shaping of American higher education: Emergence and growth of the contemporary system.* San Francisco, CA: Jossey-Bass.

Cohen, A. R. (1976). Beyond simulation: Treating the classroom as an organization. *Journal of Management Education, 2*(1), 13–19.

Collegiate Leadership Competition. (2017). Coaches. Retrieved from https://collegiateleader.org/coaches

Conger, J. (1992). *Learning to lead: The art of transforming managers into leaders.* SanFrancisco, CA: Jossey-Bass.

Conrad, D., & Hedin, D. (1990). Learning from service: Experience is the best teacher—or is it? In Jane Kendall and Associates (Eds.), *Combining service and learning: Volume I* (pp. 87–98). Raleigh, NC: National Society for Internships and Experiential Education.

Cook, L. S., & Olson, J. R. (2006). The sky's the limit: An activity for teaching project management. *Journal of Management Education, 30*(3), 404–420.

Cooper, J., Robinson, P., & McKinney, M. (1993). *Cooperative learning in the classroom.* San Francisco, CA: Jossey-Bass.

Council for the Advancement of Standards in Higher Education. (2015). Student leadership programs. In *CAS professional standards for higher education* (9th ed.). Washington, DC: Author.

Cova, B., Kassis, J., & Lanou, V. (1993). Back to pedagogy: The EAPs 20 years of European experience. *Management Education and Development, 24*, 33–47.

Covey, S. (1989). *7 habits of highly effective people.* New York: Free Press.

Cox, M. D., & Richlin, L. (1993). Emerging trends in college teaching for the 21st century: A message from the editors. *Journal on Excellence in College Teaching, 4*, 1–7.

Crenshaw, K. (1991). Mapping the margins: Intersectionality, identity politics, and violence against women of color. *Stanford Law Review*, pp. 1241–1299.

Crone, J. A. (2001). Attaining more and greater depth of discussion in the undergraduate classroom: The seminar and seminar paper. *Teaching Sociology, 29*, 229–236.

Cronin, T. E., & Genovese, M. A. (2012). *Leadership matters: Unleashing the power of paradox.* New York: Routledge.

Cross, K. P. (2002). *The role of class discussion in the learning-centered classroom.* The Cross Papers No. 6. Phoenix, AZ: League for Innovation in the Community College and Educational Testing Service.

Csikzentmihalyi, M. (1990). The domain of creativity. In M. A. Runco, & R. S. Albert (Eds.), *Theories of creativity* (pp. 190-212).Thousand Oaks, CA: SAGE.

CSIS. (2017). Seven revolutions: An ongoing research effort to identify and analyze the most important trends shaping our world out to the year 2035. Retrieved from https://www.csis.org/programs/seven-revolutions

Csongor, J. E. (1992). Mirror, mirror on the wall: Teaching self-assessment to students. *The Mathematics Teacher, 85*(8), 636–637.

Cunliffe, A. (2002). Reflexive dialogical practice in management learning. *Management Learning, 33*(1), 35–61.

Curry, B., & Moutinho, L. (1992). Using computer simulations in management education. *Management Education and Development, 23*, 155–167.

Cuyjet, M. J. (Ed.). (2006). *African American men in college.* San Francisco, CA: Jossey-Bass.

Daft, R., & Noe, R. (2001). *Organizational behavior.* Cincinnati, OH: South-Western.

Davies, S., & Guppy, N. (1997). Fields of study, college selectivity, and student inequalities in higher education. *Social Forces, 75*(4), 1417–1438.

Day, D. V. (2001). Leadership development: A review in context. *Leadership Quarterly, 11*(4), 581–613.

Day, D. V. (2011). Integrative perspectives on longitudinal investigations of leader development: From childhood through adulthood. *The Leadership Quarterly, 22*, 561–571.

Day, D. V., Fleenor, J. W., Atwater, L. E., Sturm, R. E., & McKee, R. A. (2014). Advances in leader and leadership development: A review of 25 years of research and theory. *Leadership Quarterly, 25*, 63–82.

Day, D. V., Harrison, M. M., & Halpin, S. M. (2009). *An integrative theory of leadership development: Connecting adult development, identity, and expertise.* New York: Psychology Press.

De Graaff, R., Jan Koopman, G., Anikina, Y., & Westhoff, G. (2007). An observation tool for effective L2 pedagogy in Content and Language Integrated Learning (CLIL). *International Journal of Bilingual Education and Bilingualism, 10*(5), 603–624.

Dellow, D., & Jenkins, D. M. (2014). Learning by design, Utilizing observation instruments to promote student mindfulness of leadership practices, theories, and behaviors. *Concepts & Connections, 20*(3), 11–14.

Deming, W. E. (1986). *Out of the crisis.* Boston, MA: MIT Press.

DeNeve, K. M., & Heppner, M. J. (1997). Role play simulations: The assessment of an active learning technique and comparisons with traditional lectures. *Innovative Higher Education, 21*(3), 231–246.

Dennehy, R. F., Sims, R. R, & Collins, H. E. (1998). Debriefing experiential learning exercises: A theoretical and practical guide for success. *Journal of Management Education, 22*(1), 9–25.

DeNora, T. (2003) *After Adorno: Rethinking music sociology.* Cambridge, UK: Cambridge University Press.

Densten, I. L., & Gray, J. H. (2001). Leadership development and reflection: What is the connection. *The International Journal of Educational Management, 15*(3), 119–124.

De Pree, M. (1987). *Leadership is an art.* East Lansing, MI: Michigan State University Press.

De Pree, M. (1992). *Leadership jazz: The essential elements of a great leader.* New York, NY: Dell Publishing.

DeRue, D. S., & Wellman, N. (2009). Developing leaders via experience: The role of developmental challenge, learning orientation, and feedback availability. *Journal of Applied Psychology, 94*(4), 859–875.

de Villiers, R. (2013). 7 Principles of highly effective managerial feedback: Theory and practice in managerial development interventions. *The International Journal of Management Education, 11*(2), 66–74.

Dewey, J. (1933). *How we think: A restatement of the relation of reflective thinking to the educative process.* Boston, MA: D.C. Heath and Company.

Diamond, R. M. (1989). *Designing and improving courses and curricula in higher education.* San Francisco, CA: Jossey-Bass.

Dillon, J. T. (1994). *Using discussion in classrooms.* Milton Keynes, UK: Open University Press.

DiTiberio, J. (1998). Uses of type in education. In I. Briggs, M. McCauley, N. Quenk, & A. Hammer (Eds.), *MBTI manual: A guide to the development and use of the Myers-Briggs Type Indicator®* (3rd ed., pp. 253–284). Washington, DC: Consulting Psychologists Press.

Dochy, F. J., & McDowell, L. (1997). Assessment as a tool for learning. *Studies in Educational Evaluation, 23*(4), 279–298.

Dochy, F. J. R. C., Segers, M., & Sluijsmans, D. (1999). The use of self-, peer and co-assessment in higher education: A review. *Studies in Higher education, 24*(3), 331–350.

Doh, J. P. (2003). Can leadership be taught? Perspectives from management educators. *Academy of Management: Learning & Education, 2*(1), 54–67.

Dollisso, A. D. (2011). Using an online threaded discussions model for leadership case study: Implications for student engagement and learning in an asynchronous environment. *Proceedings of the 2011 Association of Leadership Educators Conference*, pp. 247–254. Retrieved from http://leadershipeducators.org/Resources/Documents/2011%20ALE%20Conference%20Proceedings.pdf

Dover, A. G., & Pozdol, T. (2016). Teaching good kids in a mAAd world: Using hip-hop to reflect, reframe, and respond to complex realities. *English Journal, 105*(4), 43.

Doyle, M., & Straus, D. (1976). *How to make meetings work.* New York, NY: Jove.

Drew, G. (2010). Issues and challenges in higher education leadership: Engaging for change. *Australian Educational Researcher, 37*(3), 57–76.

Drew, S. A. W., & Davidson, A. (1993). Simulation-based leadership development and team development. *Journal of Management Development, 12*(8), 39–52.

DuBrin, A. J. (2012). *Leadership: Research findings, practice, and skills* (7th ed.). Boston, MA: Cengage.

DuBrin, A. J. (2016). *Leadership: Research findings, practice, and skills.* Boston, MA: Cenange.

Dudley-Marling, C. (2013). Discussion in postsecondary classrooms: A review of the literature. *SAGE Open*, pp. 1–13.

Dugan, J. P. (2006). Involvement and leadership: A descriptive analysis of socially responsible leadership. *Journal of College Student Development, 47*(3), 335–343.

Dugan, J. P. (2011). Research on college student leadership development. In S. R. Komives, J. P. Dugan, J. E. Owen, C. Slack, W. Wagner, & Associates (Eds.), *The handbook of student leadership development* (2nd ed., pp. 59–84). San Francisco, CA: Jossey-Bass.

Dugan, J. P. (2012). Exploring local to global leadership education assessment. In K. L. Guthrie & L. Osteen (Eds.), *New directions for student services no. 140: Developing students' leadership capacity* (pp. 89–101). San Francisco, CA: Jossey-Bass.

Dugan, J. P. (2017). *Leadership theory: Cultivating critical perspectives.* San Francisco, CA: Jossey-Bass. Dugan, J. P., Kodama, C., Correia, B., & Associates. (2013). *Multi-institutional study of leadership insight report: Leadership program delivery.* College Park, MD: National Clearinghouse for Leadership Programs.

Dugan, J. P., & Komives, S. R. (2011). Leadership theories. In S. R. Komives, J. P. Dugan, J. E. Owen, C. Slack, W. Wagner, & Associates (Eds.), *The handbook of student leadership development* (2nd ed., pp. 35–58). San Francisco, CA: Jossey-Bass.

Dungan, A. T., & Mundhenk, L. G. (2006). Student self-assessment: A tool for engaging management students in their learning. *Organization Management Journal, 3*, 54–73.

Dweck, C. S. (1986). Motivational processes affecting learning. *American Psychologist, 41*(10), 1040–1048.

Dweck, C. S. (2007). The perils and promises of praise. In M. Scherer (Ed.), *On formative assessment: Readings from education leadership* (pp. 66–75). Alexandria, VA: ASCD.

Dyer, W. G. (2007). *Team building: Proven strategies for improving team performance* (4th ed.). San Francisco, CA: Jossey-Bass.

Edelstein, S., & Edwards, J. (2002). If you build it, they will come: Building learning communities through threaded discussions. *Online Journal of Distance Learning Administration, 5*(1), 1–6.

Eeds, M., & Wells, D. (1991). Talking, thinking, and cooperative learning: Lessons learned from listening to children talk about books. *Social Education, 55*, 134–137.

Eich, D. (2008). A grounded theory of high-quality leadership programs: Perspectives from student leadership programs in higher education. *Journal of Leadership & Organizational Studies, 15*(2), 176–187.

Eich, D. (2012). *Root down and branch out: Best practices for leadership development programs.* Madison, WI: Darin Eich.

Eich, D. J. (2007). *A grounded theory of high quality leadership programs: Perspectives from student leadership development programs in higher education* (Doctoral dissertation). Retrieved from ProQuest Dissertations and Theses (Publication No. AAT 3279002).

Eitington, J. E. (2001). *The winning trainer winning ways to involve people in learning* (4th ed.). Boston, MA: Butterworth Heinemann.

Emiliani, M. L., & Emiliani, M. (2013). Music as a framework to better understand Lean leadership. *Leadership & Organization Development Journal, 34*(5), 407–426.

Endersby, L., Phelps, K., & Jenkins, D. M. (2017). The virtual table: A framework for online teamwork, collaboration, and communication. In J. Ahlquist & L. Endersby (Eds.), *New directions for student leadership, No. 153: Going digital in student leadership* (pp. 75–88). San Francisco, CA: Jossey-Bass.

Ennis, R. H. (1993). Critical thinking assessment. *Theory into Practice, 32*(3), 179–186.

Erenrich, S. J., & Wergin, J. F. (2017). *Grassroots leadership and the arts for social change*. Bingley, UK: Emerald.

Ericsson, K. A., & Pool, R. (2016). *Peak: Secrets from the new science of success*. New York, NY: Houghton Mifflin Harcourt.

Ericsson, K. A., Prietula, M. J., & Cokely, E. T. (2007). The making of an expert. *Harvard Business Review, 85*, 114–121.

Erikson, E. H. (1959). *Identity and the life cycle*. New York, NY: W. W. Norton.

Erskine, J. A., Leenders, M. R., & Mauffette-Leenders, L. A. (1998). *Teaching with cases*. London/Canada: Ivey.

Erwin, T. D. (1991). *Assessing student learning and development: A guide to the principles, goals, and methods of determining college outcomes*. San Francisco, CA: Jossey-Bass.

Espinola, J. B., Wells, T., & Jenkins, D. M. (2012, October). *Reflection pedagogies 3.0: New strategies for bridging knowledge and experience with meaning making*. Presentation at International Leadership Association Conference, Denver, CO.

Ewell, P. T. (1988). Outcomes, assessment, and academic improvement: In search of usable knowledge. In J. C. Smart (Ed.), *Higher education: Handbook of theory and research* (pp. 53–108). New York, NY: Agathon Press.

Ewell, P. (2002). *Applying learning outcomes concepts to higher education: An overview*. National Center for Higher Education Management Systems (NCHEMS).

Ewens, W. (2000). Teaching using discussion. In R. Neff & M. Weimer (Eds.), *Classroom communication: Collected readings for effective discussion and questioning* (pp. 21–26). Madison, WI: Atwood.

Eyler, J., & Giles, D. E. (1999). *Where's the learning in service-learning?* San Francisco, CA: Jossey-Bass.

Eyler, J., Giles, D. E., & Schmeide. (1996). *A practitioner's guide to reflection in service-learning: Student voices and reflections*. A technical assistance project funded by the Corporation for National Service. Nashville, TN: Vanderbilt University.

Facione, P. A. (1990). *The Delphi report*. Millbrae, CA: The California Academic Press.

Falchikov, N., & Goldfinch, J. (2000). Student peer assessment in higher education: A meta-analysis comparing peer and teacher marks. *Review of Educational Research, 70*(3), 287–323.

Faria, A. J., & Dickinson, J. R. (1994). Simulation gaming for sales management training. *Journal of Management Development, 13*(1), 47–59.

Fayne, H. R. (2009). Using integrated course design to build student communities of practice in a hybrid course. In L. D. Fink & A. K. Fink. (Eds.), *New directions for teaching and learning No.119: Designing courses for significant learning: Voices of experience* (pp. 53–59). San Francisco, CA: John Wiley & Sons.

Feinstein, A. H., Mann, S., & Corsun, D. L. (2002). Charting the experiential territory: Clarifying definitions and uses of computer simulation, games, and role play. *Journal of Management Development, 21*, 732–744.

Fink, L. D. (2013). *Creating significant learning experiences*. San Francisco: John Wiley & Sons.

Flavell, J. H. (1976). Metacognitive aspects of problem solving. In L. B. Resnick (Ed.), *The nature of intelligence* (pp. 231–236). Hillsdale, NJ: Lawrence Erlbaum Associates.

Fletcher, C. (1993). Testing times for the world of psychometrics. *Personnel Management, 25*(12), 46–50.

Flores, K. L., Matkin, G. S., Burbach, M. E., Quinn, C. E., Harding, H. (2012). Deficient critical thinking skills among college graduates: Implications for leadership. *Educational Philosophy and Theory, 44*(2), 212–230.

Fogarty, R. (1994). *How to teach for metacognition*. Palatine, IL: IRI/Skylight.

Forrester, J. W. (1961). *Industrial dynamics*. Cambridge, MA: MIT Press.

Foster, C. A., & Law, M. R. (2006). How many perspectives provide a compass? Differentiating 360-degree and multi-source feedback. *International Journal of Selection and Assessment, 14*(3), 288–291.

Fraiberg, A. (2010). Fiction, business studies, and leadership: From know-how to embracing the impossible. *Journal of Leadership Studies, 3*(4), 97–101.

Frederick, P. J. (2000). Motivating students by active learning in the history classroom. In A. Booth & P. Hyland (Eds.), *The practice of university history teaching* (pp. 101–111). Manchester, UK: Manchester University Press.

Freeman, M. A., & Capper, J. M. (1998). *An anonymous asynchronous web-based role play*. Paper presented at Australasian Society for Computers in Learning in Tertiary Education, Wollongong, Australia.

Frost, S., & Jean, P. (2003). Bridging the disciplines: Interdisciplinary discourse and faculty scholarship. *Journal of Higher Education, 74*(2), 119–149.

Gagnon, G. W., & Collay, M. (2006). *Constructivist learning design: Key questions for teaching to standards*. Thousand Oaks, CA: SAGE.

Gagnon, S., Vough, H. C., & Nickerson, R. (2012). Learning to lead, unscripted: Developing affiliative leadership through improvisational theatre. *Human Resource Development Review, 11*(3), 299–325.

Gallos, J. V. (2013). *Using Bolman and Deal's Reframing Organizations fifth edition: An instructor's guide to effective teaching*. San Francisco, CA: Jossey-Bass.

Gallup. (2017). *Discover your CliftonStrengths: CliftonStrengths*. Retrieved from http://www.gallup.com/products/170957/clifton-strengthsfinder.aspx

Ganz, M. (2011). Public narrative, collective action, and power. In S. Odugbeni & T. Lee (Eds.), *Accountability through public opinion: From inertia to public action* (pp. 273–289). Washington, DC: The World Bank.

Ganz, M., & Lin, E. (2011). Learning to lead: Pedagogy of practice. In S. Snook, N. Nohria, & R. Khurana (Eds.), *Handbook for teaching leadership: Knowing, doing, and being* (pp. 353–366). Los Angeles, CA: SAGE.

Gardner, J. (1990). *On leadership*. New York City: Free Press.

Gardner, R. (2013). Introduction to debriefing. *Seminars in Perinatology, 37*, 166–174.

Gardner, S. K., & Barnes, B. J. (2007). Graduate student involvement: Socialization for the professional role. *Journal of College Student Development, 48*(4), 369–387.

Gardner, W. L., & Larson, L. L. (1988). Practicing management in the classroom: Experience is the best teacher. *Journal of Management Education, 12*(3), 12–23.

Gardner, W. L., & Martinko, M. J. (1996). Using the Myers-Briggs Type Indicator to study managers: A literature review and research agenda. *Journal of Management, 22*(1), 45–83.

Garrison, Z., & Chickering, A. (1987). Seven principles for good practices in undergraduate education. *AAHE Bulletin, 39*(7), 3–7.

Garvin, D. A. (2003). *Learning in action: A guide to putting the learning organization to work*. Boston, MA: Harvard Business Review Press.

Gertsen, R., Baker, S. K., Haager, D., & Graves, A. W. (2005). Exploring the role of teacher quality in predicting the reading out comes for first-grade English learners: An observational study. *Remedial and Special Education, 26*(4), 197–206.

Gibson, K. (2003). Games students play: Incorporating the prisoner's dilemma in teaching business ethics. *Journal of Business Ethics, 48*(1), 53–64.

Gilliland, S. (1993). The perceived fairness of selection systems: An organizational justice perspective. *Academy of Management Review, 18*, 694–734.

Gilmore, T. N., & Schall, E. (1996). Staying alive to learning: Integrating enactments with case teaching to develop leaders. *Journal of Policy Analysis and Management, 15*(3), 444–457.

Goby, V. P., & Lewis, J. H. (2000). Using experiential learning theory and the Myers-Briggs Type indicator in teaching business communication. *Business Communication Quarterly, 63*(3), 39–48.

Goertzen, B. J. (2009). Assessment in academic based leadership education programs. *Journal of Leadership Education, 8*(1), 148–162.

Goertzen, B. J. (2012). Assessment adrift: Review of the current state of assessment of academically based leadership education programs. *Journal of Leadership Studies, 6*, 55–60.

Goertzen, B. J., McRay, J., & Klaus, K. (2016). Electronic portfolios as capstone experiences in a graduate program in organizational leadership. *Journal of Leadership Education, 15*(3), 42–52.

Gokhale, A. A. (1995). Collaborative learning enhances critical thinking. *Journal of Technology Education, 7*(1), 1–8.

Golde, C. M. (1998). Beginning graduate school: Explaining first-year doctoral attrition. In M. S. Anderson (Ed.), *The experience of being in graduate school: An exploration* (pp. 55–64). San Francisco, CA: Jossey-Bass.

Goleman, D., Boyatzis, R., & McKee, A. (2002). *Primal leadership: Realizing the power of emotional intelligence.* Boston, MA: Harvard Business School Press.

Goleman, D., Boyatzis, R. E., & McKee, A. (2013). *Primal leadership: Learning to lead with emotional intelligence.* Boston, MA: Harvard Business School Press.

Gollwitzer, P. M., & Kirchhof, O. (1998). The willful pursuit of identity. In J. Heckhausen & C. S. Dweck (Eds.), *Life-span perspectives on motivation and control* (pp. 389–423). New York, NY: Cambridge University Press.

Goodrich, T., Irvine, C., & Boccher-Lattimore, D. (2005). Narrative ethics as collaboration. *Families, Systems, & Health, 28*(3), 348–357.

Gopinath, C., & Sawyer, J. E. (1999). Exploring the learning from an enterprise simulation. *The Journal of Management Development, 18*(5), 477–489.

Graham, S. T., Sincoff, M. Z., Baker, B., & Ackerman, J. C. (2003). Reel leadership: Hollywood takes the leadership challenge. *Journal of Leadership Education, 2*(2), 37–45.

Gredler, M. (1992). *Designing and evaluation games and simulations: A process approach.* London, UK: Kogan Page.

Greene, J. (1999). Head games. *Hospital and Health Networks, 73*(6), 52–56.

Greenleaf, R. K. (1977). *Servant leadership.* Indianapolis, IN: Greenleaf Center for Servant Leadership.

Grisham, T. (2006). Metaphor, poetry, storytelling and cross-cultural leadership. *Management Decision, 44*(4), 486–503.

Grossman, P., Loeb, S., Cohen, J., Hammerness, K., Wyckoff, J., Boyd, D., & Lankford, H. (2010). *Measure for measure: The relationship between measures of instructional practice in middle school English language arts and teachers' value-added scores* (No. w16015). Cambridge, MA: National Bureau of Economic Research.

Gueldenzoph, L. E., & May, G. L. (2002). Collaborative peer evaluation: Best practices for group member assessments. *Business Communication Quarterly, 65*(1), 9–20.

Guthrie, K. L. (2016). Expanding leadership education: Teaching service-learning online. *ILA Member Connector, 6,* 15–17. Retrieved from http://www.ila-net. org/members/directory/downloads/newsletter/June2016MemberConnector. pdf

Guthrie, K. L., & Bertrand Jones, T. (2012). Teaching and learning: Using experiential learning and reflection for leadership education. In K. L. Guthrie & L. Osteen (Eds.), *New directions for student services no. 140: Developing students' leadership capacity* (pp. 53–64). San Francisco, CA: Jossey-Bass.

Guthrie, K. L., Bertrand Jones, T., & Osteen, L. (Eds.). (2016). Developing culturally relevant leadership learning. In K. L. Guthrie & L. Osteen (Eds.), *New directions for student leadership capacity: Developing students' leadership capacity.* San Francisco, CA: Jossey-Bass.

Guthrie, K. L., Bertrand Jones, T., & Osteen, L. (in press). The teaching, learning, and being of leadership: Exploring context and practice of the culturally relevant leadership learning model. *Journal of Leadership Studies, 11*(3), XX–XX.

Guthrie, K. L., Bertrand Jones, T. B., Osteen, L., & Hu, S. (2013). Cultivating leader identity and capacity in students from diverse backgrounds. *ASHE Higher Education Report, 39*, 4.

Guthrie, K. L., & Bovio, R. (2014). Undergraduate certificate in leadership studies: An opportunity for seamless learning. *Journal of College and Character, 15*(1), 25–31.

Guthrie, K. L., & Callahan, K. (2016). Liberal arts: Leadership education in the 21st century. In K. L. Guthrie & L. Osteen (Eds.), *New directions for higher education no. 174: Reclaiming higher education's purpose in leadership development* (pp. 21–33). San Francisco, CA: Jossey-Bass.

Guthrie, K. L., & McCracken, H. (2010a). Making a difference online: Facilitating service-learning through distance education. *The Internet and Higher Education, 13*, 153–157.

Guthrie, K. L., & McCracken, H. (2010b). Reflective pedagogy: Making meaning in experiential based online courses. *The Journal of Educators Online, 7*(2), 1–21.

Guthrie, K. L., & Osteen, L. (Eds.). (2016). Reclaiming higher education's purpose in leadership development. *New Directions for Higher Education, 174: Developing students' leadership capacity.* San Francisco, CA: Jossey-Bass.

Guthrie, K. L., & Osteen, L. (Eds.). (2012a). Developing students' leadership capacity. *New Directions for Student Services, 140: Developing students' leadership capacity.* San Francisco, CA: Jossey-Bass.

Guthrie, K. L., & Osteen, L. (2012b). Editors' notes. In K. L. Guthrie & L. Osteen (Eds.), *New directions for student services, No. 140: Developing students' leadership capacity* (pp. 1–3). San Francisco, CA: Jossey-Bass.

Guthrie, K. L., Phelps, K., & Downey, S. (2011). Virtual environments: A developmental tool for leadership education. *Journal of Leadership Studies, 5*(2), 6–13.

Guthrie, K. L., & Thompson, S. (2010). Creating meaningful environments for leadership education. *Journal of Leadership Education, 9*(2), 50–57.

Haapsalo, H., & Hyvonen, J. (2001). Simulating business and operations management: A learning environment for the electronics industry. *International Journal of Production Economics, 73*, 261–272.

Haber, P. (2011). Formal leadership programs. In S. R. Komives, J. P. Dugan, & J. E. Owen (Eds.), *The handbook for student leadership development* (pp. 231–257). San Francisco, CA: Jossey-Bass.

Haber-Curran, P., & Owen, J. E. (2013). Engaging the whole student: Student affairs and the national leadership education research agenda. *Journal of Leadership Education, 12*(3), 38–50.

Haber-Curran, P., & Tillapaugh, D. W. (2014). Student-centered transformative learning in leadership education: An examination of the teaching and learning process. *Journal of Transformative Education, 13*, 65–84.

Haberyan, A. (2007). Team-based learning in an industrial/organizational psychology course. *North American Journal of Psychology Education, 9*(1), 143–152.

Hackman M. Z., Olive, T. E., Guzman N., & Brunson, D. (1999). Ethical considerations in the development of the interdisciplinary leadership studies program. *Journal of Leadership Studies*, *6*, 36–48.

Hafford-Letchfield, T., & Bourn, D. (2011). "How am I doing?": Advancing management skills through the use of a multi-source feedback tool to enhance work-based learning on a post-qualifying post-graduate leadership and management programme. *Social Work Education*, *30*(50), 497–511.

Hafford-Letchfield, T., Couchman, W., Harries, B., et al. (2008, January 23–25). *Using arts-based methods to develop service user led learning materials for social work education*. In IRISS International Conference Proceedings, Edinburgh. Retrieved July 1, 2016, from http://content. iriss.org.uk/pepe2008/files/731_paper.pdf

Hall, B. (2008). Keep the leadership pipeline flowing: Districts can adopt these 5 strategies to streamline succession planning. *Journal of Staff Development*, *29*(3), 33.

Hall, J. L. (2010). Teaching with music: An alternative pedagogy for leadership educators. *Journal of Leadership Studies*, *3*(4), 108–110.

Halpern, D. F. (1996). *Thought and knowledge: An introduction to critical thinking*. Mahwah, NJ: Lawrence Erlbaum Associates.

Hammel, H. (1986). How to design a debriefing session. *Journal of Experiential Education*, *9*(3), 20–25.

Hammer, M. R. (2010). *The intercultural development inventory manual*. Berlin, MD: IDI, LLC.

Hanrahan, S. J., & Isaacs, G. (2001). Assessing self- and peer-assessment: The students' views. *Higher Education Research & Development*, *20*(1), 53–70.

Harding, H. E. (2011). *'A place of becoming": Leadership educators' experience teaching leadership: A phenomenological approach* (Doctoral dissertation). Retrieved from http://digitalcommons.unl.edu/aglecdiss/19

Hardman, F., & Mroz, M. (1999). Post-16 English teaching: From recitation to discussion. *Educational Review*, *51*, 283–293.

Harland, L. K. (2003), Using personality tests in leadership development: Test format effects and the mitigating impact of explanations and feedback. *Human Resource Development Quarterly*, *14*, 285–301.

Harlen, W., & James, M. (1997). Assessment and learning: Differences and relationships between formative and summative assessment. *Assessment in Education: Principles, Policy & Practice*, *4*(3), 365–379.

Haro, S. P., & Turgut, G. (2012). Expanded strategy simulations: Developing better managers. *Journal of Management Development*, *31*(3), 209–220.

Haroutunian-Gordon, S. (1991). *Turning the soul: Teaching through conversation in high school*. Chicago, IL: University Press.

Harper, S. R. (2011). Strategy and intentionality in practice. In J. H. Schuh, S. R. Jones, & S. R. Harper (Eds.), *Student services: A handbook for the profession* (5th ed., pp. 287–302). San Francisco, CA: Jossey-Bass.

Harrington, T. F. (1995). *Assessment of abilities*. Greensboro, NC: ERIC Clearinghouse on Counseling and Student Services.

Hartz, G. (1998). Real learning takes a personal touch. *Community College Week*, *10*(22), 5.

Harvard Business Publishing. (2017). Leadership and teams simulation: Everest v2. Retrieved from https://cb.hbsp.harvard.edu/cbmp/product/7000-HTM-ENG

Harvey, M., & Jenkins, D. M. (2014). Knowledge, praxis, and reflection: The three critical elements of effective leadership studies programs. *Journal of Leadership Studies, 7,* 76–85.

Harvey, M., & Riggio, R. E. (Eds.). (2011). *Leadership studies: The dialogue of disciplines.* Northampton, MA: Edward Elgar.

Hatcher, J. A., & Bringle, R. G. (1997). Reflection: Bridging the gap between service and learning. *College Teaching, 45,* 153–158.

Hattie, J., & Timperley, H. (2007). The power of feedback. *Review of Educational Research, 77*(1), 81–112.

Haworth, J. G., & Conrad, C. F. (1997). *Emblems of quality in higher education. Developing and sustaining high-quality programs.* Needham Heights, MA: Allyn & Bacon.

Heifetz, R. A., & Linsky, M. (2002). *Leadership on the line: Staying alive through the dangers of leading.* Boston, MA: Harvard Business School Press.

Heifetz, R. A., & Linsky, M. (2004). When leadership spells danger. *Educational Leadership, 61*(7), 33–37.

Heifetz, R. A., Linsky, M., & Grashow, A. (2009). *The practice of adaptive leadership: Tools and tactics for changing your organization and the world.* Boston, MA: Harvard Business School.

Hendrix, L. (1978). Studying ourselves: The questionnaire as a teaching tool. *The Family Coordinator, 27*(1), 47–54.

Herdlein, R. J., III. (2004). Survey of chief student affairs officers regarding relevance of graduate preparation of new professionals. *NASPA Journal, 42*(1), 51–71.

Herreid, C. (2007). *Start with a story: The case study method of teaching college science.* Arlington, VA: NSTA Press.

Herreid, C. F. (2011). Case study teaching. In W. Buskist & J. E. Groccia (Eds.), *New directions for teaching and learning, no. 128: Evidence-based teaching* (pp. 31–40). San Francisco, CA: Jossey-Bass.

Hess, P. W. (2007). Enhancing leadership skill development by creating practice/ feedback opportunities in the classroom. *Journal of Management Education, 31*(2), 195–213.

Hesselbein, F. (2002) *Hesselbein on leadership.* San Francisco, CA: Jossey-Bass.

Hesselbein, F., & Shinseki, E. K. (2004). *Be, know, do: Leadership the army way: Adapted from the official army leadership manual.* San Francisco, CA: Jossey-Bass.

Hettrick, J. (2012). *Online video games: Leadership development for the millennial college Student* (Doctoral dissertation). Retrieved from ProQuest Dissertations & Theses A&I (AAT 1153264568).

Higher Education Research Institute. (1996). *A social change model of leadership development* (Version III). Los Angeles, CA: University of California Higher Education Research Institute.

Hodges, T. D., & Harter, J. K. (2005). A review of the theory and research underlying the StrengthsQuest program for students. *Educational Horizons, 83,* 190–201.

Hofstadter, R., & Hardy, C. D. (1952). *The development and scope of higher education in the United States*. New York, NY: Columbia University Press.

Hogan, R., & Champagne, D. (1979). Personal style inventory. In J. Jones & J. Pfeiffer (Eds.), *The 1980 annual handbook for group facilitators*. San Diego, CA: University Associates.

Holt, C. A., & Capra, M. (2000). Classroom games: A prisoner's dilemma. *Journal of Economic Education, 31*(3), 229–236.

Holmer, L. L. (2001). Will we teach leadership or skilled incompetence? The challenge of student project teams. *Journal of Management Education, 25*(5), 590–605.

Holt, C. A., & Capra, M. (2000). Classroom games: A prisoner's dilemma. *Journal of Economic Education, 31*(3), 229–236.

hooks, b. (1994). *Teaching to transgress: Education as the practice of freedom*. New York, NY: Routledge.

Hoover, T. S., & Webster, N. (2004). Modeling service learning for future leaders of youth organizations. *Journal of Leadership Education, 3*(3), 58–62.

Howard, J. (1998). Academic service learning: A counternormative pedagogy. In R. Rhoads & J. Howard (Eds.), *Academic service learning: A pedagogy of action and reflection* (pp. 21–29). San Francisco, CA: Jossey-Bass.

Howe, C., Tolmie, A., Thurston, A., Topping, K., Christie, D., Livingston, K., Jessiman, E., & Donaldson, C. (2007). Group work in elementary science. Towards organisational principles for supporting pupil learning. *Learning and Instruction, 17*(5), 549–563.

Huffaker, J. S., & West, E. (2005). Enhancing learning in the business classroom: An adventure with improv theater techniques. *Journal of Management Education, 29*(6), 852–869.

Hughes, R. L., Ginnett, R. C., & Curphy, G. J (1999). *Leadership: Enhancing the lessons of experience* (3rd ed.). Boston, MA: Irvin McGraw-Hill.

Hughes, R., Ginnett, R., & Curphy, G. (2012). *Leadership: Enhancing the lessons of experience* (7th ed.). New York, NY: McGraw-Hill.

Humphreys, P., Greenan, K., & McIlveen, H. (1997). Developing work-based transferable skills in a university environment. *Journal of European Industrial Training, 21*(2), 63–69.

Hunsaker, P. L. (2007). Using social simulations to assess and train potential leaders to make effective decisions in turbulent environments. *Career Development International, 12*, 341–360.

Hurtado, S., Milem, J., Clayton-Pedersen, A., & Allen, W. (1999). Enacting diverse learning environments: Improving the climate for racial/ethnic diversity in higher education. *ASHE Higher Education Report, 26*, 8.

Hynes, S. (2016). Assessing leadership using national assessment tools. In D. M. Roberts & K. J. Bailey (Eds.), *New directions for student leadership no. 151: Assessing student leadership* (pp. 67–78). San Francisco, CA: Jossey-Bass.

Illeris, K. (2007). *How we learn: Learning and non-learning in school and beyond*. London, UK: Routledge.

Inter-association Leadership Education Collaborative. (2016). *Collaborative priorities and critical considerations for leadership education*. Inter-association Leadership Education Collaborative.

International Leadership Association. (2009). ILA guiding questions: Guidelines for leadership education programs. College Park, MD: Author. Retrieved from www.ila-net.org/communities/LC/GuidingQuestionsFinal.pdf

International Leadership Association. (2017). Leadership Program Directory. Retrieved from http://www.ila-net.org/Resources/LPD/index.htm

Irwin, T. H. (Trans.). (1999). *Aristotle: Nicomachean Ethics.* Indianapolis, IN: Hackett.

Isaacs, G. (2002). *Assessing group tasks.* Queensland, Australia: University of Queensland.

Ives, C. (2014, March 14). Daydreaming or deep in thought? Using formative assessment to evaluate student participation. *Faculty Focus.* Retrieved from https://www.facultyfocus.com/articles/effective-teaching-strategies/daydreaming-deep-thought-using-formative-assessment-evaluate-student-participation/

Jacoby, B. (1996). *Service-learning in higher education: Concepts and practices.* San Francisco, CA: Jossey-Bass.

Jang, Y., & Ryu, S. (2011). Exploring game experiences and game leadership in massively multiplayer online role-playing games. *British Journal of Educational Technology, 42*(4), 616–623.

Janke, K. K., Nelson, M. H., Bzowyckyj, A. S., Fuentes, D. G., Rosenberg, E., & DiCenzo, R. (2016). Deliberate integration of student leadership development in doctor of pharmacy programs. *American Journal of Pharmaceutical Education, 80*(1), 2.

Jenkins, D. M. (2012). Exploring signature pedagogies in undergraduate leadership education. *Journal of Leadership Education, 11*(1), 1–27.

Jenkins, D. M. (2013). Exploring instructional strategies in student leadership development programming. *Journal of Leadership Studies, 6*(4), 48–62.

Jenkins, D. M. (2016). Teaching leadership online: An exploratory study of instructional and assessment strategy use. *Journal of Leadership Education, 15*(2), 129–149.

Jenkins, D. M. (2017a). Comparing instructional and assessment strategy use ingraduate- and undergraduate-level leadership studies: A global study. *Journal of Leadership Education.*

Jenkins, D. (2017b). Exploring the lived experiences of becoming and being a leadership educator: A phenomenological inquiry. *Proceedings of the 2017 Association of Leadership Educators Conference, 431-445.* Retrieved from https://www.leadershipeducators.org/resources/Pictures/ALE%202017%20Conference%20Proceedings.pdf

Jenkins, D. M., & Allen, S. A. (in press). It's all about intentionality: Aligning instructional strategies with learning outcomes and leadership competencies. *New Directions for Student Leadership.*

Jenkins, D. M., & Andenoro, A. C. (2016). Developing critical thinking through leadership education. In K. L. Guthrie & L. Osteen (Eds.), *New directions for higher education, no. 174: Reclaiming higher education's purpose in leadership development* (pp. 57–67). San Francisco, CA: Jossey-Bass.

Jenkins, D. M., & Cutchens, A. B. (2011). Leading critically: A grounded theory of applied critical thinking in leadership studies. *Journal of Leadership Education, 10*(2), 1–21.

Jenkins, D. M., & Cutchens, A. B. (2012). *From theory to practice: Facilitating innovative experiential leadership theory-based role play activities.* Proceedings from the Association of Leadership Educators Conference, Key West, FL. Retrieved from http://leadershipeducators.org/Resources/Documents/2012%20ALE%20Conference%20Proceedings.pdf

Jenkins, D. M., & Dugan, J. P. (2013). Context matters: An interdisciplinary studies interpretation of the national leadership education research agenda. *Journal of Leadership Education, 12*(3), 15–29. Retrieved from http://www.journalofleadershiped.org/attachments/article/319/special_issue2013JenkinsDugan.pdf

Jenkins, D. M., & Harvey, M. (2014). Introduction. *Journal of Leadership Studies, 7*(4), 83–85.

Jenkins, D. M., O'Dell, I., & Priest, K. L. (2013, June). Leadership program assessment & evaluation: Coming to a theater near you. *SLPKC: Official Newsletter of the Student Leadership Programs Knowledge Community of NASPA.* Retrieved from http://issuu.com/naspaslpkc/docs/slpkc_newsletter_june2013

Johnson, D. W., & Johnson, R. T. (1989). *Cooperation and competition: Theory and research.* Minneapolis, MN: Interaction Book Company.

Johnson, D. W., Johnson, R. T., & Smith, K. A. (1991). *Cooperative learning: Increasing college faculty instructional productivity. ASHE-ERIC Higher Education Report, 4,* George Washington University.

Johnson, D. W., Johnson, R. T., & Smith, K. A. (2006). *Active learning: Cooperation in the college classroom* (3rd ed.). Edina, MN: Interaction Book.

Johnson, D. W., Johnson, R. T., & Smith, K. (2007). The state of cooperative learning in postsecondary and professional settings. *Educational Psychology Review, 19,* 15–29.

Jones, S. R. (1997). Voices of identity and difference: A qualitative exploration of the multiple dimensions of identity development in women college students. *Journal of College Student Development, 38*(4), 376.

Jones, S. R. (2016). Authenticity in leadership: Intersectionality of identities. In K. L. Guthrie, T. Bertrand Jones, & L. Osteen (Eds.), *New directions for student leadership, no. 152: Developing culturally relevant leadership learning* (pp. 23–34). San Francisco, CA: Jossey-Bass.

Jones, S. R., & Abes, E. S. (2004). Enduring influences of service-learning on college students' identity development. *Journal of College Student Development, 45*(2), 149–166.

Jones, S. R., & Abes, E. S. (2013). *Identity development of college students: Advancing frameworks for multiple dimensions of identity.* San Francisco, CA: John Wiley & Sons.

Jones, S. R., & McEwen, M. K. (2000). A conceptual model of multiple dimensions of identity. *Journal of College Student Development, 41,* 405–414.

Jordan, S. A. (2001). Writing the other, writing the self: Transforming consciousness through ethnographic writing. *Language and Intercultural Communication, 1*(1), 40–56.

Joyce, W. (1999). On the free-rider problem in cooperative learning. *Journal of Education for Business, 74,* 271–274.

Joyner, B., & Young, L. (2006). Teaching medical students using role play: Twelve tips for successful role plays. *Medical Teacher, 28*(3), 225–229.

Kamen, R. (1997). Psych selection. *Journal of Business Strategy, 18*(2), 22–27.

Kao, J. (1997), *Jamming—The art and discipline of business creativity*. New York, NY: Harper Business.

Kansas State University. (2017). Staley School of Leadership Studies. Retrieved from http://www.k-state.edu/leadership/

Katz, R. L. (1955). Skills of an effective administrator. *Harvard Business Review, 33*(1), 33–42.

Katz-Buonincontro, J. (2015). Decorative integration or relevant learning? A literature review of studio arts-based management education with recommendations for teaching and research. *Journal of Management Education, 39*(1), 81–115.

Katz-Buonincontro, J., Phillips, J. C., & Arnold, N. W. (2013). *Using the arts to promote social justice & problem framing practices in school leaders*. Paper presented at the American Educational Research Association Annual Convention, San Francisco, CA.

Kayes, A. B., Kayes, D. C., & Kolb, D. A. (2005). Experiential learning in teams. *Simulation and Gaming, 36*, 330–354.

Keating, K., Rosch, D., & Burgoon, L. (2014). Developmental readiness for leadership: The differential effects of leadership courses on creating "Ready, willing, and able" leaders. *Journal of Leadership Education, 13*(3), 1–16.

Keeling, R. P. (Ed.). (2004). *Learning reconsidered: A campus-wide focus on the student experience*. Washington, DC: National Association of Student Personnel Administrators.

Keesey, R. (1988). Transformations in disciplinary knowledge assumptions and their implication for reforming the undergraduate discipline. *Issues in Integrative Studies, 6*, 82–125.

Keith, S. Z. (1996). Self-assessment materials for use in portfolios. *Primus, 6*, 178–192.

Kegan, R. (1994). *In over our heads: The mental demands of modern life*. Cambridge, MA: Harvard University Press.

Kellerman, B. (2010). *Leadership: Essential selections on power, authority, and influence*. New York: McGraw-Hill Professional.

Kellerman, B. (2012). Cut off at the pass: The limits of leadership in the 21st century. *Governance Studies at Brookings Institution*, pp. 1–11. Retrieved from https://www.brookings.edu/wp-content/uploads/2016/06/0810_leadership_deficit_kellerman.pdf

Kellerman, B. (2013). Leading questions: The end of leadership–redux. *Leadership, 9*(1), 135–139.

Kelly, P. (2009). Group work and multicultural management education. *Journal of Teaching in International Business, 20*(1), 80–102.

Kennette, L. N., & Hanzuk, W. (2017, May 1). Four types of group work activities to engage students. *Faculty Focus*. Retrieved from https://www.facultyfocus.com/articles/instructional-design/group-work-collaborative-activities/

Keys, B., & Wolfe, J. (1990). The role of management games and simulations in education and research. *Journal of Management, 16*(2), 307–336.

Keyes, C. L. M., & Haidt, J. (2003). *Flourishing: Positive psychology and the life well lived*. Washington, DC: American Psychological Association.

Kezar, A. J., Carducci, R., & Contreras-McGavin, M. (2006). Rethinking the "L" word in higher education: The revolution in research in higher education. *ASHE Higher Education Report, 31*, 6.

Kezar, A. J., & Moriarty, D. (2000). Expanding our understanding of student leadership development: A study exploring gender and ethnic identity. *Journal of College Student Development, 41*(1), 55–69.

Kılıç, D. (2016). An examination of using self-, peer-, and teacher-assessment in higher education: A case study in teacher education. *Higher Education Studies, 6*(1), 136–144.

Kiili, K., & Lainema, T. (2008). Foundation for measuring engagement in educational games. *Journal of Interactive Learning Research, 19*, 469–488.

Kirk, J. J., & Orr, R. L. (2003). A primer on the effective use of threaded discussion forums. Retrieved from http://files.eric.ed.gov/fulltext/ED472738.pdf

Klein, J. T. (1990). *Interdisciplinarity: History, theory & practice*. Detroit, MI: Wayne State University Press.

Klenke, K. (1993). Leadership education at the great divide: Crossing into the twenty-first century. *The Journal of Leadership Studies, 1*(1), 110–127.

Knights, D., & Willmott, H. (1997). The hype and hope of interdisciplinary management studies. *British Journal of Management, 8*(1), 9–22.

Kolb, D. A. (1984). *Experiential learning: Experience as the source of learning and development*. Upper Saddle River, NJ: Prentice-Hall.

Komives, S. R. (2011). Advancing leadership education. In S. R. Komives, J. P. Dugan, & J. E. Owen (Eds.), *The handbook for student leadership development* (pp. 1–19). San Francisco, CA: Jossey-Bass.

Komives, S. R., Dugan, J. P., & Owen, J. E. (2011). *The handbook for student leadership development*. San Francisco, CA: Jossey-Bass.

Komives, S. R., Longerbeam, S., Owen, J. E., Mainella, F. C., & Osteen, L. (2006). A leadership identity development model: Applications from a grounded theory. *Journal of College Student Development, 47*, 401–420.

Komives, S. R., Lucas, N., & McMahon, T. R. (1998). *Exploring Leadership: For college students who want to make a difference*. San Francisco, CA: Jossey-Bass.

Komives, S. R., Lucas, N., & McMahon, T. R. (2007). *Exploring leadership: For college students who want to make a difference* (2nd ed.). San Francisco, CA: Jossey-Bass.

Komives, S. R., Lucas, N., & McMahon, T. R. (2013). *Exploring leadership: For college students who want to make a difference* (3rd ed.). San Francisco, CA: Jossey-Bass

Komives, S. R., Owen, J. E., Longerbeam, S. D., Mainella, F. C., & Osteen, L. (2005). Developing a leadership identity: A grounded theory. *Journal of College Student Development, 46*, 593–611.

Kornfeld, E. (1990, September). Representations of history: Role-playing debates in college history courses. *Perspectives on History*. Retrieved from https://www.historians.org/perspectives/issues/1990/9009/9009

Kotnour, T., Hoekstra, R., Reilly, C., Knight, R., & Selter, J. (2014). Infusing leadership education in the undergraduate engineering experience: A framework from UCF's eli2. *Journal of Leadership Studies, 7*(4), 48–57.

Kouzes, J. M., & Posner, B. Z. (1995). *The leadership challenge* (1st ed.). San Francisco, CA: Jossey-Bass.

Kouzes, J. M., & Posner, B. Z. (2003). *The student leadership challenge practices inventory*. San Francisco, CA: John Wiley and Sons.

Kouzes, J. M., & Posner, B. Z. (2010). *The student leadership challenge: Activities book* (E. Biech, Ed.). San Francisco, CA: Jossey-Bass.

Kouzes, J. M., & Posner, B. Z. (2012a). *The leadership challenge* (5th ed.). San Francisco, CA: Jossey-Bass.

Kouzes, J. M., & Posner, B. Z. (2012b). *Leadership practices inventory: Workbook* (4th ed.). San Francisco, CA: John Wiley and Sons.

Kouzes, J., & Posner, B. (2012c). *The leadership challenge workbook* (3rd ed.). San Francisco, CA: Jossey-Bass.

Kouzes, J. M., & Posner, B. Z. (2013a). *LPI: Leadership practices inventory workbook*. San Francisco, CA: John Wiley and Sons.

Kouzes, J. M., Posner, B. Z., High, B., & Morgan, G. M. (2013b). *The student leadership challenge: Facilitation and activity guide*. San Francisco, CA: Jossey-Bass.

Kouzes, J. M., Posner, B. Z., High, B., & Morgan, G. M. (2013b). *The student leadership challenge: Student workbook and personal leadership journal*. San Francisco, CA: Jossey-Bass.

Kouzes, J. M. & Posner, B. Z. (2014a). *The student leadership challenge: Five practices for becoming an exemplary leader* (2nd ed.). San Francisco, CA: John Wiley and Sons.

Kouzes, J. M., & Posner, B. Z. (2014b). *The student leadership challenge activities book*. San: Francisco CA: Jossey-Bass.

Kouzes, J. M., & Posner, B. Z. (2017). *The leadership challenge: How to make extraordinary things happen in organizations* (6th ed.). Hoboken, NJ: John Wiley & Sons.

Krauss, S. E., & Hamid, J. A. (2015). Exploring the relationship between campus leadership development and undergraduate student motivation to lead among a Malaysian sample. *Journal of Further and Higher Education, 39*(1), 1–26.

Kreie, J., Headrick, R. W., & Steiner, R. (2007). Using team learning to improve student retention. *College Education, 55*(2), 51–56.

Kuh, G. D. (1995). The other curriculum: Out-of-class experiences associated with student learning and personal development. *Journal of Higher Education, 66*(2), 123–155.

Kuh, G. D. (2008). *High-impact educational practices: What they are, who has access to them, and why they matter*. Washington, DC: Association of American College and Universities.

Laditka, S. B., & Houck, M. M. (2006). Student-developed case studies: An experiential approach for teaching ethics in management. *Journal of Business Ethics, 64*(2), 157–167.

Ladkin, D., & Taylor, S. S. (2010). Leadership as art: Variations on a theme. *Leadership, 6*(3), 235–241.

Lafferty, J. C., & Smith, H. M. (1987). *Jungle survival situation: A group problem solving simulation: Leader's guide*. Plymouth, MI: Human Synergistics.

Lake, J., Jackson, L., & Hardman, C. (2015). A fresh perspective on medical education: The lens of the arts. *Medical Education, 49*(8), 759–772.

Landreman, L. M. (2013). *The art of effective facilitation: Reflection from social justice educators.* Sterling, VA: Stylus.

Larsen, E. (1998). Feedback: Multiple purposes for management classrooms. *Journal of Management Education, 22*, 49–62.

Larson, B. E. (1997). Social studies teachers' conceptions of discussion: A grounded theory study. *Theory & Research in Social Education, 25*(2), 113–136.

Larson, B. E., & T. A. Keiper. (2002). Classroom discussion and threaded electronic discussion: Learning in two arenas. *Contemporary Issues in Technology and Teacher Education, 2*(1). Retrieved October, 28, 2010, from http://www. citejournal.org/vol2/iss1/socialstudies/article1.pdf

Lattery, M. J. (2009). Signature pedagogies in introductory physics. In R. A. R. Gurung, N. L. Chick, & A. Haynie (Eds.), *Exploring signature pedagogies: Approaches to teaching disciplinary habits of mind* (pp. 280–294). Sterling, VA: Stylus.

Lauber, L. (2007). Role-play: Principles to increase effectiveness. In M. L. Silberman (Ed.), *The handbook of experiential learning* (pp. 185–201). San Francisco, CA: John Wiley and Sons.

Laurillard, D. (1996). Multimedia and the learner's experience of narrative. *Computers in Education, 31*, 229–243.

Lean, J., Moizer, J., Towler, M., & Abbey, C. (2006). Simulations and games: Use and barriers in higher education. *Active Learning in Higher Education, 7*(3), 227–242.

Leon, L. A., & Tai, L. S. (2004). Implementing cooperative learning in a team-teaching environment. *Journal of Education for Business, 79*(5), 287–294.

Leonard, K., Hafford-Letchfield, T., & Couchman, W. (2016). The impact of the arts in social work education: A systematic review. *Qualitative Social Work,* http://journals.sagepub.com/doi/abs/10.1177/1473325016662905

Lewin, K. (1951). *Field theory in social sciences.* New York, NY: Harper & Row.

Lewis, M. A., & Maylor, H. R. (2007). Game playing and operations management education. *International Journal of Production Economics, 105*, 134–149.

Lincoln, S. (2005). Feeling the noise: Teenagers, bedrooms and music. *Leisure Studies, 24*(4), 399–414.

Lindsay, D. R., Foster, C. A., Jackson, R. J., & Hassan, A. M. (2009). Leadership education and assessment: A developmental approach. *Journal of Leadership Education, 8*(1), 16–176.

Lopes, M. C., Fialho, F. A. P., Cunha, C. J. C. A., & Niveiros, S. I. (2013). Business games for leadership development: A systematic review. *Simulation & Gaming, 44*(4), 523–543.

Lopez, S. J., & Louis, M. C. (2009). The principles of strengths-based education. *Journal of College and Character, 10*, 1–8.

Loughman, T., & Finley, J. (2010). Beowulf and the teaching of leadership. *Journal of Leadership Education, 9*(1), 155–164.

Lovell, C. D., & Kosten, L. A. (2000). Skills, knowledge, and personal traits necessary for success as a student affairs administrator: A meta-analysis of thirty years of research. *NASPA Journal, 37*(4), 353–369.

Lowry, D. (1990). *True Colors™ trainers resource guide.* Riverside, CA True Colors™ Communications Group.

Lucas, C. J. (1994). *American higher education: A history.* New York, NY: St. Martin's Press.

Luckmann, C. (1996). Defining experiential education. *Journal of Experiential Education, 19*(1), 6–7.

Ludvik, M. J. B., Gardner, M. M., & Hickmott, J. (2012). *Demonstrating student success: A practical guide to outcomes-based assessment of learning and development in student affairs.* Sterling, VA: Stylus.

Luft, J., & Ingham, H. (1955). The Johari Window, a graphic model of interpersonal awareness. In *Proceedings of the Western Training Laboratory in Group Development.* Los Angeles, CA: UCLA.

Lunken, H. P. (1993). The art and discipline of debriefing. In S. S. Gryskiewicz (Ed.), *Discovering creativity: Proceedings of the 1992 International Creativity & Innovation Networking Conference.* Center for Creative Leadership.

Lynn. A. B. (2002). *The emotional intelligence activity book: 50 activities for promoting EQ at work.* New York, NY: HRD Press.

Macpherson, K. (1999). The development of critical thinking skills in undergraduate supervisory management units: Efficacy of student peer assessment. *Assessment & Evaluation in Higher Education, 24*(3), 273–284.

Mahoney, A. D. (2016). Culturally responsive integrative learning environments: A critical displacement approach. In K. L. Guthrie, T. B. Jones, & L. Osteen (Eds.), *New directions for higher education, no. 152: Developing culturally relevant leadership learning* (pp. 47–60). San Francisco, CA: Jossey-Bass.

Mahoney, A. D. (in press). Being at the heart of the matter: Culturally relevant leadership learning, emotions and storytelling. *Journal of Leadership Studies, 11*(3), XX–XX.

Malone, D. (2011). Empirical evidence of the fairness and quality of peer evaluation. *Academy of Educational Leadership Journal, 15*(2), 129–140.

Markham, S. E., Markham, I. S., & Smith, J. W. (2015). At the crux of dyadic leadership: Self-other agreement of leaders and direct reports: Analyzing 360-degree feedback. *Leadership Quarterly, 26*(6), 958–977.

Martin, J. (1977). The development and use of classroom observation instruments. *Canadian Journal of Education, 2*(3), 43–54.

Martineau, J., & Hannum, K. (2004). *Evaluating the impact of leadership development: A professional guide* (no. 187). Center for Creative Leadership.

Marshall, S. M., & Hornak, A. M. (2008). *A day in the life of a college student leader.* Sterling, VA: Stylus Publishing.

Marzano, R. J. (2007). *The art and science of teaching: A comprehensive framework for effective instruction.* Alexandria, VA: ASCD.

Maslow, A. H. (1970). *Motivation and personality* (2nd ed.). New York, NY: Harper and Row.

Matsumura, L., Garnier, H., Slater, S., & Boston, M. (2008). Toward measuring instructional Interactions "at-scale." *Educational Assessment, 13*(4), 267–300.

Mayo, M., Kakarika, M., Pastor, J. C., & Brutus, S. (2012). Aligning or inflating your leadership self-image? A longitudinal study of responses to peer feedback in MBA teams. *Academy of Management Learning & Education, 11*(4), 631–652.

McCall, M. W. (2004). Leadership development through experience. *Academy of Management Executive, 18*(3), 127–130.

McCarthy, J. F. (2015). Introduction to the symposium on the integration of the arts into leadership studies. *Journal of Leadership Studies, 9*(1), 30–32.

McCarthy, J. F., & Carr, S. D. (2015). Igniting passion and possibilities through the arts: Conflict, collaboration and leadership through live stage performances. *Journal of Leadership Studies, 9*(1), 33–41.

McCarthy, J., O'Connell, D., & Hall, D. T. (2005). Leading beyond tragedy: The balance of personal identity and adaptability. *Leadership & Organization Development Journal, 26*(6), 458–475.

McCarthy, P. R., & McCarthy, H. M. (2006). When case studies are not enough: Integrating experiential learning into business curricula. *Journal of Education for Business, 81*(4), 201–204.

McCauley, C. D., Moxley, R., & Van Velsor, E. (Eds.). (1998). *The center for creative leadership handbook of leadership development.* San Francisco, CA: Jossey-Bass.

McCauley, C. D., & Van Velsor, E. (Eds.). (2004). *The center for creative leadership handbook of leadership development* (Vol. 29). New York: John Wiley & Sons.

McClure, L., & Werther, W. (1993). Personality variables in management development interventions. *Journal of Management Development, 12*(3), 39–47.

McDade, S. A. (February, 1995). Case study pedagogy to advance critical thinking. *Teaching of Psychology, 22*(1), 9–10.

McEnrue, M. P. (2002). Managerial skills teaching: Ten questions and twelve answers. *Journal of Management Education, 26*(6), 648–670.

McKeachie, W. J. (1986). *Teaching tips: A guidebook for the beginning college teacher.* Lexington, MA: DC. Heath & Co.

McKeachie, W. J. (1988). The need for study strategy training. In C. E. Weinstein, E. T. Goetz, & P. A. Alexander (Eds.), *Learning and study strategies: Issues in assessment, instruction, and evaluation* (pp. 3–9). New York, NY: Academic Press.

McKendall, M. (2000, May/June). Teaching groups to become teams. *Journal of Education for Business,* pp. 277–282.

McKenney, J. L. (1962). An evaluation of business games as a learning experience. *Journal of Business, 35*, 278–286.

McKenney, J. L. (1967). *Simulation gaming for management development.* Boston, MA: Harvard Business School, Division of Research.

McKenney, J. L., & Dill, W.R. (1966). Influences on learning in simulation games. *American Behavioural Scientist, 10*(2), 28–32.

McMahon, T. (2010). Peer feedback in an undergraduate programme: Using action research to over-come students' reluctance to criticise. *Educational Action Research, 18*, 273–287.

McMahon, T. R., & Bramhall, R. (2004). Using entertainment media to inform student affairs teaching and practice related to leadership. In D. S. Forney & T.W. Cawthon (Eds.), *New directions for student services, no. 108: Using entertainment media in student affairs teaching and practice* (pp. 61–70). San Francisco, CA: Jossey-Bass.

McNamara, M. J., & Deane, D. (1995). Self-assessment activities: Toward language autonomy in language learning. *TESOL Journal, 5*(1), 17–21.

McShane, S., & Von Glinow, M. (2009). *Organizational behaviors: Essentials* (2nd ed.). New York: McGraw-Hill. McWilliams, V., & Nahavandi, A. (2006). Using live cases to teach ethics. *Journal of Business Ethics, 67,* 421–433.

Meichenbaum, D. (1985). Teaching thinking: A cognitive-behavioral perspective. In S. F. Chipman, J. W. Segal, & R. Glaser (Eds.), *Thinking and learning skills, Vol. 2: Research and open questions.* Hillsdale, NJ: Lawrence Erlbaum Associates.

Meisiek, S. (2004). Which catharsis do they mean? Aristotle, Moreno, Boal and organizational theatre. *Organization Studies, 25,* 797–816.

Meixner, C., & Rosch, D. (2011). Powerful pedagogies. In S. R. Komives, J. P. Dugan, J. E. Owen, C. Slack, & W. Wagner (Eds.), *The handbook for student leadership development* (2nd ed., pp. 307–337). San Francisco, CA: Jossey-Bass.

Mendizabal, J. C., & Guthrie, K. L. (in press). Critical perspectives in practice: Balancing leadership development, community engagement, and identity work. *Concepts and Connections.*

Mercer, N. (2010). The analysis of classroom talk: Methods and methodologies. *British Journal of Educational Psychology, 80*(1), 1–14.

Mercer, N., & Howe, C. (2012). Explaining the dialogic processes of teaching and learning: The value and potential of sociocultural theory. *Learning, Culture and Social Interaction, 1,* 12–21.

Merriam, S. B., & Caffarella, R. S. (1999). *Learning in adulthood: A comprehensive guide.* San Francisco, CA: Jossey-Bass.

Merriam-Webster. (2017). Praxis. Retrieved from https://www.merriam-webster.com/dictionary/praxis

Meyer, S. R., & Marsick, V. J. (2003). Professional development in corporate training. In K. P. King & P. A. Lawler (Eds.), *New directions for adult and continuing education, no. 98: New perspectives on designing and implementing professional development of teachers of adults* (pp. 75–82). San Francisco, CA: Jossey-Bass.

The Myers & Briggs Foundation. (2017). mbti. Retrieved from http://www.myersbriggs.org/

Myers, I. B., McCaulley, M. H., Quenk, N. L., & Hammer, A. L. (1998). *MBTI manual: A guide to the development and use of the Myers-Briggs Type indicator* (3rd ed.). Palo Alto, CA: Consulting Psychologists Press.

Myers, S. A. (1997). Increasing student participation and productivity in small-group activities for psychology classes. *Teaching of Psychology, 24*(2), 105–115.

Micari, M., Gould, A. K., & Lainez, L. (2010). Becoming a leader along the way: Embedding leadership training into a large-scale peer-learning program in the STEM disciplines. *Journal of College Student Development, 51*(2), 218–230.

Michaels, S., O'Connor, C., & Resnick, L. (2008). Deliberative discourse idealized and realized: Accountable talk in the classroom and in civic life. *Studies in Philosophy & Education, 27,* 283–297.

Michaelsen, L. K., Knight, A. B., & Fink, D. L. (2004). *Team-based learning: A transformative use of small groups in college teaching.* Sterling, VA: Stylus.

Michaelsen, L. K., Parmelee, D. X., McMahon, K. K., & Levine, R. E. (Eds.). (2008). *Team-based learning for health professions education: A guide to using small groups for Iimproving learning* (1st ed.). Herndon, VA: Stylus.

Michaelsen, L. K., & Sweet, M. (2008). The essential elements of team-based learning. In L. Michaelsen, M. Sweet, & D. X. Parmelee (Eds.), *New directions for teaching and learning, no. 116: Team-based learning: Small group learning's next big step* (pp. 7–27). San Francisco, CA: Jossey-Bass.

Michaelsen, L. K., & Sweet, M. (2011). Team-based learning. In W. Buskist & J. E. Groccia (Eds.), *New directions for teaching and learning, no. 128: Evidence-based teaching* (pp. 41–51). San Francisco, CA: Jossey-Bass.

Middlebrooks, A., & Allen, S. J. (2008). Leadership education: New challenges, continuing issues. *ESSAY FROM THE FIELD, 77.*

Milem, J. F., Chang, M. J., & Antonio, A. L. (2005). *Making diversity work on campus: A research-based perspective.* Washington, DC: Association American Colleges and Universities.

Miller, R. L., & Benz, J. J. (2008). Techniques for encouraging peer collaboration: Online threaded discussion or fishbowl interaction. *Journal of Instructional Psychology, 35*(1), 87–94.

Mills, S. R., Rice, C. T., Berliner, D. C., & Rosseau, E. W. (1980). The correspondence between teacher questions and student answers in classroom discourse. *The Journal of Experimental Education, 48*(3), 194–204.

Mirvis, P. H. (2005). Large group interventions: Change as theater. *Journal of Applied Behavioral Science, 41,* 122–138.

Mitchell, R. C. (2004). Combining cases and computer simulations in strategic management courses. *Journal of Education for Business, 79*(4), 198–205.

Mitchell, T. D., Donahue, D. M., & Young-Law, C. (2012). Service learning as a pedagogy of whiteness. *Equity & Excellence in Education, 45*(4), 612–629.

Mitra, A. M. (2011). Learning how to look: The art of observation and leadership development. In M. Harvey & R. E. Riggio (Eds.), *Leadership studies: The dialogue of disciplines* (pp. 184–196). Northampton, MA: Edward Elgar.

Morehouse College. (n.d.). About. Retrieved from http://www.morehouse.edu/about/

Moore, C., Boyd, B. L., & Dooley, K. E. (2010). The effects of experiential learning with an emphasis on reflective writing on deep-level processing of leadership students. *Journal of Leadership Education, 9*(1), 36–52.

Moorehead, G., & Griffin, R. W. (2010). *Organizational behavior: Managing people and organizations.* South-Western/Cengage Learning.

Morgan, C. A., King D. L., Rudd, R. D., & Kaufman, D. K. (2013). Elements of an undergraduate agricultural leadership program: A Delphi study. *Journal of Leadership Education, 12,* 140–155.

Morehouse College. (n.d.). About. Retrieved from http://www.morehouse.edu/about/

MSL: Multi-Institutional Study of Leadership. (2017). Design. Retrieved from https://www.leadershipstudy.net/design/

MSL: Multi-Institutional Study of Leadership. (2017). Publications. Retrieved from https://www.leadershipstudy.net/publications/#publications-1

Murry, J. (1992). *Transformation and empowerment through leadership education: A study of transformation and empowerment in selected leadership education programs* (Doctoral dissertation) Available from ProQuest Dissertations and Theses database. (Publication No. AAT 9305319).

Murphy, S. E., & Johnson, S. K. (2011). The benefits of a long-lens approach to leader development: Understanding the seeds of leadership. *The Leadership Quarterly, 22*, 459–470.

Murry, J. (1992). *Transformation and empowerment through leadership education: A study of transformation and empowerment in selected leadership education programs* (Doctoral dissertation). Available from ProQuest Dissertations and Theses database. (Publication No. AAT 9305319).

Museus, S. D. (2008). Focusing on institutional fabric: Using campus culture assessments to enhance cross-cultural engagement. In S. R. Harper (Ed.), *Creating inclusive environments for cross-cultural learning and engagement in higher education*. Washington, DC: National Association of Student Personnel Administrators.

Nadler, L. (1970). *Developing human resources*. Houston, TX: Gulf Publishing.

Nadler, L. (1984). *The handbook of human resource development*. San Francisco, CA: John Wiley & Sons.

Nandan, M., & London, M. (2013). Interdisciplinary professional education: Training college students for collaborative social change. *Education & Training, 55*(8/9), 815–835.

National Association of Scholars (January 2017). Making citizens: How American universities teach civics. Retrieved from https://www.nas.org/images/documents/NAS_makingCitizens_executiveSummary.pdf

Naumann, S., & Bennett, N. (2002). The effects of procedural justice climate on work group performance. *Small Group Research, 33*, 361–377.

Naylor, G. (1982). *The women of Brewster Place*. New York, NY: Penguin.

Nestel, D., & Tierney, T. (2007). Role-play for medical students learning about communication: Guidelines for maximising benefits. *BMC Medical Education, 7*(3).

Newell, W. H. (2001). A theory of interdisciplinary studies. *Issues in Integrative Studies, 19*, 1–25.

The New York Times in Leadership. (2017). Retrieved from http://nytimesinleadership.com/

Nobbe, J., & Soria, K. M. (2016). Leadership assessment from an institutional approach. In *New directions for student leadership, no. 151: Assessing student leadership* (pp. 93–105). San Francisco, CA: Jossey-Bass.

Nohria, N., & Khurana, R. (2010). *Handbook of leadership theory and practice*. Boston, MA: Harvard Business School Press.

Northhouse, P. G. (2009). *Introduction to leaderhsip: Concepts and practices* Thousand Oaks, CA: SAGE.

Northhouse, P. G. (2014). *Introduction to leaderhsip: Concepts and practices* (3rd ed.). Thousand Oaks, CA: SAGE.

Northouse, P. G. (2015). *Leadership: Theory and practice* (7th ed.). Thousand Oaks, CA: SAGE.

Northouse, P. (2016). *Leadership: Theory and practice* (7th ed.). Thousand Oaks, CA: SAGE.

North-Samardzic, A. (2014). It's all in the game: A review of digital games and simulations for management education. Retrieved from http://www.anzam.org/wp-content/uploads/pdf-manager/1654_ANZAM-2014-205.PDF

Northwestern McCormick School of Engineering: News & Events. (2011, April 18). Learning to be a leader [Web log comment]. Retrieved from http://www.mccormick.northwestern.edu/news/articles/archive/2009-2012/article_883.html

O'Dell, I. (2009). Assessment and accountability in higher education. *Educational Considerations, 37*(1), 4–7.

Odom, S. (2015). Undergraduate student perceptions of the pedagogy used in a leadership course: a qualitative examination. *Journal of Leadership Education, 14*(2), 17–29.

O'Donnell, A. M., & Topping, K. J. (1998). Peers assessing peers: Possibilities and problems. In K. Topping & S. Ehly (Eds.), *Peer-assisted learning* (pp. 255–278). Mahwah, NJ: Lawrence Erlbaum Associates.

Online Etymology Dictionary. (2017). Experience (n.). Retrieved from http://www.etymonline.com/index.php?term=experience&allowed_in_frame=0

Online Etymology Dictionary. (2017). Pedagogy (n.). Retrieved from http://www.etymonline.com/index.php?term=pedagogy&allowed_in_frame=0

Onwuegbuzie, A. J., Collins, K. M. T., & Jiao, Q. G. (2009). Performance of cooperative learning groups in a postgraduate education research methodology course. *Active Learning in Higher Education, 10*(3), 265–277.

Oshry, B. (1996). *Seeing systems.* San Francisco, CA: Berrett-Koehler.

Ostick, D. T., & Wall, V. A. (2011). Considerations for culture and social identity dimensions. In S. R. , J. P. Dugan, J. E. Owen, C. Slack, & W. Wagner (Eds.), *The handbook for student leadership development* (2nd ed., pp. 339–368). San Francisco, CA: Jossey-Bass.

Ousager, J., & Johannessen, H. (2010). Humanities in undergraduate medical education: A literature review. *Academic Medicine, 85*(6), 988–998.

Overholt, W. A. (1971). *Towards modern concept of leadership.* Washington, DC: NASPA.

Owen, J. E. (2011). Assessment and evaluation. In S. R. Komives, J. P. Dugan, J. E. Owen, C. Slack, W. Wagner, & Associates (Eds.), *The handbook of student leadership development* (2nd ed., pp. 177–202). San Francisco, CA: Jossey-Bass.

Owen, J. E. (2015). Integrative and interdisciplinary approaches to leadership development. In J. Owen (Ed.), *New directions for student leadership, no. 145: Innovative learning for leadership development* (pp. 49–55). San Francisco, CA: Jossey-Bass.

Owen, J. E. (2016). Fostering critical reflection: Moving from a service to a social justice paradigm. In W. Wagner & J. M. Pigza (Eds.), *New directions for student leadership, no. 150: Leadership development through service-learning* (pp. 37–48). San Francisco, CA: Jossey-Bass.

Owen, J. E., Dugan, J. P., Berwager, S., & Lott, M. (2006). Lesson plans for leadership educators. In S. R. Komives, J. P. Dugan, J. E. Owen, C. Slack, & W. Wagner (Eds.), *Handbook for student leadership programs.* College Park, MD: National Clearinghouse for Leadership Programs.

Owen, J. E., Komives, S. R., Lucas, N., & McMahon, T. R. (2007). *Instructor's guide for exploring leadership: For college students who want to make a difference* (2nd ed.). San Francisco, CA: Jossey-Bass.

Palmer, P. J. (2007). *The courage to teach: Exploring the inner landscape of a teacher's life* (2nd ed.). San Francisco, CA: Jossey-Bass.

Palomba, C. A., & Banta, T. W. (1999). *Assessment essentials: Planning, implementing, and improving assessment in higher education*. San Francisco, CA: Jossey-Bass.

Palus, C. J., & Horth, D. M. (2012). *Leadership metaphor explorer: Creative conversations for better leadership facilitator's guide*. Greensboro, NC: Center for Creative Leadership.

Parks, D. S. (2005). *Leadership can be taught*. Boston, MA: Harvard Business School Press.

Parush, T., & Koivunen, N. (2014). Paradoxes, double binds, and the construction of "creative" managerial selves in art-based leadership development. *Scandinavian Journal of Management, 30*, 104–113.

Pascarella, E. T., Palmer, B., Moye, M., & Pierson, C. T. (2001). Do diversity experiences influence the development of critical thinking? *Journal of College Student Development, 42*(3), 257–271.

Pascarella, E. T., & Terenzini, P. T. (2005). *How college affects students: A third decade of Research* (2nd ed.). San Francisco, CA: Jossey-Bass.

Paswan, A. K., & Gollakota, K. (2004). Dimensions of peer evaluation, overall satisfaction, and overall evaluation: An investigation in a group task environment. *Journal of Education for Business, 79*(4), 225–231.

Payne, S. L. (1998). Interdisciplinary studies and management faculty involvement. *Journal of Education for Business, 73*, 211–214.

Peart, S. J. (2014). That "most inexhaustible of all topics": Reflections on the leadership studies curriculum at the Jepson School. *Journal of Leadership Studies, 7*(4), 71–75.

Peden, W., Reed, S., & Wolfe, K. (2017). *Rising to the LEAP challenge: Case studies of integrative pathways to student signature work*. Washington, DC: Association of American Colleges & Universities.

Pendakur, V., & Furr, S. C. (2016). Critical leadership pedagogy: Engaging power, identity, and culture in leadership education for college students of color. In K. L. Guthrie & L. Osteen (Eds.), *New directions for higher education, no. 174: Reclaiming higher education's purpose in leadership development* (pp. 45–56). San Francisco, CA: Jossey-Bass.

Perruci, G. (2014). Leadership education across disciplines: The social science perspective. *Journal of Leadership Studies, 7*(4), 43–47.

Perruci, G., & Schwartz, S. W. (2002, September). *Leadership for what? A humanistic approach to leadership development*. Paper presented at the Art of Management and Organization Conference, King's College, London, England.

Perry, M., Maffulli, N., Willson, S., et al. (2011) The effectiveness of arts-based interventions in medical education: A literature review. *Medical Education, 45*(2), 141–148.

Pescuric, A., & Byham, W. C. (1996). The new look of behavior modeling. *Training and Development, 50*(7), 24–30. Peterson, C., & Seligman, M. P. (2004). *Character strengths and virtues: A handbook and classification*. New York, NY: Oxford University Press.

Pfeiffer, W. J., & Jones, J. E. (Eds.). (1972). *The annual handbook for group facilitators*. La Jolla, CA: University Associates.

Piaget, J. (1970). *Genetic epistemology*. New York, NY: Columbia University Press.

Piatt, K. A., & Woodruff, T. R. (2016). Developing a comprehensive assessment plan. In *New directions for student leadership, no. 151: Assessing student leadership* (pp. 19–34). San Francisco, CA: Jossey-Bass.

Pierce, J. L., & Newstrom, J. W. (2008). *Leaders and the leadership process: Readings, self-assessments and applications* (5th ed.). New York, NY: McGraw-Hill/Irwin.

Pittinksy, T. L. (2009). *Crossing the divide: Intergroup leadership in a world of difference.* Boston, MA: Harvard Business Review Press.

Polkinghorne, D. E. (1996). Explorations of narrative identity. *Psychological Inquiry*, 7(4), 363–367.

Pope, R. L., & Reynolds, A. L. (1997). The student affairs core competencies: Integrating multicultural awareness, knowledge, and skills. *Journal of College Student Development, 38*, 266–277.

Posner, B. Z. (2004). A leadership development instrument for students. *Journal of College Student Development, 45*, 443–456.

Posner, B. Z. (2015a). An investigation into the leadership practices of volunteer leaders. *Leadership & Organization Development Journal, 36*(7), 885–898.

Posner, B. Z. (2015b). Bringing the rigor of research to the art of leadership: Research behind the five practices of exemplary leadership. Retrieved from http://www.leadershipchallenge.com/UserFiles/Bringing%20the%20 Rigor%20of%20Res earch%20to%20the%20Art%20of%20Leadership.pdf

Posner, B. Z. (2015b). *Bringing the rigor of research to the art of leadership: Research behind the five practices of exemplary leadership.* Retrieved from http://www. leadershipchallenge.com/UserFiles/Bringing%20the%20Rigor%20of%20 Res earch%20to%20the%20Art%20of%20Leadership.pdf

Posner, B. Z., & Brodsky, B. (1994). Leadership practices of effective student leaders: Gender makes no difference. *NASPA Journal, 31*(2), 113–120.

Prensky, M. (2001). *Digital gamebased learning*. New York, NY: McGraw-Hill.

Pressley, M., Borkowski, J. G., & Schneider, W. (1987). Cognitive strategies: Good strategy users coordinate metacognition and knowledge. In R. Vasta & G. Whitehurst (Eds.), *Annals of child development* (pp. 80–129). Greenwich, CT: JAI Press.

Preston, M., & Peck, A. (2016). Carts before horses? Remembering the primary of the student's experience in student learning. In D. M. Roberts & K. J. Bailey (Eds.), *New directions for student leadership, no. 151: Assessing student leadership* (pp. 79–91). San Francisco, CA: Jossey-Bass.

Price, M., O'Donovan, B., & Rust, C. (2007). Putting a social-constructivist assessment process model into practice: Building the feedback loop into the assessment process through peer review. *Innovations in Education and Teaching International, 44*(2), 143–152.

Priest, K., Friedel, C., & O'Dell, I. (2012). An invitation to innovation in leadership program assessment. *Proceedings of the 2012 Association of Leadership Educators Annual Conference*, pp. 383–384.

Pruetipibultham, O., & Mclean, G. N. (2010). The role of the arts in organizational settings. *Human Resource Development Review, 9*(1), 3–25.

Purg, D., & Walravens, A. (2015). Arts and leadership: Vision and practice at the IEDC-BLED school of management. *Journal of Leadership Studies, 9*(1), 42–47.

Putzel, R. (2007). XB: New-paradigm management of the classroom as a complex organization. *Journal of Business and Leadership: Research, Practice, and Teaching, 3*(1), 136–143.

Putzel, R. (2010). *XB: Manual for a learning organization.* Colchester, VT: St. Michael's College.

Race, P. (1993). Never mind the teaching—Feel the learning! *Quality Assurance in Education, 1*(2), 40–43.

Redfield, J. (2000, January 20). On discussion teaching. Retrieved from http://teaching.uchicago.edu/handbook/tac10.html

Raelin, J. A. (1997). A model of work-based learning. *Organization Science, 8*(6), 563–578.

Raffo, D. M. (2013). Teaching followership in leadership education. *Journal of Leadership Education, 12*(1), 262–273.

Rao, D., & Stupans, I. (2012). Exploring the potential of role play in higher education: Development of a typology and teacher guidelines. *Innovations in Education and Teaching International, 49*(4), 427–436.

Rath, T. (2007). *Strengthsfinder 2.0.* New York, NY: Gallup Press.

Rath, T., & Conchie, B. (2009). *Strengths based leadership: Great leaders, teams, and why people follow.* New York, NY: Gallup Press.

Rath, T., Conchie, B., & Magazine, T. (2009). Finding your leadership strengths. *Gallup Management Journal, 12-2008, 73.*

Raths, J. (1987). Enhancing understanding through debriefing. *Educational Leadership, 45*(2), 24–27.

Redfield, J. (2000, January 20). On discussion teaching. In *Teaching at Chicago: A collection of readings and practical advice for beginning teachers.* Retrieved from http://teaching.uchicago.edu/handbook/tac10.html

Reeves, B., & Malone, T. (2007, June 11). *Leadership in games and at work: Implications for the enterprise of massive multiplayer online role-playing games* (Seriosity Report). Retrieved from http://www.seriosity.com

Reeves, B., Malone, T., & O'Driscoll, T. (2008). Leadership's online labs. *Harvard Business Review, 86*(5), 59–66.

Reichard, R. J., & Walker, D. O. (2016). In pursuit: Mastering leadership through leader developmental readiness. In R. J. Reichard & S. E. Thompson (Eds.), *New directions for student leadership, no. 149: Leader developmental readiness: Pursuit of leadership excellence* (pp. 15–25). San Francisco, CA: Jossey Bass.

Rendón, L. I. (2009). *Sentipensante (sensing/thinking) pedagogy: Educating for wholeness, social justice, and liberation.* Sterling, VA: Stylus.

Reynolds, M. (1999). Critical reflection and management education: Rehabilitating less hierarchical approaches. *Journal of Management Education, 23*(5), 537–553.

Ricke-Kiely, T., & Matthias, D. C. (2013). The power of observation: Teaching leadership. *The Journal of Nonprofit Education and Leadership, 3*(2).

Riggio, R. E., Ciulla, J. B., & Sorenson, G. J. (2003). Leadership education at the undergraduate level: A liberal arts approach to leadership development. In S. E. Murphy & R. E. Riggio (Eds.), *The future of leadership development* (pp. 223–236). Mahwah, NJ: Lawrence Erlbaum Associates.

Riggio, R. E., & Mumford, M. M. (2011). Introduction to the special issue: Longitudinal studies of leadership development. *The Leadership Quarterly, 22*, 453–456.

Ritch, S., & Mengel, T. (2009). Guiding questions: Guidelines for leadership education programs. *Journal of Leadership Education, 8*(1), 216–227.

Roberto, M., & Edmondson, A. (2011). *Leadership and team simulation: Everest V2 (Software)*. Retrieved from https://cb.hbsp.harvard.edu/cbmp/product/7000-HTM-ENG

Roberts, C. (2008). Developing future leaders: The role of reflection in the classroom. *Journal of Leadership Education, 7*, 116–129. Roberts, D., & Ullom, C. (1989). Student leadership program model. *NASPA Journal, 27*(1), 67-74.

Roberts, D. C. (1981). *Student leadership programs in higher education* (no. 30). Carbondale, IL: ACPA Media, Southern Illinois University Press.

Roberts, D. C. (2007). *Deeper learning in leadership: Helping college students find the potential within.* San Francisco, CA: John Wiley & Sons.

Roberts, D. M., & Bailey, K. J. (2016). Setting the stage: The intersection of leadership and assessment. In *New directions for student leadership, no. 151: Assessing student leadership* (pp. 7–18). San Francisco, CA: Jossey-Bass.

Roberts, L. M., Wiskin, C., & Roalfe, A. (2008). Effects of exposure to mental illness in role-play on undergraduate student attitudes. *Medical School Education, 40*(7), 477–483.

Robin, B. R. (2008). Digital storytelling: A powerful technology tool for the 21st century classroom. *Theory into Practice, 47*(3), 220–228.

Robinson, A. G., & Robinson, M. M. (1994). On the tabletop improvement experiments of Japan. *Production and Operations Management, 3*(3), 201–216.

Robinson, B. D., & Schaible, R. (1993). Women and men teaching "men, women, and work." *Teaching Sociology, 21*, 363–370.

Rocca, K. A. (2010). Student participation in the college classroom: An extended multidisciplinary literature review. *Communication Education, 59*(2), 185–213.

Rodgers, C. (2002). Defining reflection: Another look at John Dewey and reflective thinking. *Teachers College Record, 104*(4), 842–866.

Rodgers, E., Bradley, C. R., & Ward, S. (2010). Poetic forms of leadership pedagogy: Rediscovering creative leadership through the arts. *Journal of Leadership Studies, 3*(4), 91–96.

Rollag, K. (2010). Teaching business cases online through discussion boards: Strategies and best practices *Journal of Management Education, 34*, 499–526.

Romanowska, J., Larsson, G., & Theorell, T. (2013). Effects on leaders of an art-based leadership intervention. *Journal of Management Development, 32*(9), 1004–1022.

Romme, A. G. L., & Putzel, R. (2003). Designing management education: Practice what you teach. *Simulation & Gaming, 34*(4), 512–530.

Roos, J., Victor, B., & Statler, M. (2004). Playing seriously with strategy. *Long Range Planning, 37*, 549–568.

Rosch, D. M., & Anthony, M.D. (2012). Leadership pedagogy: Putting theory to practice. In *New Directions for Student Services,* Vol. 2012, No. 140, Winter 2012, pp. 37–51.

Rosch, D. M., & Schwartz, L. M. (2009). Potential issues and pitfalls in outcomes assessment in leadership education. *Journal of Leadership Education, 8*(1), 177–194.

Rosse, J., Miller, J., & Stecher, M. (1994). A field study of job applicants' reactions to personality and cognitive ability testing. *Journal of Applied Psychology, 79*, 987–992.

Rosser, M. H. (2007). The magic of leadership: An exploration of Harry Potter and the *Goblet of Fire. Advances in Developing Human Resources, 9*(2), 236–250.

Rost, J. C. (1991). *Leadership for the twenty-first century.* New York, NY: Praeger.

Rost, J. C., & Barker, R. A. (2000). Leadership education in colleges: Toward a 21st century paradigm. *The Journal of Leadership Studies, 7*(1), 3–12.

Rothwell, W., & Kazanas, H. (1993). *The complete AMA guide to management development.* New York, NY: AMACOM.

Rovai, A. P. (2006). Facilitating online discussions effectively. *Internet and Higher Education, 10*, 77–88.

Rubin, R. S. (2006). The academic journal review process as a framework for student development peer feedback. *Journal of Management Education, 30*(2), 378–398.

Rudd, R., Baker, M., & Hoover, T. (2000). Undergraduate agriculture student learning styles and critical thinking abilities: Is there a relationship? *Journal of Agricultural Education, 41*(3), 2–12.

Saito, H., & Fujita, T. (2004). Characteristics and user acceptance of peer rating in EFL writing classrooms. *Language Teaching Research, 8*, 31–54.

Salas, E., Wildman, J. L., & Piccolo, R. F. (2009). Using simulation-based training to enhance management education. *Academy of Management Learning and Education, 8*(4), 559– 573.

Sanford, N. (1962). *The American college.* New York, NY: John Wiley and Sons.

Sanford, N. (1966). *Self and society: Social change and individual development.* New York, NY: Atherton.

Sargent, L. D., Allen, B. C., Frahm, J. A., & Morris, G. (2009). Enhancing the experience of student teams in large classes: Training teaching assistants to be coaches. *Journal of Management Education, 33*(5), 526–552.

Schaefer, R. A. B., & Erskine, L. (2012). Virtual team meetings: Reflections on a class exercise exploring technology choice. *Journal of Management Education, 36*(6), 777–801.

Scharff, C. (2009). Service learning: Bolstering leadership development while encouraging personal growth. *Theory in Action, 2*(2), 80–95.

Schellings, G., & van Hout-Wolters, B. (2011). Measuring strategy use with self report instruments: Theoretical and empirical considerations. *Metacognition and Learning, 6*, 83–90.

Schnaubelt, T., & Watson, J. L. (1999). Connecting service and leadership in the classroom. *Academic Exchange Quarterly, 3*, 7–15.

Schneider, C. G. (2003). Liberal education and integrative learning. *Issues in Integrative Studies, 21*, 1–8.

Schon, D. (1983). *The reflective practitioner: How professionals think in action.* New York, NY: Basic Books.

Scott, W. R., & Davis, G. R. (2007). *Organizations and organizing: Rational, natural and open systems perspectives.* Upper Saddle River, NJ: Prentice-Hall.

Seemiller, C. (2006). Impacting social change through service learning in an introductory leadership course. *Journal of Leadership Education, 5*(2), 41–49.

Seemiller, C. (2013). *The student leadership competencies guidebook: Designing intentional leadership learning and development.* San Francisco, CA: Jossey-Bass.

Seemiller, C. (2016). Complementary learning objectives: The common competencies of leadership and service-learning. In W. Wagner & J. M. Pigza (Eds.), *New directions for student leadership, no. 150: Leadership development through service-learning* (pp. 23–36). San Francisco, CA: Jossey-Bass.

Seemiller, C., & Priest, K. L. (2015). The hidden "who" in leadership education: Conceptualizing leadership educator professional identity development. *Journal of Leadership Education, 14*(3), 132–151.

Seemiller, C., & Priest, K. L. (2017). Leadership educator journeys: Expanding a model of leadership educator professional identity development. *Journal of Leadership Education, 16*(2), 1-22.

Seligman, M. E. P. (2002). *Authentic happiness: Using the new positive psychology to realize your potential for lasting fulfillment.* New York, NY: Free Press.

Senge, P. (1990). *The fifth discipline: The art and practice of the learning organisation.* New York, NY: Doubleday.

Sensory, O., & Di'Angelo, R. (2012). *Is everyone really equal: An introduction to key concepts in social justice education.* New York, NY: Teachers College Press.

Sessa, V. I., Matos, C., & Hopkins, C. A. (2009). Evaluating a college leadership course: What do students learn in a leadership course with a service-learning component and how deeply do they learn it. *Journal of Leadership Education, 7*(3), 167–200.

Shankman, M. L., Allen, S. J., & Haber-Curran, P. (2015). *Emotionally intelligent leadership for students: Facilitation and activity guide.* San Francisco, CA: Jossey-Bass.

Shankman, M. L., Allen, S. J., & Miguel, R. (2015). *Emotionally intelligent leadership for students. Inventory* (2nd ed.). San Francisco, CA: Jossey-Bass.

Shappell, A. S., & Barbato, S. (2010). Post-immersion reflective practices. *Journal of College and Character, 11*(3), 1–6.

Sheppard, J. A., & Taylor, K.M. (1999). Social loafing and expectancy-value theory. *Personality and Social Psychology Bulletin, 25,* 1147–1158.

Shively, M., & Relph, T. (2010, December). *The art of debriefing.* Workshop facilitated at the 2010 Leadership Educators Institute, Tampa, FL.

Shulman, L. S. (2005). Signature pedagogies in the professions. *Daedalus, 134*(3), 52–59.

Shushok, F., & Moore, S. H. (2010). Reading, study, and discussion of the "Great Texts" of literature, philosophy, and politics as a complement to contemporary leadership education literature. *Journal of Leadership Studies, 3*(4), 71–80.

Siciliano, J. (1999). A template for managing teamwork in courses across the curriculum. *Journal of Education for Business, 74*(5), 261–264.

Simmons, A., & Lipman, D. (2006). *The story factor.* Cambridge, MA: Perseus Books Group.

Simpson, M. L., & Nist, S. L. (2000). An update on strategic learning: It's more than textbook reading strategies. *Journal of Adolescent and Adult Literacy, 43*(6) 528–541.

Sinclair, A. (2003). The effects of justice and cooperation on team effectiveness. *Small Group Research, 34,* 74–100.

Singh, K. (2010). Metaphor as a tool in educational leadership classrooms. *Management in Education, 24*(3), 127–131.

Sitzmann, T., Ely, K., Brown, K. G., & Bauer, K. N. (2010). Self-assessment of knowledge: A cognitive learning or affective measure? *Academy of Management Learning & Education, 9,* 169–191.

Sivers, D. (2010, February 10). First follower: Leadership lessons from dancing guy. Retrieved from http://www.youtube.com/watch?v=fW8amMCVAJQ

Skendall, K. C., Ostick, D. T., Komives, S. R., & Wagner, W. (Eds.). (2017). *The social change model: Facilitating leadership development.* San Francisco, CA: Jossey-Bass.

Slavin, R. E. (1983). *Cooperative learning.* White Plains, NY: Longman.

Slavin, R. E. (1996). *Education for all: Contexts of learning.* Lisse, The Netherlands: Swets & Zeitlinger.

Sluijsmans, D., Dochy, F., & Moerkerke, G. (1999). Creating a learning environment by using self-, peer- and co-assessment. *Learning Environments Research, 1,* 293–319.

Smist, J. A. (2011). Cocurricular programs. In S. R. Komives, J. P. Dugan, & J. E. Owen (Eds.), *The handbook for student leadership development* (pp. 287–304). San Francisco, CA: Jossey-Bass.

Smith, D. N. (2015). Effectively using discussion boards to engage students in introductory leadership courses. *International Journal of Leadership in Education, 14*(2), 229.

Smith, D. N., & Roebuck, D. B. (2009). Connecting the dots of leadership through interview assignments. *Proceedings of the Association of Leadership Educators Conference, Milwaukee, WI.* Retrieved from http://www.leadershipeducators. org/Resources/Documents/Conferences/Milwuakee/Smith-Roebuck%20 FINAL.pdf

Smith, G. W. (2009). Using feature films as the primary instructional medium to teach organizational behavior. *Journal of Management Education, 33*(4), 462–489.

Sogurno, O. A. (2003). Efficacy of role-playing pedagogy in training leaders: Some reflections. *Journal of Management Development, 23*(4), 355–371.

Solórzano, D. G., & Yosso, T. J. (2002). Critical race methodology: Counter-storytelling as an analytical framework for education research. *Qualitative Inquiry, 8*(1), 23–44.

Somervell, H. (1993). Issues in assessment, enterprise and higher education: The case for self-peer and collaborative assessment. *Assessment and Evaluation in Higher Education, 18*(3), 221–233.

Sorenson, G. (2007). An intellectual history of leadership studies: The role of James MacGregor Burns. In R. Cuoto (Ed.), *Reflections on leadership* (pp. 19–30). Lanham, MD: University Press of America.

Soria, K., Roberts, J., & Reinhard, A. (2015). First-year college students' strengths awareness and perceived leadership development. *Journal of Student Affairs Research and Practice, 52*(1), 89–103.

Soria, K. M., & Stubblefield, R. (2015). Knowing me, knowing you: Building strengths awareness, belonging, and persistence in higher education. *Journal of College Student Retention: Research, Theory & Practice, 0*(0), 1–22.

Soumerai, E. N., & Mazer, R. (2006). Arts-based leadership: Theatrical tributes. In M. Klau, S. Boyd, & L. Luckow (Eds.), *New directions for youth development, no. 109: Youth leadership* (pp. 117–124). San Francisco, CA: John Wiley & Sons.

Southern Association of Colleges and Schools Commission on Colleges. (2015). *2015 annual report and proceedings.* Retrieved from http://www.sacscoc.org/pdf/2015_Annual_Report.pdf

Sowcik, M. (2012). Legitimacy, maturity, and accountability of leadership studies programs: A movement toward "good" practices. *Journal of Leadership Studies, 6*(3), 47–48.

Sowcik, M., & Allen, S. J. (2013). Getting down to business: A look at leadership education in business schools. *Journal of Leadership Education, 12*(3), 57–75.

Sowcik, M., Andenoro, A. C., McNutt, M., & Murphy, S. E. (2015). *Leadership 2050: Critical challenges, key contexts, and emerging trends.* Bingley, UK: Emerald.

Sparling, D. (2002). Simulations and supply chains: Strategies for teaching supply chain management. *Supply Chain Management, 7*(5), 334–342.

Speck, B. W. (2001). Why service-learning? In M. Canada & B. W. Speck (Eds.), *New directions for higher education, no. 114: Developing and implementing service-learning programs* (pp. 3–13). San Francisco, CA: Jossey-Bass.

Spector, P. E. (2004). Social desirability bias. In M. S. Lewis-Beck, A. Bryan, & T. F. Liao (Eds.), *The SAGE encyclopedia of social science research methods* (pp. 1045–1046). Thousand Oaks, CA: SAGE.

Springborg, C. (2010). Leadership as art-leaders coming to their senses. *Leadership, 6*(3), 243–258.

Springer, C. W., & Borthick, A. F. (2004). Business simulation to stage critical thinking in introductory accounting: Rationale, design, and implementation. *Issues in Accounting Education, 19*(3), 277–303.

statista. (2017). WoW subscription numbers 2005–2015. Retrieved from https://www.statista.com/statistics/276601/number-of-world-of-warcraft-subscribers-by-quarter/

Stanton, N., & Matthews, G. (1995). Twenty-one traits of personality: An alternative solution for the occupational personality questionnaire. *Journal of Management Development, 14*(7), 66–75.

Stanton, T. K., Giles, D. E., & Cruz, N. I. (1999). *Service-learning: A movement's pioneers reflect on its origins, practice, and future.* San Francisco, CA: Jossey-Bass

Starkey, M. (1992). Testing the tests. *Management Today,* pp. 76–80.

Stearns, L., Morgan, J., Capraro, M., & Capraro, R. (2012). A teacher observation instrument for PBL classroom instruction. *Journal of STEM Education: Innovations and Research, 13*(3), 7–16.

Stech, E. L. (2007). Leadership prescription paradigms. *Journal of Leadership Education, 6*(1), 28–37.

Stedman, N. L. P. (2009). Casting the net of critical thinking: A look into the collegiate leadership classroom. *Journal of Leadership Education*, 7(3), 201–218.

Steen, S., Bader, C., & Kubrin, C. (1999). Rethinking the graduate seminar. *Teaching Sociology, 27*, 167–192.

Stenta, D.A. (2001). *The mount leadership society: Promoting intersections of leadership and social change in a service -learning class.* Retrieved from ProQuest Dissertations & Theses Global (302257).

Stevens, D. D., & Cooper, J. E. (2009). *Journal keeping: How to use reflective writing for effective learning, teaching, professional insight, and positive change.* Sterling, VA: Stylus.

Stevens, R. (2015). Role-play and student engagement: Reflections from the classroom. *Teaching in Higher Education, 20*(5), 481–492.

Stoecker R. (2016). *Liberating service learning and the rest of higher education civic engagement.* Philadelphia, PA: Temple University Press.

Strain, C. R. (2005). Pedagogy and practice: Service-learning and students moral development. *New Directions for Teaching and Learning, 103*, 61–72.

Sturken, M., & Cartwright, L. (2003). *Practices of looking.* New York, NY: Oxford University Press.

Sutherland, I. (2013). Arts-based methods in leadership development: Affording aesthetic workspaces, reflexivity and memories with momentum. *Management Learning, 44*(1), 25–43.

Sutton, E. M., & Kimbrough, W. M. (2001). Trends in Black student involvement. *NASPA Journal, 39*(1), 30–40.

Svinicki, M., & McKeachie, W. J. (2011). *McKeachie's teaching tips: Strategies, research, and theory for college and university teachers* (13th ed.). Belmont, CA: Cengage.

Svinicki, M. D., & McKeachie, W. J. (2014). *McKeachie's teaching tips: Strategies, research, and theory for college and university teachers* (14th ed.). Belmont, CA: Wadsworth Cengage Learning.

Swann, W. B. (2012). Self-verification theory. In P. Van Lang, A. Kruglanski, & E.T. Higgins (Eds.), *Handbook of theories of social psychology* (pp. 23–42). San Francisco, CA: SAGE.

Tabak, F., & Lebron, M. (2017). Learning by doing in leadership education: Experiencing followership and effective leadership communication through role-play. *Journal of Leadership Education, 16*(2), 199–212.

Tam, M. (2000). Constructivism, instructional design, and technology: Implications for transforming distance learning. *Educational Technology & Society, 3*(2), 51–60.

Tan, Ivy, G. C., Sharan, S., & Lee, C. K. E. (2007). Group investigation effects on achievement, motivation, and perceptions of students in Singapore. *The Journal of Educational Research, 100*(3), 142–154.

Taylor, H. (1999). *Role-play cases for teaching interviewing skills in information systems analysis.* Paper presented at the HERDSA Annual International Conference. Retrieved from http://www.herdsa.org.au/wp-content/uploads/conference/1999/pdf/

Taylor, S. N. (2014). Student self-assessment and multisource feedback assessment: Exploring benefits, limitations, and remedies. *Journal of Management Education, 38*(3), 359–383.

Taylor, S. S. (2004). Presentational form in first person research: Off-line collaborative reflection using art. *Action Research, 2*(1), 71– 88.

Taylor, S. S. (2008). Theatrical performance as unfreezing: Ties that bind at the academy of management. *Journal of Management Inquiry, 17*(4), 398–406.

Taylor, S. S. (2012). *Leadership craft, leadership art.* New York, NY: Palgrave Macmillan.

Taylor, S. S. (2015). Leading to learn. *Journal of Leadership Studies, 9*(1), 52–55.

Taylor, S. S., & Ladkin, D. (2009). Understanding arts-based methods in managerial development. *Academy of Management Learning & Education, 8*(1), 55–69.

Tennyson, R. D., & Breuer K. (2002). Improving problem solving and creativity through use of complex-dynamic simulations. *Computers in Human Behavior, 18,* 650–668.

Thiagarajan, S. (1992). Using games for debriefing. *Simulation & Gaming, 23*(2), 161–173.

Thomas, R. J. (2008). *Crucibles of leadership: How to learn from experience to become a great leader.* Cambridge, MA: Harvard Business Press.

Thomas, S., & Busby, S. (2003). Do industry collaborative projects enhance students' learning? *Education + Training, 45*(4/5), 226–235.

Thompson, M. D. (2006). Student leadership process development: An assessment of contributing college resources. *Journal of College Student Development, 47*(3), 343–350.

Thompson, S., & Couto, R. (2016). Creating problem-based leadership learning across the curriculum. In K. L. Guthrie & L. Osteen (Eds.), *New directions for higher education, no. 174: Reclaiming higher education's purpose in leadership development* (pp. 35–44). San Francisco, CA: Jossey-Bass.

Thorson, K. (2014, April 4). Why do we take personality tests? [Web log comment]. Retrieved from http://psych-your-mind.blogspot.com/2014/04/why-do-we-take-personality-tests.html

Tillapaugh, D., & Haber-Curran (Eds.). (2017). Critical perspectives on gender and student leadership. In *New direction for student leadership, no. 154.* Hoboken, NJ: John Wiley & Sons.

Toegel, G., & Conger, J. A. (2003). 360-degree assessment: Time for reinvention. *Academy of Management Learning & Education, 2*(3), 297–311.

Topping, K. J. (2009). Peer assessment. *Theory into Practice, 48,* 20–27.

Torrez, M. A. (2013). Developing a multicultural mindset. In W. Wagner, D. T. Ostick, & Associates (Eds.), *Exploring leadership for college students who want to make a difference: Facilitation and activity guide* (pp. 95–99). San Francisco, CA: Jossey-Bass.

Tourangeau, A. E., & McGilton, K. (2004). Measuring leadership practices of nurses using the leadership practices inventory. *Nursing Research, 53*(3), 182–189.

Tremble, N. (n.d.). *Situational leadership.* Retrieved from https://www.vistacampus.gov/sites/default/files/legacy/50/Training/TrainingResources/LeadershipTrainingModule/situational_leadership.pdf

Trigwell, K., & Prosser, M. (1991). Improving the quality of student learning: The influence of learning context and student approaches to learning on learning outcomes. *Higher Education, 22*(3), 251–266.

Trowler, V. (2013). Leadership practices for student engagement in challenging conditions. *Perspectives: Policy and Practice in Higher Education, 17*(3), 91.

Tuckman, B. W. (1965). Developmental sequence in small groups. *Psychological Bulletin, 63*(6), 384–399.

Tyree, T. (1998). Designing an instrument to measure socially responsible leadership using the social change model of leadership development. *Dissertation Abstracts International, 59*(06), 1945 (UMI No. 9836493).

Tyson, R. H., & Janine, L. (2006). Integrating role-play into software engineering courses. *Journal of Computing in Small Colleges, 22*(2), 32–38.

University of South Florida. (2017). 2013–2018 Strategic plan. Retrieved from http://www.usf.edu/ods/documents/strategicplans/usf-strategic-plan-2013-2018.pdf

Vito, G. F., & Higgins, G. E. (2010). Examining the validity of The Leadership Challenge inventory: The case for law enforcement. *International Journal of Police Service and Management, 12*(3), 305–319.

Van Buskirk, W., & London, M. (2008). Inviting the muse into the classroom: Poetic license in management education. *Journal of Management Education, 32*, 294–315.

Van Ments, M. (1994). *The effective use of role play.* London, UK: Kogan Page.

Van Velsor, E., Ruderman, M., & Phillips, A. D. (1989). The lessons of the looking glass: Management simulations and the real world of action. *Leadership and Organization Development Journal, 10*(6), 27–31.

Velez, J. J., Moore, L. L., Bruce, J. A., & Stephens, C. A. (2014). Agricultural leadership education: Past history, present reality, and future directions. *Journal of Leadership Studies, 7*(4), 65–70.

Vito, G. F., & Higgins, G. E. (2010). Examining the validity of the leadership challenge inventory: The case for law enforcement. *International Journal of Police Science & Management, 12*(3), 305–319.

Volpe White, J., & Guthrie, K. L. (2016). Creating a meaningful learning environment: Reflection in leadership education. *Journal of Leadership Education, 15*(1), 60–75.

Wagner, W., & Ostick, D. T. (2013). *Exploring leadership: For college students who want to make a difference: Facilitation and activity guide.* San Francisco, CA: Jossey-Bass.

Wagner, W., Ostick, D. T., & Komives, S. R. (2014). *Leadership for a better world: Understanding the social change model of leadership development. Instructor's manual.* College Park, MD: National Clearinghouse for Leadership Programs. Retrieved from http://blogs.umb.edu/cesi/files/2014/11/leadership_for_a_better_world-q4hvb1.pdf

Wagner, W., & Pigza, J. M. (2016). Fostering critical reflection: Moving from a service to a social justice paradigm. In W. Wagner & J. M. Pigza (Eds.), *New directions for student leadership, no. 150: Leadership development through service-learning* (pp. 11–22). San Francisco, CA: Jossey-Bass.

Walker, J. (2005). Debriefing: Enhancing experiential learning. *Journal of Family and Consumer Sciences, 97*(1), 73–75.

Walker, K. (2002). Reflections on the history and development of ALE and JOLE. *Journal of Leadership Education, 1*(1), 11–24.

Wang, Y., & Rodgers, R. (2006). Impact of service-learning and social justice education on college students' cognitive development. *NASPA Journal, 43*(2), 316–337.

Ward, T. B. (2001). Creative cognition, conceptual combination, and the creative writing of Stephen R. Donaldson. *American Psychologist, 56*(4), 350–354.

Warner, L. S., & Grint, K. (2006). American Indian ways of leading and knowing. *Leadership, 2*(2), 225–244.

Wasserman, S. (1994). *Advances in social network analysis: Research in the social and behavioral sciences.* Thousand Oaks, CA: SAGE.

Watkins, S, R. (in press). Doctoral dissertation, Florida State University.

Weasenforth, D., Biesenbach-Lucas, S., & Meloni, C. (2002). Realizing constructivist objectives through collaborative technologies: Threaded discussions. *Language Learning & Technology, 6*(3), 58–86.

Webb, N. (1985). Student interaction and learning in small groups: A research summary. *Learning to Cooperate, Cooperating to Learn*, pp. 148–172.

Webster, N. S., Bruce, J. A., & Hoover, T. S. (2006). Understanding the perceptions of service learning with teen leaders. *The Journal of Leadership Education, 5*(1), 26–38.

Weeks, P., & Kelsey, K. (2007). Student project teams: Understanding team process through an examination of leadership practices and team culture. *Journal of Leadership Education, 6*(1), 209–225.

Weidman, J. C., Twale, D. J., & Stein, E. L. (2001). Socialization of graduate and professional students in higher education: A perilous passage. *ASHE-ERIC Higher Education Report, 28*, 3.

Weimer, M. (2013, January 9). First day of class activities that create a climate for learning. *Faculty Focus.* Retrieved from http://www.facultyfocus.com/articles/teaching-professor-blog/

Welch, M. (1999). The ABCs of reflection: A template for students and instructors to implement written reflection in service-learning. *NSEE Quarterly, 25*, 22–25.

Welch, R. L. (2000). Training a new generation of leaders. *Journal of Leadership Studies, 7*, 70–81.

Westfall, S. B. (1999). Partnerships to connect in- and out-of-class experiences. In J. H. Schuh & E. J. Whitt (Eds.), *New directions for student services, no. 87: Creating successful partnerships between academic and student affairs* (pp. 51–61). San Francisco, CA: Jossey-Bass.

Whetten, D. A., & Cameron, K. S. (2015). *Developing management skills.* New York, NY: Pearson.

White, J. V. (2012). Students' perception of the role of reflection in leadership learning. *Journal of Leadership Education, 11*(2), 140–157.

White, J. V. (2014). *Students' application of leadership learning through reflection* (Doctoral dissertation).

Wicks, P. G., & Rippin, A. (2010) Art as experience: An inquiry into art and leadership using dolls and doll-making. *Leadership, 6*(3), 259–278.

Wiggins, G., & McTighe, J. (1998). *Understanding by design*. Alexandria, VA: Association for Supervision & Curriculum Development.

Wiggins, G., & McTighe, J. (2005). *Understanding by design* (2nd ed.). Alexandria, VA: Association for Supervision and Curriculum Development.

Wilen, W. W. (Ed.). (2004). *Dynamics of effective secondary teaching*. Boston, MA: Allyn & Bacon.

Willcoxson, L. E. (2006). "It's not fair!" Assessing the dynamics and resourcing of teamwork. *Journal of Management Education, 30*(6), 798–808.

Williams, D., Ducheneaut, N., Xiong, L., Zhang, Y., Yee, N., & Nickell, E. (2006). From tree house to barracks: The social life of guilds in world of warcraft. *Games and Culture, 1*(4), 338–361.

Williams, J. R. (2006). Pirates and power: What Captain Jack Sparrow, his friends, and his foes can teach us about power bases. *Journal of Leadership Education, 5*(2), 60–68.

Willis, J. (1995). Recursive, reflective instructional design model based on constructivist-interpretivist theory. *Educational Technology, 35*(6), 5–23.

Wilson, M.C. (2004). *Closing the leadership gap: Why women can and must help run the world*. New York, NY: Viking.

Wimmer, G., Meyers, C., Porter, H., & Shaw, M. (2012). Learning vicariously: Students' reflections of the leadership lessons portrayed in *The Office. Journal of Leadership Education, 11*(2), 52–71.

Wisniewski, M. A. (2010). Leadership and the Millennials: Transforming today's technological teens in tomorrow's leaders. *Journal of Leadership Education, 9*(1), 53–68.

Wren, J. T. (1994). Teaching leadership: The art of the possible. *Journal of Leadership Studies, 1*(2), 73–93.

Wren, J. T. (1995). *The leader's companion: Insights on leadership through the ages*. New York, NY: Free Press.

Wren, J. T. (2001). *Instructor's manual to accompany the leader's companion: Insights on leadership through the ages*. Richmond, VA: University of Richmond.

Wren, J. T., Riggio, R., & Genovese, M. (2009). *Leadership and the liberal arts: Achieving the promise of a liberal education*. New York, NY: Palgrave Macmillan.

Yammarino, F. J., Dionne, S. D., Uk Chun, J., & Dansereau, F. (2005). Leadership and levels of analysis: A state-of-the-science review. *Leadership Quarterly, 16*(6), 879–919.

Yukl, G. (2006). *Leadership in organizations* (6th ed.). Saddle River, NJ: Pearson Education.

Zagorsek, H., Stough, S. J., & Jaklic, M. (2006). Analysis of the reliability of the leadership practices inventory in the item response theory framework. *International Journal of Selection and Assessment, 14*(2), 180–191.

Zantow, K., Knowlton, D. S., & Sharp, D. C. (2005). More than fun and games: Reconsidering the virtues of strategic management simulations. *Academy of Management Learning and Education, 4*(4), 451–458.

Zimmerman-Oster, K., & Burkhardt, J. (1999). Leadership in the making: Impact and insights from leadership development programs in U.S. colleges and universities. *Journal of Leadership & Organizational Studies, 6*(3–4), 50–66.

Zull, J. (2002). *The art of changing the brain*. Sterling, VA: Stylus.

ABOUT THE AUTHORS

Kathy L. Guthrie is an Associate Professor of Higher Education in the Department of Educational Leadership and Policy Studies at Florida State University. In addition to teaching in the Higher Education program, Kathy also serves as the Director of the Leadership Learning Research Center (LLRC), whose mission is to inform and support scholars, educators, and practitioners regarding leadership teaching and learning through scholarship, curriculum development, and consultation. The strength of the LLRC resides in its theory-to-practice-to-theory framework, where research is directly applied to both curricular and co-curricular leadership education. Kathy also coordinates the Undergraduate Certificate in Leadership Studies, which is a partnership between the College of Education and the Center for Leadership and Social Change. Her research focuses on the learning outcomes and environment of leadership and civic education, online teaching and learning, and professional development for Student Affairs Professionals.

Kathy has authored 29 refereed journal articles and 6 book chapters. In 2016 she co-edited a *New Directions in Student Leadership* issue titled "Culturally Relevant Leadership Learning" and a *New Directions in Higher Education* issue titled "Reclaiming Higher Education's Purpose in Leadership Development. In 2013 she co-authored "Cultivating Leader Identity and Capacity in Students From Diverse Backgrounds," and in 2012 Kathy co-edited a *New Directions in Student Services* issue titled "Developing Students' Leadership Capacity."

In her current role with Florida State University, Kathy teaches doctoral, masters, and undergraduate courses. She recently developed a course for Higher Education Master's program on being a leadership educator. She has also taught courses in the undergraduate leadership certificate, including Leadership Theory and Practice, Leadership in Groups and Communities, Leadership and Change, and Leadership Experience.

Over the course of her career, Kathy has been honored with awards including the Association of College Personnel Administrator (ACPA) Diamond Honoree Award (2017), Florida State University's Graduate Faculty Mentor Award (2017), Florida State University's Transformation through Teaching Award (2015), Florida State University College of Education Teaching Award (2014), Association of College Personnel Administrators' Emerging Scholar (2012), Seminole Faculty Award (2011), and National Association of Student Personnel Administrators (NASPA) Contributions to Student Affairs through Teaching (2010).

Kathy serves on the advisory board for the new *Journal of Campus Activities Practice and Scholarship*, is an editorial board member of the *Journal of College and Character*, and a regular reviewer for the *Journal of Leadership Education*. Currently, Kathy is the Associate Editor of the *New Directions in Student Leadership* series and Editor of the *Contemporary Perspectives in Leadership Learning* book series. Kathy is also active in several professional associations, including ACPA, NASPA, and the International Leadership Association, where she is the immediate past-Chair for the Leadership Scholarship Member Interest Group.

Prior to becoming a faculty member, Kathy served as an administrator for 10 years in various functional areas within student affairs, including campus activities, commuter services, community engagement, and leadership development. She has worked in higher education in both administrative and faculty roles for almost 20 years and loves every minute of her chosen career path. Originally from Central Illinois, Kathy currently lives in Tampa, Florida, with her incredible husband and fun 4-year-old (collectively known as Team Guthrie). She loves Chicago pizza, Jimmy Buffett, baseball (Go Cubs!), and just being with Team Guthrie.

Daniel M. Jenkins is Chair and Associate Professor of Leadership and Organizational Studies at the University of Southern Maine (USM), where he teaches undergraduate and graduate courses in leadership and organizational theory, group dynamics, and research methods. He received his doctorate in Curriculum & Instruction as well as an MA in Political Science from the University of South Florida (USF) and a BS in Communication Studies from The Florida State University. Dan's research focuses on leadership education in face-to-face, blended, and distance learning modalities, pedagogy, course and curriculum design, and assessment and evaluation, as well as critical thinking.

Dan has taught undergraduate, graduate, face-to-face, online, and blended courses, including Leadership, Organizational Theory, Foundations of Leadership Studies I & II, Leading Through Conflict, Exploring Leadership on Campus, Applied Social Policy, and Methods of Inquiry. In addition to his teaching and administrative responsibilities at USM, Dan is also the Faculty Fellow for a university-wide strengths-based education program.

Dan has 18 refereed journal articles and three book chapters. In 2013 and 2014 Dan edited two special symposia in the *Journal of Leadership Studies*. The first focused on the pedagogical challenges, trends, choices, and considerations in leadership education and included contributions from across the field, including the armed forces and the Cleveland Clinic. The second included a first-ever cross-perspective of leadership programs from various disciplines such as Engineering/STEM, Agriculture, Social Sciences, and a curricular/co-curricular partnership. Dan is also a co-author of the *National Leadership Education Research Agenda 2013–2018: Providing Strategic Direction for the Field of Leadership Education.*

Dan serves as the Associate Media Editor for the *Journal of Leadership Studies* and is a regular reviewer for the *Journal of Leadership Education*. He is also co-editor of the International Leadership Association (ILA)'s "PAUSE for Pedagogy" *Interface Newsletter* column. Additionally, Dan is a co-founder and co-chair of the ILA Leadership Education Academy and Vice-Chair of the Collegiate Leadership Competition.

Additionally, Dan is active in several professional associations, serving as the ILA Liaison to the Inter-Association Leadership Education Collaborative since 2013, was the Chair of ILA Leadership Education Member Interest Group from 2013 to 2015, was Secretary of the Association of Leadership Educators from 2014 to 2016, and was the 2012–2013 preconference committee coordinator for the NASPA SLPKC.

Prior to becoming a full-time faculty member, Dan worked as a professional academic advisor and co-director of the leadership studies minor at USF. Concurrently, Dan taught political science courses at Hillsborough Community College, including State & Local Government, American Government, and Introduction to Political Science. Plus, he has worked in the financial services industry for a Fortune 250 company, in hospitality, the Florida Legislature, and as a staff member in gubernatorial and school board election campaigns. Overall, Dan has worked in higher education in both administrative and faculty roles for more than a decade and shares Kathy's love for his chosen career path. Furthermore, Dan is a father of two, a Florida native, and enjoys the beach, classic rock and jazz, college football (Go Noles!), and spending time with his family and friends.

CPSIA information can be obtained
at www.ICGtesting.com
Printed in the USA
LVHW03s0725101018
593043LV00002B/4/P